W9-BAX-064

THE GANDHI READER

The Gandhi Reader

A SOURCE BOOK
OF HIS LIFE
AND WRITINGS

EDITED BY Homer A. Jack

INDIANA UNIVERSITY PRESS

BLOOMINGTON · 1956

Excerpts from the writings of Gandhi and others are used
with permission as indicated at the beginning of each
selection. Many of the writings of Gandhi are used with
the permission of the Navajivan Trust, Ahmedabad, India.

Manufactured in the United States of America by
American Book–Stratford Press, Inc., New York

INTRODUCTION

Mohandas K. Gandhi was one of the great men not only of our time, but of all history. Greatness is an elusive quality: a conqueror who wins great victories may scarcely be remembered in the next century; a saint who remains unknown to his countrymen may be worshiped by another generation. Gandhi's greatness, which was widely recognized during his lifetime, has not diminished and indeed is likely to increase. He lived in the first half of the twentieth century, when inventors and rulers captured men's imaginations and souls: Edison, Ford, and Marconi; Lenin, Hitler, and Stalin. Gandhi shares contemporary regard with statesmen like Churchill and Roosevelt as well as with creative thinkers like Einstein and Schweitzer. Yet when the history of this era is written in perspective, Gandhi will stand securely beside Einstein and Schweitzer as one of the truly great creative personalities of our age. He is certainly the most important figure produced in centuries by a non-Western civilization.

Although Gandhi was revered by millions in the East, he was widely known and admired in the West. He was perhaps most commonly thought of as the little brown man in a white loincloth who successfully twisted the tail of the British lion. However, the writings of Gandhi are but little known, at least in the United States—much less than those of his Indian contemporaries, Nehru and Tagore, or his intellectual peers, Einstein and Schweitzer.

Gandhi left much to posterity. His legacy consisted not of personal possessions, but of a dramatic life and penetrating ethical insights. There is an embarrassing divergence between the lives and the doctrines of many world leaders. With Gandhi, his life and his teachings were one. The best exposition of his message was his own biography, much of which, fortunately, he has related himself.

Perhaps the most important single volume written by Gandhi was his autobiography, characteristically subtitled "The Story of My Experiments with Truth." This long work was written in the Gujarati language and later translated into English. It was first published serially in *Young India*, beginning in 1925. One of its limitations is its incomplete description of Gandhi's first ex- periments with *satyagraha* (non-violent direct action) during the twenty years he was in South Africa. This is provided in a second, less-known autobiographical volume—composed when Gandhi was in prison—entitled *Satyagraha in South Africa* and published in 1928.

Gandhi's autobiography terminates in 1920, when Gandhi had almost three decades of intense activity before him. He never had the time or inclination to write further autobiographical volumes, but certain works officially compiled by his close associates de- scribe some of the climactic events in his life. These include the "great trial" of 1921, the midnight operation in 1924, the "great fast" of 1924, the London Round Table Conference in 1931, the "epic fast" in 1932, Gandhi's activity during World War II, his conferences with Jinnah over Pakistan, and his pilgrimages to Noakhali and Calcutta in 1946–47.

The great bulk of Gandhi's writings was in the form of edito- rials or short essays for his weekly newspapers. In 1903, in South Africa, he launched the English and Gujarati weekly newspaper, *Indian Opinion*. He soon found the newspaper to be an indis- pensable political tool. In India, in 1919, he helped establish the English-language *Young India* and its Gujarati edition, *Navajivan*. In 1933 *Young India* became *Harijan*—Gandhi's word for the un- touchables. Some of his editorials and articles had tremendous po- litical influence. In the 1940s, for example, *Harijan* was issued in a total of twelve editions in nine languages and, in addition, Gan- dhi's most important articles were reprinted the next day in all the newspapers of India. In his last years his own writings appeared less frequently; in their place were summaries of his speeches and talks after prayers, and descriptions of his activities by other persons.

Gandhi's writings in these newspapers have been reprinted in a number of "authorized" collections. These are available on such subjects as self-restraint, Christian missions, non-violence in war and peace, Hindu-Moslem communal unity, Hinduism, village industries, diet and diet reform, women and social injustice, and students. These collections constitute the great bulk of Gandhi's writings and comprise many thousands of pages of fascinating reading. No subject was too large for a Gandhi editorial, and none was too small. In his writings and in his talks after prayers, Gandhi delighted in the juxtaposition of the sublime with the familiar; to him anything was sublime which helped the people, even if it dealt with traditionally forbidden or unpleasant subjects.

In addition to his autobiographical and editorial writings, Gandhi was the author of a number of important miscellaneous works. In 1909, while on a voyage from London to South Africa, he composed the pamphlet *Hind Swaraj* or *Indian Home Rule*. In a sense this is Gandhi's *Mein Kampf*, for much of his later political philosophy may be found in this early pamphlet. In 1941 he published another significant pamphlet entitled *Constructive Programme: Its Meaning and Place*. This is a matured estimate of his total domestic "platform." Also in this miscellaneous category should be mentioned *Songs from Prison*, the translations that Gandhi made in prison in 1930 from the Upanishads and other Indian discourses. In 1946 the English translation of Gandhi's version of the Bhagavad Gita was issued as *The Gita According to Gandhi*.

Of the rich biographical material about Gandhi, the earliest book is Joseph J. Doke's *An Indian Patriot in South Africa*, published in 1909. The most widely known early biography was Romain Rolland's *Mahatma Gandhi* (1924). The best biography published to date is undoubtedly Louis Fischer's *The Life of Mahatma Gandhi* (1950); the longest is D. G. Tendulkar's eight-volume *Mahatma* (1951–1954). A number of other biographies have appeared in recent years, including several written especially for high school children.

A whole field of literature has developed explaining Gandhi's philosophy, beginning with C. F. Andrews' important volume, *Mahatma Gandhi's Ideas* (1929). Two historic volumes appeared in 1939 and 1944 on the occasion of Gandhi's seventieth and seventy-fifth birthdays. Finally, a number of pamphlets and books have appeared dealing with the period just before and after Gandhi's death.

Not many will now agree with Winston Churchill, who once tried to dismiss Gandhi as a "seditious fakir." Yet not all will agree as to whether Gandhi was primarily a saint or a politician. Gandhi himself said that "people describe me as a saint trying to be a politician, but the truth is the other way around." Trained in the law rather than in religion or philosophy, Gandhi nevertheless had a consuming interest in religion and sought to live a truly religious life. He not only succeeded as few men have done, but he devised a new religious approach to the problem of combating evil. Yet Gandhi was also a politician. His religion was of the market place, seldom above it. Both in South Africa and in India his efforts were unambiguously political. As Horace Alexander wisely observed, Gandhi's whole life was "a kind of dialectic," first preparing his people for freedom and then helping them to attain it.

Gandhi's patient efforts to prepare the Indian people for freedom have been called "the constructive program." This dealt at various times with a wide range of domestic reforms: Hindu-Moslem communal unity, elimination of untouchability, prohibition, home spinning, village industries, village sanitation, basic education, adult education, emancipation of women, education in health and hygiene, and other topics. Some of Gandhi's prescriptions were somewhat provincial in that they were not completely relevant to other cultures. Other aspects of his constructive program had and have universal significance.

Gandhi's greatest contribution was in the field of methodology. With the help of Hindu and Christian scriptures and insights from Henry D. Thoreau and Count Leo Tolstoy, he devised a new method of warfare—one which large or small groups, or even whole nations, could use against the greatest manifestations of evil: racism, imperialism, and war. The term satyagraha was coined by Gandhi as a more satisfactory phrase than "passive resistance" or "civil disobedience," and the method of satyagraha was evolved by him through long experimentation first in South Africa and later in India.

Here is truly an epochal social invention. Gandhi said that satyagraha is meant for the common people, not merely for saints. It is war without violence. It is based on love, not on hate: on loving one's opponents and suffering to convert them. It differentiates between the sin and the sinner, between the evil and the evildoer. It is the weapon of the brave, not of the weak. It demands discipline and may entail self-sacrifice, suffering, fasting, imprisonment, and death, yet it has the supreme virtue of providing means consonant with the highest ends.

In this anthology Gandhi is first presented through his biography—the drama of his life—and only secondarily through his message. Wherever possible, Gandhi speaks for himself. Where this has not been possible, the writings of those who knew him well have been used for the most part. Much has necessarily had to be omitted. Yet the range is wide enough to give the reader a fair sample of Gandhi's many interests as well as of the major events in his life.

This book is not meant to be a substitute for a good biography of Gandhi or for the detailed study of his writings. After reading these articles by and about him, perhaps the reader will be induced to delve further into Gandhi's life and to take to heart his life and message. Gandhi himself would wish us to devote our energies not to forming a cult in his honor, but to achieving international and domestic peace with justice by non-violent means.

HOMER A. JACK

Evanston, Illinois
October 2, 1955

CONTENTS

Chapter 19. Last Days (1948)

Chapter 20. Mourning and Homage (1948)

GLOSSARY OF INDIAN TERMS

Ahimsa	Non-violence (a, privative; himsa, violence). This is an ancient Hindu precept, proclaimed by Buddha, by disciples of Vishnu, and by Mahavira, founder of Jainism.
Ashram	Religious community or institution or school; place of discipline and service.
Ba	Familiar title for mother in Gujarati. Used as a title of respect for Mrs. Gandhi.
Bai, behn	A kindly way of addressing a woman.
Bapu	Familiar title for father in Gujarati. Used throughout India as a title of respect for Gandhi.
Bhagavad Gita	The Song of the Divine Lord. This is a poem of 700 stanzas, part of the Mahabharata.
Bhajan	Hymn.
Brahmacharya	Continence, sexual self-restraint; literally, conduct that leads one to God.
Brahman	The essence of the godhead.
Brahmin	The highest caste in Hinduism—those who have knowledge; often, though incorrectly, spelled Brahman.
Charkha	The hand spinning wheel.
Congress	The Indian National Congress, an unofficial political organization.
Crore	100 lakhs, or 10,000,000.
Darshan	A form of spiritual happiness induced by being in the presence of a cherished person, place, or thing.
Dharma	Religion or religious duty.
Dhoti	The loincloth worn by Hindu men, usually a long piece with ornamental borders that is tucked in at the waist.
Gandhiji	A title of respect for Gandhi, the ji a common suffix of respect corresponding to sir or mister. Sometimes the suffix was used after Mahatma—Mahatmaji.
Ghee, ghi	Clarified butter; it is boiled and the watery particles and the curds are skimmed off.
Gita	Song. See Bhagavad Gita.
Goondas	Rowdies.
Gujarati	Language spoken in the province of Gujarat, India, where Gandhi was born.

Guru	Spiritual guide.
Harijans	A term given by Gandhi to the untouchables (*hari*, God's; *jan*, people). See Untouchables.
Hartal	Cessation of work; a form of non-violent demonstration in which all work ceases, shops are closed, etc.
Haveli	A temple for those of the Vaishnava faith.
Hindi	The language of northern India, with Sanskrit roots.
Hindu Mabasabha	A political party of orthodox Hindus.
Hindustani	A language based on Hindi but containing many Arabic and Persian words.
Khaddar (khadi)	Hand-spun or homespun cloth.
Khan	A common suffix to the names of Moslems of all ranks.
Khilafat	A Pan-Islamic movement in India in response to the deposal of the Sultan of Turkey (who was Caliph of Islam) as a result of Turkey's defeat in World War I.
Kshattriya	The second caste in Hinduism—those who rule.
Lakh	100,000.
Lathi	A long stick, usually made of bamboo, tipped with brass or iron, often 6 to 8 feet long.
Mahabharata	The national epic of which Krishna is the divine hero. The Bhagavad Gita is part of the Mahabharata.
Mahasabha	See Hindu Mahasabha.
Mahatma	Great soul (*maha*, great; *atma*, soul).
Mantra	Magic name of God; an incantation or formula of prayer sacred to any deity.
Manusmriti	Laws of Manu, a Hindu law-giver; an ancient religious code upholding the caste system and containing accounts of creation.
Maulana	A religious teacher of Islam; man of erudition; an honorific term.
Moksha	Freedom from the cycle of death and rebirth; salvation.
Muslim	Belonging to Islam; frequent Indian spelling of Moslem.
Mussulman	Follower of Islam; frequent Indian spelling of Mohammedan. Spelled variously.
Pandit	A learned man or teacher, especially a Brahmin, in Hindu religion, law, and science.
Parsi	A Zoroastrian of India descended from Persian refugees.
Pathans	A Mohammedan Afghan people of India's northwest frontier.
Puranas	Sacred Hindu legends.
Ram Raksha	A recitation of sacred texts asking for the protection of Rama.

Rama	The divine incarnation of the Supreme Being in human form as described in the epic, Ramayana.
Ramanama	The word used for the constant repetition of the name, Rama, as an act of devotion to the Lord.
Ramayana	The sacred epic of north India.
Rupee (Rs.)	The monetary unit of India; present value about 21 cents. Three *pies* equal one *pice*; four *pice* equal one *anna*; sixteen *annas* equal one *rupee*.
Sahib	Mr. or Master; often used in speaking of or addressing Europeans.
Sanatani	An orthodox Hindu.
Sardar	A title meaning leader.
Sari	The principal garment of an Indian woman, being a long piece of cloth wrapped around the waist, a portion covering the bosom and the head.
Satyagraha	Truth-force or soul-force (*sat*, truth; *agraha*, firmness); non-violent direct action; passive resistance; civil disobedience; non-violent non-cooperation.
Satyagrahi	One who practices *satyagraha*.
Shastras	Scriptures.
Sheth	Master, a name given to Hindus of importance in Sind and other parts of West India.
Shrijut (Sjt.)	A common title equivalent to esquire; often Shri or Srj.
Shrimati	A common title for women.
Shudra	The fourth (and lowest) caste of Hinduism—those who labor.
Sikh	A member of a religious sect founded about 1500 A.D. in the Punjab.
Siva (Shiva)	A god of the Hindu triad, typifying destruction and reproduction.
Swadeshi	Belonging to, or made in, one's own country (*swa*, self; *deshi*, country); applied to movement for boycott of foreign goods.
Swaraj	Self-government (*swa*, self; *raj*, government); independence.
Tamil	A language spoken in southern India and Ceylon.
Telugu	The largest division of the Dravidian dialects in southern India.
Untouchables	Castes or communities which, through ancestry, profession, or custom, are looked upon as impure by orthodox Hindus. Also called Scheduled Castes, Depressed Classes, Pariahs, and Harijans.
Upanishads	Hindu religious philosophical discourses.
Urdu	A Persianized Moslem form of Hindustani.

Vaishnava   A sect of Hindus worshiping Vishnu as the one su-
                     preme God.
Vaishya   The third caste in Hinduism—those who trade and
                     farm.
Varna   Caste.
Varnashrama dharma   Religion of caste (varna, color; ashrama, place of
                     discipline).
Vedanta   An important Hindu philosophical system.
Vedas   Earliest Hindu religious hymns.
Vishnu   The second god of the Hindu triad; the preserver.
                     The other gods are Brahma, the creator, and Siva,
                     the destroyer and regenerator.

PRINCIPAL CHARACTERS IN THE BOOK

Alexander, Horace G. (1889–   ). An English Quaker who taught at Birmingham for twenty years, visited India several times, and returned there in 1946 at Gandhi's request.

Ali, Mohammed (1878–1930?). Prominent Moslem leader and close friend of Gandhi. His older brother was Shuakat Ali.

Ambedkar, Bhimrao Ramji (1893–   ). The leader of the untouchables of India. For a time he was Minister of Law in the Government of India.

Andrews, Charles Freer (1871–1940). An itinerant British missionary who first met Gandhi in South Africa in 1914 and was on intimate terms with him for the next quarter century. He was given the title "Deenabandhu," meaning "The Friend or Brother of Those who Deserve Compassion."

Banker, Shankarlal G. (1889–   ). The publisher of Young India who was tried and sentenced with Gandhi in 1922.

Besant, Mrs. Annie (1847–1933). A British theosophist who went to India to live. She became active in Indian politics and was president of the Indian National Congress in 1917. She founded the Central Hindu College at Benares.

Cripps, Sir Stafford (1889–1952). A wealthy lawyer and Labor Member of Parliament, who was sent to India in March 1942 by Prime Minister Winston Churchill with proposals on the postwar status of India. He was later Chancellor of the Exchequer in the Labor Government from 1947 to 1950.

Das, Chittaranjan R. (1870–1925). A leader of the Indian nationalist movement from Bengal. He was called "Deshbandhu," meaning "Friend of the Country."

Desai, Mahadev (1892–1942). For more than twenty-four years he was Gandhi's personal secretary and chronicler.

Doke, Rev. Joseph J. (1861–1913). A Baptist missionary in South Africa who befriended Gandhi and was his first biographer.

Gandhi, Devadas (1900–   ). Gandhi's fourth son, now managing editor of The Hindustan Times in New Delhi. He is married to Lakshmi, daughter of C. Rajagopalachari.

Gandhi, Harilal (1888–1948). Gandhi's eldest son, who died in a tuberculosis hospital.

Gandhi, Karamchand (1823–86). Gandhi's father, who was for a time Prime Minister of a small state in western India.

Gandhi, Kasturba[i] (1869–1942). Gandhi's wife, whom he married in 1882 and who was the mother of their four sons.

Gandhi, Maganlal (1883–1928). Gandhi's second cousin who lived with him in South Africa. He suggested the root of the term, satyagraha, and managed Gandhi's ashram in India.

Gandhi, Manilal (1892–   ). Gandhi's second son, who for many years continued his interests in South Africa, including the editorship of Indian Opinion at Phoenix, Natal.

Gandhi, Putlibai (1841–91). Gandhi's mother.

Gandhi, Ramdas (1897–   ). Gandhi's third son, now living in Nagpur, India.

Gokhale, Gopal Krishna (1866–1915). President of the Indian National Congress in 1905 and founder of the Servants of India Society, he was Gandhi's political mentor.

Jinnah, Mohammed Ali (Qaid-i-Azam) (1876–1948). A wealthy Bombay lawyer who organized the Moslem League in 1934. He was the father of Pakistan and its first Governor-General.

Kallenbach, Herman (1871–1945). An architect in South Africa, of German nationality, who became a close associate of Gandhi during the decade ending 1914.

Malaviya, Pandit Madan Mohan (1861–1946). A distinguished Brahmin leader of orthodox Hinduism who for many years worked closely with Gandhi.

Mirabehn (Madeleine Slade) (1892–   ). The daughter of a British admiral who joined Gandhi's ashram in 1925 and was associated with his work in India until his death.

Naidu, Mrs. Sarojini (1879–1949). An Indian nationalist leader and poetess who was closely associated with Gandhi. She was president of the Indian National Congress in 1925 and Governor of the United Provinces at the time of her death.

Nayyar, Dr. Sushila (1916–   ). A woman physician who attended Kasturba Gandhi in her later years and also Mahatma Gandhi. She is the sister of Pyarelal.

Nehru, Jawaharlal (1889–   ). He worked closely with Gandhi in the Indian National Congress after first meeting him in 1916. He was president of the Congress in 1936, 1937, and 1946 and was named first Prime Minister of independent India.

Nehru, Motilal (1861–1931). The father of Jawaharlal. A Kashmir Brahmin, he abandoned his wealthy law practice and became a leader of the Indian National Congress. He was a close associate of Gandhi.

Patel, Sardar Vallabhbhai (1875–1951). A lawyer in Ahmedabad, he first became associated with Gandhi in 1916 and was a leading official of the Congress after that time. He was Deputy Prime Minister of India at the time of his death.

Polak, Henry S. L. (1882–   ). An Englishman who became a close associate of Gandhi in South Africa from 1904 to 1914. He later was a lawyer and journalist in England.

Prasad, Rajendra (1884–   ). He first met Gandhi in Champaran in 1917 and was an official of the Congress and associate of Gandhi after that time. In 1950 he became the first President of India.

Pyarelal (Nayyar) (1899–   ). A secretary on Gandhi's staff who succeeded Mahadev Desai as personal secretary after Desai's death in 1942.

Rai, Lajpat (Lalaji) (1864–1928). A nationalist leader from the Punjab who was mortally wounded in a political demonstration.

Rajagopalachari, Chakravarti (1879–   ). After joining the satyagraha campaign in 1919, he became closely associated with Gandhi and his daughter married Gandhi's son, Devadas. He was Governor-General of India from 1948 to 1950.

Rolland, Romain (1866–1944). French author who received the Nobel Prize for literature in 1915 and wrote the first widely read biography of Gandhi.

Smuts, Jan Christiaan (1870–1951). South African statesman and general who opposed Gandhi during the satyagraha campaigns culminating in the Smuts-Gandhi pact in 1914.

Tagore, Rabindranath (1861–1941). Indian poet and author who was awarded the Nobel Prize for literature in 1913.

Tilak, Bal Gangadhar (1856–1920). A Brahmin scholar and mathematician who was a leader of the nationalist movement. He was called "Lokamanya," meaning "Beloved of the People."

PART ONE 1869-1914

1 THE EARLY YEARS
(1869–1892)

BIRTH AND PARENTAGE
• by M. K. Gandhi

This is the first chapter of Gandhi's well-known autobiography, entitled An Autobiography, or The Story of My Experiments with Truth. It was written in Gujarati and translated into English by Mahadev Desai, Gandhi's secretary. Begun while Gandhi was in prison in 1922, it first appeared serially in Gandhi's newspaper, Navajivan, and in English in Young India, beginning in December 1925; in America it appeared in Unity magazine. The full autobiography was first published in book form in a two-volume Indian edition, the first volume in 1927 and the second in 1929. The book is aptly named, since it very frankly reveals Gandhi's experiments in living. It is one of the most candid autobiographies ever written. Because of this, C. F. Andrews felt that "it greatly needs editing for the West," and an abridgment under his editorship was published in London in 1930 with the title His Own Story. The complete autobiography was not published in America until 1948, under the title Gandhi's Autobiography.

THE GANDHIS belong to the Bania caste and seem to have been originally grocers. But for three generations, from my grandfather,

• Reprinted with permission from Gandhi's Autobiography (Washington: Public Affairs Press, 1948), Part I, Chapter I, pp. 11-14.

✗ they have been Prime Ministers in several Kathiawad [1] States. Uttamchand Gandhi, *alias* Ota Gandhi, my grandfather, must have been a man of principle. State intrigues compelled him to leave Porbandar, where he was Diwan,[2] and to seek refuge in Junagadh. There he saluted the Nawab [3] with the left hand. Some-one, noting the apparent discourtesy, asked for an explanation, which was given thus: "The right hand is already pledged to Por-bandar."

Ota Gandhi married a second time, having lost his first wife. He had four sons by his first wife and two by his second wife. I do not think that in my childhood I ever felt or knew that these sons of Ota Gandhi were not all of the same mother. The fifth of these six brothers was Karamchand Gandhi, *alias* Kaba Gandhi, and the sixth was Tulsidas Gandhi. Both these brothers were Prime Ministers in Porbandar, one after the other. Kaba Gandhi was my father. He was a member of the Rajasthanik Court. It is now extinct, but in those days it was a very influential body for settling disputes between the chiefs and their fellow clansmen. He was for some time Prime Minister in Rajkot and then in Van-kaner. He was a pensioner of the Rajkot State when he died.

Kaba Gandhi married four times in succession, having lost his wife each time by death. He had two daughters by his first and second marriages. His last wife, Putlibai, bore him a daughter and three sons, I being the youngest.

My father was a lover of his clan, truthful, brave and generous, but short-tempered. To a certain extent he might have been even given to carnal pleasures. For he married for the fourth time when he was over forty. But he was incorruptible and had earned a name for strict impartiality in his family as well as outside. His loyalty to the state was well known. An Assistant Political Agent spoke insultingly of the Rajkot Thakore Saheb, his chief, and he stood up to the insult. The Agent was angry and asked Kaba Gandhi to apologize. This he refused to do and was therefore kept under de-tention for a few hours. But when the Agent saw that Kaba Gandhi was adamant, he ordered him to be released.

My father never had any ambition to accumulate riches and left us very little property.

He had no education, save that of experience. At best, he might be said to have read up to the fifth Gujarati standard. Of history and geography he was innocent. But his rich experience of practical affairs stood him in good stead in the solution of the most intricate questions and in managing hundreds of men. Of religious training he had very little, but he had that kind of religious culture which frequent visits to temples and listening to religious discourses make available to many Hindus. In his last days he began reading the Gita at the instance of a learned Brahman friend of the family, and he used to repeat aloud some verses every day at the time of worship.

The outstanding impression my mother has left on my memory is that of saintliness. She was deeply religious. She would not think of taking her meals without her daily prayers. Going to Haveli— the Vaishnava temple—was one of her daily duties. As far as my memory can go back, I do not remember her having ever missed the Chaturmas.[4] She would take the hardest vows and keep them without flinching. Illness was no excuse for relaxing them. I can recall her once falling ill when she was observing the Chandrayana [5] vow, but the illness was not allowed to interrupt the observance. To keep two or three consecutive fasts was nothing to her. Living on one meal a day during Chaturmas was a habit with her. Not content with that she fasted every alternate day during one Chaturmas. During another Chaturmas she vowed not to have food without seeing the sun. We children on those days would stand, staring at the sky, waiting to announce the appearance of the sun to our mother. Everyone knows that at the height of the rainy season the sun often does not condescend to show his face. And I remember days when, at his sudden appearance, we would rush and announce it to her. She would run out to see with her own eyes, but by that time the fugitive sun would be gone, thus depriving her of her meal. "That does not matter," she would say cheerfully, "God did not want me to eat today." And then she would return to her round of duties.

My mother had strong commonsense. She was well informed about all matters of state, and ladies of the court thought highly of her intelligence. Often I would accompany her, exercising the privilege of childhood, and I still remember many lively discussions she had with the widowed mother of the Thakore Saheb.

Of these parents I was born at Porbandar, otherwise known as Sudamapuri, on the 2nd October 1869. I passed my childhood in Porbandar. I recollect having been put to school. It was with some difficulty that I got through the multiplication tables. The fact that I recollect nothing more of those days than having learnt, in company with other boys, to call our teacher all kinds of names, would strongly suggest that my intellect must have been sluggish, and my memory raw.

CHILD MARRIAGE
by M. K. Gandhi

MUCH AS I WISH that I had not to write this chapter, I know that I shall have to swallow many such bitter draughts in the course of this narrative. And I cannot do otherwise, if I claim to be a worshipper of Truth. It is my painful duty to have to record here my marriage at the age of thirteen. As I see the youngsters of the same age about me who are under my care, and think of my own marriage, I am inclined to pity myself and to congratulate them on having escaped my lot. I can see no moral argument in support of such a preposterously early marriage.

Let the reader make no mistake. I was married, not betrothed. For in Kathiawad there are two distinct rites—betrothal and marriage. Betrothal is a preliminary promise on the part of the parents

• Reprinted with permission from *Gandhi's Autobiography* (Washington: Public Affairs Press, 1948), Part I, Chapter III, pp. 18-21.

of the boy and the girl to join them in marriage, and it is not inviolable. The death of the boy entails no widowhood on the girl. It is an agreement purely between the parents, and the children have no concern with it. Often they are not even informed of it. It appears that I was betrothed thrice, though without my knowledge. I was told that two girls chosen for me had died in turn, and therefore I infer that I was betrothed three times. I have a faint recollection, however, that the third betrothal took place in my seventh year. But I do not recollect having been informed about it. In the present chapter I am talking about my marriage, of which I have the clearest recollection.

It will be remembered that we were three brothers. The first was already married. The elders decided to marry my second brother, who was two or three years my senior, a cousin, possibly a year older, and me, all at the same time. In doing so there was no thought of our welfare, much less our wishes. It was purely a question of their own convenience and economy.

Marriage among Hindus is no simple matter. The parents of the bride and the bridegroom often bring themselves to ruin over it. They waste their substance, they waste their time. Months are taken up over the preparations—in making clothes and ornaments and in preparing budgets for dinners. Each tries to outdo the other in the number and variety of courses to be prepared. Women, whether they have a voice or no, sing themselves hoarse, even get ill, and disturb the peace of their neighbors. These in their turn quietly put up with all the turmoil and bustle, all the dirt and filth, representing the remains of the feasts, because they know that a time will come when they also will be behaving in the same manner.

It would be better, thought my elders, to have all this bother over at one and the same time. Less expense and greater *éclat*. For money could be freely spent if it had only to be spent once instead of thrice. My father and my uncle were both old, and we were the last children they had to marry. It is likely that they wanted to have the last best time of their lives. In view of all these con-

siderations, a triple wedding was decided upon, and as I have said
before, months were taken up in preparation for it.

It was only through these preparations that we got warning of
the coming event. I do not think it meant to me anything more
than the prospect of good clothes to wear, drum beating, marriage
processions, rich dinners and a strange girl to play with. The carnal
desire came later. I propose to draw the curtain over my shame,
except for a few details worth recording. To these I shall come
later. But even they have little to do with the central idea I have
kept before me in writing this story.

So my brother and I were both taken to Porbandar from Rajkot.
There are some amusing details of the preliminaries to the final
drama—e.g. smearing our bodies all over with turmeric paste—but
I must omit them.

My father was a Diwan, but nevertheless a servant, and all the
more so because he was in favor with the Thakore Saheb. The
latter would not let him go until the last moment. And when he
did so, he ordered for my father special stage coaches, reducing
the journey by two days. But the fates had willed otherwise.
Porbandar is 120 miles from Rajkot,—a cart journey of five days.
My father did the distance in three, but the coach toppled over
in the third stage, and he sustained severe injuries. He arrived
bandaged all over. Both his and our interest in the coming event
was half destroyed, but the ceremony had to be gone through.
For how could the marriage dates be changed? However, I forgot
my grief over my father's injuries in the childish amusement of
the wedding.

I was devoted to my parents. But no less was I devoted to the
passions that flesh is heir to. I had yet to learn that all happiness
and pleasure should be sacrificed in devoted service to my parents.
And yet, as though by way of punishment for my desire for
pleasures, an incident happened, which has ever since rankled in
my mind and which I will relate later.[6] Nishkulanand [7] sings:
"Renunciation of objects, without the renunciation of desires, is
shortlived, however hard you may try." Whenever I sing this song

or hear it sung, this bitter untoward incident rushes to my memory and fills me with shame.

My father put on a brave face in spite of his injuries, and took full part in the wedding. As I think of it, I can even today call before my mind's eye the places where he sat as he went through the different details of the ceremony. Little did I dream then that one day I should severely criticize my father for having married me as a child. Everything on that day seemed to me right and proper and pleasing. There was also my own eagerness to get married. And as everything that my father did then struck me as beyond reproach, the recollection of those things is fresh in my memory. I can picture to myself, even today, how we sat on our wedding dais, how we performed the *Saptapadi*,[8] how we, the newly wedded husband and wife, put the sweet *Kansar* [9] into each other's mouth, and how we began to live together. And oh! that first night. Two innocent children all unwittingly hurled themselves into the ocean of life. My brother's wife had thoroughly coached me about my behavior on the first night. I do not know who had coached my wife. I have never asked her about it, nor am I inclined to do so now. The reader may be sure that we were too nervous to face each other. We were certainly too shy. How was I to talk to her, and what was I to say? The coaching could not carry me far. But no coaching is really necessary in such matters. The impressions of the former birth are potent enough to make all coaching superfluous. We gradually began to know each other, and to speak freely together. We were the same age. But I took no time in assuming the authority of a husband.

EATING FORBIDDEN MEAT

• by M. K. Gandhi

. . . [A] FRIEND . . . informed me that many of our teachers
were secretly taking meat and wine. He also named many well-
known people of Rajkot as belonging to the same company. There
were also, I was told, some high-school boys among them.

I was surprised and pained. I asked my friend the reason and he
explained it thus: "We are a weak people because we do not eat
meat. The English are able to rule over us, because they are
meat-eaters. You know how hardy I am, and how great a runner
too. It is because I am a meat-eater. Meat-eaters do not have boils
or tumors, and even if they sometimes happen to have any, these
heal quickly. Our teachers and other distinguished people who eat
meat are no fools. They know its virtues. You should do likewise.
There is nothing like trying. Try, and see what strength it gives."

All these pleas on behalf of meat-eating were not advanced at a
single sitting. They represent the substance of a long and elaborate
argument which my friend was trying to impress upon me from
time to time. My elder brother had already fallen. He therefore
supported my friend's argument. I certainly looked feeble-bodied
by the side of my brother and this friend. They were both hardier,
physically stronger, and more daring. This friend's exploits cast a
spell over me. He could run long distances and extraordinarily
fast. He was an adept in high and long jumping. He could put
up with any amount of corporal punishment. He would often
display his exploits to me and, as one is always dazzled when he
sees in others the qualities that he lacks himself, I was dazzled by
this friend's exploits. This was followed by a strong desire to be

• Reprinted with permission from *Gandhi's Autobiography* (Washington: Public Affairs Press, 1948), Part I, Chapters VI and VII, pp. 32-36.

like him. I could hardly jump or run. Why should not I also be as strong as he?

Moreover, I was a coward. I used to be haunted by the fear of thieves, ghosts, and serpents. I did not dare to stir out of doors at night. Darkness was a terror to me. It was almost impossible for me to sleep in the dark, as I would imagine ghosts coming from one direction, thieves from another and serpents from a third. I could not therefore bear to sleep without a light in the room. How could I disclose my fears to my wife, no child, but already at the threshold of youth, sleeping by my side? I knew that she had more courage than I, and I felt ashamed of myself. She knew no fear of serpents and ghosts. She could go out anywhere in the dark. My friend knew all these weaknesses of mine. He would tell me that he could hold in his hand live serpents, could defy thieves, and did not believe in ghosts. And all this was, of course, the result of eating meat.

A doggerel of the Gujarati poet Narmad was in vogue amongst us schoolboys, as follows:

> Behold the mighty Englishman
> He rules the Indian small,
> Because being a meat-eater
> He is five cubits tall.

All this had its due effect on me. I was beaten. It began to grow on me that meat-eating was good, that it would make me strong and daring, and that, if the whole country took to meat-eating, the English could be overcome.

A day was thereupon fixed for beginning the experiment. It had to be conducted in secret. The Gandhis were Vaishnavas.[10] My parents were particularly staunch Vaishnavas. They would regularly visit the *Haveli*.[11] The family had even its own temples. Jainism was strong in Gujarat, and its influence was felt everywhere and on all occasions. The opposition to and abhorrence of meat-eating that existed in Gujarat among the Jains and Vaishnavas were to be seen nowhere else in India or outside in such strength. These were the traditions in which I was born and bred.

And I was extremely devoted to my parents. I knew that the moment they came to know of my having eaten meat, they would be shocked to death. Moreover, my love of truth made me extra cautious. I cannot say that I did not know then that I should have to deceive my parents if I began eating meat. But my mind was bent on the "reform." It was not a question of pleasing the palate. I did not know that it had a particularly good relish. I wished to be strong and daring and wanted my countrymen also to be such, so that we might defeat the English and make India free. The word "Swaraj" I had not yet heard. But I knew what freedom meant. The frenzy of the "reform" blinded me. And having ensured secrecy, I persuaded myself that mere hiding the deed from parents was no departure from truth.

So the day came. It is difficult fully to describe my condition. There were, on the one hand, the zeal for "reform," and the novelty of making a momentous departure in life. There was, on the other, the shame of hiding like a thief to do this very thing. I cannot say which of the two swayed me more. We went in search of a lonely spot by the river, and there I saw, for the first time in my life—meat. There was baker's bread also. I relished neither. The goat's meat was as tough as leather. I simply could not eat it. I was sick and had to leave off eating.

I had a very bad night afterwards. A horrible nightmare haunted me. Every time I dropped off to sleep it would seem as though a live goat were bleating inside me, and I would jump up full of remorse. But then I would remind myself that meat-eating was a duty and so become more cheerful.

My friend was not a man to give in easily. He now began to cook various delicacies with meat, and dress them neatly. And for dining, no longer was the secluded spot on the river chosen, but a State house, with its dining hall, and tables and chairs, about which my friend had made arrangements in collusion with the chief cook there.

This bait had its effect. I got over my dislike for bread, forswore my compassion for the goats, and became a relisher of meat-dishes, if not of meat itself. This went on for about a year. But not more than half a dozen meat-feasts were enjoyed in all; because the State house was not available every day, and there was the obvious difficulty about frequently preparing expensive savory meat-dishes. I had no money to pay for this "reform." My friend had therefore always to find the wherewithal. I had no knowledge where he found it. But find it he did, because he was bent on turning me into a meat-eater. But even his means must have been limited, and hence these feasts had necessarily to be few and far between.

Whenever I had occasion to indulge in these surreptitious feasts, dinner at home was out of the question. My mother would naturally ask me to come and take my food and want to know the reason why I did not wish to eat. I would say to her, "I have no appetite today; there is something wrong with my digestion." It was not without compunction that I devised these pretexts. I knew I was lying, and lying to my mother. I also knew that, if my mother and father came to know of my having become a meat-eater, they would be deeply shocked. This knowledge was gnawing at my heart.

Therefore I said to myself: "Though it is essential to eat meat, and also essential to take up food 'reform' in the country, yet deceiving and lying to one's father and mother is worse than not eating meat. In their lifetime, therefore, meat-eating must be out of the question. When they are no more and I have found my freedom, I will eat meat openly, but until that moment arrives I will abstain from it."

This decision I communicated to my friend, and I have never since gone back to meat. My parents never knew that two of their sons had become meat-eaters.

EARLY GLIMPSES OF RELIGION
by M. K. Gandhi

From my sixth or seventh year up to my sixteenth I was at school, being taught all sorts of things except religion. I may say that I failed to get from the teachers what they could have given me without any effort on their part. And yet I kept on picking up things here and there from my surroundings. The term "religion" I am using in its broadest sense, meaning thereby self-realization or knowledge of self.

Being born in the Vaishnava faith, I had often to go to the Haveli. But it never appealed to me. I did not like its glitter and pomp. Also I heard rumors of immorality being practised there, and lost all interest in it. Hence I could gain nothing from the Haveli.

But what I failed to get there I obtained from my nurse, an old servant of the family, whose affection for me I still recall. I have said before that there was in me a fear of ghosts and spirits. Rambha, for that was her name, suggested, as a remedy for this fear, the repetition of Ramanama.[12] I had more faith in her than in her remedy, and so at a tender age I began repeating Ramanama to cure my fear of ghosts and spirits. This was of course short-lived, but the good seed sown in childhood was not sown in vain. I think it is due to the seed sown by that good woman Rambha that today Ramanama is an infallible remedy for me.

Just about this time, a cousin of mine who was a devotee of the Ramayana[13] arranged for my second brother and me to learn Ram Raksha.[14] We got it by heart, and made it a rule to recite it every morning after the bath. The practice was kept up as long

• Reprinted with permission from Gandhi's Autobiography (Washington: Public Affairs Press, 1948), Part I, Chapter X, pp. 47-51.

as we were in Porbandar. As soon as we reached Rajkot, it was forgotten. For I had not much belief in it. I recited it partly because of my pride in being able to recite *Ram Raksha* with correct pronunciation.

What, however, left a deep impression on me was the reading of the *Ramayana* before my father. During part of his illness my father was in Porbandar. There every evening he used to listen to the *Ramayana*. The reader was a great devotee of Rama— Ladha Maharaj of Bileshvar. It was said of him that he cured himself of his leprosy not by any medicine, but by applying to the affected parts *bilva* leaves which had been cast away after being offered to the image of Mahadeva [15] in Bileshvar temple, and by the regular repetition of *Ramanama*. His faith, it was said, had made him whole. This may or may not be true. We at any rate believed the story. And it is a fact that when Ladha Maharaj began his reading of the *Ramayana* his body was entirely free from leprosy. He had a melodious voice. He would sing the *Dohas* (couplets) and *Chopais* (quatrains), and explain them, losing himself in the discourse and carrying his listeners along with him. I must have been thirteen at that time, but I quite remember being enraptured by his reading. That laid the foundation of my deep devotion to the *Ramayana*. Today I regard the *Ramayana* of Tulasidas [16] as the greatest book in all devotional literature.

A few months after this we came to Rajkot. There was no *Ramayana* reading there. The *Bhagavat*,[17] however, used to be read on every *Ekadashi* [18] day. Sometimes I attended the reading, but the reciter was uninspiring. Today I see that the *Bhagavat* is a book which can evoke religious fervor. I have read it in Gujarati with intense interest. But when I heard portions of the original read by Pandit Madan Mohan Malaviya during my twenty-one days' fast, I wished I had heard it in my childhood from such a devotee as he is, so that I could have formed a liking for it at an early age. Impressions formed at that age strike roots deep down into one's nature, and it is my perpetual regret that I was not fortunate enough to hear more good books of this kind read during that period.

In Rajkot, however, I got an early grounding in toleration for all branches of Hinduism and sister religions. For my father and mother would visit the *Haveli* as also Shiva's and Rama's temples, and would take or send us youngsters there. Jain monks also would pay frequent visits to my father, and would even go out of their way to accept food from us—non-Jains. They would have talks with my father on subjects religious and mundane.

He had, besides, Musalman and Parsi friends, who would talk to him about their own faiths, and he would listen to them always with respect, and often with interest. Being his nurse, I often had a chance to be present at these talks. These many things combined to inculcate in me a toleration for all faiths.

Only Christianity was at the time an exception. I developed a sort of dislike for it. And for a reason. In those days Christian missionaries used to stand in a corner near the high school and hold forth, pouring abuse on Hindus and their gods. I could not endure this. I must have stood there to hear them once only, but that was enough to dissuade me from repeating the experiment. About the same time, I heard of a well known Hindu having been converted to Christianity. It was the talk of the town that, when he was baptized, he had to eat beef and drink liquor, that he also had to change his clothes, and that thenceforth he began to go about in European costume including a hat. These things got on my nerves. Surely, thought I, a religion that compelled one to eat beef, drink liquor, and change one's own clothes did not deserve the name. I also heard that the new convert had already begun abusing the religion of his ancestors, their customs and their country. All these things created in me a dislike for Christianity.

But the fact that I had learnt to be tolerant to other religions did not mean that I had any living faith in God. I happened, about this time, to come across *Manusmriti* [19] which was amongst my father's collection. The story of the creation and similar things in it did not impress me very much, but on the contrary made me incline somewhat towards atheism.

There was a cousin of mine, still alive, for whose intellect I had great regard. To him I turned with my doubts. But he could not resolve them. He sent me away with this answer: "When you grow up, you will be able to solve these doubts yourself. These questions ought not to be raised at your age." I was silenced, but was not comforted. Chapters about diet and the like in *Manusmriti* seemed to me to run contrary to daily practice. To my doubts as to this also, I got the same answer. "With intellect more developed and with more reading I shall understand it better," I said to myself.

Manusmriti at any rate did not then teach me *ahimsa*.[20] I have told the story of my meat-eating. *Manusmriti* seemed to support it. I also felt that it was quite moral to kill serpents, bugs, and the like. I remember to have killed at that age bugs and such other insects, regarding it as a duty.

But one thing took deep root in me—the conviction that morality is the basis of things, and that truth is the substance of all morality. Truth became my sole objective. It began to grow in magnitude every day, and my definition of it also has been ever widening.

A Gujarati didactic stanza likewise gripped my mind and heart. Its precept—return good for evil—became my guiding principle. It became such a passion with me that I began numerous experiments in it. Here are those (for me) wonderful lines:

> For a bowl of water give a goodly meal;
> For a kindly greeting bow thou down with zeal;
> For a simple penny pay thou back with gold;
> If thy life be rescued, life do not withhold.
> Thus the words and actions of the wise regard;
> Every little service tenfold they reward.
> But the truly noble know all men as one,
> And return with gladness good for evil done.

PLAYING THE ENGLISH GENTLEMAN
by M. K. Gandhi

Gandhi graduated from high school in 1887 and enrolled in
Samaldas College in his home province. He disliked this school
and fell in with the suggestion that he study law in England.
With some difficulty he secured the blessings of his wife, mother,
and brother, but he reaped the opprobrium of his caste in Bombay. On September 4, 1888 he sailed alone from Bombay and
arrived in Southampton about three weeks later. After several
shifts, he roomed in the house of a widow in West Kensington.
He had some difficulty in adjusting himself to the new culture
and climate, as this excerpt shows.

I HAD NOT YET started upon my regular studies. I had just begun
reading newspapers, thanks to Sjt. Shukla.[21] In India I had never
read a newspaper. But here I succeeded in cultivating a liking
for them by regular reading. I always glanced over The Daily
News, The Daily Telegraph, and The Pall Mall Gazette. This took
me hardly an hour. I therefore began to wander about. I launched
out in search of a vegetarian restaurant. The landlady had told me
that there were such places in the city. I would trot ten or twelve
miles each day, go into a cheap restaurant and eat my fill of bread,
but would never be satisfied. During these wanderings I once hit
on a vegetarian restaurant in Farringdon Street. The sight of it
filled me with the same joy that a child feels on getting a thing
after its own heart. Before I entered I noticed books for sale
exhibited under a glass window near the door. I saw among them
Salt's Plea for Vegetarianism. This I purchased for a shilling and

• Reprinted with permission from Gandhi's Autobiography (Washington: Public Affairs Press, 1948), Part I, Chapters XIV and XV, pp. 66-67, 69-71.

went straight to the dining room. This was my first hearty meal since my arrival in England. God had come to my aid.

I read Salt's book from cover to cover and was very much impressed by it. From the date of reading this book, I may claim to have become a vegetarian by choice. I blessed the day on which I had taken the vow before my mother. I had all along abstained from meat in the interests of truth and of the vow I had taken, but had wished at the same time that every Indian should be a meat-eater, and had looked forward to being one myself freely and openly some day, and to enlisting others in the cause. The choice was now made in favor of vegetarianism, the spread of which henceforward became my mission. . . .

I decided . . . to become polished and make up for my vegetarianism by cultivating other accomplishments which fitted one for polite society. And for this purpose I undertook the all too impossible task of becoming an English gentleman.

The clothes after the Bombay cut that I was wearing were, I thought, unsuitable for English society, and I got new ones at the Army and Navy Stores. I also went in for a chimney-pot hat costing nineteen shillings—an excessive price in those days. Not content with this, I wasted ten pounds on an evening suit made in Bond Street, the centre of fashionable life in London; and got my good and noble-hearted brother to send me a double watch-chain of gold. It was not correct to wear a ready-made tie and I learnt the art of tying one for myself. While in India, the mirror had been a luxury permitted on the days when the family barber gave me a shave. Here I wasted ten minutes every day before a huge mirror, watching myself arranging my tie and parting my hair in the correct fashion. My hair was by no means soft, and every day it meant a regular struggle with the brush to keep it in position. Each time the hat was put on and off, the hand would automatically move towards the head to adjust the hair, not to mention the other civilized habit of the hand every now and then operating for the same purpose when sitting in polished society.

As if all this were not enough to make me look the thing, I directed my attention to other details that were supposed to go

towards the making of an English gentleman. I was told it was
necessary for me to take lessons in dancing, French and elocution.
French was not only the language of neighboring France, but it
was the *lingua franca* of the Continent over which I had a desire
to travel. I decided to take dancing lessons at a class and paid down
£3 as fees for a term. I must have taken about six lessons in three
weeks. But it was beyond me to achieve anything like rhythmic
motion. I could not follow the piano and hence found it impossible to keep time. What then was I to do? The recluse in the
fable kept a cat to keep off the rats, and then a cow to feed the
cat with milk, and a man to keep the cow and so on. My ambi-
tions also grew like the family of the recluse. I thought I should
learn to play the violin in order to cultivate an ear for Western
music. So I invested £3 in a violin and something more in fees.
I sought a third teacher to give me lessons in elocution and paid
him a preliminary fee of a guinea. He recommended Bell's *Standard Elocutionist* as the text-book, which I purchased. And I began with a speech of Pitt's.

But Mr. Bell rang the bell of alarm in my ear and I awoke.

I had not to spend a lifetime in England, I said to myself.
What then was the use of learning elocution? And how could
dancing make a gentleman of me? The violin I could learn even
in India. I was a student and ought to go on with my studies. I
should qualify myself to join the Inns of Court.[22] If my character
made a gentleman of me, so much the better. Otherwise I should
forego the ambition.

RELIGIOUS STUDIES

• by M. K. Gandhi

After a number of experiments in English living, Gandhi settled down to the frugal life of a student. He took his own rooms, and improved his weak English. He studied Latin, French, chemistry, and other subjects in a private class and passed the London matriculation examinations. In the meantime, he joined a vegetarian society and was appointed to its executive committee.

TOWARDS THE END of my second year in England I came across two Theosophists,[23] brothers, and both unmarried. They talked to me about the *Gita*. They were reading Sir Edwin Arnold's translation —*The Song Celestial*—and they invited me to read the original with them. I felt ashamed, as I had read the divine poem neither in Sanskrit nor in Gujarati. I was constrained to tell them that I had not read the *Gita*, but that I would gladly read it with them, and that though my knowledge of Sanskrit was meagre, still I hoped to be able to understand the original to the extent of telling where the translation failed to bring out the meaning. I began reading the *Gita* with them. The verses in the second chapter

If one
Ponders on objects of the sense, there springs
Attraction; from attraction grows desire,
Desire flames to fierce passion, passion breeds
Recklessness; then the memory—all betrayed—
Lets noble purpose go, and saps the mind,
Till purpose, mind, and man are all undone.

• Reprinted with permission from *Gandhi's Autobiography* (Washington: Public Affairs Press, 1948), Part I, Chapter XX, pp. 90-92.

made a deep impression on my mind, and they still ring in my ears. The book struck me as one of priceless worth. The impression has ever since been growing on me with the result that I regard it today as the book *par excellence* for the knowledge of Truth. It has afforded me invaluable help in my moments of gloom. I have read almost all the English translations of it, and I regard Sir Edwin Arnold's as the best. He has been faithful to the text, and yet it does not read like a translation. Though I read the *Gita* with these friends, I cannot pretend to have studied it then. It was only after some years that it became a book of daily reading.

The brothers also recommended *The Light of Asia* by Sir Edwin Arnold, whom I knew till then as the author only of *The Song Celestial*, and I read it with even greater interest than I did the *Bhagavadgita*. Once I had begun it I could not leave off. They also took me on one occasion to the Blavatsky Lodge and introduced me to Madame Blavatsky and Mrs. Besant. The latter had just then joined the Theosophical Society, and I was following with great interest the controversy about her conversion. The friends advised me to join the Society, but I politely declined saying, "With my meagre knowledge of my own religion I do not want to belong to any religious body." I recall having read, at the brothers' instance, Madame Blavatsky's *Key to Theosophy*. This book stimulated in me the desire to read books on Hinduism, and disabused me of the notion fostered by the missionaries that Hinduism was rife with superstition.

About the same time I met a good Christian from Manchester in a vegetarian boarding house. He talked to me about Christianity. I narrated to him my Rajkot recollections. He was pained to hear them. He said, "I am a vegetarian. I do not drink. Many Christians are meat-eaters and drink, no doubt; but neither meat-eating nor drinking is enjoined by Scripture. Do please read the Bible." I accepted his advice, and he got me a copy. I have a faint recollection that he himself used to sell copies of the Bible, and I purchased from him an edition containing maps, concordance, and other aids. I began reading it, but I could not possibly read through the Old Testament. I read the book of Genesis, and the chapters that followed invariably sent me to sleep. But just for the sake of being able to say that I had read it, I plodded through the other books with much difficulty and without the least interest or understanding. I disliked reading the book of Numbers.

But the New Testament produced a different impression, especially the Sermon on the Mount which went straight to my heart. I compared it with the *Gita*. The verses, "But I say unto you, that ye resist not evil: but whosoever shall smite thee on thy right cheek, turn to him the other also. And if any man take away thy coat let him have thy cloke too," delighted me beyond measure and put me in mind of Shamal Bhatt's [24] "For a bowl of water, give a goodly meal" etc. My young mind tried to unify the teaching of the *Gita*, the *Light of Asia* and the Sermon on the Mount. That renunciation was the highest form of religion appealed to me greatly.

This reading whetted my appetite for studying the lives of other religious teachers. A friend recommended Carlyle's *Heroes and Hero-Worship*. I read the chapter on the Hero as a prophet and learnt of the Prophet's [25] greatness and bravery and austere living.

Beyond this acquaintance with religion I could not go at the moment, as reading for the examination left me scarcely any time for outside subjects. But I took mental note of the fact that I should read more religious books and acquaint myself with all the principal religions.

And how could I help knowing something of atheism too? Every Indian knew Bradlaugh's [26] name and his so-called atheism. I read some book about it, the name of which I forget. It had no effect on me, for I had already crossed the Sahara of atheism. Mrs. Besant, who was then very much in the limelight, had turned to theism from atheism, and that fact also strengthened my aversion to atheism. I had read her book *How I Became a Theosophist*.

BEGINNING LIFE AS A LAWYER

•

by M. K. Gandhi

Gandhi made a brief trip to Paris to visit the Exhibition in 1890. He studied for his bar examinations, spending "nine months of fairly hard labor to read through the Common Law of England." Having passed his examinations, he was called to the bar on June 10, 1891, enrolled in the High Court on June 11, and sailed for India on June 12. He was met at Bombay by his elder brother, and told that his mother had died while he was in England. The news had been withheld to spare him the blow in a foreign land. Gandhi wrote, "My grief was even greater than over my father's death; most of my cherished hopes were shattered." His brother had, however, made plans for him to practice law.

MY ELDER BROTHER had built high hopes on me. The desire for wealth and name and fame was great in him. He had a big heart, generous to a fault. This, combined with his simple nature, had attracted to him many friends, and through them he expected to get me briefs. He had also assumed that I should have a swinging practice and had, in that expectation, allowed the household expenses to become top-heavy. He had also left no stone unturned in preparing the field for my practice.

The storm in my caste over my foreign voyage was still brewing. It had divided the caste into two camps, one of which immediately readmitted me, while the other was bent on keeping me out. To please the former my brother took me to Nasik before going to Rajkot, gave me a bath in the sacred river and, on reaching Rajkot, gave a caste dinner. I did not like all this. But my brother's love

• Reprinted with permission from *Gandhi's Autobiography* (Washington: Public Affairs Press, 1948), Part II, pp. 115, 116, 117, 119-20, 121, 123, 128-29.

for me was boundless, and my devotion to him was in proportion to it, and so I mechanically acted as he wished, taking his will to be law. The trouble about readmission to the caste was thus practically over. . . .

My relations with my wife were still not as I desired. Even my stay in England had not cured me of jealousy. I continued my squeamishness and suspiciousness in respect of every little thing, and hence all my cherished desires remained unfulfilled. I had decided that my wife should learn reading and writing and that I should help her in her studies, but my lust came in the way and she had to suffer for my own shortcoming. Once I went the length of sending her away to her father's house, and consented to receive her back only after I had made her thoroughly miserable. I saw later that all this was pure folly on my part.

I had planned reform in the education of children. My brother had children, and my own child which I had left at home when I went to England was now a boy of nearly four. It was my desire to teach these little ones physical exercise and make them hardy, and also to give them the benefit of my personal guidance. In this I had my brother's support and I succeeded in my efforts more or less. I very much liked the company of children, and the habit of playing and joking with them has stayed with me till today. I have ever since thought that I should make a good teacher of children. . . .

Expenses thus went up. New things were added every day. We had succeeded in tying a white elephant at our door. But how was the wherewithal to be found? To start practice in Rajkot would have meant sure ridicule. I had hardly the knowledge of a qualified vakil [27] and yet I expected to be paid ten times his fee! No client would be fool enough to engage me. And even if such a one was to be found, should I add arrogance and fraud to my ignorance, and increase the burden of debt I owed to the world?

Friends advised me to go to Bombay for some time in order to gain experience of the High Court, to study Indian law and to try to get what briefs I could. I took up the suggestion and went. . . .

Whilst in Bombay, I began, on the one hand, my study of Indian law and, on the other, my experiments in dietetics in which Virchand Gandhi, a friend, joined me. My brother, for his part, was trying his best to get me briefs.

The study of Indian law was a tedious business. The Civil Procedure Code I could in no way get on with. Not so, however, with the Evidence Act. Virchand Gandhi was reading for the Solicitor's Examination and would tell me all sorts of stories about barristers and vakils. "Sir Pherozeshah's ability," he would say, "lies in his profound knowledge of law. He has the Evidence Act by heart and knows all the cases on the thirty-second section. Badruddin Tyabji's wonderful power of argument inspires the judges with awe."

The stories of stalwarts such as these would unnerve me.

"It is not unusual," he would add, "for a barrister to vegetate for five or seven years. That's why I have signed the articles for solicitorship.[28] You should count yourself lucky if you can paddle your own canoe in three years' time."

Expenses were mounting up every month. To have a barrister's board outside the house, whilst still preparing for the barrister's profession inside, was a thing to which I could not reconcile myself. Hence I could not give undivided attention to my studies. I developed some liking for the Evidence Act and read Mayne's *Hindu Law* with deep interest, but I had not the courage to conduct a case. I was helpless beyond words, even as the bride come fresh to her father-in-law's house!

About this time, I took up the case of one Mamibai. It was a "small cause." "You will have to pay some commission to the tout," I was told. I emphatically declined.

"But even that great criminal lawyer Mr. So-and-So, who makes three to four thousand a month, pays commission!"

"I do not need to emulate him," I rejoined. "I should be content with Rs. 300 a month. Father did not get more."

"But those days are gone. Expenses in Bombay have gone up frightfully. You must be businesslike."

I was adamant. I gave no commission, but got Mamibai's case

all the same. It was an easy case. I charged Rs. 30 for my fees. The case was not likely to last longer than a day.

This was my debut in the Small Causes Court. I appeared for the defendant and had thus to cross-examine the plaintiff's witnesses. I stood up, but my heart sank into my boots. My head was reeling and I felt as though the whole court was doing likewise. I could think of no question to ask. The judge must have laughed, and the vakils no doubt enjoyed the spectacle. But I was past seeing anything. I sat down and told the agent that I could not conduct the case, that he had better engage Patel and have the fee back from me. Mr. Patel was duly engaged for Rs. 51. To him, of course, the case was child's play.

I hastened from the Court, not knowing whether my client won or lost her case, but I was ashamed of myself, and decided not to take up any more cases until I had courage enough to conduct them. Indeed I did not go to Court again until I went to South Africa. There was no virtue in my decision. I had simply made a virtue of necessity. There would be no one so foolish as to entrust his case to me, only to lose it!

. . . I wrung my hands in despair. My brother also felt much worried. We both came to the conclusion that it was no use spending more time in Bombay. I should settle in Rajkot where my brother, himself a petty pleader, could give me some work in the shape of drafting applications and memorials. And then as there was already a household at Rajkot, the breaking up of the one at Bombay meant a considerable saving. I liked the suggestion. My little establishment was thus closed after a stay of six months in Bombay. . . .

Disappointed, I left Bombay and went to Rajkot where I set up my own office. Here I got along moderately well. Drafting applications and memorials brought me in, on an average, Rs. 300 a month. For this work I had to thank influence rather than my own ability, for my brother's partner had a settled practice. All applications etc. which were, really or to his mind, of an important character, he sent to big barristers. To my lot fell the applications to be drafted on behalf of his poor clients. . . .

In the meantime a Meman [29] firm from Porbandar wrote to my brother making the following offer: "We have business in South Africa. Ours is a big firm, and we have a big case there in the Court, our claim being £40,000. It has been going on for a long time. We have engaged the services of the best vakils and barristers. If you sent your brother there, he would be useful to us and also to himself. He would be able to instruct our counsel better than ourselves. And he would have the advantage of seeing a new part of the world, and of making new acquaintances."

My brother discussed the proposition with me. I could not clearly make out whether I had simply to instruct the counsel or to appear in court. But I was tempted.

My brother introduced me to the late Sheth Abdul Karim Jhaveri, a partner of Dada Abdulla and Co., the firm in question. "It won't be a difficult job," the Sheth assured me. "We have big Europeans as our friends, whose acquaintance you will make. You can be useful to us in our shop. Much of our correspondence is in English and you can help us with that too. You will, of course, be our guest and hence will have no expense whatever."

"How long do you require my services?" I asked. "And what will be the payment?"

"Not more than a year. We will pay you a first class return fare and a sum of £105, all around."

This was hardly going there as a barrister. It was going as a servant of the firm. But I wanted somehow to leave India. There was also the tempting opportunity of seeing a new country, and of having new experience. Also I could send £105 to my brother and help in the expenses of the household. I closed with the offer without any higgling, and got ready to go to South Africa.

2 FIRST YEARS IN AFRICA (1893–1904)

ON THE WAY TO PRETORIA

• by M. K. Gandhi

Gandhi sailed for South Africa without his family in April 1893. He reached Durban toward the end of May and was met by his employer, Abdulla Sheth, a Moslem who, although unlettered, was one of the most affluent Indian businessmen in Natal. Gandhi soon left for Pretoria, capital of the Transvaal, where his presence was required in connection with the lawsuit for which he had been brought from India. The following incidents of the journey left an indelible impression in his memory.

ON THE SEVENTH or eighth day after my arrival, I left Durban. A first class seat was booked for me. It was usual there to pay five shillings extra, if one needed a bedding. Abdulla Sheth insisted that I should book one bedding but, out of obstinacy and pride and with a view to saving five shillings, I declined. Abdulla Sheth warned me. "Look, now," said he, "this is a different country from India. Thank God, we have enough and to spare. Please do not stint yourself in anything that you may need."

I thanked him and asked him not to be anxious.

The train reached Maritzburg, the capital of Natal, at about

• Reprinted with permission from *Gandhi's Autobiography* (Washington: Public Affairs Press, 1948), Part II, pp. 140-46.

9 P.M. Beddings used to be provided at this station. A railway servant came and asked me if I wanted one. "No," said I. "I have one with me." He went away. But a passenger came next, and looked me up and down. He saw that I was a "colored" man. This disturbed him. Out he went and came in again with one or two officials. They all kept quiet, when another official came to me and said, "Come along, you must go to the van compartment."

"But I have a first class ticket," said I.

"That doesn't matter," rejoined the other. "I tell you, you must go to the van compartment."

"I tell you, I was permitted to travel in this compartment at Durban, and I insist on going on in it."

"No, you won't," said the official. "You must leave this compartment, or else I shall have to call a police constable to push you out."

"Yes, you may. I refuse to get out voluntarily."

The constable came. He took me by the hand and pushed me out. My luggage was also taken out. I refused to go to the other compartment and the train steamed away. I went and sat in the waiting room, keeping my hand-bag with me, and leaving the other luggage where it was. The railway authorities had taken charge of it.

It was winter, and winter in the higher regions of South Africa is severely cold. Maritzburg being at a high altitude, the cold was extremely bitter. My overcoat was in my luggage, but I did not dare to ask for it lest I should be insulted again, so I sat and shivered. There was no light in the room. A passenger came in at about midnight and possibly wanted to talk to me. But I was in no mood to talk.

I began to think of my duty. Should I fight for my rights or go back to India, or should I go on to Pretoria without minding the insults, and return to India after finishing the case? It would be cowardice to run back to India without fulfilling my obligation. The hardship to which I was subjected was superficial—only a symptom of the deep disease of color prejudice. I should try, if possible, to root out the disease and suffer hardships in the process.

Redress for wrongs I should seek only to the extent that would be necessary for the removal of the color prejudice.

So I decided to take the next available train to Pretoria.

The following morning I sent a long telegram to the General Manager of the Railway and also informed Abdulla Sheth, who immediately met the General Manager. The Manager justified the conduct of the railway authorities, but informed him that he had already instructed the Station Master to see that I reached my destination safely. Abdulla Sheth wired to the Indian merchants in Maritzburg and to friends in other places to meet me and look after me. The merchants came to see me at the station and tried to comfort me by narrating their own hardships and explaining that what had happened to me was nothing unusual. They also said that Indians traveling first or second class had to expect trouble from railway officials and white passengers. The day was thus spent in listening to these tales of woe. The evening train arrived. There was a reserved berth for me. I now purchased at Maritzburg the bedding ticket I had refused to book at Durban.

The train reached Charlestown in the morning. There was no railway, in those days, between Charlestown and Johannesburg, but only a stage-coach, which halted at Standerton for the night en route. I possessed a ticket for the coach, which was not cancelled by the break of the journey at Maritzburg for a day; besides, Abdulla Sheth had sent a wire to the coach agent at Charlestown.

But the agent only needed a pretext for putting me off, and so, when he discovered me to be a stranger, he said, "Your ticket is cancelled." I gave him the proper reply. The reason at the back of his mind was not want of accommodation, but quite another. Passengers had to be accommodated inside the coach, but as I was regarded as a "coolie" and looked a stranger, it would be proper, thought the "leader," as the white man in charge of the coach was called, not to seat me with the white passengers. There were seats on either side of the coachbox. The leader sat on one of these as a rule. Today he sat inside and gave me his seat. I knew it was sheer injustice and an insult, but I thought it better to pocket it. I could not have forced myself inside, and if I had raised a protest, the coach would have gone off without me. This would have meant the loss of another day, and Heaven only knows what would have happened the next day. So, much as I fretted within myself, I prudently sat next the coachman.

At about three o'clock the coach reached Pardekoph. Now the leader desired to sit where I was seated, as he wanted to smoke and possibly to have some fresh air. So he took a piece of dirty sack-cloth from the driver, spread it on the footboard and, addressing me said, "Sami, you sit on this, I want to sit near the driver." The insult was more than I could bear. In fear and trembling I said to him, "It was you who seated me here, though I should have been accommodated inside. I put up with the insult. Now that you want to sit outside and smoke, you would have me sit at your feet. I will not do so, but I am prepared to sit inside."

As I was struggling through these sentences, the man came down upon me and began heavily to box my ears. He seized me by the arm and tried to drag me down. I clung to the brass rails of the coachbox and was determined to keep my hold even at the risk of breaking my wristbones. The passengers were witnessing the scene—the man swearing at me, dragging and belaboring me, and I remaining still. He was strong and I was weak. Some of the passengers were moved to pity and exclaimed: "Man, let him alone. Don't beat him. He is not to blame. He is right. If he can't stay there, let him come and sit with us." "No fear," cried the man, but he seemed somewhat crestfallen and stopped beating me. He let go my arm, swore at me a little more, and asking the Hottentot servant who was sitting on the other side of the coachbox to sit on the footboard, took the seat so vacated.

The passengers took their seats and, the whistle given, the coach rattled away. My heart was beating fast within my breast, and I was wondering whether I should ever reach my destination alive. The man cast an angry look at me now and then and, pointing his finger at me, growled: "Take care, let me once get to Standerton and I shall show you what I do." I sat speechless and prayed to God to help me.

After dark we reached Standerton and I heaved a sigh of relief on seeing some Indian faces. As soon as I got down, these friends said: "We are here to receive you and take you to Isa Sheth's shop. We have had a telegram from Dada Abdulla." I was very glad, and we went to Sheth Isa Haji Sumar's shop. The Sheth and his clerks gathered around me. I told them all that I had gone through. They were very sorry to hear it and comforted me by relating to me their own bitter experiences.

I wanted to inform the agent of the Coach Company of the whole affair. So I wrote him a letter, narrating everything that had happened, and drawing his attention to the threat his man had held out. I also asked for an assurance that he would accommodate me with the other passengers inside the coach when we started the next morning. To which the agent replied to this effect: "From Standerton we have a bigger coach with different men in charge. The man complained of will not be there tomorrow, and you will have a seat with the other passengers." This somewhat relieved me. I had, of course, no intention of proceeding against the man who had assaulted me, and so the chapter of the assault closed there.

In the morning Isa Sheth's man took me to the coach. I got a good seat and reached Johannesburg quite safely that night.

Standerton is a small village and Johannesburg a big city. Abdulla Sheth had wired to Johannesburg also, and given me the name and address of Muhammad Kasam Kamruddin's firm there. Their man had come to receive me at the stage, but neither did I see him nor did he recognize me. So I decided to go to a hotel. I knew the names of several. Taking a cab I asked to be driven to the Grand National Hotel. I saw the Manager and asked for a room. He eyed me for a moment, and politely saying, "I am very sorry, we are full up," bade me good-bye. So I asked the cabman to drive to Muhammad Kasam Kamruddin's shop. Here I found Abdul Gani Sheth expecting me, and he gave me a cordial greeting. He had a hearty laugh over the story of my experience at the hotel. "How ever did you expect to be admitted to a hotel?" he said.

"Why not?" I asked.

"You will come to know after you have stayed here a few days," said he. "Only we can live in a land like this, because, for making money, we do not mind pocketing insults, and here we are." With this he narrated to me the story of the hardships of Indians in South Africa.

RELIGIOUS FERMENT

by M. K. Gandhi

In Pretoria Gandhi attended to his legal work, but had much time for other pursuits. He spent much of his free time studying the condition of the Indian population in the Transvaal, and himself constantly experienced discrimination. A Christian legal associate, Mr. A. W. Baker, was also a lay preacher and took Gandhi to noon-day prayer meetings. There he met Mr. Coates, a Quaker, who discussed Christianity with him and introduced him to other Christian friends.

MR. BAKER WAS getting anxious about my future. He took me to the Wellington Convention. The Protestant Christians organize such gatherings every few years for religious enlightenment or, in other words, self-purification. One may call this religious restoration or revival. The Wellington Convention was of this type. The chairman was the famous divine of the place, the Rev. Andrew Murray. Mr. Baker had hoped that the atmosphere of religious exaltation at the Convention, and the enthusiasm and earnestness of the people attending it, would inevitably lead me to embrace Christianity.

But his final hope was the efficacy of prayer. He had an abiding

• Reprinted with permission from *Gandhi's Autobiography* (Washington: Public Affairs Press, 1948), Part II, Chapter XV, pp. 169-72.

faith in prayer. It was his firm conviction that God could not but listen to prayer fervently offered. He would cite the instances of men like George Muller of Bristol, who depended entirely on prayer even for his temporal needs. I listened to his discourse on the efficacy of prayer with unbiased attention, and assured him that nothing could prevent me from embracing Christianity, should I feel the call. I had no hesitation in giving him this assurance, as I had long since taught myself to follow the inner voice. I delighted in submitting to it. To act against it would be difficult and painful to me.

So we went to Wellington. Mr. Baker was hard put to it in having "a colored man" like me for his companion. He had to suffer inconveniences on many occasions entirely on account of me. We had to break the journey on the way, as one of the days happened to be a Sunday, and Mr. Baker and his party would not travel on the sabbath. Though the manager of the station hotel agreed to take me in after much altercation, he absolutely refused to admit me to the dining room. Mr. Baker was not the man to give way easily. He stood by the rights of the guests of a hotel. But I could see his difficulty. At Wellington also I stayed with Mr. Baker. In spite of his best efforts to conceal the little inconveniences that he was put up to, I could see them all.

This Convention was an assemblage of devout Christians. I was delighted at their faith. I met the Rev. Murray. I saw that many were praying for me. I liked some of their hymns, they were very sweet.

The Convention lasted for three days. I could understand and appreciate the devoutness of those who attended it. But I saw no reason for changing my belief—my religion. It was impossible for me to believe that I could go to heaven or attain salvation only by becoming a Christian. When I frankly said so to some of the good Christian friends, they were shocked. But there was no help for it.

My difficulties lay deeper. It was more than I could believe that Jesus was the only incarnate son of God, and that only he who believed in him would have everlasting life. If God could have sons, all of us were His sons. If Jesus was like God, or God Himself, then all men were like God and could be God Himself. My reason was not ready to believe literally that Jesus by his death and by his blood redeemed the sins of the world. Metaphorically there might be some truth in it. Again, according to Christianity only human beings had souls, and not other living beings, for whom death meant complete extinction; while I held a contrary belief. I could accept Jesus as a martyr, an embodiment of sacrifice, and a divine teacher, but not as the most perfect man ever born. His death on the Cross was a great example to the world, but that there was anything like a mysterious or miraculous virtue in it my heart could not accept. The pious lives of Christians did not give me anything that the lives of men of other faiths had failed to give. I had seen in other lives just the same reformation that I had heard of among Christians. Philosophically there was nothing extraordinary in Christian principles. From the point of view of sacrifice, it seemed to me that the Hindus greatly surpassed the Christians. It was impossible for me to regard Christianity as a perfect religion or the greatest of all religions.

I shared this mental churning with my Christian friends whenever there was an opportunity, but their answers could not satisfy me.

Thus if I could not accept Christianity either as a perfect, or the greatest, religion, neither was I then convinced of Hinduism being such. Hindu defects were pressingly visible to me. If untouchability could be a part of Hinduism, it could but be a rotten part or an excrescence. I could not understand the raison d'être of a multitude of sects and castes. What was the meaning of saying that the Vedas were the inspired Word of God? If they were inspired, why not also the Bible and the Koran?

As Christians friends were endeavoring to convert me, even so were Musalman friends. Abdulla Sheth had kept on inducing me to study Islam, and of course he had always something to say regarding its beauty.

I expressed my difficulties in a letter to Raychandbhai.[1] I also corresponded with other religious authorities in India and received answers from them. Raychandbhai's letter somewhat pacified me. He asked me to be patient and to study Hinduism more deeply. One of his sentences was to this effect: "On a dispassionate view of the question I am convinced that no other religion has the subtle and profound thought of Hinduism, its vision of the soul, or its charity."

I purchased Sale's translation of the Koran and began reading it. I also obtained other books on Islam. I communicated with Christian friends in England. One of them introduced me to Edward Maitland,[2] with whom I opened correspondence. He sent me *The Perfect Way*, a book he had written in collaboration with Anna Kingsford. The book was a repudiation of the current Christian belief. He also sent me another book, *The New Interpretation of the Bible*. I liked both. They seemed to support Hinduism. Tolstoy's *The Kingdom of God Is Within You* [3] overwhelmed me. It left an abiding impression on me. Before the independent thinking, profound morality, and the truthfulness of this book, all the books given me by Mr. Coates seemed to pale into insignificance.

My studies thus carried me in a direction unthought of by the Christian friends. My correspondence with Edward Maitland was fairly prolonged, and that with Raychandbhai continued until his death. I read some of the books he sent me. These included *Panchikaran*, *Maniratnamala*, *Mumukshu Prakaran* of *Yogavasishtha*, Haribhadra Suri's *Shaddarshana Samuchchaya* and others.

Though I took a path my Christian friends had not intended for me, I have remained forever indebted to them for the religious quest that they awakened in me. I shall always cherish the memory of their contact. The years that followed had more, not less, of such sweet and sacred contacts in store for me.

A PARIAH

by C. F. Andrews

[GANDHI] had himself suffered terribly in South Africa, along with the whole Indian community, many of whom were High-Caste Hindus, owing to the treatment meted out to them by Christian people. . . . How can I ever forget, for instance, the shock of horror and dismay which I had on first landing in South Africa in 1913? The Archdeacon kindly met me on the wharf and asked me to preach in his church. It was the first Sunday after Christmas, and I preached a Christmas sermon of "peace and good will to all mankind." I had no idea whatever that anything had happened while I was preaching that sermon; but Mr. Gandhi had expressed to my friend and companion, Mr. W. W. Pearson, of Manchester, that he himself would like to hear me preach. Mr. Pearson had taken him to the church door, and he had been refused an entrance even after all the circumstances of the request had been courteously explained and it was known who was being refused. Mr. Gandhi was thus a pariah in South Africa to that European Christian congregation.

• Reprinted with permission from C. F. Andrews, *Mahatma Gandhi's Ideas* (London: Allen and Unwin, 1949), pp. 177-78.

MAN PROPOSES, GOD DISPOSES

• by M. K. Gandhi

Although Gandhi was not the principal lawyer for his client in the lawsuit—for £40,000—he studied the bookkeeping involved in the case and did much translation. He concluded that his client had the stronger case, but that the interminable litigation would ruin both plaintiff and defendant. He successfully urged the appointment of an arbitrator and, in the end, his client won. Since the loser would be bankrupt if he had to pay the whole award, Gandhi induced his client to accept installment payments. Gandhi said, "My joy was boundless. I had learnt the true practice of law. I realized that the true function of a lawyer was to unite parties riven asunder."

THE CASE having been concluded, I had no reason for staying in Pretoria. So I went back to Durban and began to make preparations for my return home. But Abdulla Sheth was not the man to let me sail without a send-off. He gave a farewell party in my honor at Sydenham.

It was proposed to spend the whole day there. Whilst I was turning over the sheets of some of the newspapers I found there, I chanced to see a paragraph in a corner of one of them under the caption, "Indian Franchise." It was with reference to the Bill then before the House of Legislature, which sought to deprive the Indians of their right to elect members of the Natal Legislative Assembly. I was ignorant of the Bill, and so were the rest of the guests who had assembled there.

I inquired of Abdulla Sheth about it. He said: "What can we

• Reprinted with permission from *Gandhi's Autobiography* (Washington: Public Affairs Press, 1948), Part II, Chapter XVI, pp. 173-75.

understand in these matters? We can only understand things that affect our trade. As you know all our trade in the Orange Free State has been swept away. We agitated about it, but in vain. We are after all lame men, being unlettered. We generally take in newspapers simply to ascertain the daily market rates, etc. What can we know of legislation? Our eyes and ears are the European attorneys here."

"But," said I, "there are so many young Indians born and educated here. Do not they help you?"

"They!" exclaimed Abdulla Sheth in despair. "They never care to come to us, and to tell you the truth, we care less to recognize them. Being Christians, they are under the thumb of the white clergymen, who in their turn are subject to the Government."

This opened my eyes. I felt that this class should be claimed as our own. Was this the meaning of Christianity? Did they cease to be Indians because they had become Christians?

But I was on the point of returning home and hesitated to express what was passing through my mind in this matter. I simply said to Abdulla Sheth: "This Bill, if it passes into law, will make our lot extremely difficult. It is the first nail into our coffin. It strikes at the root of our self-respect."

"It may," echoed Sheth Abdulla. "I will tell you the genesis of the franchise question. We knew nothing about it. But Mr. Escombe, one of our best attorneys, whom you know, put the idea into our heads. It happened thus. He is a great fighter, and there being no love lost between him and the Wharf Engineer, he feared that the Engineer might deprive him of his votes and defeat him at the election. So he acquainted us with our position, and at his instance we all registered ourselves as voters, and voted for him. You will now see how the franchise has not for us the value that you attach to it. But we understand what you say. Well, then, what is your advice?"

The other guests were listening to this conversation with attention. One of them said: "Shall I tell you what should be done? You cancel your passage by this boat, stay here a month longer, and we will fight as you direct us."

All the others chimed in: "Indeed, indeed. Abdulla Sheth, you must detain Gandhibhai."

The Sheth was a shrewd man. He said: "I may not detain him now. Or rather, you have as much right as I to do so. But you are quite right. Let us *all* persuade him to stay on. But you should remember that he is a barrister. What about his fees?"

The mention of fees pained me, and I broke in: "Abdulla Sheth, fees are out of the question. There can be no fees for public work. I can stay, if at all, as a servant. And as you know, I am not acquainted with all these friends. But if you believe that they will cooperate, I am prepared to stay a month longer. There is one thing, however. Though you need not pay me anything, work of the nature we contemplate cannot be done without some funds to start with. Thus we may have to send telegrams. we may have to print some literature, some touring may have to be done, the local attorneys may have to be consulted, and as I am ignorant of your laws, I may need some law-books for reference. All this cannot be done without money. And it is clear that one man is not enough for this work. Many must come forward to help him."

And a chorus of voices was heard: "Allah is great and merciful. Money will come in. Men there are, as many as you may need. You please consent to stay, and all will be well."

The farewell party was thus turned into a working committee. I suggested finishing dinner etc. quickly and getting back home. I worked out in my own mind an outline of the campaign. I ascertained the names of those who were on the list of voters, and made up my mind to stay on for a month.

Thus God laid the foundations of my life in South Africa and sowed the seed of the fight for national self-respect.

MOBBED AT DURBAN
by M. K. Gandhi

In 1896, after Gandhi had been in South Africa three years,
he asked permission to return to India for six months. He wanted
to bring back his wife and children, who had remained in India,
and he also hoped to arouse interest in the grievances of Indians
in South Africa. To this end he wrote a popular brochure called
The Green Pamphlet. He also traveled widely in India, until, in
Calcutta, he received word to return at once to South Africa. He
sailed with his wife and two sons from Bombay at the beginning
of December 1896.

On reaching the port of Durban, his ship and another from
India were put in quarantine, ostensibly because of the plague in
Bombay, but really because of the presence of Gandhi. A garbled
report of his pamphlet had reached South Africa and the white
community was aroused against Gandhi, fearing that his returning
with two ship-loads of Indians was a plot to invade the country.
After riding at sea for twenty-three days outside Port Natal, the
ships were allowed to discharge their passengers, who had in the
meantime, together with Gandhi, received all kinds of threats.

A MESSAGE reached me from Mr. Escombe [4] advising me not to
land with the others but to wait until evening when he would
send the Superintendent of Water Police to escort me home, and
adding that my family were free to land at any time. This was not
an order according to law, but was by way of advice to the captain
not to allow me to land and of warning to me of the danger that
was hanging over my head. The captain had not the power forc-

• Reprinted with permission from M. K. Gandhi, Satyagraha in South Africa
(Madras: Ganesan, 1928), pp. 91-103.

ly to prevent me from landing. But I came to the conclusion
that I should accept this suggestion. I sent my family to the resi-
ence of my old friend and client, Parsee Rustomji, instead of to
y own place, and told them that I would meet them there. When
the passengers had disembarked, Mr. Laughton, counsel for Dada
Abdulla [5] and a personal friend of mine, came up and met me.
He asked me why I had not yet landed. I told him about Mr.
scombe's letter. He said that he did not like the idea of my wait-
ng till evening and then entering the city like a thief or offender,
that if I was not afraid, I should accompany him there and then,
nd that we could walk to the town as if nothing had happened.
I replied: "I do not think I am afraid. It is only a question of pro-
riety whether or not I should accept Mr. Escombe's suggestion.
And we should also consider whether the captain of the steamer
responsible in the matter." Mr. Laughton smiled and said:
"What has Mr. Escombe done for you that you must needs heed
his suggestion? And what reason have you to believe that he is
actuated by kindliness and not by some ulterior motive? I know
more than you what has happened in the town, and what hand
Mr. Escombe had in the happenings there." I interrupted him
with a shaking of the head. "We might assume," continued Mr.
Laughton, "that he is actuated by the best of motives. But I am
positively of opinion that if you comply with his suggestion, you
will stand humiliated. I would, therefore, advise you, if you are
ready, to accompany me just now. The captain is our man, and
his responsibility is our responsibility. He is accountable only to
Dada Abdulla. I know what they will think of the matter, as they
have displayed great courage in the present struggle." I replied:
"Let us then go. I have no preparations to make. All I have to do
is to put on my turban. Let us inform the captain and start." We
took the captain's leave.

Mr. Laughton was an old and well-known advocate of Durban.
I had come in intimate contact with him before I returned to
India. I used to consult him in difficult cases and often to engage
him as my senior. He was a brave and powerfully built man.

Our road lay through the principal street of Durban. It was

about half past four in the evening when we started. The sky was
slightly overcast and the sun was not to be seen. It would take a
pedestrian at least one hour to reach Rustomji Sheth's place. The
number of persons present about the wharf was not larger than
what is to be usually seen there. As soon as we landed, some boys
saw us. As I was the only Indian who put on a turban of a particular type, they at once recognized me, began to shout "Gandhi," "Gandhi," "thrash him," "surround him," and came up
towards us. Some began to throw pebbles at us. A few elderly
Europeans joined the boys. Gradually the party of rioters began
to grow. Mr. Laughton thought that there was danger in our going
on foot. He therefore hailed a rickshaw. I had never sat in a rickshaw before, as it was thoroughly disgusting to me to sit in a vehicle pulled by human beings. But I then felt that it was my duty
to use that vehicle. I have experienced five or seven times in my
life that one, whom God wishes to save, cannot fall even if he
will. If I did not fall I cannot take any credit for it to myself.
These rickshaws are pulled by Zulus. The elderly Europeans and
the boys threatened the rickshaw puller that if he allowed me to
sit in his rickshaw, they would beat him and smash his rickshaw
to pieces. The rickshaw boy, therefore, said "Kha" (meaning
"no") and went away. I was thus spared the shame of a rick
shaw ride.

We had no alternative now but to proceed to our destination
on foot. A mob followed us. With every step we advanced, it grew
larger and larger. The gathering was enormous when we reached
West Street. A man of powerful build took hold of Mr. Laughton
and tore him away from me. He was not therefore in a position
to come up with me. The crowd began to abuse me and shower
upon me stones and whatever else they could lay their hands on.
They threw down my turban. Meanwhile a burly fellow came up
to me, slapped me in the face and then kicked me. I was about
to fall down unconscious when I held on to the railings of a house
near by. I took breath for a while and when the fainting was over
proceeded on my way. I had almost given up the hope of reaching

home alive. But I remember well that even then my heart did not arraign my assailants.

While I was thus wending my way, the wife of the Superintendent of Police at Durban was coming from the opposite direction. We knew each other well. She was a brave lady. Although the sky was cloudy and the sun about to set, she opened her sunshade for my protection and began to walk at my side. The Europeans would not insult a lady, especially the wife of the old and popular Superintendent of Police, nor would they hurt her. They must avoid injuring her while aiming blows at me. The injuries, therefore, which I received after she joined me, were not serious. Meanwhile the Superintendent of Police came to know of the attack upon me and sent a party of constables for my protection. The police surrounded me. The Police Station was on our way. When we reached there I saw that the Superintendent of Police was waiting for us. He offered me asylum in the police station, but I declined the offer with thanks and said, "I must reach my destination. I have faith in the fair play of the citizens of Durban and in the righteousness of my own cause. I am thankful to you for sending the police party for my protection. Mrs. Alexander too has contributed to my safety."

I reached Rustomji's house without further trouble. It was nearly evening when I reached there. Dr. Dadibarjor, the medical officer of the *Courland*, who was with Rustomji Sheth, began to treat me. He examined my wounds. There were not many of them. One blind wound in particular was very painful. But I was not yet privileged to rest in peace. Thousands of Europeans gathered before Rustomji Sheth's house. After nightfall, hooligans also joined the crowd. The crowd sent word to Rustomji Sheth that if he did not hand me over to them, they would burn him and his house along with me. Rustomji Sheth was too good an Indian to be daunted. When Superintendent Alexander came to know how matters stood, he quietly joined the crowd with a number of detectives. He sent for a bench and stood upon it. Thus under the pretence of talking to the crowd, he took possession of the entrance to Rustomji's house so that none could break and enter it. He had already posted detectives at proper places. Immediately on arrival, he had instructed a subordinate to disguise himself as an Indian trader by putting on Indian dress and painting his face to see me and deliver to me the following message: "If you wish to save your friend, his guests and property, and your own family, I advise you to disguise yourself as an Indian constable, come out through Rustomji's go-down, steal through the crowd with my man and reach the Police Station. A carriage is awaiting you at the corner of the street. This is the only way in which I can save you and others. The crowd is so excited that I am not in a position to control it. If you are not prompt in following my directions, I am afraid the crowd will raze Rustomji's house to the ground and it is impossible for me to imagine how many lives will be lost and how much property destroyed."

I gauged the situation at once. I soon disguised myself as a constable and left Rustomji's house. The Police Officer and I reached the Police Station in safety. In the meantime Mr. Alexander was humoring the crowd by singing topical songs [6] and talking to them. When he knew that I had reached the Police Station, he became serious and asked:

"What do you want?"

"We want Gandhi."

"What will you do with him?"

"We will burn him."

"What harm has he done to you?"

"He has vilified us in India and wants to flood Natal with Indians."

"What if he does not come out?"

"We will then burn this house."

"His wife and children are also there. There are other men and women besides. Would you not be ashamed of burning women and children?"

"The responsibility for that will rest with you. What can we do when you make us helpless in the matter? We do not wish to hurt anyone else. It would be enough if you hand over Gandhi to us. If you do not surrender the culprit, and if others are injured in our endeavor to capture him, would it be fair on your part to blame us?"

The Superintendent gently smiled and informed the crowd that I had left Rustomji's house, passed through their midst, and reached another place already. The crowd laughed loudly and shouted, "It is a lie, it is a lie."

The Superintendent said: "If you will not believe your old Superintendent of Police, please appoint a committee of three or four men from amongst you. Let others promise that they will not enter the house, and that if the committee fail to find Gandhi in the house, you will peacefully return to your homes. You got excited today and did not obey the police. That reflects discredit on you, not on the police. The police therefore played a trick with you; it removed your prey from your midst and you have lost the game. You will certainly not blame the police for this. The police, whom you yourselves have appointed, have simply done their duty."

The Superintendent addressed the crowd with such suavity and determination, that they gave him the promise he had asked for. A committee was appointed. It searched Rustomji's house through and through, and reported to the crowd that the Superintendent was right and had beaten them in the game. The crowd was disappointed. But they kept their word and dispersed without committing any mischief. This happened on 13th January 1897.

The same morning after the quarantine on the steamers had been removed, the reporter of a Durban newspaper had seen me on the steamer. He had asked me everything. It was quite easy to dispose of the charges against me to his satisfaction. I showed to him in detail that I had not indulged in the least exaggeration. What I had done was only my duty. If I had failed to discharge it, I would be unworthy of the name of man. All this appeared in the newspapers the next day. Sensible people among the Europeans admitted their mistake. The newspapers expressed their sympathy with the standpoint of the Europeans in Natal, but at the same time fully defended my action. This enhanced my reputation as well as the prestige of the Indian community. It was proved that the Indians, poor as they were, were no cowards, and that the Indian traders were prepared to fight for their self-respect and for their country regardless of loss.

Thus though the Indian community had to suffer hardship and though Dada Abdulla incurred big losses, the ultimate result, I believe, was entirely beneficial. The community had an opportunity of measuring their own strength and their self-confidence increased in consequence. I had a most valuable experience, and whenever I think of that day, I feel that God was preparing me for the practice of Satyagraha.

The events in Natal had their repercussion in England. Mr. Chamberlain,[7] Secretary of State for the Colonies, cabled to the Government of Natal asking them to prosecute my assailants and to see that justice was done to me.

Mr. Escombe, who was Attorney-General with the Government of Natal, called me. He told me about Mr. Chamberlain's cable. He expressed his regret for the injuries I had sustained, and his pleasure that the consequences of the assault were not more serious. He added, "I can assure you that I did not at all intend that you or any other member of your community should be injured. As I feared that you might possibly be hurt, I sent you word to say that you should land at night. You did not like my suggestion. I do not wish to blame you in the least that you accepted Mr. Laughton's advice. You were perfectly entitled to do what you thought fit. The Government of Natal fully accepts Mr. Chamberlain's demand. We desire that the offenders should be brought to book. Can you identify any of your assailants?"

I replied: "I might perhaps be able to identify one or two of them. But I must say at once before this conversation proceeds that I have already made up my mind not to prosecute my assailants. I cannot see that they are at fault. What information they had, they had obtained from their leaders. It is too much to expect them to judge whether it was correct or otherwise. If all that they heard about me was true, it was natural for them to be excited and do something wrong in a fit of indignation. I would not blame them for it. Excited crowds have always tried to deal out justice in that manner. If any one is to blame it is the Committee of Europeans, you yourself and therefore, the Government of Natal. Reuter might have cabled any distorted account. But when you knew that I was coming to Natal, it was your duty and duty of the Committee to question me about the suspicions you entertained with regard to my activities in India, to hear what I had to say and then do what might appear proper in the circumstances. Now I cannot prosecute you or the Committee for the assault. And even if I could, I would not seek redress in a court of law. You took such steps as seemed advisable to you for safeguarding the interests of the Europeans of Natal. That is a political matter, and it remains for me to fight with you in the political field and to convince you and the other Europeans that the Indians who constitute a large proportion of the population of the British Empire wish to preserve their self-respect and safeguard their rights without injuring the Europeans in the least."

Mr. Escombe said, "I quite understand what you say, and I appreciate it. I was not prepared to hear that you were not willing to prosecute your assailants. I would not have been displeased in the least had you prosecuted them. But when you have signified your determination not to prosecute, I do not hesitate to say not only that you have come to a right decision in the matter, but you will render further service to your community by your self-restraint. I must at the same time admit that your refusal to prosecute your assailants will save the Government of Natal from a most awkward position. If you so desire, the Government will see that your assailants are arrested, but it is scarcely necessary to tell you that it would irritate the Europeans and give rise to all manner of criticism, which no Government would relish. But if you have finally made up your mind not to prosecute, you should write to me a note signifying your intention to that effect. I cannot defend my Government merely by sending Mr. Chamberlain a summary of our conversation. I should cable to him a summary of your note. I am not, however, asking you to let me have the note just now. You had better consult your friends. You consult Mr. Laughton also. And if after such consultations you still adhere to your resolution not to prosecute, you write to me. But

your note should clearly state that you, on your own responsibility, refuse to prosecute your assailants. Then only can I make
use of it."

I said: "I had no idea that you had sent for me in this connection. I have not consulted anyone on the subject, nor do I wish
to consult anyone now. When I decided to land and proceed
with Mr. Laughton, I had made up my mind that I should not
feel aggrieved in case I was injured. Prosecuting my assailants is
therefore out of the question. This is a religious question with me,
and I believe with you that I shall serve my community as well as
myself by this act of self-restraint. I propose, therefore, to take all
the responsibility on my shoulders and to give you the note you
ask for here and now." I then obtained blank paper from him,
wrote out the desired note and handed it over to him.

FAMILY LIFE
by M. K. Gandhi

*Gandhi was separated a great deal from his family in his
early life. For this and other reasons, his family is only occasionally
mentioned in his autobiography. Following are several separated
narratives of family life between the time he brought his wife and
children to South Africa in 1897 and his return to India in 1901–2.*

WHEN I landed at Durban in January 1897, I had three children
with me, my sister's son ten years old, and my own sons nine and
five years of age. Where was I to educate them?

I could have sent them to the schools for European children,
but only as a matter of favor and exception. No other Indian

• Reprinted with permission from *Gandhi's Autobiography* (Washington: Public Affairs Press, 1948), Part III, pp. 245-46, 250-51, 261-63, 338-40.

children were allowed to attend them. For these there were schools established by Christian missions, but I was not prepared to send my children there, as I did not like the education imparted in those schools. For one thing, the medium of instruction would be only English, or perhaps incorrect Tamil or Hindi; this too could only have been arranged with difficulty. I could not possibly put up with this and other disadvantages. In the meantime I was making my own attempt to teach them. But that was at best irregular, and I could not get hold of a suitable Gujarati teacher.

I was at my wits' end. I advertised for an English teacher who should teach the children under my direction. Some regular instruction was to be given them by this teacher, and for the rest they should be satisfied with what little I could give them irregularly. So I engaged an English governess on £7 a month. This went on for some time, but not to my satisfaction. The boys acquired some knowledge of Gujarati through my conversation and intercourse with them, which was strictly in the mother-tongue. I was loath to send them back to India, for I believed even then that young children should not be separated from their parents. The education that children naturally imbibe in a well-ordered household is impossible to obtain in hostels. I therefore kept my children with me. I did send my nephew and elder son to be educated at residential schools in India for a few months, but I soon had to recall them. Later, the eldest son, long after he had come of age, broke away from me, and went to India to join a High School in Ahmedabad. I have an impression that the nephew was satisfied with what I could give him. Unfortunately he died in the prime of youth after a brief illness. The other three of my sons have never been at a public school, though they did get some regular schooling in an improvised school which I started for the children of Satyagrahi parents in South Africa. . . .

The question of the rearing of children had been ever before me. I had two sons born in South Africa, and my service in the hospital was useful in solving the question of their upbringing.

My independent spirit was a constant source of trial. My wife and I had decided to have the best medical aid at the time of her delivery, but if the doctor and the nurse were to leave us in the lurch at the right moment, what was I to do? Then the nurse had to be an Indian. And the difficulty of getting a trained Indian nurse in South Africa can be easily imagined from the similar difficulty in India. So I studied the things necessary for safe labor. I read Dr. Tribhuvandas' book, Ma-ne Shikhaman—Advice to a Mother—and I nursed both my children according to the instructions given in the book, tempered here and there by such experience as I had gained elsewhere. The services of a nurse were utilized—not for more than two months each time—chiefly for helping my wife, and not for taking care of the babies, which I did myself.

The birth of the last child put me to the severest test. The travail came on suddenly. The doctor was not immediately available, and some time was lost in fetching the midwife. Even if she had been on the spot, she could not have helped delivery. I had to see through the safe delivery of the baby. My careful study of the subject in Dr. Tribhuvandas' work was of inestimable help. I was not nervous.

I am convinced that for the proper upbringing of children the parents ought to have a general knowledge of the care and nursing of babies. At every step I have seen the advantages of my careful study of the subject. My children would not have enjoyed the general health that they do today, had I not studied the subject and turned my knowledge to account. We labor under a sort of superstition that the child has nothing to learn during the first five years of its life. On the contrary the fact is that the child never learns in after life what it does in its first five years. The education of the child begins with conception. The physical and mental states of the parents at the moment of conception are reproduced in the baby. Then during the period of pregnancy it continues to be affected by the mother's moods, desires and temperament, as also by her ways of life. After birth the child imitates the parents, and for a considerable number of years entirely depends on them for its growth. . . .

I had started on a life of ease and comfort, but the experiment was short-lived. Although I had furnished the house with care, yet it failed to have any hold on me. So no sooner had I launched forth on that life, than I began to cut down expenses. The washerman's bill was heavy, and as he was besides by no means noted for his punctuality, even two to three dozen shirts and collars proved insufficient for me. Collars had to be changed daily and shirts, if not daily, at least every alternate day. This meant a double expense, which appeared to me unnecessary. So I equipped myself with a washing outfit to save it. I bought a book on washing, studied the art and taught it also to my wife. This no doubt added to my work, but its novelty made it a pleasure.

I shall never forget the first collar that I washed myself. I had used more starch than necessary, the iron had not been made hot enough, and for fear of burning the collar I had not pressed it sufficiently. The result was that, though the collar was fairly stiff, the superfluous starch continually dropped off it. I went to court with the collar on, thus inviting the ridicule of brother barristers, but even in those days I could be impervious to ridicule. . . .

In the same way, as I freed myself from slavery to the washerman, I threw off dependence on the barber. All people who go to England learn there at least the art of shaving, but none, to my knowledge, learn to cut their own hair. I had to learn that too. I once went to an English hair-cutter in Pretoria. He contemptuously refused to cut my hair. I certainly felt hurt, but immediately purchased a pair of clippers and cut my hair before the mirror. I succeeded more or less in cutting the front hair, but I spoiled the back. The friends in the court shook with laughter.

"What's wrong with your hair, Gandhi? Rats have been at it?"

"No. The white barber would not condescend to touch my black hair," said I, "so I preferred to cut it myself, no matter how badly." . . .

When I was practicing in Durban, my office clerks often stayed with me, and there were among them Hindus and Christians, or to describe them by their provinces, Gujaratis and Tamilians. I do not recollect having ever regarded them as anything but my kith and kin. I treated them as members of my family, and had unpleasantness with my wife if ever she stood in the way of my treating them as such. One of the clerks was a Christian, born of Panchama [8] parents.

The house was built after the Western model and the rooms rightly had no outlets for dirty water. Each room had therefore chamber-pots. Rather than have these cleaned by a servant or a sweeper, my wife or I attended to them. The clerks who made themselves completely at home would naturally clean their own pots, but the Christian clerk was a newcomer, and it was our duty to attend to his bedroom. My wife managed the pots of the others, but to clean those used by one who had been a Panchama seemed to her to be the limit, and we fell out. She could not bear the pots being cleaned by me, neither did she like doing it herself. Even today I can recall the picture of her chiding me, her eyes red with anger, and pearl drops streaming down her cheeks, as she descended the ladder, pot in hand. But I was a cruelly kind husband. I regarded myself as her teacher, and so harassed her out of my blind love for her.

I was far from being satisfied by her merely carrying the pot. I would have her do it cheerfully. So I said, raising my voice: "I will not stand this nonsense in my house."

The words pierced her like an arrow.

She shouted back: "Keep your house to yourself and let me go." I forgot myself, and the spring of compassion dried up in me. I caught her by the hand, dragged the helpless woman to the gate, which was just opposite the ladder, and proceeded to open it with the intention of pushing her out. The tears were running down her cheeks in torrents, and she cried: "Have you no sense of shame? Must you so far forget yourself? Where am I to go? I have no parents or relatives here to harbor me. Being your wife, you think I must put up with your cuffs and kicks? For Heaven's sake behave yourself, and shut the gate. Let us not be found making scenes like this!"

I put on a brave face, but was really ashamed and shut the gate. If my wife could not leave me, neither could I leave her. We have had numerous bickerings, but the end has always been peace between us. The wife, with her matchless powers of endurance, has always been the victor.

Today I am in a position to narrate the incident with some detachment, as it belongs to a period out of which I have fortunately emerged. I am no longer a blind, infatuated husband, I am no more my wife's teacher. Kasturba can, if she will, be as unpleasant to me today, as I used to be to her before. We are tried friends, the one no longer regarding the other as the object of lust. She has been a faithful nurse throughout my illnesses, serving without any thought of reward. . . .

THE MAGIC SPELL OF A BOOK
• by M. K. Gandhi

In 1904 the journal, Indian Opinion, was launched in South Africa. Gandhi paid most of the deficits and wrote for it as well. "Week after week," he says, "I poured out my soul in its columns." At this time, in a vegetarian restaurant, Gandhi made the acquaintance of Mr. Henry S. L. Polak, of whom he later wrote, "We seemed to hold closely similar views on the essential things of life."

MR. POLAK . . . came to see me off at the station, and left with me a book to read during the journey, which he said I was sure to like. It was Ruskin's *Unto This Last.*

• Reprinted with permission from *Gandhi's Autobiography* (Washington: Public Affairs Press, 1948), Part IV, Chapters XVIII and XIX, pp. 364-68.

The book was impossible to lay aside, once I had begun it. It gripped me. Johannesburg to Durban was a twenty-four hours' journey. The train reached there in the evening. I could not get any sleep that night. I determined to change my life in accordance with the ideals of the book.

This was the first book of Ruskin I had ever read. During the days of my education I had read practically nothing outside textbooks, and after I launched into active life I had very little time for reading. I cannot therefore claim much book knowledge. However, I believe I have not lost much because of this enforced restraint. On the contrary, the limited reading may be said to have enabled me thoroughly to digest what I did read. Of these books, the one that brought about an instantaneous and practical transformation in my life was *Unto This Last*. I translated it later into Gujarati, entitling it *Sarvodaya* (the welfare of all).

I believe that I discovered some of my deepest convictions reflected in this great book of Ruskin, and that is why it so captured me and made me transform my life. A poet is one who can call forth the good latent in the human breast. Poets do not influence all alike, for everyone is not evolved in an equal measure.

The teaching of *Unto This Last* I understood to be:

1. That the good of the individual is contained in the good of all.
2. That a lawyer's work has the same value as the barber's, inasmuch as all have the same right of earning their livelihood from their work.
3. That a life of labor, i.e., the life of the tiller of the soil and the handicraftsman, is the life worth living.

The first of these I knew. The second I had dimly realized. The third had never occurred to me. *Unto This Last* made it as clear as daylight for me that the second and third were contained in the first. I arose with the dawn, ready to reduce these principles to practice.

I talked over the whole thing with Mr. West,[9] described to him the effect *Unto This Last* had produced on my mind, and proposed that *Indian Opinion* should be removed to a farm, on which everyone should labor, drawing the same living wage, and attending to the press work in spare time. Mr. West approved of the proposal, and £3 was laid down as the monthly allowance per head, irrespective of color or nationality.

But it was a question whether all the ten or more workers in the press would agree to go and settle on an out-of-the-way farm, and be satisfied with bare maintenance. We therefore proposed that those who could not fit in with the scheme should continue to draw their salaries and gradually try to reach the ideal of becoming members of the settlement.

I talked to the workers in the terms of this proposal. It did not appeal to Sjt. Madanjit,[10] who considered my proposal to be foolish and held that it would ruin a venture on which he had staked his all, that the workers would bolt, *Indian Opinion* would come to a stop, and the press would have to be closed down.

Among the men working in the press was Chhaganlal Gandhi, one of my cousins. I had put the proposal to him at the same time as to West. He had a wife and children, but he had from childhood chosen to be trained and to work under me. He had full faith in me. So without any argument he agreed to the scheme and has been with me ever since. The machinist Govindaswami also fell in with the proposal. The rest did not join the scheme, but agreed to go wherever I removed the press.

I do not think I took more than two days to fix up these matters with the men. Thereafter I at once advertised for a piece of land situated near a railway station in the vicinity of Durban. An offer came in respect of Phoenix. Mr. West and I went to inspect the estate. Within a week we purchased twenty acres of land. It had a nice little spring and a few orange and mango trees. Adjoining it was a piece of 80 acres which had many more fruit trees and a dilapidated cottage. We purchased this too, the total cost being a thousand pounds.

The late Mr. Rustomji always supported me in such enterprises. He liked the project. He placed at my disposal second-hand corrugated iron sheets of a big godown and other building material, with which we started work. Some Indian carpenters and masons, who had worked with me in the Boer War, helped me in erecting a shed for the press. This structure, which was 75 feet long and 50 feet broad, was ready in less than a month. Mr. West and others, at great personal risk, stayed with the carpenters and masons. The place, uninhabited and thickly overgrown with grass, was infested with snakes and obviously dangerous to live in. At first all lived under canvas. We carted most of our things to Phoenix in about a week. It was fourteen miles from Durban, and two and a half miles from Phoenix station.

Only one issue of *Indian Opinion* had to be printed outside, in the Mercury press.

I now endeavored to draw to Phoenix those relations and friends who had come with me from India to try their fortune, and who were engaged in business of various kinds. They had come in search of wealth, and it was therefore difficult to persuade them; but some agreed. Of these I can single out here only Maganlal Gandhi's name. The others went back to business. Maganlal Gandhi left his business for good to cast in his lot with me, and by ability, sacrifice and devotion stands foremost among my original coworkers in my ethical experiments. As a self-taught handicraftsman his place among them is unique.

Thus the Phoenix Settlement was started in 1904, and there in spite of numerous odds *Indian Opinion* continues to be published.

3 BEGINNINGS OF *SATYAGRAHA* (1906-1908)

THE ADVENT OF *SATYAGRAHA*

by M. K. Gandhi

In August 1906 the Transvaal government Gazette printed a proposed ordinance which would require all Indians to register with the authorities and to carry a certificate at all times, on penalty of imprisonment or deportation from the Transvaal. This ordinance was named "the Black Act" and Gandhi, on first reading it, felt that if it were adopted it would mean "absolute ruin for the Indians of South Africa." The leading Indians held a small meeting and after Gandhi explained the meaning of the ordinance to them, it was agreed to hold a public meeting at which a number of resolutions about the Black Act would be proposed.

THE MEETING was duly held on the 11th September 1906. It was attended by delegates from various places in the Transvaal. But I must confess that even I myself had not then understood all the implications of the resolutions I had helped to frame; nor had I gauged all the possible conclusions to which they might lead. The old Empire Theatre was packed from floor to ceiling. I could read in every face the expectation of something strange to be done or to happen. Mr. Abdul Gani, Chairman of the Transvaal British Indian Association, presided. He was one of the oldest Indian

• Reprinted with permission from M. K. Gandhi, *Satyagraha in South Africa* (Madras: Ganesan, 1928), Chapter XII, pp. 161-73.

residents of the Transvaal, and partner and manager of the Johannesburg branch of the well-known firm of Mamad Kasam Kamrudin. The most important among the resolutions passed by the meeting was the famous Fourth Resolution, by which the Indians solemnly determined not to submit to the Ordinance in the event of its becoming law in the teeth of their opposition and to suffer all the penalties attaching to such non-submission.

I fully explained this resolution to the meeting and received a patient hearing. The business of the meeting was conducted in Hindi or Gujarati; it was impossible therefore that anyone present should not follow the proceedings. For the Tamils and Telugus who did not know Hindi there were Tamil and Telugu speakers who fully explained everything in their respective languages. The resolution was duly proposed, seconded and supported by several speakers one of whom was Sheth Haji Habib. He too was a very old and experienced resident of South Africa and made an impassioned speech. He was deeply moved and went so far as to say that we must pass this resolution with God as witness and must never yield a cowardly submission to such degrading legislation. He then went on solemnly to declare in the name of God that he would never submit to that law, and advised all present to do likewise. Others also delivered powerful and angry speeches in supporting the resolution.

When in the course of his speech Sheth Haji Habib came to the solemn declaration, I was at once startled and put on my guard. Only then did I fully realize my own responsibility and the responsibility of the community. The community had passed many a resolution before and amended such resolutions in the light of further reflection or fresh experience. There were cases in which resolutions passed had not been observed by all concerned. Amendments in resolutions and failure to observe resolutions on the part of persons agreeing thereto are ordinary experiences of public life all the world over. But no one ever imports the name of God into such resolutions. In the abstract there should not be any distinction between a resolution and an oath taken in the name of God. When an intelligent man makes a resolution deliberately he never swerves from it by a hair's breadth. With him his resolution carries as much weight as a declaration made with God as witness does. But the world takes no note of abstract principles and imagines an ordinary resolution and an oath in the name of God to be as poles asunder. A man who makes an ordinary resolution is not ashamed of himself when he deviates from it, but a man who violates an oath administered to him is not only ashamed of himself, but is also looked upon by society as a sinner. This imaginary distinction has struck such a deep root in the human mind that a person making a statement on oath before a judge is held to have committed an offence in law if the statement is proved to be false and receives drastic punishment.

Full of these thoughts as I was, possessing as I did much experience of solemn pledges, having profited by them, I was simply taken aback by Sheth Haji Habib's suggestion of an oath. I thought out the possible consequences of it in a single moment. My perplexity gave place to enthusiasm. And although I had no intention of taking an oath or inviting others to do so when I went to the meeting, I warmly approved of the Sheth's suggestion. But at the same time it seemed to me that the people should be apprised of all the consequences and should have explained to them clearly the meaning of a pledge. And if even then they were prepared to pledge themselves, they should be encouraged to do so; otherwise I must understand that they were not still ready to stand the final test. I therefore asked the President for permission to explain to the meeting the implications of Sheth Haji Habib's suggestion. The President readily granted it and I rose to address the meeting. I give below a summary of my remarks just as I can recall them now:

"I wish to explain to this meeting that there is a vast difference between this resolution and every other resolution we have passed up to date and that there is a wide divergence also in the manner of making it. It is a very grave resolution we are making, as our existence in South Africa depends upon our fully observing it. The manner of making the resolution suggested by our friend is as much of a novelty as of a solemnity. I did not come to the meeting with a view to getting the resolution passed in that manner, which redounds to the credit of Sheth Haji Habib as well as it lays a burden of responsibility upon him. I tender my congratulations to him. I deeply appreciate his suggestion, but if you adopt it you too will share his responsibility. You must understand what is this responsibility, and as an adviser and servant of the community, it is my duty fully to explain it to you.

"We all believe in one and the same God, the differences of nomenclature in Hinduism and Islam notwithstanding. To pledge ourselves or to take an oath in the name of that God or with Him as witness is not something to be trifled with. If having taken such an oath we violate our pledge we are guilty before God and man. Personally I hold that a man, who deliberately and intelligently takes a pledge and then breaks it, forfeits his manhood. And just as a copper coin treated with mercury not only becomes valueless when found out but also makes its owner liable to punishment, in the same way a man who lightly pledges his word and then breaks it becomes a man of straw and fits himself for punishment here as well as hereafter. Sheth Haji Habib is proposing to administer an oath of such a serious character. There is no one in this meeting who can be classed as an infant or as wanting in understanding. You are all well advanced in age and have seen the world; many of you are delegates and have discharged responsibilities in a greater or lesser measure. No one present, therefore, can ever hope to excuse himself by saying that he did not know what he was about when he took the oath.

"I know that pledges and vows are, and should be, taken on rare occasions. A man who takes a vow every now and then is sure to stumble. But if I can imagine a crisis in the history of the Indian community of South Africa when it would be in the fitness of things to take pledges that crisis is surely now. There is wisdom in taking serious steps with great caution and hesitation. But caution and hesitation have their limits, which we have now passed. The Government have taken leave of all sense of decency. We would only be betraying our unworthiness and cowardice, if we cannot stake our all in the face of the conflagration which envelopes us and sit watching it with folded hands. There is no doubt, therefore, that the present is a proper occasion for taking pledges. But every one of us must think out for himself if he has the will and the ability to pledge himself. Resolutions of this nature cannot be passed by a majority vote. Only those who take a pledge can be bound by it. This pledge must not be taken with a view to produce an effect on outsiders. No one should trouble to consider what impression it might have upon the Local Government, the Imperial Government, or the Government of India. Every one must only search his own heart, and if the inner voice assures him that he has the requisite strength to carry him through, then only should he pledge himself and then only would his pledge bear fruit.

"A few words now as to the consequences. Hoping for the best, we may say that if a majority of the Indians pledge themselves to resistance and if all who take the pledge prove true to themselves, the Ordinance may not even be passed and, if passed, may be soon repealed. It may be that we may not be called upon to suffer at all. But if on the one hand who takes a pledge must be a robust optimist, on the other hand he must be prepared for the worst. It is therefore that I would give you an idea of the worst that might happen to us in the present struggle. Imagine that all of us present here numbering 3,000 at the most pledge ourselves. Imagine again that the remaining 10,000 Indians take no such pledge. We will only provoke ridicule in the beginning. Again, it is quite possible that in spite of the present warning some or many of those who pledge themselves might weaken at the very first trial. We might have to go to jail, where we might be insulted. We might have to go hungry and suffer extreme heat or cold. Hard labor might be imposed upon us. We might be flogged by rude warders. We might be fined heavily and our property might be attached and held up to auction if there are only a few resisters left. Opulent today we might be reduced to abject poverty tomorrow. We might be deported. Suffering from starvation and similar hardships in jail, some of us might fall ill and even die. In short, therefore, it is not at all impossible that we might have to endure every hardship that we can imagine, and wisdom lies in pledging ourselves on the understanding that we shall have to suffer all that and worse. If some one asks me when and how the struggle may end, I may say that if the entire community manfully stands the test, the end will be near. If many of us fall back under storm and stress, the struggle will be prolonged. But I can boldly declare, and with certainty, that so long as there is even a handful of men true to their pledge, there can only be one end to the struggle, and that is victory.

"A word about my personal responsibility. If I am warning you of the risks attendant upon the pledge, I am at the same time inviting you to pledge yourselves, and I am fully conscious of my responsibility in the matter. It is possible that a majority of those present here might take the pledge in a fit of enthusiasm or indignation but might weaken under the ordeal, and only a handful might be left to face the final test. Even then there is only one course open to the like of me, to die but not to submit to the law. It is quite unlikely but even if everyone else flinched leaving me alone to face the music, I am confident that I would never violate my pledge. Please do not misunderstand me. I am not saying this out of vanity, but I wish to put you, especially the leaders upon the platform, on your guard. I wish respectfully to suggest it to you that if you have not the will or the ability to stand firm even when you are perfectly isolated, you must not only not take the pledge yourselves but you must declare your opposition before the resolution is put to the meeting and before its members begin to take pledges and you must not make yourselves parties to the resolution. Although we are going to take the pledge in a body, no one should imagine that default on the part of one or many can absolve the rest from their obligation. Everyone should fully realize his responsibility, then only pledge himself independently of others and understand that he himself must be true to his pledge even unto death, no matter what others do."

I spoke to this effect and resumed my seat. The meeting heard me word by word in perfect quiet. Other leaders too spoke. All dwelt upon their own responsibility and the responsibility of the audience. The President rose. He too made the situation clear, and at last all present, standing with upraised hands, took an oath with God as witness not to submit to the Ordinance if it became law. I can never forget the scene, which is present before my mind's eye as I write. The community's enthusiasm knew no bounds. The very next day there was some accident in the theatre in consequence of which it was wholly destroyed by fire. On the third day friends brought me the news of the fire and congratulated the community upon this good omen, which signified to them that the Ordinance would meet the same fate as the theatre. I have never been influenced by such so-called signs and therefore did not attach any weight to the coincidence. I have taken note of it here only as a demonstration of the community's courage and faith. The reader will find in the subsequent chapters many proofs of these two high qualities of the people. . . .

None of us knew what name to give to our movement. I then used the term "passive resistance" in describing it. I did not quite understand the implications of "passive resistance" as I called it. I only knew that some new principle had come into being. As the struggle advanced, the phrase "passive resistance" gave rise to confusion and it appeared shameful to permit this great struggle to be known only by an English name. Again, that foreign phrase could hardly pass as current coin among the community. A small prize was therefore announced in *Indian Opinion* to be awarded to the reader who invented the best designation for our struggle. We thus received a number of suggestions. The meaning of the struggle had been then fully discussed in *Indian Opinion* and the competitors for the prize had fairly sufficient material to serve as a basis for their exploration. Sr. Maganlal Gandhi was one of the competitors and he suggested the word "Sadagraha," meaning "firmness in a good cause." I liked the word, but it did not fully represent the whole idea I wished it to connote. I therefore corrected it to "Satyagraha." Truth (Satya) implies love and firmness (Agraha) engenders and therefore serves as a synonym for force. I thus began to call the Indian movement "Satyagraha," that is to say, the Force which is born of Truth and Love or non-violence, and gave up the use of the phrase "passive resistance," in connection with it, so much so that even in English writing we often avoided it and used instead the word "Satyagraha" itself or some other equivalent English phrase. This then was the genesis of the movement which came to be known as Satyagraha, and of the word used as a designation for it. . . .

FIRST IMPRISONMENT
by M. K. Gandhi

The Black Act was put into effect in July 1907, and called for the registration of all Asians in South Africa. When only a few Indians registered, the government decided to make arrests to enforce the Act. During Christmas week, 1907, some of the leaders of the Indian community, including Gandhi, were served with a notice to appear before the magistrate to show cause why, having failed to apply for registration as required by the new law, they should not be ordered to leave the Transvaal.

The magistrate conducted each case separately, and ordered all the accused to leave the Transvaal within forty-eight hours in some cases and seven or fourteen days in others.

The time limit expired on 10th January, 1908 and the same day we were called upon to attend court for sentence.

None of us had to offer any defence. All were to plead guilty to the charge of disobeying the order to leave the Transvaal within the stated period, issued by the Magistrate, on failure to satisfy him that they were lawful holders of certificates of registration.

I asked leave to make a short statement, and on its being

• Reprinted with permission from M. K. Gandhi, Satyagraha in South Africa (Madras: Ganesan, 1928), pp. 230-38.

granted, I said I thought there should be a distinction made between my case and those that were to follow. I had just heard from Pretoria that my compatriots there had been sentenced to three months' imprisonment with hard labor, and had been fined a heavy amount, in lieu of payment of which they would receive a further period of three months' hard labor. If these men had committed an offence, I had committed a greater offence and I therefore asked the Magistrate to impose upon me the heaviest penalty. The Magistrate, however, did not accede to my request and sentenced me to two months' simple imprisonment. I had some slight feeling of awkwardness due to the fact that I was standing as an accused in the very Court where I had often appeared as counsel. But I well remember that I considered the former role as far more honorable than the latter, and did not feel the slightest hesitation in entering the prisoner's box.

In the Court there were hundreds of Indians as well as brother members of the Bar in front of me. On the sentence being pronounced I was at once removed in custody and was then quite alone. The policeman asked me to sit on a bench kept there for prisoners, shut the door on me and went away. I was somewhat agitated and fell into deep thought. Home, the Courts where I practiced, the public meeting—all these passed away like a dream, and I was now a prisoner. What will happen in two months? Will I have to serve the full term? If the people courted imprisonment in large numbers, as they had promised, there would be no question of serving the full sentence. But if they failed to fill the prisons, two months would be as tedious as an age. These thoughts passed through my mind in less than one hundredth of the time that it has taken me to dictate them. And they filled me with shame. How vain I was! I, who had asked the people to consider the prisons as His Majesty's hotels, the suffering consequent upon disobeying the Black Act as perfect bliss, and the sacrifice of one's all and of life itself in resisting it as supreme enjoyment! Where had all this knowledge vanished today? This second train of thought acted upon me as a bracing tonic, and I began to laugh at my own folly. I began to think what kind of imprisonment would be awarded to the others and whether they would be kept with me in the prison. But I was disturbed by the police officer who opened the gate and asked me to follow him, which I did. He then made me go before him, following me himself, took me to the prisoner's closed van and asked me to take my seat in it. I was driven to Johannesburg jail.

In jail I was asked to put off my own private clothing. I knew that convicts were made naked in jails. We had all decided as Satyagrahis voluntarily to obey all jail regulations so long as they were not inconsistent with one's self-respect or with one's religious convictions. The clothes which were given to me to wear were very dirty. I did not like to put them on at all. It was not without pain that I reconciled myself to them from an idea that I must put up with some dirt. After the officers had recorded my name and address, I was taken to a large cell, and in a short time was joined by my compatriots who came laughing and told me how they received the same sentence as myself, and what took place after I had been removed. I understood from them that when my case was over, the Indians, some of whom were excited, took out a procession with black flags in their hands. The police disturbed the procession and flogged some of its members. We were all happy at the thought that we were kept in the same jail and in the same cell.

The cell door was locked at 6 o'clock. The door was not made up of bars but was quite solid, there being high up in the wall a small aperture for ventilation, so that we felt as if we had been locked up in a safe.

No wonder the jail authorities did not accord us the good treatment which they had meted out to Rama Sundara. As Rama Sundara was the first Satyagrahi prisoner, the authorities had no idea even as to how he was to be treated. Our batch was fairly large and further arrests were in contemplation. We were therefore kept in the Negro ward. In South Africa only two classes of convicts are recognized, namely Whites and Blacks, i.e. the Negroes, and the Indians were classed with Negroes.

The next morning we found that prisoners without hard labor

had the right to keep on their own private clothing, and if they would not exercise this right, they were given special jail clothing assigned to that class of prisoners. We decided that it was not right to put on our own clothing and that it was appropriate to take the jail uniform, and we informed the authorities accordingly. We were therefore given the clothes assigned to Negro convicts not punished with hard labor. But Negro prisoners sentenced to simple imprisonment are never numerous, and hence there was a shortage of simple imprisonment prisoners' clothing as soon as other Indians sentenced to simple imprisonment began to arrive. As the Indians did not wish to stand upon ceremony in this matter, they readily accepted clothing assigned to hard labor prisoners. Some of those who came in later preferred to keep on their own clothing rather than put on the uniform of the hard labor convicts. I thought this improper, but did not care to insist upon their following the correct procedure in the matter.

From the second or third day Satyagrahi prisoners began to arrive in large numbers. They had all courted arrest and were most of them hawkers. In South Africa, every hawker, Black or White, has to take out a license, always to carry it with him and show it to the police when asked to do so. Nearly every day some policeman would ask to see the licenses and arrest those who had none to show. The community had resolved to fill up the jail after our arrests. In this the hawkers took the lead. It was easy for them to be arrested. They must refuse to show their licenses and that was enough to ensure their arrest. In this way the number of Satyagrahi prisoners swelled to more than a hundred in one week. And as some few were sure to arrive every day, we received the daily budget of news without a newspaper. When Satyagrahis began to be arrested in large numbers, they were sentenced to imprisonment with hard labor, either because the magistrates lost patience, or because, as we thought, they received some such instructions from the Government. Even today, I think we were right in our conjecture, as, if we leave out the first few cases in which simple imprisonment was awarded, never afterwards throughout the long drawn out struggle was there pronounced a sentence of simple imprisonment, even ladies having been punished with hard labor. If all the magistrates had not received the same orders or instructions, and if yet by mere coincidence they sentenced all men and women at all times to hard labor, that must be held to be almost a miracle.

In Johannesburg jail prisoners not condemned to hard labor got "mealie pap" in the morning. There was no salt in it, but each prisoner was given some salt separately. At noon the prisoners were given four ounces of rice, four ounces of bread, one ounce of ghi and a little salt, and in the evening "mealie pap" and some vegetable, chiefly potatoes of which two were given if they were small and only one if they were big in size. None of us were satisfied with this diet. The rice was cooked soft. We asked the prison medical officer for some condiments, and told him that condiments were allowed in the jails in India. "This is not India," was the stern answer. "There is no question of taste about prison diet and condiments therefore cannot be allowed." We asked for pulse on the ground that the regulation diet was lacking in muscle-building properties. "Prisoners must not indulge in arguments on medical grounds," replied the doctor. "You do get muscle-building food, as twice a week you are served boiled beans instead of maize." The doctor's argument was sound if the human stomach was capable of extracting the various elements out of various foods taken at various times in a week or fortnight. As a matter of fact he had no intention whatever of looking to our convenience. The Superintendent permitted us to cook our food ourselves. We elected Thambi Naidoo [1] as our chef, and as such he had to fight many a battle on our behalf. If the vegetable ration issued was short in weight, he would insist on getting full weight. On vegetable days which were two in a week we cooked twice and on other days only once, as we were allowed to cook other things for ourselves only for the noonday meal. We were somewhat better off after we began to cook our own food.

But whether or not we succeeded in obtaining these conveniences, everyone of us was firm in his resolution of passing his term in jail in perfect happiness and peace. The number of Satyagrahi prisoners gradually rose to over 150. As we were all simple imprisonment convicts, we had no work to do except keeping the cells etc. clean. We asked the Superintendent for work, and he replied: "I am sorry I cannot give you work, as, if I did, I should be held to have committed an offense. But you can devote as much time as you please to keeping the place clean." We asked for some such exercise as drill, as we had observed even the Negro prisoners with hard labor being drilled in addition to their usual work. The Superintendent replied, "If your warder has time and if he gives you drill, I will not object to it; nor will I require him to do it, as he is hard worked as it is, and your arrival in unexpectedly large numbers has made his work harder still." The warder was a good man and this qualified permission was quite enough for him. He began to drill us every morning with great interest. This drill must be performed in the small yard before our cells and was therefore in the nature of a merry-go-round. When the warder finished the drill and went away, it was continued by a Pathan compatriot of ours named Nawabkhan, who made us all laugh with his quaint pronunciation of English words of command. He rendered "Stand at ease" as "sundlies." We could not for the life of us understand what Hindustani word it was, but afterwards it dawned upon us that it was not Hindustani but only Nawabkhani English.

FIRST ATTACK ON HIS LIFE

• by M. K. Gandhi

Gandhi was in prison less than three weeks when he was summoned to Pretoria to confer with General Jan Christiaan

• Reprinted with permission from M. K. Gandhi, *Satyagraha in South Africa* (Madras: Ganesan, 1928), pp. 257-63, 288-89.

Smuts. A compromise was reached whereby if the Asians in South
Africa would register voluntarily, Smuts promised to repeal the
Black Act. Gandhi was immediately released from prison, but
encountered much opposition in trying to convince his fellow Indians that this was a reasonable compromise. Gandhi, however,
announced that he would be the first to register and give his
fingerprints under the new agreement.

On the morning of 10th February 1908 some of us got ready to
go and take out certificates of registration.[2] The supreme necessity of getting through the registration business with all possible
expedition had been fully impressed on the community, and it
had been agreed, that the leaders should be the first to take out
certificates on the first day, with a view to break down shyness,
to see if the officers concerned discharged their duties with courtesy and generally to have an eye over all the arrangements.

When I reached my office, which was also the office of the
Satyagraha Association, I found Mir Alam and his companions
standing outside the premises. Mir Alam was an old client of
mine, and used to seek my advice in all his affairs. Many Pathans
in the Transvaal employed laborers to manufacture straw or coir[3]
mattresses, which they sold at a good profit, and Mir Alam did
the same. He was fully six feet in height and of a large and powerful build. Today for the first time I saw Mir Alam outside my
office instead of inside it, and although his eyes met mine, he
for the first time refrained from saluting me. I saluted him and
he saluted me in return. As usual I asked him, "How do you
do?", and my impression is that he said he was all right. But he
did not today wear his usual smile on the face. I noticed his angry
eyes and took a mental note of the fact. I thought that something
was going to happen. I entered the office. The Chairman Mr.
Essop Mian and other friends arrived, and we set out for the
Asiatic Office. Mir Alam and his companions followed us.

The Registration Office was at Von Brandis Square, less than a
mile away from my office. On our way to it we had to pass through
high roads. As we were going along Von Brandis Street, outside

the premises of Messrs. Arnot and Gibson, not more than three minutes' walk from the Registration Office, Mir Alam accosted me and asked me, "Where are you going?"

"I propose to take out a certificate of registration, giving the ten finger-prints," I replied. "If you will go with me, I will first get you a certificate, with an impression only of the two thumbs, and then I will take one for myself, giving the finger-prints."

I had scarcely finished the last sentence when a heavy cudgel blow descended on my head from behind. I at once fainted with the words *He Rama* (Oh God!) on my lips, lay prostrate on the ground and had no notion of what followed. But Mir Alam and his companions gave me more blows and kicks, some of which were warded off by Essop Mian and Thambi Naidoo with the result that they too became a target for attack in their turn. The noise attracted some European passers-by to the scene. Mir Alam and his companions fled but were caught by the Europeans. The police arrived in the meanwhile and took them in custody. I was picked up and carried into Mr. J. C. Gibson's private office. When I regained consciousness, I saw Mr. Doke[4] bending over me. "How do you feel?" he asked me.

"I am all right," I replied, "but there is pain in the teeth and the ribs. Where is Mir Alam?"

"He has been arrested along with the rest."

"They should be released."

"That is all very well. But here you are in a stranger's office with your lip and cheek badly lacerated. The police are ready to take you to the hospital, but if you will go to my place, Mrs. Doke and I will minister to your comforts as best we can."

"Yes, please take me to your place. Thank the police for their offer but tell them that I prefer to go with you."

Mr. Chamney the Registrar of Asiatics too now arrived on the scene. I was taken in a carriage to this good clergyman's residence in Smit Street and a doctor was called in. Meanwhile I said to Mr. Chamney: "I wished to come to your office, give ten finger-prints and take out the first certificate of registration, but God willed it otherwise. However, I have now to request you to bring

the papers and allow me to register at once. I hope that you will
not let anyone else register before me."

"Where is the hurry about it?" asked Mr. Chamney. "The doctor will be here soon. You please rest yourself and all will be well.
I will issue certificates to others but keep your name at the head
of the list."

"Not so," I replied. "I am pledged to take out the first certificate if I am alive and if it is acceptable to God. It is therefore
that I insist upon the papers being brought here and now."

Upon this Mr. Chamney went away to bring the papers.

The second thing for me to do was to wire to the Attorney-
General that I did not hold Mir Alam and others guilty for the
assault committed upon me, that in any case I did not wish them
to be prosecuted and that I hoped they would be discharged for
my sake. But the Europeans of Johannesburg addressed a strong
letter to the Attorney-General saying that whatever views Gandhi
might hold as regards the punishment of criminals, they could not
be given effect to in South Africa. Gandhi himself might not take
any steps, but the assault was committed not in a private place
but on the high roads and was therefore a public offense. Several
Englishmen too were in a position to tender evidence and the
offenders must be prosecuted. Upon this the Attorney-General re-
arrested Mir Alam and one of his companions who were sentenced to three months' hard labor. Only I was not summoned
as a witness.

But let us return to the sick room. Dr. Thwaites came in while
Mr. Chamney was still away. He examined me and stitched up
the wounds in the cheek and on the upper lip. He prescribed
some medicine to be applied to the ribs and enjoined silence upon
me so long as the stitches were not removed. He restricted my diet
to liquids only. He said that none of the injuries was serious, that
I should be able to leave my bed and take up my ordinary activities in a week, but that I should be careful not to undertake much
physical strain for two months more. So saying he left.

Thus speech was forbidden me, but I was still master of my

hands. I addressed a short note as follows to the community through the Chairman and sent it for publication:

"I am well in the brotherly and sisterly hands of Mr. and Mrs. Doke. I hope to take up my duty shortly.

"Those who have committed the act did not know what they were doing. They thought that I was doing what was wrong. They have had their redress in the only manner they know. I therefore request that no steps be taken against them.

"Seeing that the assault was committed by a Mussalman or Mussalmans, the Hindus might probably feel hurt. If so, they would put themselves in the wrong before the world and their Maker. Rather let the blood spilt today cement the two communities indissolubly—such is my heartfelt prayer. May God grant it.

"Assault or no assault, my advice remains the same. The large majority of Asiatics ought to give finger-prints. Those who have real conscientious scruples will be exempted by the Government. To ask for more would be to show ourselves as children.

"The spirit of Satyagraha rightly understood should make the people fear none and nothing but God. No cowardly fear therefore should deter the vast majority of sober-minded Indians from doing their duty. The promise of repeal of the Act against voluntary registration having been given, it is the sacred duty of every good Indian to help the Government and the Colony to the uttermost."

Mr. Chamney returned with the papers and I gave my finger-prints but not without pain. I then saw that tears stood in Mr. Chamney's eyes. I had often to write bitterly against him, but this showed me how man's heart may be softened by events.

The reader will easily imagine that all this did not take more than a few minutes. Mr. Doke and his good wife were anxious that I should be perfectly at rest and peaceful, and were therefore pained to witness my mental activity after the assault. They were afraid that it might react in a manner prejudicial to my health. They, therefore, by making signs and similar devices, removed all persons from near my bed, and asked me not to write or do anything. I made a request in writing, that before and in order that I might lie down quietly, their daughter Olive, who was then only a little girl, should sing for me my favorite English hymn, "Lead, kindly light." Mr. Doke liked this very much and acceded to my request with a sweet smile. He called Olive by signs and asked her to stand at the door and sing the hymn in a low tone. The whole scene passes before my eyes as I dictate this, and the melodious voice of little Olive reverberates in my ears. . . .

Just suppose that Mir Alam and his friends, instead of only wounding, had actually destroyed my body. And suppose also that the community had deliberately remained calm and unperturbed, and forgiven the offenders perceiving that according to their lights they could not behave otherwise than they did. Far from injuring the community, such a noble attitude would have greatly benefited them. All misunderstanding would have disappeared, and Mir Alam and party would have had their eyes opened to the error of their ways. As for me, nothing better can happen to a Satyagrahi than meeting death all unsought in the very act of Satyagraha, i.e., pursuing Truth. All these propositions are true only of a struggle like the Satyagraha movement, where there is no room for hatred, where self-reliance is the order of the day, where no one has to look expectantly at another, where there are no leaders and hence no followers, or where all are leaders and all are followers, so that the death of a fighter, however eminent, makes not for slackness but on the other hand intensifies the struggle.

A BONFIRE OF CERTIFICATES
by M. K. Gandhi

General Smuts did not carry out his part of the compromise; he refused to take steps for the repeal of the Black Act. The dissatisfaction of the Asian community grew and the Indians

• Reprinted with permission from M. K. Gandhi, *Satyagraha in South Africa* (Madras: Ganesan, 1928), pp. 310-14.

were ready to resume the struggle and, if necessary, go to jail
again. They finally sent a so-called ultimatum to General Smuts
indicating that, if the decision to repeal the Act were not communicated to the Indian community by a specific date—August 16,
1908—the voluntary certificates would be collected and burned.

THE ULTIMATUM was to expire on the same day that the new Asiatic bill was to be carried through the Legislature. A meeting had
been called some two hours after the expiry of the time limit to
perform the public ceremony of burning the certificates. The Satyagraha Committee thought that the meeting would not be
fruitless even if quite unexpectedly perhaps a favorable reply was
received from the Government, as in that case the meeting could
be utilized for announcing the Government's favorable decision
to the community.

The Committee however believed that the Government would
not reply to the ultimatum at all. We had all reached the place
of meeting early, and arranged for the Government's reply by
wire, if any, to be brought promptly to the meeting, which was
held at four o'clock on the grounds of the Hamidia Mosque at
Johannesburg (16th August 1908). Every inch of space available
was taken up by Indians of all classes. The Negroes of South
Africa take their meals in iron cauldrons resting on four legs. One
such cauldron of the largest size available in the market had been
requisitioned from an Indian trader's shop and set up on a platform in a corner of the grounds in order to burn the certificates.

As the business of the meeting was about to commence, a volunteer arrived on a cycle with a telegram from the Government in
which they regretted the determination of the Indian community
and announced their inability to change their line of action. The
telegram was read to the audience which received it with cheers,
as if they were glad that the auspicious opportunity of burning
the certificates did not after all slip out of their hands as it would
have if the Government had complied with the demands formu-
lated in the ultimatum. It is difficult to pronounce any categorical
opinion on the propriety or the reverse of such a feeling of glad-

ness without a knowledge of the motives which prompted each of the audience who greeted the Government reply with applause. This much however can be said, that these cheers were a happy sign of the enthusiasm of the meeting. The Indians had now some consciousness of their strength.

The meeting began. The chairman put the meeting on their guard and explained the whole situation to them. Appropriate resolutions were adopted. I clearly detailed the various stages of the protracted negotiations and said, "If there is any Indian who has handed his certificate to be burnt but wants it to be returned to him, let him step forward and have it. Merely burning the certificates is no crime, and will not enable those who court imprisonment to win it. By burning the certificates we only declare our solemn resolution never to submit to the Black Act and divest ourselves of the power of even showing the certificates. But it is open to anyone to take a copy tomorrow of the certificate that may be burned to ashes today, and if there are any persons here who contemplate such a cowardly act or doubt their own ability to stand the ordeal, there is still time for them to have their certificates back, and these can be given back to them. No one need be ashamed of getting his certificate back just now, as in doing so he will be exhibiting a certain kind of courage. But it would be not only shameful but also detrimental to the best interests of the community to get a copy of the certificate afterwards. Again let us take note that this is going to be a protracted struggle. We know that some of us have fallen out of the marching army, and the burden of those who remain has been made heavier to that extent. I would advise you to ponder over all these considerations and only then to take the plunge proposed today."

Even during my speech there were voices saying, "We do not want the certificates back, burn them." Finally I suggested that if anyone wanted to oppose the resolution, he should come forward, but no one stood up. Mir Alam too was present at this meeting. He announced that he had done wrong to assault me as he did, and to the great joy of the audience, handed his original certificate to be burnt, as he had not taken a voluntary certificate. I took hold of his hand, pressed it with joy, and assured him once more that I had never harbored in my mind any resentment against him.

The Committee had already received upwards of 2,000 certificates to be burnt. These were all thrown into the cauldron, saturated with paraffin and set ablaze by Mr. Essop Mian. The whole assembly rose to their feet and made the place resound with the echoes of their continuous cheers during the burning process. Some of those who had still withheld their certificates brought them in numbers to the platform, and these too were consigned to the flames. When asked why he handed his certificate only at the last moment, one of these friends said that he did so as it was more appropriate and would create a greater impression on the onlookers. Another frankly admitted his want of courage and a feeling that the certificates might not be burnt after all. But he could not possibly withhold the certificate after he had seen the bonfire and gave it up, from an idea that the fate of all might well be his own fate too. Such frankness was a matter of frequent experience during this struggle.

The reporters of English newspapers present at the meeting were profoundly impressed with the whole scene and gave graphic descriptions of the meeting in their papers. A description of the meeting was sent to *The Daily Mail* (London) by its Johannesburg correspondent, in course of which he compared the act of the Indians in burning their certificates with that of the Boston Tea Party. I do not think this comparison did more than justice to the Indians, seeing that if the whole might of the British Empire was ranged against the hundreds of thousands of able Europeans in America, here in South Africa a helpless body of 13,000 Indians had challenged the powerful Government of the Transvaal. The Indians' only weapon was a faith in the righteousness of their own cause and in God. There is no doubt that this weapon is all-sufficient and all-powerful for the devout, but so long as that is not the view of the man in the street, 13,000 unarmed Indians might appear insignificant before the well-armed Europeans of America. As God is the strength of the weak, it is as well that the world despises them.

THE MAN HIMSELF

by Joseph J. Doke

Reverend Joseph J. Doke was a Baptist minister in Johan-
nesburg who was a friend and co-worker of Gandhi. He was his
first biographer. This biography of Gandhi, entitled An Indian
Patriot in South Africa, was published in London in 1909. The
following excerpts tell of Doke's first encounter with Gandhi in
1907 and of his efforts to induce Gandhi to give him material for
the biography.

IT WAS late in December, 1907, when I saw Mr. Gandhi for the
first time. Rumor had been very busy with his name. The Passive
Resistance movement had come into prominence. Some small stir
had been made in the newspapers by the imprisonment of a Pundit, and in one way or another, Mr. Gandhi's name had been
bandied from lip to lip. One evening, a friend raised the Asiatic
Question at the supper-table, and as we were comparatively new
to Johannesburg, although not new to the country, he told us what
he thought of the Indians. His account was so strange and so
completely opposed to all our previous experience, that it made us
curious, and more than anything else decided me to interview the
leader.

The office, at the corner of Rissik and Anderson Streets, I found
to be like other offices. It was intended for work and not for show.
The windows and door were adorned with the name of the occupant with the denomination of Attorney attached to it. The first
room was given up to a lady-typist; the second, into which I was
ushered, was the SANCTUM SANCTORUM. It was meagerly furnished

• Reprinted from Joseph J. Doke, *An Indian Patriot in South Africa* (London:
London Indian Chronicle, 1909), pp. 5-10.

and dusty. A few pictures were scattered along the walls. They were chiefly photographs of no great merit. The Indian Stretcher-bearer Corps was in evidence—photographs of Mrs. Besant, Sir William Wilson Hunter, and Justice Ranade—several separate Indian portraits—and a beautiful picture of Jesus Christ. Some indifferent chairs, and shelves filled with law books completed the inventory.

All this I confess to have noted afterwards. Just then, my whole attention was centered in the man who greeted me, and in an effort to readjust my ideas to unexpected experiences. Having travelled in India, I had almost unconsciously selected some typical face and form as likely to confront me, probably a tall and stately figure, and a bold, masterful face, in harmony with the influence which he seemed to exert in Johannesburg. Perhaps a bearing haughty and aggressive. Instead of this, to my surprise, a small, lithe, spare figure stood before me, and a refined, earnest face looked into mine. The skin was dark, the eyes dark, but the smile which lighted up the face, and that direct fearless glance, simply took one's heart by storm. I judged him to be of some thirty-eight years of age, which proved correct. But the strain of his work showed its traces in the sprinkling of silver hairs on his head. He spoke English perfectly, and was evidently a man of great culture.

Asking me to be seated, he listened to an explanation of my visit, noting the points raised with a nod of the head, and a quick "Yes," until I had done. Then he went straight to the mark. Using his fingers to emphasize his thoughts, he gave the most luminous statement of the Asiatic position, in a few crisp sentences, that I have ever heard. I was anxious to know what the religious elements in the struggle were, and he gave them with convincing clearness, explaining patiently every little involved issue, and satisfying himself that I understood each before dealing with the next. Once, when he paused longer than usual, to see whether I had grasped the thought or had only assented for the sake of courtesy, I closed my note-book, thinking he had finished. "Don't close it," he said, "the chief point is yet to come."

There was a quiet assured strength about him, a greatness of heart, a transparent honesty, that attracted me at once to the Indian leader. We parted friends.

When I think of him now, one or two scenes stand out more vividly than others.

There is the trial in the "B" Criminal Court, a great mass of excited Asiatics crushed in at the door, and spreading to a great crowd outside. The cynical Magistrate, with his face flushed, presiding at the Bench; the horseshoe of legal offices below.

Then I can see again that spare, lithe form responding to the call, "Mohandas Karamchand Gandhi," and taking the prisoner's place with alacrity to receive a sentence of "two months' imprisonment" for the sake of his suffering people. Just prior to this, he had addressed these words to the hundreds of Asiatics who had gathered at the Mosque: "No matter what may be said, I will always repeat that it is a struggle for religious liberty. By religion, I do not mean formal religion, or customary religion, but that religion which underlies all religions, which brings us face to face with our Maker. If you cease to be men, if, on taking a deliberate vow, you break that vow, in order that you remain in the Transvaal without physical inconvenience, you undoubtedly forsake God. To repeat again the words of the Jew of Nazareth, those who would follow God have to leave the world, and I call upon my countrymen, in this particular instance, to leave the world and cling to God, as a child clings to its mother's breast." Notable and brave words.

Another scene recurs to my mind with equal vividness. The Pathans had attacked him, striking him down and beating him with savage brutality. When he recovered consciousness, he was lying in an office near by to which he had been carried. I saw him a moment later. He was helpless and bleeding, the doctor was cleansing his wounds, the police officers watching and listening beside him, while he was using what little strength he had to insist that no action should be taken to punish his would-be murderers. "They thought they were doing right," he said, "and I have no desire to prosecute them." They were punished, but Mr. Gandhi took no part in it.

These are scenes one can never forget; they serve to reveal the man. Our Indian friend lives on a higher plane than most men do. His actions, like the actions of Mary of Bethany, are often counted eccentric, and not infrequently misunderstood. Those who do not know him think there is some unworthy motive behind, some Oriental "slimness," to account for such profound unworldliness. But those who know him well are ashamed of themselves in his presence.

Money, I think, has no charm for him. His compatriots are angry; they say, "He will take nothing. The money we gave him when he went as our deputy to England he brought back to us again. The presents we made him in Natal, he handed over to our public funds. He is poor because he will be poor."

They wonder at him, grow angry at his strange unselfishness, and love him with the love of pride and trust. He is one of those outstanding characters, with whom to walk is a liberal education, whom to know is to love.

This morning, as usual, the sanctum was full of Indians when I entered, discussing earnestly the latest phase of the Asiatic difficulty. When, however, it became clear that Mr. Gandhi and I wished for a quiet chat, with the well-bred instinct of Orientals they silently left the room. Mr. Gandhi swung round on his office-chair and faced me, his dark eyes alert and watchful, his hair a little more silvered, I thought, than yesterday, his whole attitude alert and expectant.

"My friend," I began, "I want to ask you a strange question—how far are you prepared to make a martyr of yourself for the good of the cause?" He looked a little surprised, but said quietly, "I think you should know that by this time." "No," I said, "candidly I do not." "Well," said he, his face kindling, "it is a matter with me of complete surrender. I am nothing, I am willing to die at any time, or to do anything for the cause." "Take care," I rejoined, "perhaps I shall ask something too great." "You cannot do that," he replied, calmly. Then I saw my opportunity, and drew the toils about him. "Listen," I said. "It appears to me that what

we are doing now is merely tinkering at the Asiatic settlement—
our fight with this Government is only part of a much greater
fight, to be fought out on a larger battlefield. The question of the
status of British Indians throughout the whole Empire will have
to be solved, and in the settlement of that vast problem, you
should have much to say. The question is—how can we best prepare for that future?" He nodded in his own quick, incisive way.
I proceeded: "You know very well that, with us Europeans, character and personality are of the first importance. It is so here, and
it must be so at home. You yourself are the chief asset of the Indian cause. It is a great thing to know and trust the leader of such
a movement." He was about to speak, but I stopped him. "Let me
continue," I said. "Your position as leader makes your personality
of great importance to the cause. It has occurred to me that if I
could write a short book—bright, graphic, and reliable—making
your personality real to the people of England, it might do something to help the cause in the great struggle that is to come." The
emphatic nods became appreciably weaker, but they did not altogether cease, so I went on; "You will see, however, that my
power to do this depends altogether upon yourself. You must tell
me about your childhood and youth, allow me to picture your
personality, and depict your character, and if I know anything of
you, to submit to this will be the severest kind of martyrdom that
you can suffer." "Ah," he said, as my purpose dawned upon him,
"you have caught me completely." "But," said I, "would this help
your people?" He thought a moment, and then replied. "Yes, in
England." "Well, can you go so far?" "For the cause, I can," he
said. And then, "What do you want me to do? You don't want
me to write anything, do you?" "No," I replied, "not a word; just
let me question you about that Indian city where you were born,
that beautiful home of yours far away in the East, the very
thoughts of your heart, your struggles and sacrifices and victories.
What you cannot tell me, others will help me to discover." So,
silently, with a grip of the hand, we confirmed the bond, and this
is how this story was born.

4 SOUTH AFRICAN CLIMAX (1913-1914)

PREPARING FOR THE MARCH
by M. K. Gandhi

By early 1913 the Indians in South Africa had three main grievances: a ban on Asian immigrants, a three-pound annual tax to be paid by each indentured laborer who remained in South Africa as a free man, and a court decision holding that only Christian marriages were legal. Indian women, especially, protested this last issue, and groups of them marched across the borders of the Transvaal and Natal to court arrest. Those entering the Transvaal were arrested, but those entering Natal were not detained and went to Newcastle, where they urged the indentured miners to strike. When the government arrested these women, the strike of the miners spread. Gandhi arrived in Newcastle and advised the miners to leave the compounds and begin a march to Charlestown, on the Natal-Transvaal border, and thence into the Transvaal in order to court arrest. While preparations for the march were being made, Gandhi was invited by the mine-owners to confer with them in Durban, but no settlement was reached.

I RETURNED TO NEWCASTLE. Laborers were still pouring in from all directions. I clearly explained the whole situation to the "army."

• Reprinted with permission from M. K. Gandhi, *Satyagraha in South Africa* (Madras: Ganesan, 1928), pp. 444-46, 452-53, 455-56.

I said they were still free to return to work if they wished. I told them about the threats held out by the coalowners, and pictured before them the risks of the future. I pointed out that no one could tell when the struggle would end. I described to the men the hardships of jail, and yet they would not flinch. They fearlessly replied that they would never be down-hearted so long as I was fighting by their side, and they asked me not to be anxious about them as they were inured to hardships.

It was now only left for us to march. The laborers were informed one evening that they were to commence the march early next morning (28th October 1913), and the rules to be observed on the march were read to them. It was no joke to control a multitude of five or six thousand men. I had no idea of the exact number, nor did I know their names or places of residence. I was merely content with as many of them as chose to remain. I could not afford to give them anything on the road beyond a daily ration of one pound and a half of bread and an ounce of sugar per each "soldier." If possible I would try to get something more from the Indian traders on the way. But if I failed they must rest content with bread and sugar. My experience of the Boer war and the Zulu "rebellion" [1] stood me in good stead on the present occasion. None of the "invaders" was to keep with him any more clothes than necessary. None was to touch any one's property on the way. They were to bear it patiently if any official or non-official European met them and abused or even flogged them. They were to allow themselves to be arrested if the police offered to arrest them. The march must continue even if I was arrested. All these points were explained to the men and I also announced the names of those who should successively lead the "army" in place of me.

The men understood the instructions issued to them, and our caravan safely reached Charlestown where the traders rendered us great help. They gave us the use of their houses, and permitted us to make our cooking arrangements on the grounds of the mosque. The ration supplied on the march would be exhausted when camp was reached and therefore we were in need of cooking pots, which were cheerfully supplied by the traders. We had with us a plentiful store of rice etc. to which also the traders contributed their share. . . .

I wrote to the Government, that we did not propose to enter the Transvaal with a view to domicile, but as an effective protest against the minister's breach of pledge and as a pure demonstration of our distress at the loss of our self-respect. Government would be relieving us of all anxiety if they were good enough to arrest us where we then were, that is in Charlestown. But if they did not arrest us, and if any of us surreptitiously entered the Transvaal, the responsibility would not be ours. There was no secrecy about our movement. None of us had a personal axe to grind. We would not like it if any of us secretly entered the Transvaal. But we could not hold ourselves responsible for the acts of any as we had to deal with thousands of unknown men and as we could not command any other sanction but that of love. Finally I assured the Government that if they repealed the £3 tax, the strike would be called off and the indentured laborers would return to work, as we would not ask them to join the general struggle directed against the rest of our grievances.

The position therefore was quite uncertain, and there was no knowing when the Government would arrest us. But at a crisis like this we could not await the reply of the Government for a number of days, but only for one or two returns of the post. We therefore decided to leave Charlestown and enter the Transvaal at once if the Government did not put us under arrest. If we were not arrested on the way, the "army of peace" was to march twenty to twenty-four miles a day for eight days together, with a view to reach Tolstoy Farm, and to stop there till the struggle was over and in the meanwhile to maintain themselves by working the Farm. . . .

When all the preparations for the march were completed, I made one more effort to achieve a settlement. I had already sent letters and telegrams. I now decided to 'phone even at the risk of my overtures being answered by an insult. From Charlestown I 'phoned to General Smuts in Pretoria. I called his secretary and said: "Tell General Smuts that I am fully prepared for the march.

The Europeans in Volksrust are excited and perhaps likely to violate even the safety of our lives. They have certainly held out such a threat. I am sure that even the General would not wish any such untoward event to happen. If he promises to abolish the £3 tax, I will stop the march, as I will not break the law merely for the sake of breaking it but I am driven to it by inexorable necessity. Will not the General accede to such a small request?" I received this reply within half a minute: "General Smuts will have nothing to do with you. You may do just as you please." With this the message closed.

I had fully expected this result, though I was not prepared for the curtness of the reply. I hoped for a civil answer, as my political relations with the General since the organization of Satyagraha had now subsisted for six years. But as I would not be elated by his courtesy, I did not weaken in the face of his incivility. The strait and narrow path I had to tread was clear before me. The next day (6th November 1913) at the appointed stroke of the hour (6:30) we offered prayers and commenced the march in the name of God. The pilgrim band was composed of 2,037 men, 127 women and 57 children.

THE GREAT MARCH
by M. K. Gandhi

THE CARAVAN of pilgrims thus started punctually at the appointed hour. There is a small spruit [2] one mile from Charlestown, and as soon as one crosses it, one has entered Volksrust or the Transvaal. A small patrol of mounted policemen was on duty at the border gate. I went up to them, leaving instructions with the

• Reprinted with permission from M. K. Gandhi, *Satyagraha in South Africa* (Madras: Ganesan, 1928), pp. 457-63, 466-71, 472-73.

"army" to cross over when I signaled to them. But while I was still talking with the police, the pilgrims made a sudden rush and crossed the border. The police surrounded them, but the surging multitude was not easy of control. The police had no intention of arresting us. I pacified the pilgrims and got them to arrange themselves in regular rows. Everything was in order in a few minutes and the march into the Transvaal began.

Two days before this the Europeans of Volksrust held a meeting where they offered all manner of threats to the Indians. Some said that they would shoot the Indians if they entered the Transvaal. Mr. Kallenbach [3] attended this meeting to reason with the Europeans who were however not prepared to listen to him. Indeed some of them even stood up to assault him. Mr. Kallenbach is an athlete, having received physical training at the hands of Sandow,[4] and it was not easy to frighten him. One European challenged him to a duel. Mr. Kallenbach replied, "As I have accepted the religion of peace, I may not accept the challenge. Let him who will come and do his worst with me. But I will continue to claim a hearing at this meeting. You have publicly invited all Europeans to attend, and I am here to inform you that not all Europeans are ready as you are to lay violent hands upon innocent men. There is one European who would like to inform you that the charges you level at the Indians are false. The Indians do not want what you imagine them to do. The Indians are not out to challenge your position as rulers. They do not wish to fight with you or to fill the country. They only seek justice pure and simple. They propose to enter the Transvaal not with a view to settle there, but only as an effective demonstration against the unjust tax which is levied upon them. They are brave men. They will not injure you in person or in property, they will not fight with you, but enter the Transvaal they will, even in the face of your gunfire. They are not the men to beat a retreat from the fear of your bullets or your spears. They propose to melt, and I know they will melt, your hearts by self-suffering. This is all I have to say. I have had my say and, I believe, thus rendered you a service. Beware and save yourselves from perpetrating a wrong." With these words Mr. Kallenbach resumed his seat. The audience was rather abashed. The pugilist who had invited Mr. Kallenbach to a single combat became his friend.

We had heard about this meeting and were prepared for any mischief by the Europeans in Volksrust. It was possible that the large number of policemen massed at the border was intended as a check upon them. However that may be, our procession passed through the place in peace. I do not remember that any European attempted even a jest. All were out to witness this novel sight, while there was even a friendly twinkle in the eyes of some of them.

On the first day we were to stop for the night at Palmford about eight miles from Volksrust, and we reached the place at about five o'clock in the evening. The pilgrims took their ration of bread and sugar, and spread themselves in the open air. Some were talking while others were singing bhajans. Some of the women were thoroughly exhausted by the march. They had dared to carry their children in their arms, but it was impossible for them to proceed further. I therefore, according to my previous warning, kept them as lodgers with a good Indian shopkeeper who promised to send them to Tolstoy Farm if we were permitted to go there, and to their homes if we were arrested.

As the night advanced, all noises ceased and I too was preparing to retire when I heard a tread. I saw a European coming lantern in hand. I understood what it meant, but had no preparations to make. The police officer said,

"I have a warrant of arrest for you. I want to arrest you."

"When?" I asked.

"Just now."

"Where will you take me?"

"To the adjoining railway station now, and to Volksrust when we get a train for it."

"I will go with you without informing anyone, but I will leave some instructions with one co-worker."

"You may do so."

I roused P. K. Naidoo who was sleeping near me. I informed

him about my arrest and asked him not to awake the pilgrims before morning. At daybreak they must regularly resume the march.
The march would commence before sunrise, and when it was time
for them to halt and get their rations, he must break to them the
news of my arrest. He might inform anyone who inquired about
me in the interval. If the pilgrims were arrested, they must allow
themselves to be arrested. Otherwise they must continue the
march according to the program. Naidoo had no fears at all. I
also told him what was to be done in case he was arrested. Mr.
Kallenbach too was in Volksrust at the time.

I went with the police officer, and we took the train for
Volksrust the next morning. I appeared before the Court in
Volksrust, but the prosecutor himself asked for a remand until
the 14th as he was not still ready with the evidence. The case was
postponed accordingly. I applied for bail as I had over 2,000 men,
122 women and 50 children in my charge whom I should like to
take on to their destination within the period of postponement.
The Public Prosecutor opposed my application. But the Magistrate was helpless in the matter, as every prisoner not charged with
a capital offense is in law entitled to be allowed to give bail for
his appearance, and I could not be deprived of that right. He
therefore released me on bail of £50. Mr. Kallenbach had already
kept a car ready for me, and he took me at once to rejoin the
"invaders." The special reporter of *The Transvaal Leader* wanted
to go with us. We took him in the car, and he published at the
time a vivid description of the case, the journey, and the meeting
with the pilgrims, who received me with enthusiasm and were
transported with joy. Mr. Kallenbach at once returned to Volksrust, as he had to look after the Indians stopping at Charlestown
as well as fresh arrivals there.

We continued the march, but it could not suit the Government to leave me in a state of freedom. I was therefore re-arrested
at Standerton on the 8th. Standerton is comparatively a bigger
place. There was something rather strange about the manner of
my arrest here. I was distributing bread to the pilgrims. The Indian storekeepers at Standerton presented us with some tins of

marmalade, and the distribution therefore took more time than usual. Meanwhile the Magistrate came and stood by my side. He waited till the distribution of rations was over, and then called me aside. I knew the gentleman, who, I thought, perhaps wanted to talk with me. He laughed and said,

"You are my prisoner."

"It would seem I have received promotion in rank," I said, "as magistrates take the trouble to arrest me instead of mere police officials. But you will try me just now."

"Go with me," replied the Magistrate, "the courts are still in session."

I asked the pilgrims to continue their march, and then left with the Magistrate. As soon as I reached the court room, I found that some of my co-workers had also been arrested. There were five of them there, P. K. Naidoo, Biharilal Maharaj, Ramnarayan Sinha, Raghu Narasu and Rahimkhan.

I was at once brought before the court and applied for remand and bail on the same grounds as in Volksrust. Here too the application was strongly opposed by the Public Prosecutor and here too I was released on my own recognizance of £50 and the case was remanded till the 21st. The Indian traders had kept a carriage ready for me and I rejoined the pilgrims again when they had hardly proceeded three miles further. The pilgrims thought, and I thought too, that we might now perhaps reach Tolstoy Farm. But that was not to be. It was no small thing however that the invaders got accustomed to my being arrested. The five co-workers remained in jail. . . .

Mr. Polak [5] joined us on the 9th at Teakworth between Standerton and Greylingstad. We were in the midst of our consultation and had nearly done with it. It was about 3 o'clock in the afternoon. Polak and I were walking at the head of the whole body of pilgrims. Some of the co-workers were listening to our conversation. Polak was to take the evening train for Durban. But God does not always permit man to carry out his plans. Rama had to retire to the forest on the very day that was fixed for his coronation. While we were thus engaged in talking, a Cape cart came and stopped before us and from it alighted Mr. Chamney, the Principal Immigration Officer of the Transvaal and a police officer. They took me somewhat aside and one of them said, "I arrest you."

I was thus arrested thrice in four days.

"What about the marchers?" I asked.

"We shall see to that," was the answer.

I said nothing further. I asked Polak to assume charge of and go with the pilgrims. The police officer permitted me only to inform the marchers of my arrest. As I proceeded to ask them to keep the peace etc., the officer interrupted me and said,

"You are now a prisoner and cannot make any speeches."

I understood my position, but it was needless. As soon as he stopped me speaking, the officer ordered the driver to drive the cart away at full speed. In a moment the pilgrims passed out of my sight.

The officer knew that for the time being I was master of the situation, for trusting to our non-violence, he was alone in this desolate veld [6] confronted by two thousand Indians. He also knew that I would have surrendered to him even if he had sent me a summons in writing. Such being the case, it was hardly necessary to remind me that I was a prisoner. And the advice which I would have given the pilgrims would have served the Government's purpose no less than our own. But how could an officer forego an opportunity of exercising his brief authority? I must say, however, that many officers understood us better than this gentleman. They knew that not only had arrest no terrors for us but on the other hand we hailed it as the gateway of liberty. They therefore allowed us all legitimate freedom and thankfully sought our aid in conveniently and expeditiously effecting arrests. The reader will come across apposite cases of both kinds in these pages.

I was taken to Greylingstad, and from Greylingstad via Balfour to Heidelberg where I passed the night.

The pilgrims with Polak as leader resumed their march and halted for the night at Greylingstad where they were met by Sheth Amad Mamad Kachhalia and Sheth Amad Bhayat who had come to know that arrangements were complete for arresting the whole body of marchers. Polak therefore thought that when his responsibility ceased in respect of the pilgrims upon their arrest, he could reach Durban even if a day later and take the steamer for India after all. But God had willed otherwise. At about 9 o'clock in the morning on the 10th the pilgrims reached Balfour where three special trains were drawn up at the station to take them and deport them to Natal. The pilgrims were there rather obstinate. They asked for me to be called and promised to be arrested and to board the trains if I advised them to that effect. This was a wrong attitude. And the whole game must be spoiled and the movement must receive a setback unless it was given up. Why should the pilgrims want me for going to jail? It would ill become soldiers to claim to elect their commanders or to insist upon their obeying only one of them. Mr. Chamney approached Mr. Polak and Kachhalia Sheth to help him in arresting them. These friends encountered difficulty in explaining the situation to the marchers. They told them that jail was the pilgrims' goal and they should therefore appreciate the Government's action when they were ready to arrest them. Only thus could the Satyagrahis show their quality and bring their struggle to a triumphant end. They must realize that no other procedure could have my approval. The pilgrims were brought round and all entrained peacefully.

I, on my part, was again hauled up before the Magistrate. I knew nothing of what transpired after I was separated from the pilgrims. I asked for a remand once again. I said that a remand had been granted by two courts, and that we had not now much to go to reach our destination. I therefore requested that either the Government should arrest the pilgrims or else I should be permitted to see them safe in Tolstoy Farm. The Magistrate did not comply with my request, but promised to forward it at once to the Government. This time I was arrested on a warrant from Dundee where I was to be prosecuted on the principal charge of inducing indentured laborers to leave the province of Natal. I was therefore taken to Dundee by rail the same day.

Mr. Polak was not only not arrested at Balfour but he was even thanked for the assistance he had rendered to the authorities. Mr. Chamney even said, that the Government had no intention of arresting him. But these were Mr. Chamney's own views or the views of the Government in so far as they were known to that officer. Government in fact would be changing their mind every now and then. And finally they reached the decision that Mr. Polak should not be allowed to sail for India and should be arrested along with Mr. Kallenbach who was working most energetically on behalf of the Indians. Mr. Polak therefore was arrested in Charlestown whilst waiting for the corridor train. Mr. Kallenbach was also arrested and both these friends were confined in Volksrust jail.

I was tried in Dundee on the 11th and sentenced to nine months' imprisonment with hard labor. I had still to take my second trial at Volksrust on the charge of aiding and abetting prohibited persons to enter the Transvaal. From Dundee I was therefore taken on the 13th to Volksrust where I was glad to meet Kallenbach and Polak in the jail.

I appeared before the Volksrust court on the 14th. The beauty of it was that the charge was proved against me only by witnesses furnished by myself at Kromdraai. The police could have secured witnesses but with difficulty. They had therefore sought my aid in the matter. The courts here would not convict a prisoner merely upon his pleading guilty.

This was arranged as regards me, but who would testify against Mr. Kallenbach and Mr. Polak? It was impossible to convict them in the absence of evidence, and it was also difficult at once to secure witnesses against them. Mr. Kallenbach intended to plead guilty as he wished to be with the pilgrims. But Mr. Polak was bound for India, and was not deliberately courting jail at this moment. After a joint consultation therefore we three resolved that we should say neither yes nor no in case we were asked whether Mr. Polak was guilty of the offense with which he was charged.

I provided the evidence for the crown against Mr. Kallenbach and I appeared as witness against Mr. Polak. We did not wish that the cases should be protracted, and we therefore did our best to see that each case was disposed of within a day. The proceedings against me were completed on the 14th, against Kallenbach on the 15th and against Polak on the 17th, and the Magistrate passed sentence of three months' imprisonment on all three of us. We now thought we could live together in Volksrust jail for these three months. But the Government could not afford to allow it. . . .

Government would not like that men should thus be attracted to jail, nor did they appreciate the fact that prisoners upon their release should carry my messages outside. They therefore decided to separate Kallenbach, Polak and me, send us away from Volksrust, and take me in particular to a place where no Indian could go and see me. I was sent accordingly to the jail in Bloemfontein, the capital of Orangia, where there were not more than 50 Indians, all of them serving as waiters in hotels. I was the only Indian prisoner there, the rest being Europeans and Negroes. I was not troubled at this isolation but hailed it as a blessing. There was no need now for me to keep my eyes or ears open, and I was glad that a novel experience was in store for me. Again, I never had had time for study for years together, particularly since 1893, and the prospect of uninterrupted study for a year filled me with joy.

FAREWELL SPEECH
• by M. K. Gandhi

Although Gandhi was confined to prison after the Great March, several of his associates avoided arrest in order to com-

• Reprinted with permission from *Souvenir of the Passive Resistance Movement in South Africa (1906–14)* (Golden Number, *Indian Opinion*, Natal: Phoenix Farm, 1914), pp. 10-12.

municate with India and England. Increasing pressure was put on the government of South Africa to come to terms with the Indians. Suddenly, on December 18, 1913, Gandhi, Kallenbach, and Polak were released from prison, and a commission was appointed to investigate the grievances of the Indian community. After prolonged negotiations between Smuts and Gandhi, an agreement was reached on June 30, 1914. This agreement became, with the support of Smuts, the basis of the Indian Relief Act, which went into effect in July 1914. The Act made non-Christian marriages valid, abolished the three-pound tax on indentured laborers who remained in Natal, banned the importation of indentured laborers from India after 1920, and allowed Indians born in South Africa to enter the Cape Colony, although otherwise Indians could not move freely from one South African province to another.

Having achieved this partial victory, Gandhi resolved to leave South Africa forever. Accompanied by his wife and Kallenbach, he sailed for England on July 18, 1914. Before he left, he was everywhere feted by the Indian community. One of the biggest demonstrations was in Johannesburg, where he made a farewell speech which, unfortunately for posterity, is recorded only in the third person.

MR. GANDHI said that they or circumstances had placed him that evening in a most embarrassing position. Hitherto those who had known him in Johannesburg had known him in the capacity of one of many hosts at gatherings of that kind, but that evening they had placed him in the unfortunate position of being a guest, and he did not know how he would be able to discharge that duty. For the other he thought long experience had fitted him, if he might say so with due humility, most admirably; but the present position was entirely new to him and Mrs. Gandhi, and he was exceedingly diffident as to how he was going to discharge the new duty that had been imposed upon him. So much had been said about Mrs. Gandhi and himself, their so-called devotion, their so-called self-sacrifice, and many other things. There was one injunction of his religion, and he thought it was true of all reli-

gions, and that was that when one's praises were sung one should
fly from those praises, and, if one could not do that, one should
stop one's ears, and if one could not do either of these things, one
should dedicate everything that was said in connection with one
to the Almighty, the Divine Essence, which pervaded everyone
and everything in the Universe, and he hoped that Mrs. Gandhi
and he would have the strength to dedicate all that had been
said that evening to the Divine Essence. . . .

Johannesburg was not a new place to him. . . . It was in
Johannesburg that he had found his most precious friends. It was
in Johannesburg that the foundation for the great struggle of
Passive Resistance was laid in the September of 1906. . . . It was
last, but not least, Johannesburg that had given Valiamma,[7] that
young girl, whose picture rose before him even as he spoke, who
had died in the cause of truth. Simple-minded in faith—she had
not the knowledge that he had, she did not know what Passive
Resistance was, she did not know what it was the community
would gain, but she was simply taken up with unbounded enthusiasm for her people—went to jail, came out of it a wreck, and
within a few days died. It was in Johannesburg again that produced a Nagappan [8] and Naryansamy, two lovely youths hardly
out of their teens, who also died. But both Mrs. Gandhi and he
stood living before them. He and Mrs. Gandhi had worked in the
limelight; those others had worked behind the scenes, not knowing where they were going, except this, that what they were
doing was right and proper, and, if any praise was due anywhere
at all, it was due to those three who died. . . .

No wonder if Passive Resistance had fired and quickened the
conscience of South Africa! And, therefore, whenever he had
spoken, he had said that, if the Indian community had gained
anything through this settlement, it was certainly due to Passive
Resistance; but it was certainly not due to Passive Resistance
alone. He thought that the cablegram that had been read
that evening showed that they had to thank that noble Viceroy, Lord Hardinge, for his great effort. He thought, too, that
they had to thank the Imperial Government, who, during the past

few years, in season and out of season, had been sending dispatches to General Botha,[9] and asking him to consider their standpoint— the Imperial standpoint. They had to thank also the Union Government for the spirit of justice they had adopted that time. They had, too, to thank the noble members of both Houses of the Legislature who had made those historic speeches and brought about the settlement; and, lastly, they had to thank the Opposition also for their cooperation with the Government in bringing about the passage of the Bill, in spite of the jarring note produced by the Natal members.

When one considered all those things, the service that he and Mrs. Gandhi might have rendered could be only very little. They were but two out of many instruments that had gone to make this settlement. And what was that settlement? In his humble opinion, the value of the settlement, if they were to examine it, would consist not in the intrinsic things they had received, but in the sufferings and the sorrows long drawn out that were necessary in order to achieve those things. . . . What was there to gloat over in having an intolerable burden removed which might have been removed years ago? What was there in a lawful wife's being recognized in a place like South Africa? . . . Behind that struggle for concrete rights lay the great spirit which asked for an abstract principle, and the fight which was undertaken in 1906, although it was a fight against a particular law, was a fight undertaken in order to combat the spirit that was seen about to over-shadow the whole of South Africa, and to undermine the glorious British Constitution, of which the Chairman had spoken so loftily that evening, and about which he [the speaker] shared his views.

It was his knowledge, right or wrong, of the British Constitution, which bound him to the Empire. Tear that Constitution to shreds and his loyalty also would be torn to shreds. Keep that Constitution intact, and they held him bound a slave to that Constitution. He had felt that the choice lay for himself and his fellow-countrymen between two courses, when his spirit was brooding over South Africa, either to sunder themselves from the

British Constitution, or to fight in order that the ideals of that Constitution might be preserved—but only the ideals. Lord Ampthill [10] had said, in a preface to Mr. Doke's book, that the theory of the British Constitution must be preserved at any cost if the British Empire was to be saved from the mistakes that all the previous Empires had made. Practice might bend to the temporary aberration through which local circumstances might compel them to pass, it might bend before unreasoning or unreasonable prejudice, but theory once recognized could never be departed from, and this principle must be maintained at any cost. And it was that spirit which had been acknowledged now by the Union Government, and acknowledged now nobly and loftily.

The words that General Smuts so often emphasized still rang in his ears. He had said, "Gandhi, this time we want no misunderstanding, we want no mental or other reservations, let all the cards be on the table, and I want you to tell me wherever you think that a particular passage or word does not read in accordance with your own reading," and it was so.

That was the spirit in which he approached the negotiations. When he remembered General Smuts of a few years ago, when he told Lord Crewe [11] that South Africa would not depart from its policy of racial distinction, that it was bound to retain that distinction, and that, therefore, the sting that lay in this Immigration Law would not be removed, many a friend, including Lord Ampthill, asked whether they could not for the time being suspend their activity. He had said, "No." If they did that it would undermine his loyalty, and even though he might be the only person he would still fight on. Lord Ampthill had congratulated him, and that great nobleman had never deserted the cause even when it was at its lowest ebb, and they saw the result that day. They had not by any means to congratulate themselves on a victory gained. There was no question of a victory gained, but the question of the establishment of the principle that, so far as the Union of South Africa at least was concerned, its legislation would never contain the racial taint, would never contain the color disability. The practice would certainly be different.

There was the Immigration Law—it recognized no racial distinctions, but in practice they had arranged, they had given a promise, that there should be no undue influx from India as to immigration. That was a concession to present prejudice. Whether it was right or wrong was not for him to discuss then. But it was the establishment of that principle which had made the struggle so important to the British Empire, and the establishment of that principle which had made those sufferings perfectly justifiable and perfectly honorable, and he thought that, when they considered the struggle from that standpoint, it was a perfectly dignified thing for any gathering to congratulate itself upon such a vindication of the principles of the British Constitution.

One word of caution he wished to utter regarding the settlement. The settlement was honorable to both parties. He did not think there was any room left for misunderstanding, but whilst it was final in the sense that it closed the great struggle, it was not final in the sense that it gave to Indians all that they were entitled to. There was still the Gold Law [12] which had many a sting in it. There was still the Licensing Laws throughout the Union, which also contained many a sting. There was still a matter which the Colonial-born Indians especially could not understand or appreciate, namely, the water-tight compartments in which they had to live; whilst there was absolutely free inter-communication and inter-migration between the Provinces for Europeans, Indians had to be cooped up in their respective Provinces. Then there was undue restraint on their trading activity. There was the prohibition as to holding landed property in the Transvaal, which was degrading, and all these things took Indians into all kinds of undesirable channels. These restrictions would have to be removed. But for that, he thought, sufficient patience would have to be exercised. Time was now at their disposal, and how wonderfully the tone had been changed! And here he had been told in Capetown, and he believed it implicitly, the spirit of Mr. Andrews had pervaded all those statesmen and leading men whom he saw. He came and went away after a brief period, but he certainly fired those whom he saw with a sense of their duty to the Empire of which they were members. . . .

To his countrymen he would say that they should wait and nurse the settlement, which he considered was all that they could possibly and reasonably have expected, and that they would now live to see, with the cooperation of their European friends, that what was promised was fulfilled, that the administration of the existing laws was just, and that vested rights were respected in the administration; that after they had nursed these things, if they cultivated European public opinion, making it possible for the Government of the day to grant a restoration of the other rights of which they had been deprived, he did not think that there need be any fear about the future. He thought that, with mutual cooperation, with mutual goodwill, with due response on the part of either party, the Indian community need never be a source of weakness to that Government or to any Government. On the contrary, he had full faith in his countrymen that, if they were well treated, they would always rise to the occasion and help the Government of the day. If they had insisted on their rights on many an occasion, he hoped that the European friends who were there would remember that they had also discharged the responsibilities which had faced them.

And now it was time for him to close his remarks and say a few words of farewell only. He did not know how he could express those words. The best years of his life had been passed in South Africa. India, as his distinguished countryman, Mr. Gokhale, had reminded him, had become a strange land to him. South Africa he knew, but not India. He did not know what impelled him to go to India, but he did know that the parting from them all, the parting from the European friends who had helped him through thick and thin, was a heavy blow, and one he was least able to bear; yet he knew he had to part with them. He could only say farewell and ask them to give him their blessing, to pray for them that their heads might not be turned by the praise they had received, that they might still know how to do their duty to the best of their ability, that they might still learn that first, second, and last should be the approbation of their own conscience, and that then whatever might be due to them would follow in its own time.

5 "INDIAN HOME RULE" (1909)

• "INDIAN HOME RULE" (1909)
by M. K. Gandhi

The first important work written by Gandhi was a pamphlet entitled Hind Swaraj, or Indian Home Rule, composed in 1909, which has been frequently reprinted. Its genesis and evolution are best described in "A Word of Explanation" written by Gandhi himself in 1921: [1]

"It is certainly my good fortune that this booklet of mine is receiving wide attention. The original is in Gujarati. It has a checkered career. It was first published in the columns of the Indian Opinion of South Africa. It was written in 1908 [2] during my return voyage from London to South Africa in answer to the Indian school of violence and its prototype in South Africa. I came in contact with every known Indian anarchist in London. Their bravery impressed me, but I felt that their zeal was misguided. I felt that violence was no remedy for India's ills, and that her civilization required the use of a different and higher weapon for self-protection. The Satyagraha of South Africa was still an infant hardly two years old. But it had developed sufficiently to permit me to write of it with some degree of confidence. What I

• Reprinted with permission from M. K. Gandhi, Hind Swaraj, or Indian Home Rule (Ahmedabad: Navajivan, 1946), pp. 24-27, 43-46, 56-63, 71-76.

wrote was so much appreciated that it was published as a booklet. It attracted some attention in India. The Bombay Government prohibited its circulation. I replied by publishing its translation. I thought that it was due to my English friends that they should know its contents. In my opinion it is a book which can be put into the hands of a child. It teaches the gospel of love in place of that of hate. It replaces violence with self-sacrifice. It pits soul force against brute force. It has gone through several editions and I commend it to those who would care to read it. I withdraw nothing except one word of it, and that in deference to a lady friend. The booklet is a severe condemnation of 'modern civilization.' It was written in 1908. My conviction is deeper today than ever. I feel that if India will discard 'modern civilization' she can only gain by doing so."

Of the twenty chapters in this pamphlet, only portions of four can be given here.

CIVILIZATION (Chapter VI)

READER: . . . Now will you tell me something of what you have read and thought of this civilization?

EDITOR: Let us first consider what state of things is described by the word "civilization." Its true test lies in the fact that people living in it make bodily welfare the object of life. We will take some examples. The people of Europe today live in better-built houses than they did a hundred years ago. This is considered an emblem of civilization, and this is also a matter to promote bodily happiness. Formerly, they wore skins, and used spears as their weapons. Now, they wear long trousers, and, for embellishing their bodies, they wear a variety of clothing, and, instead of spears, they carry with them revolvers containing five or more chambers. If people of a certain country, who have hitherto not been in the habit of wearing much clothing, boots, etc., adopt European clothing, they are supposed to have become civilized out of savagery. Formerly, in Europe, people ploughed their lands mainly by manual labor. Now, one man can plough a vast tract by means of steam engines and can thus amass great wealth. This is called a sign of civilization. Formerly, only a few men wrote valuable books. Now, anybody writes and prints anything he likes and poisons people's minds. Formerly, men traveled in wagons. Now, they fly through the air in trains at the rate of four hundred and more miles per day. This is considered the height of civilization. It has been stated that, as men progress, they shall be able to travel in airships and reach any part of the world in a few hours. Men will not need the use of their hands and feet. They will press a button, and they will have their clothing by their side. They will press another button, and they will have their newspaper. A third, and a motor-car will be in waiting for them. They will have a variety of delicately dished up food. Everything will be done by machinery. Formerly, when people wanted to fight with one another, they measured between them their bodily strength; now it is possible to take away thousands of lives by one man working behind a gun from a hill. This is civilization. Formerly, men worked in the open air only as much as they liked. Now thousands of workmen meet together and for the sake of maintenance work in factories or mines. Their condition is worse than that of beasts. They are obliged to work, at the risk of their lives, at most dangerous occupations, for the sake of millionaires. Formerly, men were made slaves under physical compulsion. Now they are enslaved by temptation of money and of the luxuries that money can buy. There are now diseases of which people never dreamt before, and an army of doctors is engaged in finding out their cures, and so hospitals have increased. This is a test of civilization. Formerly, special messengers were required and much expense was incurred in order to send letters; today, anyone can abuse his fellow by means of a letter for one penny. True, at the same cost, one can send one's thanks also. Formerly, people had two or three meals consisting of home-made bread and vegetables; now, they require something to eat every two hours so that they have hardly leisure for anything else. What more need I say? All this you can ascertain from several authoritative books. These are all true tests of civilization. And if anyone speaks to the contrary, know that he is ignorant. This civilization takes note neither of morality nor of religion. Its votaries calmly state that their business is not to teach religion. Some even consider it to be a superstitious growth. Others put on the cloak of religion, and prate about morality. Even a child can understand that in all I have described above there can be no inducement to morality. Civilization seeks to increase bodily comforts, and it fails miserably even in doing so.

This civilization is irreligion, and it has taken such a hold on the people in Europe that those who are in it appear to be half mad. They lack real physical strength or courage. They keep up their energy by intoxication. They can hardly be happy in solitude. Women, who should be the queens of households, wander in the streets or they slave away in factories. For the sake of a pittance, half a million women in England alone are laboring under trying circumstances in factories or similar institutions. This awful fact is one of the causes of the daily growing suffragette movement.

This civilization is such that one has only to be patient and it will be self-destroyed. According to the teaching of Mahomed this would be considered a Satanic Civilization. Hinduism calls it the Black Age. I cannot give you an adequate conception of it. It is eating into the vitals of the English nation. It must be shunned. Parliaments are really emblems of slavery. If you will sufficiently think over this, you will entertain the same opinion and cease to blame the English. They rather deserve our sympathy. They are a shrewd nation and I therefore believe that they will cast off the evil. They are enterprising and industrious, and their mode of thought is not inherently immoral. Neither are they bad at heart. I therefore respect them. Civilization is not an incurable disease, but it should never be forgotten that the English people are at present afflicted by it.

WHAT IS TRUE CIVILIZATION? (Chapter XIII)

READER: You have denounced railways, lawyers and doctors. I can see that you will discard all machinery. What, then, is civilization?
EDITOR: The answer to that question is not difficult. I believe that

the civilization India has evolved is not to be beaten in the world. Nothing can equal the seeds sown by our ancestors. Rome went, Greece shared the same fate; the might of the Pharaohs was broken; Japan has become westernized; of China nothing can be said; but India is still, somehow or other, sound at the foundation. The people of Europe learn their lessons from the writings of the men of Greece or Rome, which exist no longer in their former glory. In trying to learn from them, the Europeans imagine that they will avoid the mistakes of Greece and Rome. Such is their pitiable condition. In the midst of all this India remains immovable and that is her glory. It is a charge against India that her people are so uncivilized, ignorant and stolid, that it is not possible to induce them to adopt any changes. It is a charge really against our merit. What we have tested and found true on the anvil of experience, we dare not change. Many thrust their advice upon India, and she remains steady. This is her beauty: it is the sheet-anchor of our hope.

Civilization is that mode of conduct which points out to man the path of duty. Performance of duty and observance of morality are convertible terms. To observe morality is to attain mastery over our mind and our passions. So doing, we know ourselves. The Gujarati equivalent for civilization means "good conduct."

If this definition be correct, then India, as so many writers have shown, has nothing to learn from anybody else, and this is as it should be. We notice that the mind is a restless bird; the more it gets the more it wants, and still remains unsatisfied. The more we indulge our passions the more unbridled they become. Our ancestors, therefore, set a limit to our indulgences. They saw that happiness was largely a mental condition. A man is not necessarily happy because he is rich, or unhappy because he is poor. The rich are often seen to be unhappy, the poor to be happy. Millions will always remain poor. Observing all this, our ancestors dissuaded us from luxuries and pleasures. We have managed with the same kind of plough as existed thousands of years ago. We have retained the same kind of cottages that we had in former times and our indigenous education remains the same as before. We have

had no system of life-corroding competition. Each followed his
own occupation or trade and charged a regulation wage. It was not
that we did not know how to invent machinery, but our fore-
fathers knew that, if we set our hearts after such things, we would
become slaves and lose our moral fibre. They, therefore, after
due deliberation decided that we should only do what we could
with our hands and feet. They saw that our real happiness and
health consisted in a proper use of our hands and feet. They
further reasoned that large cities were a snare and a useless en-
cumbrance and that people would not be happy in them, that
there would be gangs of thieves and robbers, prostitution and vice
flourishing in them and that poor men would be robbed by rich
men. They were, therefore, satisfied with small villages. They saw
that kings and their swords were inferior to the sword of ethics,
and they, therefore, held the sovereigns of the earth to be inferior
to the Rishis [3] and the Fakirs.[4] A nation with a constitution like
this is fitter to teach others than to learn from others. This nation
had courts, lawyers and doctors, but they were all within bounds.
Everybody knew that these professions were not particularly
superior; moreover, these vakils and vaids [5] did not rob people;
they were considered people's dependents, not their masters. Justice
was tolerably fair. The ordinary rule was to avoid courts. There
were no touts to lure people into them. This evil, too, was notice-
able only in and around capitals. The common people lived
independently and followed their agricultural occupation. They
enjoyed true Home Rule. . . .

Now you see what I consider to be real civilization. Those who
want to change conditions such as I have described are enemies
of the country and are sinners.

READER: It would be all right if India were exactly as you have
described it, but it is also India where there are hundreds of child
widows, where two year old babies are married, where twelve
year old girls are mothers and house wives, where women practice
polyandry, where the practice of Niyoga [6] obtains, where, in the
name of religion, girls dedicate themselves to prostitution, and
in the name of religion, sheep and goats are killed. Do you con-

sider these also symbols of the civilization that you have described?
EDITOR: You make a mistake. The defects that you have shown
are defects. Nobody mistakes them for ancient civilization. They
remain in spite of it. Attempts have always been made and will be
made to remove them. We may utilize the new spirit that is born
in us for purging ourselves of these evils. But what I have described
to you as emblems of modern civilization are accepted as such by
its votaries. The Indian civilization, as described by me, has been
so described by its votaries. In no part of the world, and under
no civilization, have all men attained perfection. The tendency
of the Indian civilization is to elevate the moral being, that of the
Western civilization is to propagate immorality. The latter is
godless, the former is based on a belief in God. So understanding
and so believing, it behooves every lover of India to cling to the
old Indian civilization even as a child clings to the mother's
breast.

PASSIVE RESISTANCE (Chapter XVII)

READER: Is there any historical evidence as to the success of what
you have called soul-force or truth-force? No instance seems to
have happened of any nation having risen through soul-force. I
still think that the evil-doers will not cease doing evil without
physical punishment.
EDITOR: The poet Tulsidas has said: "Of religion, pity, or love, is
the root, as egotism of the body. Therefore, we should not abandon
pity so long as we are alive." This appears to me to be a scientific
truth. I believe in it as much as I believe in two and two being
four. The force of love is the same as the force of the soul or
truth. We have evidence of its working at every step. The universe
would disappear without the existence of that force. But you ask
for historical evidence. It is, therefore, necessary to know what
history means. The Gujarati equivalent means; "It so happened."
If that is the meaning of history, it is possible to give copious
evidence. But, if it means the doings of kings and emperors, there
can be no evidence of soul-force or passive resistance in such
history. You cannot expect silver ore in a tin mine. History, as

we know it, is a record of the wars of the world, and so there is a proverb among Englishmen that a nation which has no history, that is, no wars, is a happy nation. How kings played, how they became enemies of one another, how they murdered one another, is found accurately recorded in history, and if this were all that had happened in the world, it would have been ended long ago. If the story of the universe had commenced with wars, not a man would have been found alive today. Those people who have been warred against have disappeared as, for instance, the natives of Australia of whom hardly a man was left alive by the intruders. Mark, please, that these natives did not use soul-force in self-defense, and it does not require much foresight to know that the Australians will share the same fate as their victims. "Those that take the sword shall perish by the sword." With us the proverb is that professional swimmers will find a watery grave.

The fact that there are so many men still alive in the world shows that it is based not on the force of arms but on the force of truth or love. Therefore, the greatest and most unimpeachable evidence of the success of this force is to be found in the fact that, in spite of the wars of the world, it still lives on.

Thousands, indeed tens of thousands, depend for their existence on a very active working of this force. Little quarrels of millions of families in their daily lives disappear before the exercise of this force. Hundreds of nations live in peace. History does not and cannot take note of this fact. History is really a record of every interruption of the even working of the force of love or of the soul. Two brothers quarrel; one of them repents and re-awakens the love that was lying dormant in him; the two again begin to live in peace; nobody takes note of this. But if the two brothers, through the intervention of solicitors or some other reason, take up arms or go to law—which is another form of the exhibition of brute force—their doings would be immediately noticed in the press, they would be the talk of their neighbors and would probably go down to history. And what is true of families and communities is true of nations. There is no reason to believe that there is one law for families and another for nations. History, then, is a record of an interruption of the course of nature. Soul-force, being natural, is not noted in history.

READER: According to what you say, it is plain that instances of this kind of passive resistance are not to be found in history. It is necessary to understand this passive resistance more fully. It will be better, therefore, if you enlarge upon it.

EDITOR: Passive resistance is a method of securing rights by personal suffering; it is the reverse of resistance by arms. When I refuse to do a thing that is repugnant to my conscience, I use soul-force. For instance, the Government of the day has passed a law which is applicable to me. I do not like it. If by using violence I force the Government to repeal the law, I am employing what may be termed body-force. If I do not obey the law and accept the penalty for its breach, I use soul-force. It involves sacrifice of self.

Everybody admits that sacrifice of self is infinitely superior to sacrifice of others. Moreover, if this kind of force is used in a cause that is unjust, only the person using it suffers. He does not make others suffer for his mistakes. Men have before now done many things which were subsequently found to have been wrong. No man can claim that he is absolutely in the right or that a particular thing is wrong because he thinks so, but it is wrong for him so long as that is his deliberate judgment. It is therefore meet that he should not do that which he knows to be wrong, and suffer the consequence whatever it may be. This is the key to the use of soul-force.

READER: You would then disregard laws—this is rank disloyalty. We have always been considered a law-abiding nation. You seem to be going even beyond the extremists. They say that we must obey the laws that have been passed, but that if the laws be bad, we must drive out the law-givers even by force.

EDITOR: Whether I go beyond them or whether I do not is a matter of no consequence to either of us. We simply want to find out what is right and to act accordingly. The real meaning of the statement that we are a law-abiding nation is that we are passive resisters. When we do not like certain laws, we do not break the heads of law-givers but we suffer and do not submit to the laws. That we should obey laws whether good or bad is a new-fangled notion. There was no such thing in former days. The people disregarded those laws they did not like and suffered the penalties for their breach. It is contrary to our manhood if we obey laws repugnant to our conscience. Such teaching is opposed to religion and means slavery. If the Government were to ask us to go about without any clothing, should we do so? If I were a passive resister, I would say to them that I would have nothing to do with their law. But we have so forgotten ourselves and become so compliant that we do not mind any degrading law.

A man who has realized his manhood, who fears only God, will fear no one else. Man-made laws are not necessarily binding on him. Even the Government does not expect any such thing from us. They do not say: "You must do such and such a thing," but they say: "If you do not do it, we will punish you." We are sunk so low that we fancy that it is our duty and our religion to do what the law lays down. If man will only realize that it is unmanly to obey laws that are unjust, no man's tyranny will enslave him. This is the key to self-rule or home-rule.

It is a superstition and ungodly thing to believe that an act of a majority binds a minority. Many examples can be given in which acts of majorities will be found to have been wrong and those of minorities to have been right. All reforms owe their origin to the initiation of minorities in opposition to majorities. If among a band of robbers a knowledge of robbing is obligatory, is a pious man to accept the obligation? So long as the superstition that men should obey unjust laws exists, so long will their slavery exist. And a passive resister alone can remove such a superstition.

To use brute-force, to use gunpowder, is contrary to passive resistance, for it means that we want our opponent to do by force that which we desire but he does not. And if such a use of force is justifiable, surely he is entitled to do likewise by us. And so we should never come to an agreement. We may simply fancy, like the blind horse moving in a circle round a mill, that we are making progress. Those who believe that they are not bound to obey laws which are repugnant to their conscience have only the remedy of passive resistance open to them. Any other must lead to disaster.

READER: From what you say I deduce that passive resistance is a splendid weapon of the weak, but that when they are strong they may take up arms.

EDITOR: This is a gross ignorance. Passive resistance, that is, soul-force, is matchless. It is superior to the force of arms. How, then, can it be considered only a weapon of the weak? Physical-force men are strangers to the courage that is requisite in a passive resister. Do you believe that a coward can ever disobey a law that he dislikes? Extremists are considered to be advocates of brute force. Why do they, then, talk about obeying laws? I do not blame them. They can say nothing else. When they succeed in driving out the English and they themselves become governors, they will want you and me to obey their laws. And that is a fitting thing for their constitution. But a passive resister will say he will not obey a law that is against his conscience, even though he may be blown to pieces at the mouth of a cannon.

What do you think? Wherein is courage required—in blowing others to pieces from behind a cannon, or with a smiling face to approach a cannon and be blown to pieces? Who is the true warrior—he who keeps death always as a bosom-friend, or he who controls the death of others? Believe me that a man devoid of courage and manhood can never be a passive resister.

This, however, I will admit: that even a man weak in body is capable of offering this resistance. One man can offer it just as well as millions. Both men and women can indulge in it. It does not require the training of an army; it needs no jiu-jitsu. Control over the mind is alone necessary, and when that is attained, man is free like the king of the forest and his very glance withers the enemy.

Passive resistance is an all-sided sword, it can be used anyhow; it blesses him who uses it and him against whom it is used. Without drawing a drop of blood it produces far-reaching results.

It never rusts and cannot be stolen. Competition between passive resisters does not exhaust. The sword of passive resistance does not require a scabbard. It is strange indeed that you should consider such a weapon to be a weapon merely of the weak. . . .

READER: From what you say, then, it would appear that it is not a small thing to become a passive resister, and, if that is so, I should like you to explain how a man may become one.

EDITOR: To become a passive resister is easy enough but it is also equally difficult. I have known a lad of fourteen years become a passive resister; I have known also sick people do likewise; and I have also known physically strong and otherwise happy people unable to take up passive resistance. After a great deal of experience it seems to me that those who want to become passive resisters for the service of the country have to observe perfect chastity, adopt poverty, follow truth, and cultivate fearlessness.

Chastity is one of the greatest disciplines without which the mind cannot attain requisite firmness. A man who is unchaste loses stamina, becomes emasculated and cowardly. He whose mind is given over to animal passions is not capable of any great effort. . . .

Just as there is necessity for chastity, so is there for poverty. Pecuniary ambition and passive resistance cannot go well together. Those who have money are not expected to throw it away, but they are expected to be indifferent about it. They must be prepared to lose every penny rather than give up passive resistance.

Passive resistance has been described in the course of our discussion as truth-force. Truth, therefore, has necessarily to be followed and that at any cost. In this connection, academic questions such as whether a man may not lie in order to save a life, etc., arise, but these questions occur only to those who wish to justify lying. Those who want to follow truth every time are not placed in such a quandary; and if they are, they are still saved from a false position.

Passive resistance cannot proceed a step without fearlessness. Those alone can follow the path of passive resistance who are free

from fear, whether as to their possessions, false honor, their relatives, the government, bodily injuries or death.

These observances are not to be abandoned in the belief that
they are difficult. Nature has implanted in the human breast
ability to cope with any difficulty or suffering that may come to
man unprovoked. These qualities are worth having, even for those
who do not wish to serve the country. Let there be no mistake,
as those who want to train themselves in the use of arms are also
obliged to have these qualities more or less. Everybody does not
become a warrior for the wish. A would-be warrior will have to
observe chastity and to be satisfied with poverty as his lot. A
warrior without fearlessness cannot be conceived of. It may be
thought that he would not need to be exactly truthful, but that
quality follows real fearlessness. When a man abandons truth, he
does so owing to fear in some shape or form. The above four
attributes, then, need not frighten anyone. It may be as well here
to note that a physical-force man has to have many other useless
qualities which a passive resister never needs. And you will find
that whatever extra effort a swordsman needs is due to lack of
fearlessness. If he is an embodiment of the latter, the sword will
drop from his hand that very moment. He does not need its support. One who is free from hatred requires no sword. A man
with a stick suddenly came face to face with a lion and instinctively
raised his weapon in self-defense. The man saw that he had only
prated about fearlessness when there was none in him. That
moment he dropped the stick and found himself free from all
fear.

CONCLUSION (Chapter XX)

READER: From your views I gather that you would form a third
party. You are neither an extremist nor a moderate.

EDITOR: That is a mistake. I do not think of a third party at all.
We do not all think alike. We cannot say that all the moderates
hold identical views. And how can those who want only to serve
have a party? I would serve both the moderates and the extremists.

Where I differ from them, I would respectfully place my position before them and continue my service.

READER: What, then, would you say to both the parties?

EDITOR: I would say to the extremists: "I know that you want Home Rule for India; it is not to be had for your asking. Everyone will have to take it for himself. What others get for me is not Home Rule but foreign rule; therefore, it would not be proper for you to say that you have obtained Home Rule if you have merely expelled the English. I have already described the true nature of Home Rule. This you would never obtain by force of arms. Brute-force is not natural to Indian soil. You will have, therefore, to rely wholly on soul-force. You must not consider that violence is necessary at any stage for reaching our goal."

I would say to the moderates: "Mere petitioning is derogatory; we thereby confess inferiority. To say that British rule is indispensable, is almost a denial of the Godhead. We cannot say that anybody or anything is indispensable except God. Moreover, common sense should tell us that to state that, for the time being, the presence of the English in India is a necessity, is to make them conceited.

"If the English vacated India, bag and baggage, it must not be supposed that she would be widowed. It is possible that those who are forced to observe peace under their pressure would fight after their withdrawal. There can be no advantage in suppressing an eruption; it must have its vent. If, therefore, before we can remain at peace, we must fight amongst ourselves, it is better that we do so. There is no occasion for a third party to protect the weak. It is this so-called protection which has unnerved us. Such protection can only make the weak weaker. Unless we realize this, we cannot have Home Rule. I would paraphrase the thought of an English divine and say that anarchy under Home Rule were better than orderly foreign rule. Only, the meaning that the learned divine attached to Home Rule is different from Indian Home Rule according to my conception. We have to learn, and to teach others, that we do not want the tyranny of either English rule or Indian rule."

If this idea were carried out, both the extremists and the moderates could join hands. There is no occasion to fear or distrust one another.

READER: What then, would you say to the English?

EDITOR: To them I would respectfully say: "I admit you are my rulers. It is not necessary to debate the question whether you hold India by the sword or by my consent. I have no objection to your remaining in my country, but although you are the rulers, you will have to remain as servants of the people. It is not we who have to do as you wish, but it is you who have to do as we wish. You may keep the riches that you have drained away from this land, but you may not drain riches henceforth. Your function will be, if you so wish, to police India; you must abandon the idea of deriving any commercial benefit from us. We hold the civilization that you support to be the reverse of civilization. We consider our civilization to be far superior to yours. If you realize this truth, it will be to your advantage and, if you do not, according to your own proverb, you should only live in our country in the same manner as we do. You must not do anything that is contrary to our religions. It is your duty as rulers that for the sake of the Hindus you should eschew beef, and for the sake of Mahomedans you should avoid bacon and ham. We have hitherto said nothing because we have been cowed down, but you need not consider that you have not hurt our feelings by your conduct. We are not expressing our sentiments either through base selfishness or fear, but because it is our duty now to speak out boldly. We consider your schools and law courts to be useless. We want our own ancient schools and courts to be restored. The common language of India is not English but Hindi. You should, therefore, learn it. We can hold communication with you only in our national language.

"We cannot tolerate the idea of your spending money on railways and the military. We see no occasion for either. You may fear Russia; we do not. When she comes we shall look after her. If you are with us, we may then receive her jointly. We do not need any European cloth. We shall manage with articles produced and manufactured at home. You may not keep one eye on Manchester and the other on India. We can work together only if our interests are identical.

"This has not been said to you in arrogance. You have great military resources. Your naval power is matchless. If we wanted to fight with you on your own ground, we should be unable to do so, but if the above submissions be not acceptable to you, we cease to play the part of the ruled. You may, if you like, cut us to pieces. You may shatter us at the cannon's mouth. If you act contrary to our will, we shall not help you; and without our help, we know that you cannot move one step forward.

"It is likely that you will laugh at all this in the intoxication of your power. We may not be able to disillusion you at once; but if there be any manliness in us, you will see shortly that your intoxication is suicidal and that your laugh at our expense is an aberration of intellect. We believe that at heart you belong to a religious nation. We are living in a land which is the source of religions. How we came together need not be considered, but we can make mutual good use of our relations.

"You, English, who have come to India are not good specimens of the English nation, nor can we, almost half-Anglicized Indians, be considered good specimens of the real Indian nation. If the English nation were to know all you have done, it would oppose many of your actions. The mass of the Indians have had few dealings with you. If you will abandon your so-called civilization and search into your own scriptures, you will find that our demands are just. Only on condition of our demands being fully satisfied may you remain in India; and if you remain under those conditions, we shall learn several things from you and you will learn many from us. So doing we shall benefit each other and the world. But that will happen only when the root of our relationship is sunk in a religious soil."

READER: What will you say to . . . those of us who are affected by European civilization, and who are eager to have Home Rule[?]

EDITOR: To these I would say, "It is only those Indians who are imbued with real love who will be able to speak to the English in the above strain without being frightened, and only those can be said to be so imbued who conscientiously believe that Indian civilization is the best and that the European is a nine days' wonder. Such ephemeral civilizations have often come and gone and will continue to do so. Those only can be considered to be so imbued who, having experienced the force of the soul within themselves, will not cower before brute-force, and will not, on any account, desire to use brute-force. Those only can be considered to have been so imbued who are intensely dissatisfied with the present pitiable condition, having already drunk the cup of poison.

"If there be only one such Indian, he will speak as above to the English and the English will have to listen to him.

"These are not demands, but they show our mental state. We shall get nothing by asking; we shall have to take what we want, and we need the requisite strength for the effort. . . ."

READER: This is a large order. When will all carry it out?

EDITOR: You make a mistake. You and I have nothing to do with the others. Let each do his duty. If I do my duty, that is, serve myself, I shall be able to serve others. Before I leave you, I will take the liberty of repeating:

1. Real home-rule is self-rule or self-control.

2. The way to it is passive resistance; that is soul-force or love-force.

3. In order to exert this force, Swadeshi [7] in every sense is necessary.

4. What we want to do should be done, not because we object to the English or because we want to retaliate but because it is our duty to do so. Thus, supposing that the English remove the salt-tax, restore our money, give the highest posts to Indians, withdraw the English troops, we shall certainly not use their machine-made goods, nor use the English language, nor many of their industries. It is worth noting that these things are, in their nature, harmful; hence we do not want them. I bear no enmity towards the English but I do towards their civilization.

In my opinion, we have used the term "Swaraj" [8] without understanding its real significance. I have endeavored to explain it as I understand it, and my conscience testifies that my life henceforth is dedicated to its attainment.

PART TWO 1915–1931

6   A NEW START IN INDIA (1915-1918)

ADMITTING AN UNTOUCHABLE

· by M. K. Gandhi

Gandhi arrived in England, from South Africa, just at the beginning of the first World War. He organized an Indian Ambulance Corps in England, but was obliged to leave the British Isles and sail for India because of pleurisy. By May 1915 he was settled enough in India to establish his first religious community— the Satyagraha Ashram—at Kochrab, near Ahmedabad, in his native district of Gujarat.

THE ASHRAM had been in existence only a few months when we were put to a test such as I had scarcely expected. I received a letter from Amritlal Thakkar to this effect: "A humble and honest untouchable family is desirous of joining your Ashram. Will you accept them?"

I was perturbed. I had never expected that an untouchable family with an introduction from no less a man than Thakkar Bapa would so soon be seeking admission to the Ashram. I shared the letter with my companions. They welcomed it.

I wrote to Amritlal Thakkar expressing our willingness to ac-

· Reprinted with permission from Gandhi's Autobiography (Washington: Public Affairs Press, 1948), Part V, Chapter X, pp. 485-87.

cept the family, provided all the members were ready to abide by the rules of the Ashram.

The family consisted of Dudabhai, his wife Danibehn and their daughter Lakshmi,[1] then a mere toddling babe. Dudabhai had been a teacher in Bombay. They all agreed to abide by the rules and were accepted.

But their admission created a flutter amongst the friends who had been helping the Ashram. The very first difficulty was found with regard to the use of the well, which was partly controlled by the owner of the bungalow. The man in charge of the water-lift objected that drops of water from our bucket would pollute him. So he took to swearing at us and molesting Dudabhai. I told everyone to put up with the abuse and continue drawing water at any cost. When he saw that we did not return his abuse, the man became ashamed and ceased to bother us.

All monetary help, however, was stopped. The friend who had asked that question about an untouchable being able to follow the rules of the Ashram had never expected that any such would be forthcoming.

With the stopping of monetary help came rumors of proposed social boycott. We were prepared for all this. I had told my companions that, if we were boycotted and denied the usual facilities, we would not leave Ahmedabad. We would rather go and stay in the untouchables' quarter and live on whatever we could get by manual labor.

Matters came to such a pass that Maganlal Gandhi one day gave me this notice: "We are out of funds and there is nothing for the next month."

I quietly replied: "Then we shall go to the untouchables' quarter."

This was not the first time I had been faced with such a trial. On all such occasions God has sent help at the last moment. One morning, shortly after Maganlal had given me warning of our monetary plight, one of the children came and said that a Sheth [2] who was waiting in a car outside wanted to see me. I went out to him. "I want to give the Ashram some help. Will you accept it?" he asked.

"Most certainly," said I. "And I confess I am at the present moment at the end of my resources."

"I shall come tomorrow at this time," he said. "Will you be here?"

"Yes," said I, and he left.

Next day, exactly at the appointed hour, the car drew up near our quarters, and the horn was blown. The children came with the news. The Sheth did not come in. I went out to see him. He placed in my hands currency notes of the value of Rs. 13,000 and drove away.

I had never expected this help, and what a novel way of rendering it! The gentleman had never before visited the Ashram. So far as I can remember, I had met him only once. No visit, no enquiries, simply rendering help and going away! This was a unique experience for me. The help deferred the exodus to the untouchables' quarter. We now felt quite safe for a year.

Just as there was a storm outside, so was there a storm in the Ashram itself. Though in South Africa untouchable friends used to come to my place and live and feed with me, my wife and other women did not seem quite to relish the admission into the Ashram of the untouchable friends. My eyes and ears easily detected their indifference, if not their dislike, towards Danibehn. The monetary difficulty had caused me no anxiety; but this internal storm was more than I could bear. Danibehn was an ordinary woman. Dudabhai was a man with slight education but of good understanding. I liked his patience. Sometimes he did flare up, but on the whole I was well impressed with his forbearance. I pleaded with him to swallow minor insults. He not only agreed, but prevailed upon his wife to do likewise.

The admission of this family proved a valuable lesson to the Ashram. In the very beginning we proclaimed to the world that the Ashram would not countenance untouchability. Those who wanted to help the Ashram were thus put on their guard, and the work of the Ashram in this direction was considerably sim-

128 THE GANDHI READER

plified. The fact that it is mostly the real orthodox Hindus who have met the daily growing expenses of the Ashram is perhaps a clear indication that untouchability is shaken to its foundation. There are indeed many other proofs of this, but the fact that good Hindus do not scruple to help an Ashram where we go the length of dining with the untouchables is no small proof.

BENARES UNIVERSITY SPEECH
by M. K. Gandhi

During World War I, although most Indians remained loyal to the government, the demand for home rule was growing and seditious activity was suppressed by the authorities. Indian nationalists were divided between moderate reformists and extremists who advocated direct action. Professor G. K. Gokhale, Gandhi's political mentor, advised him to spend his first year with "his ears open but his mouth shut." Gandhi traveled a great deal and kept his ears open, but did not always heed Gokhale's advice. He was moving toward the conviction that the British had no right to rule India, but that many evils in Indian society would have to be corrected before India would be fit to govern herself. Some of these ideas found expression in a speech delivered on February 4, 1916 at the dedication of the Hindu Central University College at Benares, a great ceremony attended by the Viceroy, Lord Hardinge, and other notables. Mrs. Annie Besant, the famous Englishwoman who became a religious and political leader in India (and who had founded the college in 1892), presided at the meeting. Gandhi's frankness in criticizing both British and Indian shortcomings led to such an uproar in the audience that he was unable to finish his speech.

· Reprinted with permission from M. K. Gandhi, To the Students (Ahmedabad: Navajivan, 1949), pp. 14-22.

FRIENDS. I WISH to tender my humble apology for the long delay that took place before I am able to reach this place. And you will readily accept the apology when I tell you that I am not responsible for the delay, nor is any human agency responsible for it. [Laughter] The fact is that I am like an animal on show and my keepers in their over-kindness always manage to neglect a necessary chapter in this life and that is pure accident. In this case, they did not provide for the series of accidents that happened to us—to me, my keepers, and my carriers. Hence, this delay.

Friends, under the influence of the matchless eloquence of the lady [Mrs. Besant] who has just sat down, pray, do not believe that our University has become a finished product and that all the young men who are to come to the University that has yet to rise and come into existence, have also come and returned from it finished citizens of a great Empire. Do not go away with any such impression, and, if you, the student world, to which my remarks are supposed to be addressed this evening, consider for one moment that the spiritual life, for which this country is noted and for which this country has no rival, can be transmitted through the lip, pray, believe me, you are wrong. You will never be able merely through the lip to give the message that India, I hope, will one day deliver to the world. I myself have been "fed up" with speeches and lectures. I except the lectures that have been delivered here during the last two days from this category, because they were necessary. But I do venture to suggest to you that we have now reached almost the end of our resources in speech-making, and it is not enough that our ears are feasted, that our eyes are feasted, but it is necessary that our hearts have got to be touched and that our hands and feet have got to be moved. We have been told during the last two days how necessary it is, if we are to retain our hold upon the simplicity of Indian character, that our hands and feet should move in unison with our hearts. But this is only by way of preface.

I wanted to say it is a matter of deep humiliation and shame

for us that I am compelled this evening, under the shadow of
this great college in this sacred city, to address my countrymen
in a language that is foreign to me. I know that if I was
appointed an examiner to examine all those who have been
attending during these two days this series of lectures, most
of those who might be examined upon these lectures would
fail. And why? Because they have not been touched. I was
present at the sessions of the great Congress [3] in the month of
December. There was a much vaster audience, and will you believe me when I tell you that the only speeches that touched
that huge audience in Bombay were the speeches that were delivered in Hindustani? In Bombay, mind you, not in Benares
where everybody speaks Hindi. But between the vernaculars of
the Bombay Presidency on the one hand, and Hindi on the other,
no such great dividing line exists as there does between English
and the sister languages of India; and the Congress audience was
better able to follow the speakers in Hindi. I am hoping that this
University will see to it that the youths who come to it will receive their instruction through the medium of their vernaculars.
Our language is the reflection of ourselves, and if you tell me
that our languages are too poor to express the best thought, then
I say that the sooner we are wiped out of existence the better
for us. Is there a man who dreams that English can ever become
the national language of India? [Cries of "Never"] Why this
handicap on the nation? Just consider for one moment what
an unequal race our lads have to run with every English lad. I
had the privilege of a close conversation with some Poona pro-
fessors. They assured me that every Indian youth, because he
reached his knowledge through the English language, lost at
least six precious years of life. Multiply that by the number of
students turned out by our schools and colleges and find out for
yourselves how many thousand years have been lost to the nation. The charge against us is that we have no initiative. How
can we have any if we are to devote the precious years of our
life to the mastery of a foreign tongue? We fail in this attempt
also. Was it possible for any speaker yesterday and today to

impress his audience as was possible for Mr. Higginbotham? It was not the fault of the previous speakers that they could not engage the audience. They had more than substance enough for us in their addresses. But their addresses could not go home to us. I have heard it said that after all it is English-educated India which is leading and which is doing all the things for the nation. It would be monstrous if it were otherwise. The only education we receive is English education. Surely, we must show something for it. But suppose that we had been receiving, during the past fifty years, education through our vernaculars, what should we have today? We should have today a free India, we should have our educated men, not as if they were foreigners in their own land but speaking to the heart of the nation; they would be working among the poorest of the poor, and whatever they would have gained during the past fifty years would be a heritage for the nation. [Applause] Today even our wives are not the sharers in our best thought. Look at Professor Bose and Professor Ray [4] and their brilliant researches. Is it not a shame that their researches are not the common property of the masses? Let us now turn to another subject.

The Congress has passed a resolution about self-government, and I have no doubt that the All-India Congress Committee and the Moslem League will do their duty and come forward with some tangible suggestions. But I, for one, must frankly confess that I am not so much interested in what they will be able to produce, as I am interested in anything that the student world is going to produce or the masses are going to produce. No paper contribution will ever give us self-government. No amount of speeches will ever make us fit for self-government. It is only our conduct that will fit us for it. [Applause] And, how are we trying to govern ourselves? I want to think audibly this evening. I do not want to make a speech, and if you find me this evening speaking without reserve, pray, consider that you are only sharing the thoughts of a man who allows himself to think audibly, and if you think that I seem to transgress the limits that courtesy imposes upon me, pardon me for the liberty I may be taking. I visited the Viswanath Temple last evening and as I was walking through those lanes, these were the thoughts that touched me. If a stranger dropped from above on to this great Temple and he had to consider what we as Hindus were, would he not be justified in condemning us? Is not this great Temple a reflection of our own character? I speak feelingly as a Hindu. Is it right that the lanes of our sacred Temple should be as dirty as they are? The houses round about are built anyhow. The lanes are tortuous and narrow. If even our temples are not models of roominess and cleanliness, what can our self-government be? Shall our temples be abodes of holiness, cleanliness and peace as soon as the English have retired from India, either of their own pleasure or by compulsion, bag and baggage?

I entirely agree with the President of the Congress that before we think of self-government, we shall have to do the necessary plodding. In every city there are two divisions, the cantonment and the city proper. The city mostly is a stinking den. But we are a people unused to city life. But if we want city life, we cannot reproduce the easy-going hamlet life. It is not comforting to think that people walk about the streets of Indian Bombay under the perpetual fear of dwellers in the storied buildings spitting upon them. I do a great deal of railway travelling. I observe the difficulty of third class passengers. But the Railway Administration is by no means to blame for all their hard lot. We do not know the elementary laws of cleanliness. We spit anywhere on the carriage floor, irrespective of the thought that it is often used as sleeping space. We do not trouble ourselves as to how we use it; the result is indescribable filth in the compartment. The so-called better class passengers over-awe their less fortunate brethren. Among them I have seen the student world also. Sometimes they behave no better. They can speak English and they have worn Norfolk jackets and, therefore, claim the right to force their way in and command seating accommodation. I have turned the searchlight all over, and as you have given me the privilege of speaking to you, I am laying my heart bare. Surely, we must set these things right in our progress towards self-government.

I now introduce you to another scene. His Highness the Maharajah, who presided yesterday over our deliberations, spoke about the poverty of India. Other speakers laid great stress upon it. But what did we witness in the great *pandal* [5] in which the foundation ceremony was performed by the Viceroy? Certainly a most gorgeous show, an exhibition of jewellery which made a splendid feast for the eyes of the greatest jeweller who chose to come from Paris. I compare with the richly bedecked noblemen the millions of the poor. And I feel like saying to those noblemen: "There is no salvation for India unless you strip yourselves of this jewellery and hold it in trust for your countrymen in India." [Hear, hear and applause] I am sure it is not the desire of the King-Emperor or Lord Hardinge that, in order to show the truest loyalty to our King-Emperor, it is necessary for us to ransack our jewellery-boxes and to appear bedecked from top to toe. I would undertake, at the peril of my life, to bring to you a message from King George himself that he expects nothing of the kind. Sir, whenever I hear of a great palace rising in any great city of India, be it in British India or be it in India which is ruled by our great chiefs, I become jealous at once and I say: "Oh, it is the money that has come from the agriculturists." Over 75 per cent of the population are agriculturists, and Mr. Higginbotham told us last night in his own felicitous language that they are the men who grow two blades of grass in the place of one. But there cannot be much spirit of self-government about us if we take away or allow others to take away from them almost the whole of the results of their labor. Our salvation can only come through the farmer. Neither the lawyers, nor the doctors, nor the rich landlords are going to secure it.

Now, last but not the least, it is my bounden duty to refer to what agitated our minds during these two or three days. All of us have had many anxious moments while the Viceroy was going through the streets of Benares. There were detectives stationed in many places. We were horrified. We asked ourselves: "Why this distrust. Is it not better that even Lord Hardinge should die than live a living death?" But a representative of a

mighty Sovereign may not. He might find it necessary even to
live a living death. But why was it necessary to impose these
detectives on us? We may foam, we may fret, we may resent,
but let us not forget that India of today in her impatience has
produced an army of anarchists. I myself am an anarchist, but
of another type. But there is a class of anarchists amongst us,
and if I was able to reach this class, I would say to them that
their anarchism has no room in India, if India is to conquer the
conqueror. It is a sign of fear. If we trust and fear God, we
shall have to fear no one, not Maharajahs, not Viceroys, not the
detectives, not even King George. I honor the anarchist for his
love of the country. I honor him for his bravery in being willing
to die for his country; but I ask him: "Is killing honorable? Is
the dagger of an assassin a fit precursor of an honorable death?"
I deny it. There is no warrant for such methods in any scriptures.
If I found it necessary for the salvation of India that the English
should retire, that they should be driven out, I would not hesitate to declare that they would have to go, and I hope, I would
be prepared to die in defense of that belief. That would, in my
opinion, be an honorable death. The bomb-thrower creates secret
plots, is afraid to come out into the open, and when caught pays
the penalty of misdirected zeal. I have been told: "Had we not
done this, had some people not thrown bombs, we should never
have gained what we have got with reference to the Partition
Movement." [Mrs. Besant: "Please stop it"] This was what I said
in Bengal when Mr. Lyon presided at the meeting. I think what
I am saying is necessary. If I am told to stop I shall obey. [Turn-
ing to the Chairman] I await your orders. If you consider that
by my speaking as I am, I am not serving the country and the
Empire, I shall certainly stop. [Cries of "Go on"] [The chairman:
"Please explain your object"] I am explaining my object. I am
simply—[another interruption]. My friends, please do not resent
this interruption. If Mrs. Besant this evening suggests that I
should stop, she does so because she loves India so well, and
she considers that I am erring in thinking audibly before you,
young men. But even so, I simply say this, that I want to purge

India of the atmosphere of suspicion on either side; if we are to
reach our goal, we should have an empire which is to be based
upon mutual love and mutual trust. Is it not better that we
talk under the shadow of this college than that we should be
talking irresponsibly in our homes? I consider that it is much
better that we talk these things openly. I have done so with excellent results before now. I know that there is nothing that the
students are not discussing. There is nothing that the students
do not know. I am, therefore, turning the searchlight towards
ourselves. I hold the name of my country so dear to me that I
exchange these thoughts with you, and submit to you that there
is no reason for anarchism in India. Let us frankly and openly
say whatever we want to say to our rulers and face the consequences, if what we have to say does not please them. But let
us not abuse. I was talking the other day to a member of the
much-abused Civil Service. I have not very much in common
with the members of that Service; but I could not help admiring the manner in which he was speaking to me. He said: "Mr.
Gandhi, do you for one moment suppose that all we, Civil
Servants, are a bad lot, that we want to oppress the people whom
we have come to govern?" "No," I said. "Then, if you get an
opportunity put in a word for the much-abused Civil Service."
And I am here to put in that word. Yes, many members of the
Indian Civil Service are most decidedly over-bearing; they are
tyrannical, at times thoughtless. Many other adjectives may be
used. I grant all these things and I grant also that, after having
lived in India for a certain number of years, some of them become
somewhat degraded. But what does that signify? They were gentlemen before they came here, and if they have lost some of
the moral fibre, it is a reflection upon ourselves. [Cries of "No"]
Just think out for yourselves, if a man who was good yesterday
has become bad after having come in contact with me, is he responsible that he has deteriorated or am I? The atmosphere of
sycophancy and falsity that surrounds them on their coming to
India demoralizes them, as it would many of us. It is well to
take the blame sometimes. If we are to receive self-government

we shall have to take it. We shall never be granted self-government. Look at the history of the British Empire and the British nation; freedom-loving as it is, it will not be a party to give freedom to a people who will not take it themselves. Learn your lessons, if you wish to, from the Boer War. Those who were enemies of that empire only a few years ago, have now become friends. [At this point there was an interruption and there was a movement on the platform to leave; the speech, therefore, ended here abruptly.]

THE *SATYAGRAHA ASHRAM*
by M. K. Gandhi

An ashram is a religious community or retreat. In India, many spiritual leaders have established their own ashrams as a living embodiment of their spiritual ideas. In South Africa Gandhi organized two communities which were, in effect, ashrams: Phoenix Farm in 1904 near Durban and Tolstoy Farm in 1910 near Johannesburg. Returning to India in 1914, Gandhi transferred many of his entourage to Shantiniketan, Rabindranath Tagore's ashram near Calcutta.

In May 1915 Gandhi established his own Satyagraha Ashram with twenty-five inmates in a rented bungalow at Kochrab, a small village near Ahmedabad, in his native Gujarati-speaking section of India. Because of an outbreak of plague, this ashram in 1917 was removed to Sabarmati, across the river of that name from Ahmedabad. This ashram was under his direction until 1933, when it was disbanded and given for a center for the removal of untouchability. Gandhi then established his headquarters at

· Reprinted with permission from C. F. Andrews, *Mahatma Gandhi's Ideas* (London: Allen and Unwin, 1929), pp. 101-11.

Wardha, a small town in the Central Provinces. In 1936 he visited Segaon, a village near Wardha and decided to settle there. This was renamed Sevagram in 1940 and eventually became an ashram.

Early in the establishment of the Satyagraha Ashram Gandhi devised certain rules and regulations for inhabitants of this retreat.

No WORK done by any man, however great, will really prosper unless it has a distinct religious backing. But what is Religion? I for one would answer: "Not the Religion you will get after reading all the scriptures of the world. Religion is not really what is grasped by the brain, but a heart grasp."

Religion is a thing not alien to us. It has to be evolved out of us. It is always within us: with some, consciously so; with others, quite unconsciously. But it is always there. And whether we wake up this religious instinct in us through outside assistance or by inward growth, no matter how it is done, it has got to be done, if we want to do anything in the right manner, or to achieve anything that is going to persist.

Our scriptures have laid down certain rules as maxims of human life. They tell us that without living according to these maxims we are incapable of having a reasonable perception of Religion. Believing in these implicitly, I have deemed it necessary to seek the association of those who think with me in founding this Institution [the Satyagraha Ashram]. The following are the rules that have been drawn up and have to be observed by everyone who seeks to be a member.

The first and foremost is

THE VOW OF TRUTH

Not simply as we ordinarily understand it, not truth which merely answers the saying, "Honesty is the best policy," implying that if it is not the best policy we may depart from it. Here Truth as it is conceived means that we may have to rule our life by this law of Truth at any cost; and in order to satisfy the definition I have drawn upon the celebrated illustration of the life of Prahlad.[6] For the sake of Truth he dared to oppose his own father; and he defended himself, not by paying his father back in his own coin. Rather, in defense of Truth as he knew it, he was prepared to die without caring to return the blows that he had received from his father, or from those who were charged with his father's instructions. Not only that, he would not in any way even parry the blows; on the contrary, with a smile on his lips, he underwent the innumerable tortures to which he was subjected, with the result that at last Truth rose triumphant. Not that he suffered the tortures because he knew that some day or other in his very lifetime he would be able to demonstrate the infallibility of the Law of Truth. That fact was there; but if he had died in the midst of tortures he would still have adhered to Truth. That is the Truth which I would like to follow. In our Ashram we make it a rule that we must say "No" when we mean No, regardless of consequences.

Then we come to

THE DOCTRINE OF AHIMSA

Literally speaking, Ahimsa means "non-killing." But to me it has a world of meaning, and takes me into realms much higher, infinitely higher. It really means that you may not offend anybody; you may not harbor an uncharitable thought, even in connection with one who may consider himself to be your enemy. To one who follows this doctrine there is no room for an enemy. But there may be people who consider themselves to be his enemies. So it is held that we may not harbor an evil thought even in connection with such persons. If we return blow for blow we depart from the doctrine of Ahimsa. But I go farther. If we resent a friend's action, or the so-called enemy's action, we still fall short of this doctrine. But when I say we should not resent, I do not say that we should acquiesce: by the word "resenting" I mean wishing that some harm should be done to the enemy; or that he should be put out of the way, not even by any action of ours, but by the action of somebody else, or, say, by divine agency. If we harbor even this thought we depart from this doctrine of Non-Violence. Those who join the Ashram have literally to accept that meaning.

This does not mean that we practice that doctrine in its entirety. Far from it. It is an ideal which we have to reach, and it is an ideal to be reached even at this very moment, if we are capable of doing so. But it is not a proposition in Geometry; it is not even like solving difficult problems in higher mathematics— it is infinitely more difficult. Many of us have burnt the midnight oil in solving those problems. But if you want to follow out this doctrine you will have to do much more than burn the midnight oil. You will have to pass many a sleepless night, and go through many a mental torture, before you can even be within measurable distance of this goal. It is the goal, and nothing less than that, which you and I have to reach, if we want to understand what a religious life means.

A man who believes in the efficacy of this doctrine finds in the ultimate stage, when he is about to reach the goal, the whole world at his feet. If you express your love—Ahimsa—in such a manner that it impresses itself indelibly upon your so-called enemy, he must return that love. Under this rule there is no room for organized assassinations, or for murders openly committed, or for any violence for the sake of your country, and even for guarding the honor of precious ones that may be under your charge. After all, that would be a poor defense of their honor. This doctrine tells us that we may guard the honor of those under our charge by delivering our own lives into the hands of the man who would commit the sacrilege. And that requires far greater courage than delivering of blows. If you do not retaliate, but stand your ground between your charge and the opponent, simply receiving the blows without retaliating, what happens? I give you my promise that the whole of his violence will be expended on you, and your friend will be left unscathed. Under this plan of life there is no conception of patriotism which justifies such wars as you witness today in Europe.

Then again there is

THE VOW OF CELIBACY

Those who want to perform national service, or to have a gleam of the real religious life, must lead a celibate life, whether married or unmarried. Marriage only brings a woman closer to man, and they become friends in a special sense, never to be parted either in this life or in the lives to come. But I do not think that, in our conception of marriage, our lusts should enter. Be that as it may, that is what is placed before those who come to the Ashram. I do not deal with it at any length.

Then we have, further,

THE VOW OF THE CONTROL OF THE PALATE

A man who wants to control his animal passions easily does so if he controls his palate. I fear this is one of the most difficult vows to follow. Unless we are prepared to rid ourselves of stimulating, heating, and exciting condiments we shall certainly not be able to control the over-abundant, unnecessary, and exciting stimulation of the animal passions. If we do not do that we are likely to abuse the sacred trust of our bodies that has been given us, and to become less than animals and brutes, eating, drinking, and indulging in passions which we share with animals. But have you ever seen a horse or cow indulging in the abuse of the palate as we do? Do you suppose that it is a sign of civilization, a sign of real life, that we should multiply our eatables so far that we do not even know where we are; and seek dishes until at last we have become absolutely mad and run after the newspaper sheets which give us advertisements about these dishes?

Then we have once more

THE VOW OF NON-THIEVING

I suggest that we are thieves in a way. If I take anything that I do not need for my own immediate use and keep it, I thieve it from somebody else. It is the fundamental law of Nature, without exception, that Nature produces enough for our wants from day to day; and if only everybody took enough for himself and nothing more there would be no pauperism in this world, there would be no man dying of starvation. I am no Socialist, and I do not want to dispossess those who have got possessions; but I do say that personally those of us who want to see light out of darkness have to follow this rule. I do not want to dispossess anybody; I should then be departing from the rule of Non-Violence. If somebody else possesses more than I do, let him. But so far as my own life has to be regulated I dare not possess anything which I do not want. In India we have got many millions of people who have to be satisfied with one meal a day, and that meal consisting of a *chapatti* [7] containing no fat in it and a pinch of salt. You and I have no right to anything that we really have until these many millions are clothed and fed. You and I, who ought to know better, must adjust our wants, and even undergo voluntary privation, in order that they may be nursed, fed, and clothed.

Then there is the "Vow of Non-Possession," which follows as a matter of course, and needs no further explanation at this point, where only a brief summary of various difficulties and their answer is being given.

Then I go to

THE VOW OF SWADESHI

The vow of Swadeshi is a necessary vow. We are departing from one of the sacred laws of our being when we leave our neighborhood and go somewhere else to satisfy our wants. If a man comes from Bombay and offers you wares, you are not justified in supporting the Bombay merchant so long as you have got a merchant at your very door, born and bred in Madras.

That is my view on Swadeshi. In your village you are bound to support your village barber to the exclusion of the finished barber who may come to you from Madras. If you find it necessary that your village barber should reach the attainments of the barber from Madras you may train him to that. Send him to Madras by all means, if you wish, in order that he may learn his calling. Until you do that you are not justified in going to another barber. That is Swadeshi. So when we find that there are many things that we cannot get in India we must try to do without them. We may have to do without many things; but, believe me, when you have that frame of mind you will find a great burden taken off your shoulders, even as the Pilgrim did in that inimitable book *Pilgrim's Progress*. There came a time when the mighty burden that the Pilgrim was carrying unconsciously dropped from him, and he felt a freer man than he was when he started on the journey. So will you feel freer men than you are now, if immediately you adopt this Swadeshi life.

We have also

THE VOW OF FEARLESSNESS

I found, through my wanderings in India, that my country is seized with a paralyzing fear. We may not open our lips in public; we may only talk about our opinions secretly. We may do anything we like within the four walls of our house; but those things are not for public consumption.

If we had taken a vow of silence I would have nothing to say. I suggest to you that there is only One whom we have to fear; that is God. When we fear God, then we shall fear no man, however high-placed he may be; and if you want to follow the vow of Truth, then fearlessness is absolutely necessary. Before we can aspire to guide the destinies of India we shall have to adopt this habit of fearlessness.

And then we have also

THE VOW REGARDING THE "UNTOUCHABLES"

There is an ineffaceable blot that Hinduism today carries with it. I have declined to believe that it has been handed down to us from immemorial times. I think that this miserable, wretched, enslaving spirit of "untouchableness" must have come to us when we were at our lowest ebb. This evil has stuck to us and still remains with us. It is, to my mind, a curse that has come to us;

and as long as that curse remains with us, so long I think we are bound to consider that every affliction in this sacred land is a proper punishment for the indelible crime that we are committing. That any person should be considered untouchable because of his calling passes my comprehension; and you, the student world, who receive all this modern education, if you become a party to this crime, it were better that you received no education whatsoever.

EDUCATION THROUGH THE VERNACULARS

In Europe every cultured man learns, not only his own language, but also other languages. In order to solve the problem of language in India, we in this Ashram must make it a point to learn as many Indian vernaculars as possible. The trouble of learning these languages is nothing compared to that of mastering English. How dare we rub off from our memory all the years of our infancy? But that is precisely what we do when we commence our higher life through the medium of a foreign tongue. This creates a breach for which we shall have to pay dearly. And you will see now the connection between this education and untouchability—this persistence of the latter in spite of the spread of knowledge and education. Education has enabled us to see the horrible crime, but we are seized with fear, and therefore we cannot take this doctrine to our homes.

THE VOW OF KHADDAR [8]

You may ask, "Why should we use our hands?" You may say, "Manual work has got to be done by those who are illiterate. I can only occupy myself with reading literature and political essays." We have to realize the dignity of labor. If a barber or shoemaker attends a college he ought not to abandon his profession. I consider that such professions are just as good as the profession of medicine.

Last of all, when you have conformed to these rules you may come to

THE RELIGIOUS USE OF POLITICS

Politics, divorced from religion, has absolutely no meaning. If the student world crowd the political platforms of this country, that is not necessarily a healthy sign of national growth; but this does not mean that you, in your student life, ought not to study politics. Politics are a part of our being; we ought to understand our national institutions. We may do this from our infancy. So in our Ashram every child is taught to understand the political institutions of our country and to know how the country is vibrating with new emotions, with new aspirations, with new life. But we want also the steady light, the infallible light of religious faith; not a faith which merely appeals to the intelligence, but a faith which is indelibly inscribed on the heart. First we want to realize our religious consciousness, and immediately we have done that the whole department of life is open to us; and it should then be a sacred privilege of all, so that when young men grow to manhood they may do so properly equipped to battle with life. Today what happens is this: much of the political life is confined to the students, but immediately they cease to be students they sink into oblivion, seeking miserable employments, knowing nothing about God, nothing of fresh air or bright light, or of real vigorous independence, such as comes out of obedience to those laws that I have placed before you on this occasion.

FACE TO FACE WITH *AHIMSA*

• by M. K. Gandhi

While Gandhi was attending the annual meetings of the Indian National Congress at Lucknow in December 1916, he was approached by a peasant. He later recalled the incident as follows: ". . . a peasant came up to me looking like any other peasant in India, poor and emaciated, and said, 'I am Rajkumar Shulka. I am from Champaran, and I want you to come to my district.'" This was in Bihar, in the Himalayan foothills, near Nepal. Gandhi had other immediate plans, but Shulka followed him around India so persistently that finally Gandhi yielded and in 1917 took a train for Bihar.

There Gandhi found that the Indian peasants, who were in effect sharecroppers, were very poor and complained of unjust treatment by the English landlords. They had to plant 15 per cent of their land in indigo, which was turned over to the landlords as rent. With aniline dyes lessening the value of natural indigo, some of the peasants were released from this obligation, but only on condition of paying a lump sum in cash. Gandhi's arrival aroused new hopes in the peasants and they flocked to tell him their story.

[ONE] DAY we heard that about five miles from Motihari a tenant had been ill-treated. It was decided that, in company with Babu Dharanidhar Prasad, I should go and see him the next morning, and we accordingly set off for the place on elephant's back. An elephant, by the way, is about as common in Champaran as a bullock-cart in Gujarat. We had scarcely gone half way when

• Reprinted with permission from Gandhi's Autobiography (Washington: Public Affairs Press, 1948), pp. 502-503, 505-507.

a messenger from the Police Superintendent overtook us and said that the latter had sent his compliments. I saw what he meant. Having left Dharanidharbabu to proceed to the original destination, I got into the hired carriage which the messenger had brought. He then served on me a notice to leave Champaran, and drove me to my place. On his asking me to acknowledge the service of the notice, I wrote to the effect that I did not propose to comply with it and leave Champaran till my inquiry was finished. Thereupon I received a summons to take my trial the next day for disobeying the order to leave Champaran.

I kept awake that whole night writing letters and giving necessary instructions to Babu [9] Brajkishore Prasad.

The news of the notice and the summons spread like wildfire, and I was told that Motihari that day witnessed unprecedented scenes. Gorakhbabu's house and the court house overflowed with men. Fortunately I had finished all my work during the night and so was able to cope with the crowds. My companions proved the greatest help. They occupied themselves with regulating the crowds, for the latter followed me wherever I went.

A sort of friendliness sprang up between the officials—Collector, Magistrate, Police Superintendent—and myself. I might have legally resisted the notices served on me. Instead I accepted them all, and my conduct towards the officials was correct. They thus saw that I did not want to offend them personally, but that I wanted to offer civil resistance to their orders. In this way they were put at ease, and instead of harassing me they gladly availed themselves of my and my co-worker's cooperation in regulating the crowds. But it was an ocular demonstration to them of the fact that their authority was shaken. The people had for the moment lost all fear of punishment and yielded obedience to the power of love which their new friend exercised. . . .

The trial began. The Government pleader, the Magistrate and other officials were on tenterhooks. They were at a loss to know what to do. The Government pleader was pressing the Magistrate to postpone the case. But I interfered and requested the Magistrate not to postpone the case, as I wanted to plead guilty to having disobeyed the order to leave Champaran, and read a brief statement as follows:

"With the permission of the Court I would like to make a brief statement showing why I have taken the very serious step of seemingly disobeying the order passed under Sec. 144 of Cr. P. C. In my humble opinion it is a question of difference of opinion between the Local Administration and myself. I have entered the country with motives of rendering humanitarian and national service. I have done so in response to a pressing invitation to come and help the ryots,[10] who urge they are not being fairly treated by the indigo planters. I could not render any help without studying the problem. I have, therefore, come to study it with the assistance, if possible, of the Administration and the planters. I have no other motive, and cannot believe that my coming can in any way disturb public peace and cause loss of life. I claim to have considerable experience in such matters. The Administration, however, have thought differently. I fully appreciate their difficulty, and I admit too that they can only proceed upon information they received. As a law-abiding citizen my first instinct would be, as it was, to obey the order served upon me. But I could not do so without doing violence to my sense of duty to those for whom I have come. I feel that I could just now serve them only by remaining in their midst. I could not, therefore, voluntarily retire. Amid this conflict of duties I could only throw the responsibility for removing me from them on the Administration. I am fully conscious of the fact that a person holding, in the public life of India, a position such as I do, has to be most careful in setting an example. It is my firm belief that in the complex constitution under which we are living, the only safe and honorable course for a self-respecting man is, in the circumstances such as face me, to do what I have decided to do, that is, to submit without protest to the penalty of disobedience.

"I venture to make this statement not in any way in extenuation of the penalty to be awarded against me, but to show that I have disregarded the order served upon me not for want of respect for lawful authority, but in obedience to the higher law of our being, the voice of conscience."

There was now no occasion to postpone the hearing, but as both Magistrate and the Government pleader had been taken by surprise, the Magistrate postponed judgment. Meanwhile I had wired full details to the Viceroy, to Patna friends, as also to Pandit Madan Mohan Malaviya and others.

Before I could appear before the Court to receive the sentence, the Magistrate sent a written message that the Lieutenant Governor had ordered the case against me to be withdrawn, and the Collector wrote to me saying that I was at liberty to conduct the proposed inquiry, and that I might count on whatever help I needed from the officials. None of us was prepared for this prompt and happy issue. . . .

The country thus had its first direct object-lesson in Civil Disobedience.

GANDHI IN BIHAR
•
by Rajendra Prasad

After continuing to hear many witnesses about the injustices in Champaran, Gandhi asked the Governor either to redress the peasant grievances or appoint an official commission of inquiry. The Governor appointed a commission, with Gandhi as a member representing the peasants. In the end, the Commission recommended that the planters should repay part of the money they had previously exacted from the peasants and that the compulsory growing of indigo should be abolished. Thus Gandhi won his first major struggle on Indian soil. Later he commented: "What

• Reprinted with permission from Rajendra Prasad, Mahatma Gandhi and Bihar (Bombay: Hind Kitabs, 1949), pp. 24-29.

I did was a very ordinary thing. I declared that the British could not order me around in my own country."

Gandhi also worked among the peasants and gathered a number of helpers around him. Among these was Rajendra Prasad, a Bihar lawyer, who was to become his lifelong associate and later President of the Indian National Congress and first President of the Republic of India. At Bihar also Gandhi was joined by Mahadev Desai, who was to be his personal secretary for more than two decades.

[THE] PURELY SOCIAL WORK [which Gandhi did in Champaran] was remarkable though it did not attract much attention at the time. Bihar was a province in which orthodoxy reigned supreme among the Hindus. We also have our mode of living which, we found, was not helpful in the kind of work we were engaged in. As soon as Mahatmaji [Gandhi] discovered that a large number of workers would be required to assist him who would have to make a prolonged stay with him, he made up his mind that we should have a separate house and establishment where we could stay and work instead of billeting ourselves on friends as we did on our arrival at Motihari. He said a house must be found and, if necessary, taken on rent, and he fixed the day on which we should shift. A house was found and everything was ready for removal, but according to our habits of procrastination, and busy as we had been the whole day, we felt it would be better if we shifted the next day. But Mahatmaji had fixed the day for removal and that day had passed and it was about 9 o'clock at night. He felt that if we did not move that night the first decision of moving that day would remain unfulfilled on account of our laziness. The next day we would have again a large number of ryots anxious to get their statements recorded who would have to be kept waiting while we were busy shifting to another house. So at about 10 o'clock at night the order went forth that we must move the same night and when he found us hesitating and discussing how to get a carriage or laborers to carry our things, he rose, packed his bedding and started, carrying the load. We had no option but to run after him with whatever we could carry. Fortunately, the new house was at a short distance. On reaching there we found that it was not as clean as it should be. He immediately took a broom and started sweeping. We were shamed into taking away the broom from him and sweeping the house clean. This was the first of the many lessons which we had to learn from him.

It is an inveterate habit with Biharees [11] to depend upon servants for personal service even in small matters. We had several of us our own servants and so the number of inmates of the camp or Ashram, as you might call it, was practically double that of workers. We had besides a cook who came a few days later. Our orthodoxy was such that none of us had taken *kachi* [12] food from the hands of anyone except a Brahmin or a fellow caste-man. And this we had carried and preserved in spite of the fact that some of us had been educated in Calcutta and spent years in that big metropolis, and in spite of the fact that some of us had taken part in the agitation for the readmission of English-returned gentlemen to caste. The question was—were we going to keep our caste intact? Mahatmaji was of course living on groundnuts, dates and fresh fruits and so when this question arose, there was no difficulty on his account. Mahatmaji saw our orthodoxy and told us that when we were engaged in public work of the kind we were doing in Champaran, we all became of one caste, namely, the caste of the co-workers, and it was not desirable for us to stick to the lifeless custom of not eating particular things touched by particular persons. At any rate so long as we were in Champaran, our work should not be allowed to suffer, our time should not be wasted and the expenses of establishment should not be permitted to mount up just for the sake of preserving our castes. And so for the first time we began to eat rice and *dal* [13] touched by others without distinction, although we happened to have amongst us Kayasthas, Rajputs, Agarwals, Goalas, Gujerati Banias,[14] and possibly some others whom I forget now. We discovered soon afterwards that this change in our habits was necessary and useful as without it we would have found great difficulty in carrying on the work which became more and more heavy and exacting.

The next question was about the servants—should we keep so many of them? Mahatmaji again told us that if we wanted to serve the country this dependence on servants should also go. In any case we could not afford to have so many servants in the camp both because it was expensive and because there was not sufficient accommodation. Besides, it was wholly unnecessary.

One after another the servants were sent away and only one kitchen servant was employed to clean and wash and help in sundry other ways. We were thrown upon our own resources for everything else. It thus became necessary for us to draw water for our use from the well, to wash our own clothes after bath, to wash our plates after meals and to clean the rooms. It was a novel experience to all of us and though it was irksome to begin with, we easily reconciled ourselves to it. It had a splendid effect on the ryots who used to assemble in their hundreds every day to give their statements.

The cook was also sent away afterwards when Srimati Kasturba Gandhi (Mahatmaji's wife) arrived. He told us that she would cook for all and that some of us would only have to assist her. It appeared to us to be hard on her to have to cook for so many of us, and when we protested, he silenced us by saying that she was used to cooking for larger numbers and there would be no difficulty. So some of us had to help her in the kitchen and we used to see how with our wood-fuel she would be busy in the kitchen fanning the fire which would smoke and cause tears in her and her assistant's eyes. Mahatmaji also used to help in feeding us, as he took it upon himself to serve out the food when we sat for dinner, particularly at the evening meal. He would take particular pleasure in doing so. It was a sight to see about a dozen of us seated with our plates, Mahatmaji serving out rice and *dal*, and Ba, as we soon learnt to call her, handing over the different dishes to him to serve. Before and after meals we were required to clean and wash our utensils and to wash the floor where we used to dine, and restore the whole place to a clean and tidy condition. I remember that there were occasions when we had to wash the cooking pots also during the absence or indisposition of the single servant who was retained for the purpose.

I remember a funny story. One morning I was busy cleaning a tiffin-carrier [15] at the well. It had been left unwashed for some days and it was taking time to make it quite clean and bright. Mahatmaji came to the well for water and seeing that I was hard at work, laughed his usual hearty laugh and said: "Well, is it not creditable that I have made High Court Vakils scrape and wash their pots?" And so it was. It used to be an interesting sight for the villagers to see us doing all this with our own hands. They knew many of us as Vakil Sahebs who had houses and establishments and servants and cooks of our own at our homes, but we were drudging like common folks. Many of them would offer to help us and do all that for us. But Mahatmaji said we were having a lesson in self-help and should not spoil it by taking service from villagers even when voluntarily offered. Were we not there to serve them? Why then should we take service from them?

But this was not all. There was a corresponding change in our food also. In the beginning Mahatmaji was living on groundnuts, dates and fresh fruits. Later on he began to take rice and boiled vegetables without salt and without any spices. Our food also became very simple. Although our vegetables were not merely boiled with water—there used to be some ghee [16] added—spices, except perhaps for turmeric (haldi) and salt were practically excluded. We thus used to have two simple and healthy meals, one at about 8:30 or 9:00 in the morning and the other at about 5:00 in the evening before sunset. In between we used sometimes to have some fruits or other things of the season but this was irregular and occasional. The principal meals were in the morning and evening. We ate nothing during the night. The result was that in spite of the hard work we had to put in, we preserved excellent health and our living was cheap.

Apart from occasional visits, which we had to pay to villages either with Mahatmaji or by ourselves, our routine used to be a full day's work. We used to rise early, Mahatmaji earliest of all.

We did not have congregational prayers then as we used to have later, wherever we happened to be with Mahatmaji. He would have his prayers while we were all asleep in the small hours of the morning and, after morning ablutions, would begin writing or reading. We would rise later, yet early enough to be ready for bath, etc. by about 6:30, and sit to work. We would have put in about two hours' work before breakfast between 8:00 and 9:00 and thereafter we would continue our work till it was time for the evening meal, with occasional breaks according to the exigencies of work during the afternoon. By the time the evening meal was finished the day's post would have arrived along with newspapers. About 6:30 or 7:00 P.M. we would go out with Mahatmaji for a walk of about 2 or 3 miles. This used to be the time when we would talk to Mahatmaji about various matters not necessarily connected with the enquiry and discuss items of news published in the papers. After returning we would again sit to work for an hour or more, according as the work of the day was light or heavy, and then retire about 9:00 or 10:00 at night to rise the next day and continue as on the day before. Mahatmaji would not waste a single minute of his time and his hard work used to help and inspire us when we were inclined to be lazy. . . .

7 INDIAN PROBLEMS

A STRIKE AT AHMEDABAD
by M. K. Gandhi

Toward the beginning of 1918 Gandhi received word of unrest on the part of the workers in the textile mills of Ahmedabad.
He studied the situation and found that the case of the millhands
was strong. He was—as he wrote—"in a most delicate situation"
since he was a close friend of Ambalal Sarabhai, the principal
millowner. He advised the millowners to agree to arbitrate the
dispute, but they refused. So Gandhi advised the workers to go
on strike, exacting from them a pledge not to return to work
until either their terms were accepted or the millowners agreed
to refer the dispute to arbitration.

Gandhi attended the daily meetings of the strikers under the
shade of a tree on the bank of the Sabarmati River and reminded
them of their pledge. It was here that Gandhi first became well
acquainted with Sardar Vallabhbhai Patel, a rich Ahmedabad
attorney, who was to be associated with him for the next three
decades and to become Deputy Prime Minister of India.

FOR THE FIRST two weeks the millhands exhibited great courage
and self-restraint and daily held monster meetings. On these

• Reprinted with permission from Gandhi's Autobiography (Washington: Public Affairs Press, 1948), pp. 526-29.

154

occasions I used to remind them of their pledge, and they would shout back to me the assurance that they would rather die than break their word.

But at last they began to show signs of flagging. Just as physical weakness in men manifests itself in irascibility, their attitude towards the blacklegs [1] became more and more menacing as the strike seemed to weaken, and I began to fear an outbreak of rowdyism on their part. The attendance at their daily meetings also began to dwindle by degrees, and despondency and despair were writ large on the faces of those who did attend. Finally the information was brought to me that the strikers had begun to totter. I felt deeply troubled and set to thinking furiously as to what my duty was in the circumstances. I had had experience of a gigantic strike in South Africa, but the situation that confronted me here was different. The mill-hands had taken the pledge at my suggestion. They had repeated it before me day after day, and the very idea that they might now go back upon it was to me inconceivable. Was it pride or was it my love for the laborers and my passionate regard for the truth that was at the back of this feeling—who can say?

One morning—it was at a mill-hands' meeting—while I was still groping and unable to see my way clearly, the light came to me. Unbidden and all by themselves the words came to my lips: "Unless the strikers rally," I declared to the meeting, "and continue the strike till a settlement is reached, or till they leave the mills altogether, I will not touch any food."

The laborers were thunderstruck. Tears began to course down Anasuyabehn's [2] cheeks. The laborers broke out, "Not you but we shall fast. It would be monstrous if you were to fast. Please forgive us for our lapse, we will now remain faithful to our pledge to the end."

"There is no need for you to fast," I replied. "It would be enough if you could remain true to your pledge. As you know we are without funds, and we do not want to continue our strike by living on public charity. You should therefore try to eke out a bare existence by some kind of labor, so that you may be able to remain unconcerned, no matter how long the strike may continue. As for my fast, it will be broken only after the strike is settled."

In the meantime Vallabhbhai [Patel] was trying to find some employment for the strikers under the Municipality, but there was not much hope of success there. Maganlal Gandhi suggested that, as we needed sand for filling the foundation of our weaving school in the Ashram, a number of them might be employed for that purpose. The laborers welcomed the proposal. Anasuya-behn led the way with a basket on her head and soon an endless stream of laborers carrying baskets of sand on their heads could be seen issuing out of the hollow of the riverbed. It was a sight worth seeing. The laborers felt themselves infused with a new strength, and it became difficult to cope with the task of paying out wages to them.

My fast was not free from a grave defect. For as I have already mentioned . . . I enjoyed very close and cordial relations with the millowners, and my fast could not but affect their decision. As a Satyagrahi I knew that I might not fast against them, but ought to leave them free to be influenced by the mill-hands' strike alone. My fast was undertaken not on account of a lapse of the mill-owners, but on account of that of the laborers in which, as their representative, I felt I had a share. With the millowners, I could only plead; to fast against them would amount to coercion. Yet in spite of my knowledge that my fast was bound to put pressure upon them, as in fact it did, I felt I could not help it. The duty to undertake it seemed to me to be clear.

I tried to set the millowners at ease. "There is not the slightest necessity for you to withdraw from your position," I said to them. But they received my words coldly and even flung keen, delicate bits of sarcasm at me, as indeed they had a perfect right to do.

The principal man at the back of the millowners' unbending attitude towards the strike was Sheth Ambalal. His resolute will and transparent sincerity were wonderful and captured my heart. It was a pleasure to be pitched against him. The strain produced by my fast upon the opposition, of which he was the head, cut me, therefore, to the quick. And then, Sarladevi, his wife, was attached to me with the affection of a blood-sister, and I could not bear to see her anguish on account of my action.

Anasuyabehn and a number of other friends and laborers shared the fast with me on the first day. But after some difficulty I was able to dissuade them from continuing it further.

The net result of it was that an atmosphere of goodwill was created all round. The hearts of the millowners were touched, and they set about discovering some means for a settlement. Anasuyabehn's house became the venue of their discussions. Sjt. Anand-shankar Dhruva intervened and was in the end appointed arbitrator, and the strike was called off after I had fasted only for three days. The millowners commemorated the event by distributing sweets among the laborers, and thus a settlement was reached after 21 days' strike. . . .[3]

THE CONDITION OF LABOR
by M. K. Gandhi

Two PATHS are open before India today, either to introduce the western principle of "Might is right" or to uphold the eastern principle that truth alone conquers, that truth knows no mishap, that the strong and the weak have alike a right to secure justice. The choice is to begin with the laboring class. Should the laborers obtain an increment in their wages by violence? Even if that be possible, they cannot resort to anything like violence, howsoever legitimate may be their claims. To use violence for securing rights may seem an easy path, but it proves to be thorny in the long run. Those who live by the sword die also by the sword. . . .

• An article published in *Young India*, June 1, 1921; reprinted with permission. Also in M. K. Gandhi, *Young India, 1919–1922* (New York: B. W. Huebsch, 1923), pp. 727-31.

What shall we do then? The laborers in Bombay made a fine stand. I was not in a position to know all the facts. But this much I could see that they could fight in a better way. The millowner may be wholly in the wrong. In the struggle between capital and labor, it may be generally said that more often than not the capitalists are in the wrong box. But when labor comes fully to realize its strength, I know it can become more tyrannical than capital. The millowners will have to work on the terms dictated by labor, if the latter could command intelligence of the former. It is clear, however, that labor will never attain to that intelligence. If it does, labor will cease to be labor and become itself the master. The capitalists do not fight on the strength of money alone. They do possess intelligence and tact.

The question before us is this: When the laborers, remaining what they are, develop a certain consciousness, what should be their course? It would be suicidal if the laborers rely upon their numbers or brute-force, i.e., violence. By so doing, they will do harm to industries in the country. If, on the other hand, they take their stand on pure justice and suffer in their person to secure it, not only will they always succeed but they will reform their masters, develop industries and both master and men will be as members of one and the same family. A satisfactory solution of the condition of labor must include the following:

1. The hours of labor must leave the workmen some hours of leisure.
2. They must get facilities for their own education.
3. Provision should be made for an adequate supply of milk, clothing and necessary education for their children.
4. There should be sanitary dwellings for the workmen.
5. They should be in a position to save enough to maintain themselves during their old age.

None of these conditions is satisfied today. For this both the parties are responsible. The masters care only for the service they get. What becomes of the laborer does not concern them. All their endeavors are generally confined to obtaining maximum service with minimum payment. The laborer, on the other hand, tries to hit upon all tricks whereby he can get maximum pay with minimum work. The result is that although the laborers get an increment there is no improvement in the work turned out. The relations between the two parties are not purified and the laborers do not make proper use of the increment they get.

A third party has sprung up between these two parties. It has become the laborer's friend. There is need for such a party. Only to the extent to which this party has disinterested friendship for the laborers can it befriend them.

A time has come now when attempts will be made to use labor as a pawn in more ways than one. The occasion demands consideration at the hands of those that would take part in politics. What will they choose? Their own interest or the service of labor and the nation? Labor stands in sore need of friends. It cannot proceed without a lead. What sort of men give this lead will decide the condition of labor.

Strikes, cessation of work and hartal [4] are wonderful things no doubt, but it is not difficult to abuse them. Workmen ought to organize themselves into strong Labor Unions, and on no account shall they strike work without the consent of these Unions. Strikes should not be risked without previous negotiations with the millowners. If the millowners resort to arbitration, the principle of *Panchayat* [5] should be accepted. And once the *Panch* [6] are appointed, their decision must be accepted by both the parties alike, whether they like it or not.

Readers, if you are interested in ameliorating the condition of labor, if you want to befriend the workman and serve him, you will see from the above that there is only one royal road before you, viz., to elevate the workmen by creating between the two parties family relationship. And to secure this end there is no path like Truth. Mere increase in wages should not satisfy you; you must also watch by what means they get it and how they spend it.

STRIKES

•

by M. K. Gandhi

STRIKES ARE the order of the day. They are a symptom of the
existing unrest. All kinds of vague ideas are floating in the air. A
vague hope inspires all, and great will be the disappointment if
that vague hope does not take definite shape. The labor world in
India, as elsewhere, is at the mercy of those who set up as advisers
and guides. The latter are not always scrupulous, and not always
wise even when they are scrupulous. The laborers are dissatisfied
with their lot. They have every reason for dissatisfaction. They are
being taught, and justly, to regard themselves as being chiefly
instrumental in enriching their employers. And so it requires
little effort to make them lay down their tools. The political
situation too is beginning to affect the laborers of India. And
there are not wanting labor leaders who consider that strikes may
be engineered for political purposes.

In my opinion, it will be a most serious mistake to make use
of labor strikes for such a purpose. I don't deny that such strikes
can serve political ends. But they do not fall within the plan of
non-violent non-cooperation. It does not require much effort of
the intellect to perceive that it is a most dangerous thing to make
political use of labor until laborers understand the political condition of the country and are prepared to work for the common
good. This is hardly to be expected of them all of a sudden and
until they have bettered their own condition so as to enable them
to keep body and soul together in a decent manner. The greatest
political contribution, therefore, that laborers can make is to

• An article published in Young India, February 16, 1921; reprinted with permission. Also in M. K. Gandhi, Young India, 1919–1922 (New York: B. W.
Huebsch, 1923), pp. 736-41.

improve their own condition, to become better informed, to insist on their rights, and even to demand proper use by their employers of the manufactures in which they have had such an important hand. The proper evolution, therefore, would be for the laborers to raise themselves to the status of part proprietors. Strikes, therefore, for the present should only take place for the direct betterment of laborers' lot and, when they have acquired the spirit of patriotism, for the regulation of prices of their manufactures.

The conditions of a successful strike are simple. And when they are fulfilled, a strike need never fail.

1. The cause of the strike must be just.

2. There should be practical unanimity among the strikers.

3. There should be no violence used against non-strikers.

4. Strikers should be able to maintain themselves during the strike period without falling back upon Union funds and should therefore occupy themselves in some useful and productive temporary occupation.

5. A strike is no remedy when there is enough other labor to replace strikers. In that case, in the event of unjust treatment or inadequate wages or the like, resignation is the remedy.

6. Successful strikes have taken place even when all the above conditions have not been fulfilled, but that merely proves that the employers were weak and have a guilty conscience. We often make terrible mistakes by copying bad examples. The safest thing is not to copy examples of which we have rarely complete knowledge but to follow the conditions which we know and recognize to be essential for success.

It is the duty of every well wisher of the country, if we are to attain *Swaraj* during the year, not to precipitate any action that may even by a day retard the fulfillment of the great national purpose.

THE UNTOUCHABLES
by M. K. Gandhi

Gandhi was deeply concerned with the problem of untouchability almost as soon as he returned to India from South Africa. He increasingly considered the elimination of untouchability as part of the national campaign for freedom. In 1921, at Ahmedabad, he made the following memorable address before a convention of the untouchables—the Suppressed Class Conference.

I REGARD untouchability as the greatest blot on Hinduism. This idea was not brought home to me by my bitter experiences during the South African struggle. It is not due to the fact that I was once an agnostic. It is equally wrong to think, as some people do, that I have taken my views from my study of Christian religious literature. These views date as far back as the time when I was neither enamoured of, nor was acquainted with, the Bible or the followers of the Bible.

I was hardly yet twelve when this idea had dawned on me. A scavenger named Uka, an untouchable, used to attend our house for cleaning latrines. Often I would ask my mother why it was wrong to touch him, why I was forbidden to touch him. If I accidentally touched Uka, I was asked to perform the ablutions, and though I naturally obeyed, it was not without smilingly protesting that untouchability was not sanctioned by religion, that it was impossible that it should be so. I was a very dutiful and obedient child and so far as it was consistent with respect for parents, I often had tussles with them on this matter. I told

• Reprinted with permission from an article published in *Young India*, April 27, 1921. Also in M. K. Gandhi, *Young India, 1919–1922* (New York: B. W. Huebsch, 1923), pp. 472-77.

my mother that she was entirely wrong in considering physical contact with Uka as sinful.

While at school I would often happen to touch the "untouchables," and as I never would conceal the fact from my parents, my mother would tell me that the shortest cut to purification after the unholy touch was to cancel the touch by touching any Mussalman passing by. And simply out of reverence and regard for my mother I often did so, but never did so believing it to be a religious obligation. After some time we shifted to Porbandar, where I made my first acquaintance with Sanskrit. I was not yet put to an English school, and my brother and I were placed in charge of a Brahmin, who taught us *Ramraksha* and *Vishnu Punjar*.[7] The texts "*jale Vishnuh*" "*sthale Vishnuh*" (there is the Lord [present] in water, there is the Lord [present] in earth) have never gone out of my memory. . . . I could never believe then that there was any text in the *Ramraksha* pointing to the contact of the "untouchables" as a sin. . . .

The *Ramayana* used to be regularly read in our family. A Brahmin called Ladha Maharaj used to read it. He was stricken with leprosy, and he was confident that a regular reading of the *Ramayana* would cure him of leprosy, and, indeed he was cured of it. "How can the *Ramayana*," I thought to myself, "in which one who is regarded now-a-days as an untouchable took Rama across the Ganges in his boat, countenance the idea of any human beings being untouchable on the ground that they were polluted souls?" The fact that we addressed God as the "purifier of the polluted" and by similar appellations, shows that it is a sin to regard any one born in Hinduism as polluted or untouchable— that it is satanic to do so. I have hence been never tired of repeating that it is a great sin. I do not pretend that this thing had crystallized as a conviction in me at the age of twelve, but I do say that I did then regard untouchability as a sin. I narrate this story for the information of the *Vaishnavas* and Orthodox Hindus.

I have always claimed to be a *Sanatani* [8] Hindu. It was not that I am quite innocent of the scriptures. I am not a profound scholar of Sanskrit. I have read the *Vedas* and the *Upanishads* only in translations. Naturally therefore, mine is not a scholarly study of them. My knowledge of them is in no way profound, but I have studied them as I should do as a Hindu and I claim to have grasped their true spirit. By the time I had reached the age of 21, I had studied other religions also.

There was a time when I was wavering between Hinduism and Christianity. When I recovered my balance of mind, I felt that to me salvation was possible only through the Hindu religion and my faith in Hinduism grew deeper and more enlightened.

But even then I believed that untouchability was no part of Hinduism; and that, if it was, such Hinduism was not for me.

True, Hinduism does not regard untouchability as a sin. I do not want to enter into any controversy regarding the interpretation of the shastras.[9] It might be difficult for me to establish my point by quoting authorities from the Bhagwat[10] or Manusmriti. But I claim to have understood the spirit of Hinduism. Hinduism has sinned in giving sanction to untouchability. It has degraded us, made us the pariahs of the Empire. Even the Mussalmans caught the sinful contagion from us; and in South Africa, in East Africa and in Canada, the Mussalmans no less than Hindus came to be regarded as pariahs. All this evil has resulted from the sin of untouchability.

I may here recall my proposition, which is this: So long as the Hindus wilfully regard untouchability as part of their religion, so long as the mass of Hindus consider it a sin to touch a section of their brethren, Swaraj is impossible of attainment. Yudhish-thira[11] would not enter heaven without his dog. How can, then, the descendants of that Yudhishthira expect to obtain Swaraj, without the untouchables? What crimes, for which we condemn the Government as satanic, have not we been guilty or toward our untouchable brethren?

We are guilty of having suppressed our brethren; we make them crawl on their bellies; we have made them rub their noses on the ground; with eyes red with rage, we push them out of railway compartments—what more than this has British Rule done? What charge, that we bring against Dyer and O'Dwyer,[12] may not others, and even our own people, lay at our doors? We ought to purge ourselves of this pollution. It is idle to talk of Swaraj so long as we do not protect the weak and the helpless, or so long as it is possible for a single Swarajist to injure the feelings of any individual. Swaraj means that not a single Hindu or Muslim shall for a moment arrogantly think that he can crush with impunity meek Hindus or Muslims. Unless this condition is fulfilled, we will gain Swaraj only to lose it the next moment. We are no better than the brutes until we have purged ourselves of the sins we have committed against our weaker brethren.

But I have faith in me still. In the course of my peregrinations in India, I have realized that the spirit of kindness of which 'the Poet Tulsidas sings so eloquently, which forms the corner-stone of the Jain and Vaishnava religions, which is the quintessence of the *Bhagavat* and which every verse of the Gita is saturated with—this kindness, this love, this charity, is slowly but steadily gaining ground in the hearts of the masses of this country. . . .

If it can bring any comfort to you, my untouchable brethren, I would say that your question does not cause so much stir as it used to do formerly. That does not mean that I expect you to cease to have misgivings about the Hindus. How can they deserve to be not mistrusted having wronged you so much? Swami Vivekananda [13] used to say that the untouchables were not depressed, they were suppressed by the Hindus who in turn had suppressed themselves by suppressing them.

I suppose I was at Nellore [14] on the 6th of April. I met the untouchables there and I prayed that day as I have done today. I do want to attain *Moksha*.[15] I do not want to be reborn. But if I have to be reborn, I should be born an untouchable, so that I may share their sorrows, sufferings, and the affronts levelled at them, in order that I may endeavor to free myself and them from that miserable condition. I, therefore, prayed that, if I should be born again, I should do so not as a *Brahmin, Kshatriya, Vaishya,* or *Shudra*, but as an *Atishudra*.[16] . . .

I love scavengering.[17] In my Ashram, an eighteen-year-old Brahmin lad is doing the scavenger's work in order to teach the Ashram scavenger cleanliness. The lad is no reformer. He was born and bred in orthodoxy. He is a regular reader of the Gita and faithfully performs Sandhyavandana.[18] His pronunciation of Sanskrit verses is more faultless than mine. When he conducts the prayer, his soft sweet melodies melt one into love. But he felt that his accomplishments were incomplete until he had become also a perfect sweeper and that if we wanted the Ashram sweeper to do his work well, he must do it himself and set an example.

You should realize that you are cleaning Hindu society. You have therefore to purify your lives. You should cultivate the habits of cleanliness, so that no one may point his finger at you. Use alkali-ash or earth, if you cannot afford to use soap, to keep yourselves clean. Some of you are given to drinking and gambling which you must get rid of. You will point your finger at the Brahmins and say even they are given to these vices. But they are not looked upon as polluted and you are. You must not ask the Hindus to emancipate you as a matter of favor. Hindus must do so, if they want, in their own interest. You should, therefore, make them feel ashamed by your own purity and cleanliness. I believe that we shall have purified ourselves within the next five months. If my expectations are not fulfilled, I will think that, although my proposition was fundamentally correct, yet I was wrong in my calculation; and I will again say that I had erred in my calculation.

You claim to be Hindus; you read the Bhagavat; if, therefore, the Hindus oppress you, then you should understand that the fault does not lie in the Hindu religion but in those who profess it. In order to emancipate yourselves, you shall have to purify yourselves. You shall have to get rid of evil habits like drinking.

If you want to ameliorate your condition, if you want to obtain Swaraj, you should be self-reliant. I was told in Bombay that some of you are opposed to the N.C.O.[19] and believe that salvation is only possible through the British Government. Let me tell you that you will never be able to obtain redress by discarding Hindu Religion and courting the favor of a third party. Your emancipation lies in your own hands.

I have come in contact with the untouchables all over the country and I have observed that immense possibilities lie latent in them of which neither they nor the rest of the Hindus seem to be aware. Their intellect is of virginal purity. I ask you to learn spinning and weaving, and if you take them up as a profession, you will keep poverty from your doors. As regards your attitude towards the *Bhangis*,[20] I will repeat what I said at Godhra. I cannot understand why you should yourselves countenance the distinction between *Dheds* [21] and *Bhangis*. There is no difference between them. Even in normal times their occupation is as honorable as that of lawyers or Government servants. . . .

The Hindus are not sinful by nature; they are sunk in ignorance. Untouchability must be extinct in this very year. Two of the strongest desires that keep me in flesh and bone are the emancipation of the untouchables and the protection of the cow. When these two desires are fulfilled, there is Swaraj, and therein lies my own *Moksha*. May God give you strength to work out your salvation.

HINDUISM
by M. K. Gandhi

Gandhi could never disentangle his religious from his political interests, and when he was most deeply immersed in politics, he was often also most deeply concerned with religion. In 1921, in the midst of a major struggle with the British, he wrote an essay on Hinduism which was published in Young India.

• An article published in *Young India*, October 6, 1921; reprinted with permission. Also in C. F. Andrews, *Mahatma Gandhi's Ideas* (London: Allen and Unwin, 1929), pp. 35-42.

I CALL MYSELF a Sanatani Hindu because—

1. I believe in the Vedas, the Upanishads, the Puranas,[22] and all that goes by the name of Hindu Scriptures and therefore in Avataras (divine incarnations) and rebirth.

2. I believe in Varnashrama Dharma [23] in a sense strictly Vedic, but not in its present popular and crude sense.

3. I believe in "Cow Protection" in a much larger sense than the popular belief.

4. I do not disbelieve in "idol-worship."

5. I believe implicitly in the Hindu aphorism that no one truly knows the Scriptures who has not attained perfection in Innocence (Ahimsa), Truth (Satya), and Self-control (Brahmacharya), and who has not renounced all acquisition or possession of wealth.

6. I believe, along with every Hindu, in God and His Oneness, in rebirth and salvation.

That which distinguishes Hinduism from every other religion is its "Cow Protection," even more than its Varnashrama. Varnashrama is in my opinion inherent in human nature, and Hinduism has simply reduced it to a science. It attaches to birth. A man cannot change "Varna" by choice. Not to abide by Varna is to disregard the law of heredity.

I do not believe in the exclusive divinity of the Vedas. I believe the Bible, the Koran, and the Zend Avesta [24] to be as much divinely inspired as the Vedas. My belief in the Hindu Scriptures does not require me to accept every word and every sense as divinely inspired. Nor do I claim to have any first-hand knowledge of these wonderful books. But I do claim to know and feel the truths of the essential teaching of the Scriptures. I decline to be bound by any interpretation, however learned it may be, if it is repugnant to reason or moral sense.

I do not believe that interdining, or even intermarriage, necessarily deprives a man of the Caste status that his birth has given him. The four divisions, Brahmin, Kshattriya, Vaishya, Shudra, define a man's calling; they do not restrict or regulate social intercourse. The divisions define duties; they confer no privileges. It is, I hold, against the genius of Hinduism to arrogate to oneself a higher status, or assign to another a lower status. All are born to serve God's creation—a Brahmin with his knowledge, a Kshattriya with his power of protection, a Vaishya with his commercial ability, and a Shudra with his bodily labor.

This, however, does not mean that a Brahmin is absolved from bodily labor, or the duty of protecting himself and others. His birth makes a Brahmin predominantly a man of knowledge, the fittest by heredity and training to impart it to others. There is nothing, again, to prevent the Shudra from acquiring all the knowledge he wishes. Only he will best serve with his body, and need not envy others their special qualities for service. But a Brahmin who claims superiority by right of knowledge falls, and has no knowledge. And so with the others, who pride themselves upon their special qualities. Varnashrama implies self-restraint, conservation, and economy of energy.

Though, therefore, Varnashrama is not affected by interdining or intermarriage, Hinduism does most emphatically discourage these things.

Hinduism has reached the highest limit of self-restraint. It is undoubtedly a religion of renunciation of the flesh, so that the spirit may be set free. By restricting a Hindu's choice of a bride for his son to a particular group he exercises rare self-restraint.

Hinduism does not regard the married state as by any means essential for salvation. Marriage is a "fall" even as "birth" is a fall. Salvation is freedom from birth and hence from death also.

Prohibition against intermarriage and interdining is essential for a rapid evolution of the soul. But this self-denial is no test of Varna (Caste). A Brahmin may remain a Brahmin, though he may dine with his Shudra brother, provided he has not left off his duty of service by knowledge. It follows from what I have said above that restraint in matters of marriage and dining is not based upon notions of superiority. A Hindu who refuses to dine with another from a sense of superiority altogether misrepresents his Hindu religion.

Unfortunately, today Hinduism seems to consist merely in "eating" and "not eating." Hinduism is in danger of losing its substance; it is resolving itself into a matter of elaborate rules as to what and with whom to eat. Abstemiousness from meat is undoubtedly a great aid to the evolution of the spirit; but it is by no means an end in itself. Many a man eating meat and dining with everybody, but living in the fear of God, is nearer to his salvation than a man religiously abstaining from meat and many other things, but blaspheming God in every one of his acts.

The central fact of Hinduism, however, is "Cow Protection." "Cow Protection" to me is one of the most wonderful phenomena in all human evolution; for it takes the human being beyond his species. The cow to me means the entire sub-human world. Man through the cow is enjoined to realize his identity with all that lives. Why the cow was selected for apotheosis is obvious to me. The cow was in India the best companion. She was the giver of plenty. Not only did she give milk, but she also made agriculture possible. The cow is a poem of pity. One reads pity in the gentle animal. She is the "mother" to millions of Indian mankind. Protection of the cow means protection of the whole dumb creation of God. The ancient seer, whoever he was, began in India with the cow. The appeal of the lower order of creation is all the more forcible because it is speechless. "Cow Protection" is the gift of Hinduism to the world; and Hinduism will live so long as there are Hindus to protect the cow.

Hindus are enjoined to protect the cow by self-purification, by self-sacrifice. The present day "Cow Protection" has degenerated into a perpetual feud with the Mussalmans, whereas true cow protection means conquering the Mussalmans by our love.

A Mussalman friend sent me some time ago a book detailing the inhumanities practiced by us on the cow and her progeny; how we bleed her to take the last drop of milk from her; how we starve her to emaciation; how we ill-treat the calves; how we deprive them of their portion of milk; how cruelly we treat the oxen; how we castrate them; how we beat them; how we overload them. If they had speech they would bear witness to our crimes against them which would stagger the world. By every act of cruelty to our cattle we disown God and Hinduism; I do not know that the condition of the cattle in any other part of the world is so bad as in unhappy India. We may not blame the Englishman for this; we may not plead poverty in our defense. Criminal negligence is the only cause of the miserable condition of our cattle. Our cow-shelters, though they are an answer to our instinct of mercy, are a clumsy demonstration of its execution. Instead of being model dairy farms and great profitable national institutions they are merely depots for receiving decrepit cattle.

Hindus will be judged, not by their correct chanting of sacred texts, not by their pilgrimages, not by their most punctilious observance of Caste rules, but by their ability to protect the cow. Whilst professing the religion of "Cow Protection" we have enslaved the cow and her progeny and have become slaves ourselves.

I can no more describe my feeling for Hinduism than for my own wife. She moves me as no other woman in the world can. Not that she has no faults; I dare say she has many more than I see myself. But the feeling of an indissoluble bond is there. Even so I feel for and about Hinduism with all its faults and limitations. Nothing elates me so much as the music of the Gita or Tulsidas's Ramayana, the only two books in Hinduism I may be said really to know. When on one occasion I fancied I was taking my last breath the Gita was my solace.

I know the vice that is going on today in all the great Hindu shrines, but I love them in spite of their unspeakable failings. There is an interest which I take in them and in no other. I am a reformer through and through. But my zeal never leads me to the rejection of any of the essential things of Hinduism.

I have said I do not disbelieve in idol-worship. An idol does not excite any feeling of veneration in me. But I think that idol-worship is part of human nature. We hanker after symbolism. Why should one be more composed in a church than elsewhere? Images are an aid to worship. No Hindu considers an image to be God. I do not consider idol-worship sin.

It is clear from the foregoing that Hinduism is not an exclusive religion. In it there is room for the worship of all the prophets of the world. It is not a missionary religion in the ordinary sense of the term. It has no doubt absorbed many tribes in its fold, but this absorption has been of an evolutionary, imperceptible character. Hinduism tells everyone to worship God according to his own faith, and so it lives at peace with all the religions. . . .

"Untouchability" is repugnant to reason and to the instinct of pity or love. A religion that establishes the worship of the cow cannot possibly countenance or warrant a cruel and unhuman boycott of human beings; and I should be content to be torn to pieces rather than disown the suppressed classes. Hindus will certainly never deserve freedom, nor get it, if they allow their noble religion to be disgraced by the retention of the taint of untouchability; and, as I love Hinduism dearer than life itself, the taint has become for me an intolerable burden. Let us not deny God by denying to a fifth of our race the right of association on an equal footing.

A STUDENT'S FOUR QUESTIONS

• by Mahadev Desai

During Gandhi's fast at Delhi in 1924, one of C. F. Andrews' students came to assist Andrews while Andrews was serving Gandhi as nurse and editor. This student, Ramachandran, was the son of an official in Travancore, and had studied with both Andrews and Rabindranath Tagore at Shantiniketan. Some questions arose in Ramachandran's mind about the differences in outlook between Tagore and Gandhi. Ramachandran was hesitant to

• An article published in Young India, November 13, 1924; reprinted with permission. Also in C. F. Andrews, Mahatma Gandhi's Ideas (London: Allen and Unwin, 1929), pp. 331-42.

talk to Gandhi about these matters, but after the fast was over Andrews arranged for him to have a morning with Gandhi. Mahadev Desai, Gandhi's personal secretary, was present during this interview, taking careful notes as usual.

AMONG THOSE who visited Delhi during the weeks of fasting, penance, and prayer there was a young student from Shantiniketan named Ramachandran. He is one of the pupils of Mr. Andrews, and had no difficulty in persuading his teacher to permit him to stay at Delhi for some time after the fast was over. In the end Mr. Andrews took Ramachandran upstairs and said to Gandhiji, "I have not even introduced Ramachandran as yet to you. But he has been all the while with us, helping us devotedly with true love. He wants to ask you some questions, and I shall be so glad if you could have a talk with him before he leaves tomorrow to go back to Shantiniketan." Gandhiji at once gave his consent.

"How is it," asked Ramachandran, "that many intelligent and eminent men, who love and admire you, hold that you have ruled out of the scheme of national regeneration all considerations of Art?"

"I am sorry," replied Gandhiji, "that in this matter I have been generally misunderstood. Let me explain. There are two aspects, the outward and the inward. It is purely a matter of emphasis with me. The outward has no meaning to me at all except in so far as it helps the inward. All true Art is the expression of the soul. The outward forms have value only in so far as they are the expression of the inner spirit of man."

Ramachandran hesitatingly suggested, "The great artists themselves have declared that Art is the translation of the urge and unrest in the soul of the artists into words, colors, shapes."

"Yes," said Gandhiji, "Art of that nature has the greatest possible appeal for me. But I know that many call themselves artists in whose works there is absolutely no trace of the soul's upward urge and unrest."

"Have you any instance in mind?"

"Yes," said Gandhiji, "take Oscar Wilde. I can speak of him

because I was in England at the time that he was being discussed and talked about."

"I have been told," put in Ramachandran, "that Oscar Wilde was one of the greatest literary artists of modern times."

"Yes, that is just my trouble. Wilde saw the highest Art only in outward forms, and therefore succeeded in beautifying immorality. All true Art must help the soul to realize its inner self. In my own case I find that I can do entirely without external forms in my soul's realization. I can claim, therefore, that there is truly sufficient Art in my life, though you might not see what you call works of Art about me. My room may have blank walls; and I may even dispense with the roof, so that I may gaze out upon the starry heavens overhead that stretch in an unending expanse of beauty. What conscious Art of man can give me the scene that opens before me when I look up to the sky above with all its shining stars? This, however, does not mean that I refuse to accept the value of human productions of Art, but only that I personally feel how inadequate these are compared with the eternal symbols of beauty in Nature."

"But the artists claim to see and to find Truth through outward beauty," said Ramachandran. "Is it possible to see and find Truth in that way?"

"I would reverse the order," Gandhiji immediately answered: "I see and find beauty through Truth. All Truths, not merely true ideas, but truthful faces, truthful pictures, truthful songs, are highly beautiful. Whenever men begin to see Beauty in Truth, then Art will arise."

"But cannot Beauty," Ramachandran asked, "be separated from Truth and Truth from Beauty?"

"I should want to know exactly what is Beauty," Gandhiji replied. "If it is what people generally understand by that word, then they are wide apart. Is a woman with fair features necessarily beautiful?"

"Yes," replied Ramachandran without thinking.

"Even," asked Bapu, continuing his question, "if she may be of an ugly character?"

Ramachandran hesitated. "But her face," he said, "in that case cannot be beautiful."

"You are begging the whole question," Gandhiji replied. "You now admit that mere outward form may not make a thing beautiful. To a true artist only that face is beautiful which, quite apart from its exterior, shines with the Truth within the soul. There is then, as I have said, no Beauty apart from Truth. On the other hand, Truth may manifest itself in forms which may not be outwardly beautiful at all. Socrates, we are told, was the most truthful man of his time, and yet his features are said to have been the ugliest in Greece. To my mind he was beautiful because all his life was a striving after Truth; and you may remember that his outward form did not prevent Phidias from appreciating the beauty of Truth in him, though as an artist he was accustomed to see Beauty in outward forms also!"

"But, Bapuji," said Ramachandran eagerly, "the most beautiful things have often been created by men whose lives were not beautiful."

"That," said Gandhiji, "only means that Truth and Untruth often co-exist; good and evil are often found together. In an artist also not seldom the right perception of things and the wrong co-exist. Truly beautiful creations only come when right perception is at work. If these moments are rare in life they are also rare in Art."

"Is there Truth, Bapuji, in things that are neither moral nor immoral in themselves? For instance, is there Truth in a sunset, or a crescent moon that shines amid the stars at night?"

"Indeed," replied Gandhiji, "these beauties are truthful inasmuch as they make me think of the Creator at the back of them. How could these be beautiful but for the Truth that is in the center of creation? When I admire the wonder of a sunset or the beauty of the moon, my soul expands in worship of the Creator. I try to see Him and His mercies in all these creations. But even the sunsets and sunrises would be mere hindrances if they did not help me to think of Him. Anything which is a hindrance to the flight of the soul is a delusion and a snare; even like the body, which often does actually hinder you in the path of salvation."

"Are you against all machinery, Bapuji?" asked Ramachandran.

"How can I be," he answered, smiling at Ramachandran's naive question, "when I know that even the body is a most delicate piece of machinery? The spinning-wheel itself is a machine. What I object to is the craze for machinery, not machinery as such. The craze is for what they call labor-saving machinery. Men go on 'saving labor' till thousands are without work and thrown on the open streets to die of starvation. I want to save time and labor, not for a fraction of mankind, but for all. I want the concentration of wealth, not in the hands of a few, but in the hands of all. Today machinery merely helps a few to ride on the backs of millions. The impetus behind it all is not the philanthropy to save labor but greed. It is against this constitution of things that I am fighting with all my might."

"Then, Bapuji," said Ramachandran, "you are fighting not against machinery as such, but against its abuses, which are so much in evidence today?"

"I would unhesitatingly say 'yes'; but I would add that scientific truths and discoveries should first of all cease to be the mere instruments of greed. Then laborers will not be overworked, and machinery, instead of becoming a hindrance, will be a help. I am aiming, not at the eradication of all machinery, but its limitation."

Ramachandran said: "When logically argued out that would seem to imply that all complicated power-driven machinery should go."

"It might have to go," admitted Gandhiji, "but I must make one thing clear. The supreme consideration is man. The machine should not tend to make atrophied the limbs of men. For instance, I would make intelligent exceptions. Take the case of the Singer Sewing Machine. It is one of the few useful things ever invented, and there is a romance about the device itself. Mr. Singer saw his wife laboring over the tedious process of sewing with her own hands, and simply out of his love for her he devised the sewing machine, in order to save her from unnecessary labor. He, however, saved not only her labor, but also the labor of everyone who could purchase a sewing machine."

"But, in that case," said Ramachandran, "there would have to be a factory for making these Singer Sewing Machines, and it would have to contain power-driven machinery of ordinary type."

"Yes," said Bapu, smiling at Ramachandran's eager opposition. "But I am Socialist enough to say that such factories should be nationalized. They ought only to be working under the most attractive conditions, not for profit, but for the benefit of humanity, love taking the place of greed as the motive-power. It is an alteration in the conditions of labor that I want. This mad rush for wealth must cease; and the laborer must be assured, not only of a living wage, but of a daily task that is not a mere drudgery. The machine will, under these conditions, be as much a help to the man working it as to the State. The present mad rush will cease, and the laborers will work (as I have said) under attractive and ideal conditions. This is but one of the exceptions I have in mind. The sewing machine had love at its back. The individual is the one supreme consideration. The saving of labor of the individual should be the object, and honest humanitarian considerations and not greed the motive-power. Thus, for instance, I would welcome any day a machine to straighten crooked spindles. Not that blacksmiths will cease to make supplies; they will continue to provide the spindles; but when the spindle gets wrong every spinner will have a machine of his own to get it straight. Therefore replace greed by love and everything will come right."

"The third question," said Ramachandran, "that I would like to ask you is whether you are against the institution of marriage."

"I shall have to answer this question at some length," said Bapu. "The aim of human life is deliverance. As a Hindu, I believe that Moksha, or deliverance, is freedom from birth, by breaking the bonds of the flesh, by becoming one with God. Now marriage is a hindrance in the attainment of this supreme object, inasmuch as it only tightens the bonds of flesh. Celibacy is a great help, inasmuch as it enables one to lead a life of full surrender to God. What is the object generally understood of marriage except a repetition of one's own kind? And why need you advocate marriage? It propagates itself. It requires no agency to promote its growth."

"But must you advocate celibacy and preach it to one and all?"

"Yes," said Gandhiji. Ramachandran looked perplexed. "Then you fear there will be an end of creation? No. The extreme logical result would be not extinction of the human species, but the transference of it to a higher plane."

"But may not an artist, or a poet, or a great genius leave a legacy of his genius to posterity through his own children?"

"Certainly not," said Bapu, with emphasis. "He will have more disciples than he can ever have children; and through those disciples all his gifts to the world will be handed down in a way that nothing else can accomplish. It will be the soul's marriage with the spirit; the progeny being the disciple, a sort of divine procreation. No! You must leave marriage to take care of itself. Repetition and not growth would be the result, for lust has come to play the most important part in marriage."

"Mr. Andrews," said Ramachandran, "does not like your emphasis on celibacy."

"Yes, I know," said Gandhiji. "That is the legacy of his Protestantism. Protestantism did many good things; but one of its few evils was that it ridiculed celibacy."

"That," rejoined Ramachandran, "was because it had to fight the abuses in which the clergy of the Middle Ages had sunk."

"But all that was not due to any inherent evil of celibacy," said Bapu. "It is celibacy that has kept Catholicism green up to the present day."

Ramachandran's next question was about the much-discussed "Spinning Franchise" which Gandhiji had enjoined, insisting that none should be a member of the National Congress who did not spin with his own hands. Ramachandran assured Gandhiji at the outset that he was a spinner, but had to confess that he, with three friends at Shantiniketan, only began spinning after they had heard of the fast. He also affirmed that he believed in universal spinning. But he could not understand how the Congress should compel its members to spin. Persuasion and not compulsion should be the method.

"I see," said Gandhiji, "you even go farther than Charlie Andrews. He would not have the Congress to compel its members; but he would fain become a member of a voluntary spinning association. You object to any such association whatsoever?"

Ramachandran sat silent.

"Well, then," replied Gandhiji, enjoying the argument. "I ask you, has the Congress any right to say that its members shall not drink? Will that be a restriction of the freedom of the individual, too? If the Congress exercised that right of enjoining abstinence from drinking there would be no objection. Why? Because the evils of drink are obvious. Well, I say that in India today, where millions are on the brink of starvation, it is perhaps a much worse evil to import foreign cloth. Think of the starving millions of Orissa. When I went there I saw the famine-stricken. Thanks to a kind superintendent who was in charge of an industrial home, I saw also their children, bright, healthy, and merry, working away at their carpets, baskets, etc. There was no spinning because these other things were much in vogue at the time. But on their faces there was the luster of joyful work. But when I came to the famine-stricken, what did I see? They were merely skin and bone, only waiting to die. They were then in that condition because they would under no circumstances work. Even though you had threatened to shoot them if they refused to work, I am sure they would have preferred to be shot rather than do any honest work. This aversion from work is a greater evil than drink itself. You can take some work out of a drunkard. A drunkard retains something of a heart. He has intelligence. These starved men, refusing to work, were like mere animals. Now, how can we solve the problem of getting work out of people like this? I see no way except that of universalizing spinning. Every yard of foreign cloth brought into India is one bit of bread snatched out of the mouths of these starving poor. If you could visualize, as I can, the supreme need of the hour, which is to give India's starving millions a chance to earn their bread with joy and gladness, you would not object to the Spinning Franchise."

Ramachandran still appeared doubtful, but changed the subject. "So, Bapuji," he said, resuming the first point in the conversation, "Beauty and Truth are not merely separate aspects of the same thing?"

"Truth," repeated Gandhiji, "is the first thing to be sought for, and Beauty and Goodness will then be added unto you. That is what Christ really taught in the Sermon on the Mount. Jesus was to my mind a supreme artist because he saw and expressed Truth; and so was Muhammad. Scholars say that the Koran is the most perfect composition in all Arabic literature. Because both of them strove first for Truth, therefore the grace of expression naturally came in. Yet neither Jesus nor Muhammad wrote on Art. That is the Truth and Beauty I crave for, live for, and would die for."

Ramachandran then reverted to his difficulties as to Gandhiji's logical position with regard to machinery. "If you make an exception of the Singer Sewing Machine and your spindle," he said, "where would these exceptions end?"

Gandhiji replied: "Just where they cease to help the individual and encroach upon his individuality. The machine should not be allowed to cripple the limbs of man."

"But I was not thinking just now of the practical side, Bapuji," said Ramachandran. "Ideally would you not rule out all machinery? When you except the sewing machine, will you not have to make an exception of the motor-car?"

"No," said Bapu, "because it does not satisfy any of the primary wants of man; for it is not the primary need of man to traverse distances with the rapidity of a motor-car. The needle, on the contrary, happens to be an essential thing in life—a primary need. Ideally, however, I would rule out all machinery, even as I would reject this very body, which is not helpful to salvation, and seek the absolute liberation of the soul. From that point of view I would reject all machinery; but machines will remain because, like the body, they are inevitable. The body itself, as I told you, is the purest piece of mechanism; but if it is a hindrance to the highest flights of the soul it has to be rejected!"

"Why is the body a necessary evil?" asked Ramachandran. "There I don't understand you. But let me return to my earlier point. May not, after all, some artists be able to see Truth itself in and through Beauty, rather than Beauty in and through Truth?"

"Some may," said Gandhiji, "but here too, just as elsewhere, I must think in terms of the millions. And to the millions we cannot give that training to acquire a perception of Beauty in such a way as to see Truth in it. Show them Truth first and they will see Beauty afterwards. The famine-stricken skeletons of men and women in Orissa haunt me in my waking hours and in my dreams. Whatever can be useful to those starving millions is beautiful to my mind. Let us give today first the vital things of life, and all the graces and ornaments of life will follow."

Here the long conversation ended, and early the next morning Ramachandran started on his way back to Shantiniketan, rich with Bapu's blessings, wondering how far the teaching of his own Gurudev,[25] Rabindranath Tagore, would harmonize with that which he had just heard, and how far there was a fundamental difference between them.

8 SEDITION
(1919-1924)

A "HIMALAYAN MISCALCULATION"
• by M. K. Gandhi

The first nation-wide civil disobedience campaign in India was launched by Gandhi on April 6, 1919 in protest against the Rowlatt Act, which continued in time of peace restrictions on civil liberties that had been imposed during the World War. Thousands rose to Gandhi's call for non-violent protest and did not resist arrest or punishment. In several places, however, Indians resorted to mob violence, killing, looting, and sabotage, and the British took harsh reprisals, including the terrible Amritsar massacre on April 13. The excesses committed by Indians were to Gandhi like "a rapier run through my body," and at length convinced him that the people of India needed further training before they would be ready to practice satyagraha. Confessing that he had been guilty of "Himalayan miscalculation," he called off the movement on April 18.

NEWS WAS RECEIVED that the Rowlatt Bill had been published as an Act. That night I fell asleep while thinking over the question. Towards the small hours of the morning I woke up somewhat

• Reprinted with permission from *Gandhi's Autobiography* (Washington: Public Affairs Press, 1948), pp. 562-63, 565-66, 573-77.

earlier than usual. I was still in that twilight condition between sleep and consciousness when suddenly the idea broke upon me— it was as if in a dream. Early in the morning I related the whole story to Rajagopalachari.[1]

"The idea came to me last night in a dream that we should call upon the country to observe a general *hartal*. Satyagraha is a process of self-purification, and ours is a sacred fight, and it seems to me to be in the fitness of things that it should be commenced with an act of self-purification. Let all the people of India, therefore, suspend their business on that day and observe the day as one of fasting and prayer. The Musalmans may not fast for more than one day; so the duration of the fast should be 24 hours. It is very difficult to say whether all the provinces would respond to this appeal of ours or not, but I feel fairly sure of Bombay, Madras, Bihar and Sindh. I think we should have every reason to feel satisfied even if all these places observe the *hartal* fittingly."

Rajagopalachari was at once taken up with my suggestion. Other friends too welcomed it when it was communicated to them later. I drafted a brief appeal. The date of the *hartal* was first fixed on the 30th of March 1919, but was subsequently changed to 6th April. The people thus had only a short notice of the *hartal*. As the work had to be started at once, it was hardly possible to give longer notice.

But who knows how it all came about? The whole of India from one end to the other, towns as well as villages, observed a complete *hartal* on that day. It was a most wonderful spectacle. . . .

Needless to say the *hartal* in Bombay was a complete success. Full preparation had been made for starting civil disobedience. Two or three things had been discussed in this connection. It was decided that civil disobedience might be offered in respect of such laws only as easily lent themselves to being disobeyed by the masses. The salt tax was extremely unpopular and a powerful movement had been for some time past going on to secure its repeal. I therefore suggested that the people might prepare salt from sea-water in their own houses in disregard of the salt laws. My other suggestion was about the sale of proscribed literature. Two of my books, viz., *Hind Swaraj* and *Sarvodaya* (Gujarati adaptation of Ruskin's *Unto This Last*), which had been already proscribed, came handy for this purpose. To print and sell them openly seemed to be the easiest way of offering civil disobedience. A sufficient number of copies of the books was therefore printed, and it was arranged to sell them at the end of the monster meeting that was to be held that evening after the breaking of the fast.

On the evening of the 6th an army of volunteers issued forth accordingly with this prohibited literature to sell it among the people. Both Shrimati Sarojini Devi [2] and I went out in cars. All the copies were soon sold out. The proceeds of the sale were to be utilized for furthering the civil disobedience campaign. Both these books were priced at four annas per copy, but I hardly remember anybody having purchased them from me at their face value merely. Quite a large number of people simply poured out all the cash that was in their pockets to purchase their copy. Five and ten rupee notes just flew out to cover the price of a single copy, while in one case I remember having sold a copy for fifty rupees! It was duly explained to the people that they were liable to be arrested and imprisoned for purchasing the proscribed literature. But for the moment they had shed all fear of jail-going.

It was subsequently learnt that the Government had conveniently taken the view that the books that had been proscribed by it had not in fact been sold, and that what we had sold was not held as coming under the definition of proscribed literature. The reprint was held by the Government to be a new edition of the books that had been proscribed, and to sell them did not constitute an offense under the law. This news caused general disappointment. . . .

. . . I proceeded to Ahmedabad. I learnt that an attempt had been made to pull up the rails near the Nadiad railway station, that a Government officer had been murdered in Viramgam, and that Ahmedabad was under martial law. The people were terror-stricken. They had indulged in acts of violence and were being made to pay for them with interest.

A police officer was waiting at the station to escort me to Mr. Pratt, the Commissioner. I found him in a state of rage. I spoke to him gently, and expressed my regret for the disturbances. I suggested that martial law was unnecessary, and declared my readiness to cooperate in all efforts to restore peace. I asked for permission to hold a public meeting on the grounds of the Sabarmati Ashram. The proposal appealed to him, and the meeting was held, I think, on Sunday, the 13th of April, and martial law was withdrawn the same day or the day after. Addressing the meeting, I tried to bring home to the people the sense of their wrong, declared a penitential fast of three days for myself, appealed to the people to go on a similar fast for a day, and suggested to those who had been guilty of acts of violence to confess their guilt.

I saw my duty as clear as daylight. It was unbearable for me to find that the laborers, amongst whom I had spent a good deal of my time, whom I had served, and from whom I had expected better things, had taken part in the riots, and I felt I was a sharer in their guilt.

Just as I suggested to the people to confess their guilt, I suggested to the Government to condone the crimes. Neither accepted my suggestion.

The late Sir Ramanbhai and other citizens of Ahmedabad came to me with an appeal to suspend Satyagraha. The appeal was needless, for I had already made up my mind to suspend Satyagraha so long as people had not learnt the lesson of peace. The friends went away happy.

There were, however, others who were unhappy over the decision. They felt that, if I expected peace everywhere and regarded it as a condition precedent to launching Satyagraha, mass Satyagraha would be an impossibility. I was sorry to disagree with them. If those amongst whom I worked, and whom I expected to be prepared for non-violence and self-suffering, could not be non-violent, Satyagraha was certainly impossible. I was firmly of opinion that those who wanted to lead the people to Satyagraha ought to be able to keep the people within the limited non-violence expected of them. I hold the same opinion even today.

Almost immediately after the Ahmedabad meeting I went to Nadiad. It was here that I first used the expression of "Himalayan miscalculation" which obtained such a wide currency afterwards. Even at Ahmedabad I had begun to have a dim perception of my mistake. But when I reached Nadiad and saw the actual state of things there and heard reports about a large number of people from Kheda district [3] having been arrested, it suddenly dawned upon me that I had committed a grave error in calling upon the people in the Kheda district and elsewhere to launch upon civil disobedience prematurely, as it now seemed to me. I was addressing a public meeting. My confession brought down upon me no small amount of ridicule. But I have never regretted having made that confession. For I have always held that it is only when one sees one's own mistakes with a convex lens, and does just the reverse in the case of others, that one is able to arrive at a just relative estimate of the two. I further believe that a scrupulous and conscientious observance of this rule is necessary for one who wants to be a Satyagrahi.

Let us now see what that Himalayan miscalculation was. Before one can be fit for the practice of civil disobedience one must have rendered a willing and respectful obedience to the state laws. For the most part we obey such laws out of fear of the penalty for their breach, and this holds good particularly in respect of such laws as do not involve a moral principle. For instance, an honest, respectable man will not suddenly take to stealing, whether there is a law against stealing or not, but this very man will not feel any remorse for failure to observe the rule about carrying head-lights on bicycles after dark. Indeed it is doubtful whether he would even accept advice kindly about being more careful in this respect. But he would observe any obligatory rule of this kind, if only to escape the inconvenience of facing a prosecution for a breach of the rule. Such compliance is not, however, the willing and spontaneous obedience that is required of a Satyagrahi. A Satyagrahi obeys the laws of society intelligently and of his own free will, because he considers it to be his sacred duty to do so. It is only when a person has thus obeyed the laws of society scrupulously that he is in a position to judge as to which particular rules are good and just and which unjust and iniquitous. Only then does the right accrue to him of the civil disobedience of certain laws in well-defined circumstances. My error lay in my failure to observe this necessary limitation. I had called on the people to launch upon civil disobedience before they had thus qualified themselves for it, and this mistake seemed to me of Himalayan magnitude. As soon as I entered the Kheda district, all the old recollections of the Kheda Satyagraha [4] struggle came back to me, and I wondered how I could have failed to perceive what was so obvious. I realized that before a people could be fit for offering civil disobedience, they should thoroughly understand its deeper implications. That being so, before re-starting civil disobedience on a mass scale, it would be necessary to create a band of well-tried, pure-hearted volunteers who thoroughly understood the strict conditions of Satyagraha. They could explain these to the people, and by sleepless vigilance keep them on the right path.

With these thoughts filling my mind I reached Bombay, raised a corps of Satyagrahi volunteers through the Satyagraha Sabha [5] there, and with their help commenced the work of educating the people with regard to the meaning and inner significance of Satyagraha. This was principally done by issuing leaflets of an educative character bearing on the subject.

But whilst this work was going on, I could see that it was a difficult task to interest the people in the peaceful side of Satyagraha. The volunteers too failed to enlist themselves in large numbers. Nor did all those who actually enlisted take anything like a regular systematic training, and as the days passed by, the number of fresh recruits began gradually to dwindle instead of to grow. I realized that the progress of the training in civil disobedience was not going to be as rapid as I had at first expected.

THREE SEDITIOUS ARTICLES

During the disturbances surrounding the hartals in April 1919 two local Congress Party leaders were deported from the Punjab and, as a result, an Indian mob raged through the streets of Amritsar in that province and three Englishmen were killed. Two days later General R. E. H. Dyer arrived in Amritsar and issued an order prohibiting public meetings. On April 13, in defiance of the ban, a large but peaceful crowd gathered in the Jallianwalla Bagh, a vacant lot with few exits. General Dyer, without giving the crowd any warning to disperse, ordered his troops to open fire on the crowd. The firing continued for about ten minutes and approximately 379 persons were killed and 1,137 wounded. Other stern measures were taken throughout the Punjab. These included General Dyer's famous "crawling order," to the effect that any Indian passing through a street in Amritsar where an Englishwoman had been beaten up by an Indian mob must crawl on all fours. C. F. Andrews wrote, "No one can understand Mahatma Gandhi's attitude towards Great Britain and the British Empire unless he has come to realize that 'Amritsar' was the critical event which changed Mahatma Gandhi from a whole-hearted supporter into a pronounced opponent."

In 1920 the Congress Party, under Gandhi's leadership, decided to boycott the elections to be held under the new Montagu-Chelmsford constitutional reforms, which accorded severely limited self-government on the provincial level. At the same time the Congress launched a second nation-wide non-cooperation movement with the goal of securing full self-government for India, within the Empire or outside it if necessary. So far as practicable Indians were urged to boycott various government activities such as schools and law courts. Gandhi, in a symbolic gesture, returned to the Viceroy the Kaisar-i-Hind Gold Medal which had been conferred on him for his humanitarian work in South Africa.

The civil disobedience campaign continued until 1922. Thousands were thrown into jail and some violence occurred, but Swaraj seemed little nearer. Late in 1921 many Congress leaders urged that the pressure be stepped up by organizing non-violent mass demonstrations of non-cooperation throughout the country. Gandhi, fearing that such a movement might get out of control, persuaded them to confine it to one district, Bardoli, near Bombay, so that he could personally supervise the operation. On February 1, 1922 he informed the Viceroy, Lord Reading, that mass non-cooperation was about to start in Bardoli. On February 5, at a town called Chauri Chaura about 800 miles from Bardoli, an Indian mob burned the city hall and killed several constables. Gandhi thereupon suspended the civil disobedience movement in Bardoli and elsewhere. Many of his associates, including Nehru, accepted this decision with great reluctance, while some people maintained that he had shrewdly used the Chauri Chaura incident as an excuse to call off a campaign that was flagging in any case.

Shortly afterward Gandhi was arrested and tried for sedition. The evidence against him included three articles, reproduced below, which he had published in Young India in 1921–22. The first article refers to the arrest in September 1921 of one of Gandhi's close associates, Mohammed Ali, for attempting to persuade Moslems not to serve in the British Army. Gandhi also mentions two major Indian grievances, namely, the harsh reprisals taken by the British in the Punjab and the severe terms imposed by the Allies upon Turkey after World War I. Indian Moslems protested against the latter in what was known as the Khilafat movement (in defense of the Mohammedan Caliphate). Gandhi supported this movement and sought, in this period with great success, to promote close cooperation between Hindus and Moslems in the struggle against the British.

TAMPERING WITH LOYALTY
• by M. K. Gandhi

HIS EXCELLENCY the Governor of Bombay had warned the public sometime ago, that he "meant business," that he was not going to tolerate the speeches that were being made. In his note on the Ali Brothers and others he has made clear his meaning. The Ali Brothers are to be charged with having tampered with the loyalty of the sepoy [6] and with having uttered sedition. I must confess that I was not prepared for the revelation of such hopeless ignorance on the part of the Governor of Bombay. It is evident that he has not followed the course of Indian history during the past twelve months. He evidently does not know that the National Congress began to tamper with the loyalty of the sepoy in September last year, that the Central Khilafat Committee began it earlier still, for I must be permitted to take the credit or the odium of suggesting that India had a right openly to tell the sepoy and everyone who served the Government in any capacity whatsoever, that he participated in the wrongs done by the Government. The Conference at Karachi merely repeated the Congress declaration in terms of Islam, but speaking for Hinduism and speaking for nationalism I have no hesitation in saying that it is sinful for anyone, either as soldier or civilian, to serve this Government which has proved treacherous to the Mussalmans of India and which had been guilty of the inhumanities of the Punjab. I have said this from many a platform in the presence of sepoys. And if I have not asked individual sepoys to come out, it has not been due to want of will but of ability to support them.

• Published in Young India September 19, 1921; reprinted with permission. Also in M. K. Gandhi, Young India, 1919–1922 (New York: B. W. Huebsch, 1923), Appendix, pp. 9-11.

I have not hesitated to tell the sepoy that, if he could leave the service and support himself without the Congress or the Khilafat aid, he should leave at once. And I promise that, as soon as the spinning wheel finds an abiding place in every home and Indians begin to feel that weaving gives anybody any day an honorable livelihood, I shall not hesitate, at the peril of being shot, to ask the Indian sepoy individually to leave his service and become a weaver. For, has not the sepoy been used to hold India under subjection, has he not been used to murder innocent people at Jallianwala Bagh, has he not been used to drive away innocent men, women and children during that dreadful night at Chandpur,[7] has he not been used to subjugate the proud Arab of Mesopotamia, has he not been utilized to crush the Egyptians? How can any Indian having a spark of humanity in him and any Mussalman having any pride in his religion feel otherwise than as the Ali Brothers have done? The sepoy has been used more often as a hired assassin than as a soldier defending the liberty or the honor of the weak and the helpless. The Governor has pandered to the basest in us by telling us what would have happened in Malabar [8] but for the British soldier or sepoy. I venture to inform His Excellency that Malabar Hindus would have fared better without the British bayonets, that Hindus and Mussalmans would have jointly appeased the Moplahs, that possibly there being no Khilafat question there would have been no Moplah riot at all, that at the worst supposing that Mussalmans had common cause with the Moplahs, Hinduism would have relied upon its creed of non-violence and turned every Mussalman into a friend, or Hindu valor would have been tested and tried. The Governor of Bombay has done a disservice to himself and his cause (whatever it might be) by fomenting Hindu-Mussalman disunion, and has insulted the Hindus as well, by letting them infer from his note, that Hindus are helpless creatures unable to die for or defend their hearth, home or religion. If however the Governor is right in his assumptions, the sooner the Hindus die out the better for humanity. But let me remind His Excellency that he has pronounced the greatest condemnation upon British rule, in

that it finds Indians today devoid of enough manliness to defend
themselves against looters, whether they are Moplahs, Mussalmans
or infuriated Hindus of Arrah.[9]

His Excellency's reference to the sedition of Ali Brothers is only
less pardonable than his reference to the tampering. For he must
know that sedition has become the creed of the Congress. Every
Non-cooperator is pledged to preach disaffection towards the
Government established by law. Non-cooperation, though a religious and strictly moral movement, deliberately aims at the overthrow of the Government, and it is therefore legally seditious in
terms of the Indian Penal Code. But this is no new discovery. Lord
Chelmsford knew it. Lord Reading knows it. It is unthinkable that
the Governor of Bombay does not know it. It was common cause
that so long as the movement remained non-violent nothing
would be done to interfere with it.

But it may be urged that the Government has a right to change
its policy when it finds that the movement is really threatening
its very existence as a system. I do not deny its right. I object
to the Governor's note, because it is so worded as to let the un-
knowing public think that tampering with the loyalty of the
sepoy and sedition were fresh crimes committed by the Ali
Brothers and brought for the first time to His Excellency's notice.

However, the duty of the Congress and Khilafat workers is
clear. We ask for no quarter; we expect none from the Government. We did not solicit the promise of immunity from prison
so long as we remained non-violent. We may not now complain,
if we are imprisoned for sedition. Therefore our self-respect and
our pledge require us to remain calm, unperturbed and non-
violent. We have our appointed course to follow. We must reiterate from a thousand platforms the formula of the Ali Brothers
regarding the sepoys, and we must spread disaffection openly
and systematically till it pleases the Government to arrest us.
And this we do not by way of angry retaliation but because it
is our Dharma. We must wear Khadi even as the Brothers have
worn it, and spread the Gospel of Swadeshi. The Mussalmans
must collect for Smyrna Relief and the Angora Government. We

must spread like the Ali Brothers the Gospel of Hindu-Muslim Unity and of non-violence for the purpose of attaining Swaraj and the redress of the Khilafat and the Punjab wrongs.

We have almost reached the crisis. It is well with a patient who survives a crisis. If on the one hand we remain firm as a rock in the presence of danger, and on the other observe the greatest self-restraint, we shall certainly attain our end this very year.

A PUZZLE AND ITS SOLUTION
by M. K. Gandhi

LORD READING is puzzled and perplexed. Speaking in reply to the addresses from the British Indian Association and the Bengal National Chamber of Commerce at Calcutta, His Excellency said: "I confess that when I contemplate the activities of a section of the community, I find myself still, notwithstanding persistent study ever since I have been in India, puzzled and perplexed. I ask myself what purpose is served by flagrant breaches of the law for the purpose of challenging the Government and in order to compel arrest?" The answer was partly given by Pandit Motilal Nehru [10] when he said on being arrested that he was being taken to the house of freedom. We seek arrest because the so-called freedom is slavery. We are challenging the might of this Government because we consider its activity to be wholly evil. We want to overthrow the Government. We want to compel its submission to the people's will. We desire to show that the Government exists to serve the people, not the people the Government. Free life under the Government has become intolerable, for the price exacted for

• Published in *Young India* December 15, 1921; reprinted with permission. Also in M. K. Gandhi, *Young India, 1919–1922* (New York: B. W. Huebsch, 1923), Appendix, pp. 11-15.

the retention of freedom is unconscionably great. Whether we are one or many, we must refuse to purchase freedom at the cost of our self-respect or our cherished convictions. I have known even little children become unbending when an attempt has been made to cross their declared purpose, be it ever so flimsy in the estimation of their parents.

Lord Reading must clearly understand that the Non-cooperators are at war with the Government. They have declared rebellion against it in as much as it has committed a breach of faith with the Mussalmans, it has humiliated the Punjab and it insists upon imposing its will upon the people and refuses to repair the breach and repent of the wrong done in the Punjab.

There were two ways open to the people, the way of armed rebellion and the way of peaceful revolt. Non-cooperators have chosen, some out of weakness, some out of strength, the way of peace, i.e., voluntary suffering.

If the people are behind the sufferers, the Government must yield or be overthrown. If the people are not with them, they have at least the satisfaction of not having sold their freedom. In an armed conflict the more violent is generally the victor. The way of peace and suffering is the quickest method of cultivating public opinion, and therefore when victory is attained it is for what the world regards as Truth. Bred in the atmosphere of law courts, Lord Reading finds it difficult to appreciate the peaceful resistance to authority. His Excellency will learn by the time the conflict is over that there is a higher court than courts of justice and that is the court of conscience. It supersedes all other courts.

Lord Reading is welcome to treat all the sufferers as lunatics who do not know their own interest. He is entitled therefore to put them out of harm's way. It is an arrangement that entirely suits the lunatics and it is an ideal situation if it also suits the Government. He will have cause to complain if having courted imprisonment, Non-cooperators fret and fume or "whine for favors" as Lalaji [11] puts it. The strength of a Non-cooperator lies in his going to jail uncomplainingly. He loses his case if having courted imprisonment he begins to grumble immediately his courtship is rewarded.

The threats used by His Excellency are unbecoming. This is a fight to the finish. It is a conflict between the reign of violence and of public opinion. Those who are fighting for the latter are determined to submit to any violence rather than surrender their opinion.

SHAKING THE MANES
by M. K. Gandhi

How CAN THERE BE any compromise whilst the British Lion continues to shake his gory claws in our faces? Lord Birkenhead [12] reminds us that Britain has lost none of her hard fibre. Mr. Montagu [13] tells us in the plainest language that the British are the most determined nation in the world, who will brook no interference with their purpose. Let me quote the exact words telegraphed by Reuter:

"If the existence of our Empire were challenged, the discharge of responsibilities of the British Government to India prevented and demands were made in the very mistaken belief that we contemplated retreat from India, then India would not challenge with success the most determined people in the world, who would once again answer the challenge with all the vigor and determination at its command."

Both Lord Birkenhead and Mr. Montagu little know that India is prepared for all the hard fibre that can be transported across the seas and that her challenge was issued in the September of 1920 at Calcutta that India would be satisfied with nothing less

• Published in Young India February 23, 1922; reprinted with permission. Also in M. K. Gandhi, Young India, 1919–1922 (New York: B. W. Huebsch, 1923), Appendix, pp. 15-16.

than Swaraj and full redress of the Khilafat and the Punjab wrongs. This does involve the existence of the Empire and if the present custodians of the British Empire are not satisfied with its quiet transformation into a true Commonwealth of free nations, each with equal rights and each having the power to secede at will from an honorable and friendly partnership, all the determination and vigor of "the most determined people in the world" and the "hard fibre" will have to be spent in India in a vain effort to crush the spirit that has risen and that will neither bend nor break. It is true that we have no "hard fibre." The rice-eating puny millions of India seem to have resolved upon achieving their own destiny without any further tutelage and without arms. In the Lokamanya's language it is their "birthright," and they will have it in spite of the "hard fibre" and in spite of the vigor and determination with which it may be administered. India cannot and will not answer this insolence with insolence, but if she remains true to her pledge, her prayer to God to be delivered from such a scourge will certainly not go in vain. No empire intoxicated with red wine of power and plunder of weaker races has yet lived long in this world, and this British Empire, which is based upon organized exploitation of physically weaker races of the earth and upon a continuous exhibition of brute force, cannot live if there is a just God ruling the universe. Little do these so-called representatives of the British nation realize that India has already given many of her best men to be dealt with by the British "hard fibre." Had Chauri Chaura not interrupted the even course of the national sacrifice, there would have been still greater and more delectable offerings placed before the Lion, but God has willed it otherwise. There is nothing, however, to prevent all those representatives in Downing Street and Whitehall from doing their worst. I am aware that I have written strongly about the insolent threat that has come from across the seas, but it is high time that the British people were made to realize that the fight that was commenced in 1920 is a fight to the finish, whether it lasts one month or one year or many months or many years, and whether the representatives of Britain re-enact all the indescribable orgies of the Mutiny days with redoubled force or whether they do not. I shall only hope and pray that God will give India sufficient humility and sufficient strength to remain non-violent to the end. Submission to the insolent challenges that are cabled out on due occasions is now an utter impossibility.

THE GREAT TRIAL
by K. P. K. Menon

Lord Reading, the Viceroy of India, had considerable respect for Gandhi, whom he interviewed in 1921, and of whom he wrote: "His religious and moral views are admirable and indeed are on a remarkably high altitude, though I must confess that I find it difficult to understand his practice of them in politics." Lord Reading was under great pressure from the home government in London to place Gandhi under arrest, but hesitated to do so until Gandhi should commit some overt act. At length, however, he gave the order. Gandhi was arrested on March 10, 1922, together with S. G. Banker, the printer of Young India. Only the day before he had published an article in Young India entitled "If I Am Arrested." At the preliminary hearing on March 11, Gandhi pleaded guilty to writing seditious articles. He gave his age as fifty-three and his profession as "farmer and weaver." He was kept in jail for a week until the trial, which was held at Ahmedabad on March 18 before Justice C. N. Broomfield.

AT THE CIRCUIT HOUSE at Shahi Bag, the trial of Mr. Gandhi and Mr. Banker commenced on Saturday noon, 18th March 1922,

• Abridged and reprinted from K. P. K. Menon, editor, *The Great Trial of Mahatma Gandhi and Mr. Banker* (Madras: Ganesh, 1922). Also found, in slightly abridged form, in Ronald Duncan, editor, *Selected Writings of Mahatma Gandhi* (Boston: Beacon Press, 1951), pp. 137-47.

before Mr. C. N. Broomfield, I. C. S.,[14] District and Sessions Judge of Ahmedabad.

Sir J. T. Strangman with Rao Bahadur Girdharlal conducted the prosecution, while the accused were undefended. The Judge took his seat at 12 noon, and said there was a slight mistake in the charges framed, which he corrected. The charges were then read out by the Registrar, the offense being in three articles published in the *Young India* of September 29th, December 15th, of 1921 and February 23rd, 1922. The offending articles were then read out: first of them was "Tampering with Loyalty"; the second, "A Puzzle and Its Solution"; and the last was "Shaking the Manes."

The Judge said the law required that the charge should not only be read out, but explained. In this case, it would not be necessary for him to say much by way of explanation. The charge in each case was that of bringing or attempting to bring into hatred or contempt or exciting or attempting to excite disaffection towards His Majesty's Government, established by law in British India. Both the accused were charged with the three offences under Section 124A, contained in the articles read out, written by Mr. Gandhi and printed by Mr. Banker. The words "hatred and contempt" were words the meaning of which was sufficiently obvious. The word "disaffection" was defined under the section, where they were told that disaffection included disloyalty and feelings of enmity. . . . The charges having been read out, the Judge . . . asked Mr. Gandhi whether he pleaded guilty or claimed to be tried.

Mr. Gandhi: "I plead guilty to all the charges. . . ."

The Judge: "Mr. Banker, do you plead guilty, or do you claim to be tried?"

Mr. Banker: "I plead guilty."

Sir J. T. Strangman then wanted the Judge to proceed with the trial fully, but the Judge said he did not agree with what had been said by the Counsel. The Judge said that from the time he knew he was going to try the case, he had thought over the question of sentence, and he was prepared to hear anything that the

Counsel might have to say, or Mr. Gandhi wished to say, on the sentence. He honestly did not believe that the mere recording of evidence in the trial which Counsel had called for would make a difference to them, one way or the other. He, therefore, proposed to accept the pleas.

Mr. Gandhi smiled at this decision.

The Judge said nothing further remained but to pass sentence, and before doing so, he liked to hear Sir J. T. Strangman. He was entitled to base his general remarks on the charges against the accused and on their pleas.

Sir J. T. Strangman: The first point, he said, he wanted to make out, was that the matter which formed the subject of the present charges formed a part of the campaign to spread disaffection openly and systematically to render government impossible and to overthrow it. The earliest article that was put in from *Young India* was dated 25th May 1921, which said that it was the duty of a non-cooperator to create disaffection towards the Government. The Counsel then read out portions of articles written by Mr. Gandhi in the *Young India*. . . .

Sir J. T. Strangman said he wanted to show that these articles were not isolated. They formed part of an organized campaign, but so far as *Young India* was concerned, they would show that from the year 1921. The Counsel then read out extracts from the paper, dated June 8th, on the duty of a non-cooperator, which was to preach disaffection towards the existing Government and preparing the country for civil disobedience. Then in the same number, there was an article on disobedience. Then in the same number there was an article on "Disaffection—a virtue" or something to that effect. Then there was an article on 28th July 1921, in which it was stated that "we have to destroy the system." Again, on 30th September 1921, there was an article headed "Punjab Prosecutions," where it was stated that a non-cooperator worth his name should preach disaffection. That was all so far as *Young India* was concerned. They were earlier in date than the article, "Tampering with Loyalty," and it was referred to the Government of Bombay. Continuing, he said the accused was a man of

high educational qualifications and evidently from his writings a
recognized leader. The harm that was likely to be caused was
considerable. They were the writings of an educated man, and not
the writings of an obscure man, and the court must consider to
what the results of a campaign of the nature disclosed in the
writings must inevitably lead. They had examples before them in
the last few months. He referred to the occurrences in Bombay
last November and Chauri Chaura, leading to murder and destruction of property, involving many people in misery and misfortune. It is true that in the course of those articles they would
find non-violence was insisted upon as an item of the campaign
and as an item of the creed. But what was the use of preaching non-
violence when he preached disaffection towards government or
openly instigated others to overthrow it? The answer to that question appeared to him to come from Chauri Chaura, Madras and
Bombay. These were circumstances which he asked the court to
take into account in sentencing the accused, and it would be for
the court to consider those circumstances which involve sentences
of severity.

As regards the second accused, his offense was lesser. He did the
publication and he did not write. His offence nevertheless was a
serious one. His instructions were that he was a man of means
and he asked the court to impose a substantial fine in addition to
such term of imprisonment as might be inflicted. He quoted Section 10 of the Press Act as bearing on the question of fine. When
making a fresh declaration, he said a deposit of Rs. 1,000 to Rs.
10,000 was asked in many cases.

Court: "Mr. Gandhi, do you wish to make a statement on the
question of sentence?"

Mr. Gandhi: "I would like to make a statement."

Court: "Could you give it in writing to put it on record?"

Mr. Gandhi: "I shall give it as soon as I finish reading it."

Before reading his written statement, Mr. Gandhi spoke a few
words as introductory remarks to the whole statement. He said:

"Before I read this statement, I would like to state that I entirely endorse the learned Advocate-General's remarks in connec-

tion with my humble self. I think that he was entirely fair to me in all the statements that he has made, because it is very true and I have no desire whatsoever to conceal from this court the fact that to preach disaffection towards the existing system of government has become almost a passion with me, and the learned Advocate-General is also entirely in the right when he says that my preaching of disaffection did not commence with my connection with *Young India*, but that it commenced much earlier; and in the statement that I am about to read it will be my painful duty to admit before this court that it commenced much earlier than the period stated by the Advocate-General. It is the most painful duty with me, but I have to discharge that duty knowing the responsibility that rests upon my shoulders.

"I wish to endorse all the blame that the learned Advocate-General has thrown on my shoulders in connection with the Bombay occurrences, Madras occurrences and the Chauri Chaura occurrences. Thinking over these deeply and sleeping over them night after night, it is impossible for me to dissociate myself from the diabolical crimes of Chauri Chaura or the mad outrages of Bombay. He is quite right when he says that as a man of responsibility, a man having received a fair share of education, having had a fair share of experience of this world, I should have known the consequences of every one of my acts. I knew that I was playing with fire. I ran the risk, and if I was set free, I would still do the same. I have felt it this morning that I would have failed in my duty, if I did not say what I said here just now.

"I wanted to avoid violence. Non-violence is the first article of my faith. It is also the last article of my creed. But I had to make my choice. I had either to submit to a system which I considered had done an irreparable harm to my country, or incur the risk of the mad fury of my people bursting forth, when they understood the truth from my lips. I know that my people have sometimes gone mad. I am deeply sorry for it and I am therefore here to submit not to a light penalty but to the highest penalty. I do not ask for mercy. . . ."

The written statement was then read:

"I owe it perhaps to the Indian public and to the public in England, to placate which this prosecution is mainly taken up, that I should explain why from a staunch loyalist and cooperator I have become an uncompromising disaffectionist and non-cooperator. To the court too I should say why I plead guilty to the charge of promoting disaffection towards the Government established by law in India.

"My public life began in 1893 in South Africa in troubled weather. My first contact with British authority in that country was not of a happy character. I discovered that as a man and an Indian I had no rights. More correctly, I discovered that I had no rights as a man, because I was an Indian.

"But I was not baffled. I thought that this treatment of Indians was an excrescence upon a system that was intrinsically and mainly good. I gave the Government my voluntary and hearty cooperation, criticizing it freely where I felt it was faulty but never wishing its destruction.

"Consequently when the existence of the Empire was threatened in 1899 by the Boer challenge, I offered my services to it, raised a volunteer ambulance corps and served at several actions that took place for the relief of Ladysmith.[15] Similarly in 1906, at the time of the Zulu revolt, I raised a stretcher-bearer party and served till the end of the "rebellion."[*] On both these occasions I received medals and was even mentioned in dispatches. For my work in South Africa I was given by Lord Hardinge a Kaisar-i-Hind gold medal. When the war broke out in 1914 between England and Germany, I raised a volunteer ambulance corps in London consisting of the then resident Indians in London, chiefly students. Its work was acknowledged by the authorities to be valuable. Lastly, in India, when a special appeal was made at the War Conference in Delhi in 1918 by Lord Chelmsford for recruits, I struggled at the cost of my health to raise a corps in Kheda [16] and the response was being made when the hostilities ceased and orders were received that no more recruits were wanted. In all these efforts at service I was actuated by the belief that it was possible by such services to gain a status of full equality in the Empire for my countrymen.

"The first shock came in the shape of the Rowlatt Act, a law designated to rob the people of all real freedom. I felt called upon to lead an intensive agitation against it. Then followed the Punjab horrors beginning with the massacre at Jallianwala Bagh and culminating in crawling orders, public floggings and other indescribable humiliations. I discovered too that the plighted word of the Prime Minister to the Mussulmans of India regarding the integrity of Turkey and the holy places of Islam was not likely to be fulfilled. But in spite of the forebodings and the grave warnings of friends, at the Amritsar Congress in 1919, I fought for cooperation in working the Montagu-Chelmsford reforms, hoping that the Prime Minister would redeem his promise to the Indian Mussulmans, that the Punjab wound would be healed and that the reforms, inadequate and unsatisfactory though they were, marked a new era of hope in the life of India.

"But all that hope was shattered. The Khilafat promise was not to be redeemed. The Punjab crime was whitewashed and most culprits went not only unpunished but remained in service and in some cases continued to draw pensions from the Indian revenue, and in some cases were even rewarded. I saw too that not only did the reforms not mark a change of heart, but they were only a method of further draining India of her wealth and of prolonging her servitude.

"I came reluctantly to the conclusion that the British connection had made India more helpless than she ever was before, politically and economically. A disarmed India has no power of resistance against any aggressor if she wanted to engage in an armed conflict with him. So much is this the case that some of our best men consider that India must take generations before she can achieve Dominion status. She has become so poor that she has little power of resisting famines. Before the British advent, India spun and wove in her millions of cottages just the supplement she needed for adding to her meagre agricultural resources. This cottage industry, so vital for India's existence, has been ruined by incredibly heartless and inhuman processes as described by English witnesses. Little do town dwellers know how the semi-starved masses of India are slowly sinking to lifelessness. Little do they know that their miserable comfort represents the brokerage they get for the work they do for the foreign exploiter, that the profits and the brokerage are sucked from the masses. Little do they realize that the Government established by law in British India is carried on for this exploitation of the masses. No sophistry, no jugglery in figures can explain away the evidence that the skeletons in many villages present to the naked eye. I have no doubt whatsoever that both English and the town dwellers of India will have to answer, if there is a God above, for this crime against humanity which is perhaps unequalled in history. The law itself in this country has been used to serve the foreign exploiter. My unbiased examination of the Punjab Martial Law cases has led me to believe that at least 95 per cent of convictions were wholly bad. My experience of political cases in India leads me to the conclusion that in nine out of ten the condemned men were totally innocent. Their crime consisted in the love of their country. In 99 cases out of a hundred justice has been denied to Indians as against Europeans in the courts of India. This is not an exaggerated picture. It is the experience of almost every Indian who has had anything to do with such cases. In my opinion, the administration of the law is thus prostituted consciously or unconsciously for the benefit of the exploiter.

"The greatest misfortune is that Englishmen and their Indian associates in the administration of the country do not know that they are engaged in the crime I have attempted to describe. I am satisfied that many Englishmen and Indian officials honestly believe that they are administering one of the best systems devised in the world and that India is making steady though slow progress. They do not know that a subtle but effective system of terrorism and an organized display of force on the one hand, and the deprivation of all powers of retaliation or self-defense on the other, have emasculated the people and induced in them the habit of simulation. This awful habit has added to the ignorance and the self-deception of the administrators. Section 124A under which I am happily charged is perhaps the prince among the political sections of the Indian Penal Code designed to suppress the liberty of the citizen. Affection cannot be manufactured or regulated by law. If one has no affection for a person or system, one should be free to give the fullest expression to his disaffection, so long as he does not contemplate, promote or incite to violence. But the section under which Mr. Banker and I are charged is one under which mere promotion of disaffection is a crime. I have studied some of the cases tried under it, and I know that some of the most loved of India's patriots have been convicted under it. I consider it a privilege, therefore, to be charged under that section. I have endeavored to give in their briefest outline the reasons for my disaffection. I have no personal ill-will against any single administrator, much less can I have any disaffection toward the King's person. But I hold it to be a virtue to be disaffected towards a government which in its totality has done more harm to India than any previous system. India is less manly under the British rule than she ever was before. Holding such a belief, I consider it to be a sin to have affection for the system. And it has been a precious privilege for me to be able to write what I have in the various articles tendered in evidence against me.

"In fact, I believe that I have rendered a service to India and England by showing in non-cooperation the way out of the unnatural state in which both are living. In my humble opinion, non-cooperation with evil is as much a duty as is cooperation with good. But in the past, non-cooperation has been deliberately expressed in violence to the evil doer. I am endeavoring to show to my countrymen that violent non-cooperation only multiplies evil and that as evil can only be sustained by violence, withdrawal of support of evil requires complete abstention from violence. Non-violence implies voluntary submission to the penalty for non-cooperation with evil. I am here, therefore, to invite and submit cheerfully to the highest penalty that can be inflicted upon me for what in law is a deliberate crime and what appears to me to be the highest duty of a citizen. The only course open to you, the Judge, is either to resign your post and thus dissociate your-self from evil, if you feel that the law you are called upon to ad-minister is an evil and that in reality I am innocent; or to inflict on me the severest penalty if you believe that the system and the law you are assisting to administer are good for the people of this country and that my activity is therefore injurious to the public weal."

Mr. Banker: "I only want to say that I had the privilege of printing these articles and I plead guilty to the charge. I have got nothing to say as regards the sentence."

The Judge: "Mr. Gandhi, you have made my task easy in one way by pleading guilty to the charge. Nevertheless, what remains, namely, the determination of a just sentence, is perhaps as diffi-cult a proposition as a judge in this country could have to face. The law is no respecter of persons. Nevertheless, it will be im-possible to ignore the fact that you are in a different category from any person I have ever tried or am likely to have to try. It would be impossible to ignore the fact that, in the eyes of millions of your countrymen, you are a great patriot and a great leader. Even those who differ from you in politics look upon you as a man of high ideals and of noble and even saintly life. I have to deal with you in one character only. It is not my duty and I do not presume to judge or criticize you in any other character. It is my duty to judge you as a man subject to the law, who by his own admission has broken the law and committed what to an ordi-nary man must appear to be grave offence against the State. I do not forget that you have consistently preached against violence and that you have on many occasions, as I am willing to believe, done much to prevent violence. But having regard to the nature of your political teaching and the nature of many of those to whom it was addressed, how you could have continued to believe that violence would not be the inevitable consequence, it passes my capacity to understand.

"There are probably few people in India who do not sin-cerely regret that you should have made it impossible for any gov-ernment to leave you at liberty. But it is so. I am trying to balance what is due to you against what appears to me to be necessary in the interest of the public, and I propose in passing sentence to follow the precedent of a case in many respects similar to this case that was decided some 12 years ago, I mean the case against Bal Gangadhar Tilak [17] under the same section. The sentence that was passed upon him as it finally stood was a sentence of simple imprisonment for six years. You will not consider it unreasonable, I think, that you should be classed with Mr. Tilak, i.e., a sentence of two years' simple imprisonment on each count of the charge; six years in all, which I feel it my duty to pass upon you; and I should like to say in doing so that, if the course of events in India should make it possible for the Government to reduce the period and release you, no one will be better pleased than I."

The Judge to Mr. Banker: "I assume you have been to a large extent under the influence of your chief. The sentence that I propose to pass upon you is simple imprisonment for six months on each of the first two counts, that is to say, simple imprisonment for one year and a fine of a thousand rupees on the third count, with six months' simple imprisonment in default."

Mr. Gandhi said: "I would say one word. Since you have done me the honor of recalling the trial of the late Lokamanya Bal Gangadhar Tilak, I just want to say that I consider it to be the proudest privilege and honor to be associated with his name. So far as the sentence itself is concerned, I certainly consider that it is as light as any judge would inflict on me, and so far as the whole proceedings are concerned, I must say that I could not have expected greater courtesy."

A minute passed after the pronouncement of the sentence. The Judge . . . got up, bowed and departed. Then followed the last scene—the farewell. Friends and followers, one after another, both men and women, passed before him. He had a kind word or a cutting joke to everybody. The leave-taking nearly took one hour. The military officers with an automobile were waiting for Gandhi. They were not only courteous to him, but were respectful and deferential. At about two o'clock, Gandhi entered the car with his devoted wife, Pandit Malaviya, Banker, and Mrs. Naidu. The eager crowds standing in front of the court-house attempted to shout, "Mahatma Gandhi *ki jai*," but stopped at his request. He was taken to Sabarmati prison.

MRS. GANDHI'S MESSAGE
by Kasturbai Gandhi

MY DEAR Countrymen and Countrywomen,

My dear husband has been sentenced today to six years simple imprisonment. While I cannot deny that this heavy sentence has to some extent told upon me, I have consoled myself with the thought that it is not beyond our powers to reduce that sentence and release him by our own exertions long before his term of imprisonment is over.

I have no doubt that, if India wakes up and seriously undertakes to carry out the constructive program of the Congress, we shall succeed not only in releasing him, but also in solving to our satisfaction all the three issues for which we have been fighting and suffering for the last 18 months or more.

The remedy, therefore, lies with us. If we fail, the fault will be ours. I, therefore, appeal to all men and women who feel for me and have regard for my husband to wholeheartedly concentrate on the constructive program and make it a success.

Among all the items of the program, he laid the greatest emphasis on the spinning wheel and *khaddar*. Our success in these will not only solve the economic problem of India in relation to the masses, but also free us from our political bondage. In-

• Published in *Young India* March 23, 1922; reprinted with permission. Also in M. K. Gandhi, *Young India, 1919–1922* (New York: B. W. Huebsch, 1923), pp. 1066-67.

dia's first answer, then, to Mr. Gandhi's conviction should be that:

(a) All men and women give up their foreign cloth and adopt *khaddar* and persuade others to do so.
(b) All women make it a religious duty to spin and produce yarn every day and persuade others to do so.
(c) All merchants cease trading in foreign piece-goods.

Kasturbai Gandhi

MIDNIGHT OPERATION AT SASSOON HOSPITAL

• by V. S. Srinivasa Sastri

Gandhi entered Yeravda Central Jail on March 20, 1922. After being confined there for almost two years, he developed acute appendicitis, and was suddenly transferred to the Sassoon Hospital in nearby Poona on January 10, 1924. V. S. Srinivasa Sastri, who described this operation, was head of the Servants of India Society.

DR. V. B. GOKHALE came to me at about 8:45 P.M. just as I was finishing my dinner and told me how the Yeravda authorities had removed Mr. Gandhi to the Sassoon Hospital where he was in charge. He was about to be operated upon for appendicitis. As the case was serious, the patient had been asked whether he would like any doctor friends of his to be sent for. He had mentioned Dr. Dalal of Bombay and Dr. Jivraj Mehta who was in Baroda. Both had been wired to; and attempts had been made, but in

• Reprinted with permission from Chandrashanker Shukla, editor, *Gandhiji As We Know Him* (Bombay: Vora, 1945), pp. 55-60.

vain, to get at Dr. Dalal by means of the phone. Meanwhile, in view of the patient's temperature and pulse, it had been decided to perform the operation immediately, and he was asked whether he would like to have any friends brought to see him. He mentioned me, Dr. Phatak of the Non-cooperation Party, and Mr. N. C. Kelkar. Dr. Gokhale and I started at once and took Dr. Phatak on the way, Mr. Kelkar being away at Satara. On my entering the room we greeted each other, and I enquired how he felt as to the operation. He answered firmly that the doctors had come to a definite conclusion, and that he was content to abide by it. In reply to further inquiry he said that he had full confidence in the medical men about him, and that they had been very kind and very careful. Should there arise any public agitation, he added, then it should be made known that he had no complaint whatsoever to make against the authorities, and that so far as the care of his body went their treatment left nothing to be desired.

Then I enquired if Mrs. Gandhi had been informed of his condition. He said that she did not know the latest developments, but she knew that for some time he had not been well, and he expected to hear from her. He then made enquiries of my wife and of my colleagues in the Servants of India Society, viz., Messrs. Devadhar, Joshi, Patwardhan and Kunzru. "Have your frequent journeys out of India benefited your health?" asked the Mahatma.

Dr. Phatak then read a draft statement to be signed by Mr. Gandhi conveying his consent to the operation. After hearing it once, Mr. Gandhi put on his spectacles and read it himself. Then he said he would like the wording changed, and asked Col. Maddock who was in the room what he thought. The Colonel said that, since Mr. Gandhi knew best how to put it in appropriate language, his own suggestion would not be of much value. Then he [Gandhi] dictated a longish statement which I took down in pencil. It was addressed to Col. Maddock who was to perform the operation. The letter acknowledged the exceeding kindness and attention which he had received from Col. Maddock, the Surgeon-General, and other medical officers and attendants, and stated that he had the utmost confidence in Col. Maddock. It proceeded to thank the Government for their consideration in allowing him to send for his own doctors, but as they could not be got in spite of the best attempts made by Col. Maddock, and as delay would in the opinion of the Colonel involve serious risk, Mr. Gandhi requested him to perform the operation at once. When it was finished I read it out to him once. Then he called Col. Maddock to his side, and I read it again at his desire. Col. Maddock was quite satisfied and remarked: "Of course, you know best how to put it in proper language." He then drew up his knees in posture for signing the paper which he did in pencil. His hand shook very much, and I noticed that he did not dot the "i" at the end. He remarked to the doctor: "See how my hand trembles. You will have to put this right." Col. Maddock answered: "Oh, we will put tons and tons of strength into you."

As the operation room was being got ready, the doctors went out, and I found myself nearly alone with the Mahatma. After a remark or two of a purely personal nature I asked him whether he had anything particular to say. I noticed a touch of eagerness as he replied, as though he was waiting for an opportunity to say something. "If there is an agitation," he said, "for my release after the operation, which I do not wish, let it be on proper lines. My quarrel with the Government is there and will continue so long as the originating causes exist. Of course there can't be any conditions. If Government think they have kept me long enough, they may let me go. That would be honorable. If they think that I am an innocent man and that my motives have been good, that while I have a deep quarrel with the Government I love Englishmen and have many friends amongst them, they may release me. But it must not be on false issues. Any agitation must be kept on proper non-violent lines. Perhaps I have not expressed myself quite well, but you had better put it in your own inimitable style." I mentioned the motions of which notice had been given in the Assembly, and added that though Government might in other circumstances have opposed it, I expected that they would take a different line.

I then pressed him again for a message to his people, his followers or the country. He was surprisingly firm on this subject. He said he was a prisoner of Government and he must observe the prisoner's code of honor scrupulously. He was supposed to be civilly dead. He had no knowledge of outside events, and he could not have anything to do with the public. He had no message.

"How is it then that Mr. Mahomed Ali communicated a message as from you the other day?" The words were scarcely out of my mouth when I regretted them. But recall was impossible. He was obviously astonished at my question and exclaimed: "Mr. Mahomed Ali! A message from me!" Luckily at this point the nurse came in with some articles of apparel for him, and signalled me to depart. In a few minutes he was shifted to the operation room. I sat outside marvelling at the exhibition I had witnessed of highmindedness, forgiveness, chivalry and love transcending ordinary human nature; and what mercy it was that the non-cooperation movement should have had a leader of such serene vision and sensitiveness to honor! The Surgeon-General and the Inspector-General of Prisons were also there. I could see from their faces how anxious they were at the tremendous responsibility that lay on them. They said that the patient had borne the operation very well indeed, that some pus had come out, and that it was a matter of congratulation that the operation had not been delayed any longer. The patient had morphia and was expected to sleep soundly for some time longer, when we dispersed. I learnt from the doctor this morning that the patient's condition was thoroughly satisfactory.

AFTER THE OPERATION

by Mahadev Desai

GOD IN HIS infinite mercy has spared to us our Bapu. These have been days which will live in our annals. . . .

I have had the privilege of being with Bapu these ten days, though not of serving him. That privilege is being entirely monopolized by the hospital nurses. One of them is an Englishwoman of long experience. He cannot help smiling as she approaches him. One day, she comes talking about her pet dogs, and draws Bapu into a conversation about the different varieties of dogs and their usefulness. Another day, she talks about her experience in English and African hospitals, and tells him how she has lived throughout her life the lesson that her doctors taught her of never trying to be popular. A third day she decorates the room with the finest flowers and asks Bapu to admire her work. There was another nurse much younger, but equally fond of Bapu, who prided herself on having Mr. Gandhi as her first "private" patient after passing out as a trained nurse. "Nursing is not always a joy, at times it is a task," she used to say, "but it has been a pure joy and a privilege to nurse Mr. Gandhi. The doctor comes and tells me, 'You did not use to print your reports like this ever before,' and I tell him straightway, 'Nor had I such a patient before.'" Another day she told me, "My friends were chaffing me for getting so fond of Mr. Gandhi; I told them they would do the same if they had the privilege of serving him."

And the Surgeon's love for him is as undisguised as that of the nurses. The Civil Surgeon has had letters and telegrams pouring

• Reprinted with permission from C. F. Andrews, *Mahatma Gandhi: His Own Story* (New York: Macmillan, 1930), pp. 358-62.

in on him to congratulate him for the way in which he was serving Mahatmaji, and it is not without a blush that he says, "How
am I to reply to all of them? Shall I do it through the Press?"

I do not know if any one attending Bapu has the slightest consciousness that he is serving a state prisoner. For he is still under
a guard. A compelling love chokes all other consciousness.

But why? Even he who has to look upon him as a prisoner
seemed scarcely different in his manner from the rest. Col. Murray, the Yeravda Superintendent, came to see Bapu the other day.
"Do you think, Mr. Gandhi, I have neglected you? No. I thought
I should not disturb you. And as I see you now after some days
I find you very much better. The Colonel also assures me you are
quickly improving. Your friends remember you. Mr. Gani especially asked me to tell you that he still gets up at four o'clock
for prayers. Every one of them is happy, and misses you—I hope
they do so permanently." "Thank you, Col. Murray," said Bapu,
"but I assure you nothing will please me better than to be up
and doing and under your kind care once again at Yeravda." You
never could tell, if you did not know him, that a jail superintendent was speaking to one of his prisoners, and you could almost
visualize the atmosphere of love created by Bapu in his prison-
cell at Yeravda. . . .

And need I say anything concerning the torrents of love that
have taken their course to Poona from all the parts of India?
Devadas, who should be privileged to be with his father all the
time, has to content himself by attending to the numerous letters
and telegrams coming day and night enquiring after Bapu's health.
But the telegrams and letters do not exhaust these acts of affection. One day residents of far off Tanjore write to say that they
did their devotions in a particular temple for Mahatmaji, Hindus
from Shiyali, Tirupur, and Dindigul, vie in their love with their
Mussalman brethren of Nagore who send special food that has
been blessed for him to take. A Parsi sister writes offering her
blood if the surgeons thought it necessary to put blood in Mahatmaji; while an English lady writes detailed instructions about
Bapu's diet, and Mrs. Gokhale from Bombay writes to say that

she will spin an extra couple of hours every day, now that Mahatmaji cannot spin.

One of the constant visitors at the hospital is an Englishman, an old military pensioner, who makes it a point to come every other day with a bouquet of flowers, and gets into Bapu's room unobstructed by any one. It is simply impossible to stop him. Impatiently he rushes to Bapu, shakes his hand, and delivers his message of cheer in a few seconds and walks away. "Cheer up!" he cries "I see that you are very much better than yesterday. I know you must get better. How old are you? Fifty-five. Oh it is nothing. You know I am 82. Get better, please do." One day he stopped and asked, "Can I do anything for you, Mr. Gandhi?" "No," said Bapu. "Please pray for me." "That I will, but tell me if I can do anything for you. Please do tell me. Trust me to be your brother." To which Bapu replies with a smile, "Believe me, I have amongst my friends a number of Englishmen whom I regard as more than my brothers." The man is deeply touched, moves out assuring us that he prays thrice every day that Mr. Gandhi may live up to his own age, and also telling us that many Englishmen pray for him, and many officers enquire after him.

The picture would be incomplete if I did not say a word about the illustrious leaders who are now flocking to Poona to see their leader. They did not come until now, as they knew it would not be well to disturb him. A man like Mr. Jayakar [18] says, "I will now come, but will only have a sight of him at a distance; for I must not do anything to tire him in his present weakness." And Pandit Jawaharlal [Nehru] assures Devadas that he will come last of all. The big brother, Shawkat Ali, comes, and insists lovingly that Mahatmaji should not talk to him for fear of his becoming too tired. Pandit Motilal Nehru has no heart to get away without bidding him good-bye a second time, and deliberately misses a train. Lajpat Rai comes, eager to have a talk with him, but stands aside, almost in spite of himself, so that he may not draw him into a talk with him. He visits him again before leaving Poona. There is something in him which is struggling to find expression. Probably it checks the tears, or the tears check it. But ultimately it succeeds and bursts out. Bapu with his inimitable smile says, "Lalaji, the joke is too big for my stomach. I would have a hearty laugh, but for the wound and the stitches." Lalaji, who would have departed otherwise with a heavy heart, goes away with a much lighter heart, not without assuring others also, that we may not be sad now, but rejoice that God in His infinite mercy has blessed us by preserving the life of the one whom we all love best in the world.

Although the operation was successful, an abscess developed and Gandhi was released from prison unconditionally. Since Hindu-Moslem rioting had increased, he went to Delhi and there on September 18, 1924 he began a fast of twenty-one days as an act of penance for the sins of his people. This has been called "The Great Fast," and was reported in articles by C. F. Andrews in Young India, *October 9, 16, 1924.*

9 GANDHI AND TAGORE

THE POET'S ANXIETY
by M. K. Gandhi

Rabindranath Tagore was perhaps Gandhi's most famous Indian contemporary, who traveled widely and was well known abroad. Born in 1861, and thus eight years older than Gandhi, Tagore became a noted novelist and poet, and received the Nobel Prize for literature in 1913. He founded and presided over Shantiniketan, a religious community and school in Bengal. Tagore was referred to, by Gandhi and others, simply as The Poet and also as Gurudev—a great teacher.

John Haynes Holmes once compared Tagore and Gandhi as follows: "As different as Erasmus and Luther, these two men, each in his own distinctive way, labor to bring in that new period of world history which must mark an epoch in the annals of mankind." Although Gandhi and Tagore were great enough men to remain good friends all of their lives—and had the services of C. F. Andrews to act as an intermediary between them for a quarter of a century—they had their sharp differences. Andrews felt that there was, between these two men, a "difference of temperament

• Published in Young India June 1, 1921; reprinted with permission. Also in M. K. Gandhi, Young India, 1919–1922 (New York: B. W. Huebsch, 1923), pp. 608-13.

so wide that it was extremely difficult to arrive at a common intellectual understanding, though the moral ties of friendship remained entirely unbroken."

During the early satyagraha campaign, Tagore detected excesses
and frankly told Gandhi so in three different letters. Gandhi answered these publicly in the columns of Young India on June 1,
1921. Tagore in a sense replied in a manifesto entitled "The Call
of Truth" published in the Modern Review in October 1921.
Gandhi promptly answered this article in Young India on October
13, 1921.

THE POET OF ASIA, as Lord Hardinge called Dr. Tagore, is
fast becoming, if he has not already become, the Poet of the
world. Increasing prestige has brought him increasing responsibility. His greatest service to India must be his poetic interpretation of India's message to the world. The Poet is therefore sincerely anxious that India should deliver no false or feeble message
in her name. He is naturally jealous of his country's reputation.
He says he has striven hard to find himself in tune with the present movement. He confesses that he is baffled. He can find nothing for his lyre in the din and the bustle of Non-cooperation. In
three forceful letters he has endeavored to give expression to his
misgivings, and he has come to the conclusion that Non-cooperation is not dignified enough for the India of his vision, that it is
a doctrine of negation and despair. He fears that it is a doctrine
of separation, exclusiveness, narrowness and negation.

No Indian can feel anything but pride in the Poet's exquisite
jealousy of India's honor. It is good that he should have sent to
us his misgivings in language at once beautiful and clear.

In all humility, I shall endeavor to answer the Poet's doubts.
I may fail to convince him or the reader who may have been
touched by his eloquence, but I would like to assure him and
India that Non-cooperation in conception is not any of the things
he fears, and he need have no cause to be ashamed of his country
for having adopted Non-cooperation. If, in actual application, it

appears in the end to have failed, it will be no more the fault of
the doctrine, than it would be of Truth, if those who claim to
apply it in practice do not appear to succeed. Non-cooperation
may have come in advance of its time. India and the world must
then wait, but there is no choice for India save between violence
and Non-cooperation.

Nor need the Poet fear that Non-cooperation is intended to
erect a Chinese wall between India and the West. On the contrary, Non-cooperation is intended to pave the way to real, honorable and voluntary cooperation based on mutual respect and trust.
The present struggle is being waged against compulsory cooperation, against one-sided combination, against the armed imposition
of modern methods of exploitation masquerading under the name
of civilization.

Non-cooperation is a protest against an unwitting and unwilling
participation in evil.

The Poet's concern is largely about the students. He is of opinion that they should not have been called upon to give up Government schools before they had other schools to go to. Here I
must differ from him. I have never been able to make a fetish of
literary training. My experience has proved to my satisfaction that
literary training by itself adds not an inch to one's moral height
and that character-building is independent of literary training. I
am firmly of opinion that the Government schools have un-
manned us, rendered us helpless and Godless. They have filled us
with discontent, and providing no remedy for the discontent,
have made us despondent. They have made us what we were intended to become—clerks and interpreters. A Government builds
its prestige upon the apparently voluntary association of the governed. And if it was wrong to cooperate with the Government in
keeping us slaves, we were bound to begin with those institutions
in which our association appeared to be most voluntary. The
youth of a nation are its hope. I hold that, as soon as we discovered that the system of Government was wholly, or mainly evil,
it became sinful for us to associate our children with it.

It is no argument against the soundness of the proposition laid down by me that the vast majority of the students went back after the first flush of enthusiasm. Their recantation is proof rather of the extent of our degradation than of the wrongness of the step. Experience has shown that the establishment of national schools has not resulted in drawing many more students. The strongest and the truest of them came out without any national schools to fall back upon, and I am convinced that these first withdrawals are rendering service of the highest order.

But the Poet's protest against the calling out of the boys is really a corollary to his objection to the very doctrine of Non-cooperation. He has a horror of everything negative. His whole soul seems to rebel against the negative commandments of religion. I must give his objection in his own inimitable language. "R in support of the present movement has often said to me that passion for rejection is a stronger power in the beginning than the acceptance of an ideal. Though I know it to be a fact, I cannot take it as a truth. . . . Brahmavidya [1] in India has for its object Mukti (emancipation), while Buddhism has Nirvana (extinction). Mukti draws our attention to the positive and Nirvana to the negative side of truth. Therefore, he emphasized the fact of duhkha (misery) which had to be avoided and the Brahmavidya emphasized the fact of Ananda (joy) which had to be attained." In these and kindred passages, the reader will find the key to the Poet's mentality. In my humble opinion, rejection is as much an ideal as the acceptance of a thing. It is as necessary to reject untruth as it is to accept truth. All religions teach that two opposite forces act upon us and that the human endeavor consists in a series of eternal rejections and acceptances. Non-cooperation with evil is as much a duty as cooperation with good. I venture to suggest that the Poet has done an unconscious injustice to Buddhism in describing Nirvana as merely a negative state. I make bold to say that Mukti (emancipation) is as much a negative state as Nirvana. Emancipation from or extinction of the bondage of the flesh leads to Ananda (eternal bliss). Let me close this part of my argument by drawing attention to the fact that the final word of the Upanishads (Brahmavidya) is Not. Neti [2] was the best description the authors of the Upanishads were able to find for Brahman.

I therefore think that the Poet has been unnecessarily alarmed at the negative aspect of Non-cooperation. We had lost the power of saying "no." It had become disloyal, almost sacrilegious to say "no" to the Government. This deliberate refusal to cooperate is like the necessary weeding process that a cultivator has to resort to before he sows. Weeding is as necessary to agriculture as sowing. Indeed, even whilst the crops are growing, the weeding fork, as every husbandman knows, is an instrument almost of daily use. The nation's Non-cooperation is an invitation to the Government to cooperate with it on its own terms as is every nation's right and every good government's duty. Non-cooperation is the nation's notice that it is no longer satisfied to be in tutelage. The nation has taken to the harmless (for it), natural and religious doctrine of Non-cooperation in the place of the unnatural and irreligious doctrine of violence. And if India is ever to attain the Swaraj of the Poet's dream, she will do so only by Non-violent Non-cooperation. Let him deliver his message of peace to the world, and feel confident that India, through her Non-cooperation, if she remains true to her pledge, will have exemplified his message. Non-cooperation is intended to give the very meaning to patriotism that the Poet is yearning after. An India prostrate at the feet of Europe can give no hope to humanity. An India awakened and free has a message of peace and goodwill to a groaning world. Non-cooperation is designed to supply her with a platform from which she will preach the message.

THE CALL OF TRUTH

by Rabindranath Tagore

... THE MOVEMENT, which has now succeeded the Swadeshi agitation, is ever so much greater and has moreover extended its influence all over India. Previously, the vision of our political leaders had never reached beyond the English-knowing classes, because the country meant for them only that bookish aspect of it which is to be found in the pages of the Englishman's history. Such a country was merely a mirage born of vaporings in the English language, in which flitted about thin shades of Burke and Gladstone, Mazzini and Garibaldi. Nothing resembling self-sacrifice or true feeling for their countrymen was visible. At this juncture, Mahatma Gandhi came and stood at the cottage door of the destitute millions, clad as one of themselves, and talking to them in their own language. Here was the truth at last, not a mere quotation out of a book. So the name of Mahatma, which was given to him, is his true name. Who else has felt so many men of India to be of his own flesh and blood? At the touch of Truth the pent-up forces of the soul are set free. As soon as true love stood at India's door, it flew open; all hesitation and holding back vanished. Truth awakened truth.

Stratagem in politics is a barren policy—this was a lesson of which we were sorely in need. All honor to the Mahatma, who made visible to us the power of Truth. But reliance on tactics is so ingrained in the cowardly and the weak, that, in order to eradicate it, the very skin must be sloughed off. Even today, our worldly-wise men cannot get rid of the idea of utilizing the Mahatma as a secret and more ingenious move in their political gam-

• Reprinted from The Modern Review (Calcutta), October 1921, pp. 423-33. Only a portion of the essay is reproduced here.

ble. With their minds corroded by untruth, they cannot understand what an important thing it is that the Mahatma's supreme love should have drawn forth the country's love. The thing that has happened is nothing less than the birth of freedom. It is the gain by the country of itself. In it there is no room for any thought, as to where the Englishman is, or is not. This love is self-expression. It is pure affirmation. It does not argue with negation; it has no need for argument.

Some notes of the music of this wonderful awakening of India by love, floated over to me across the seas. It was a great joy to me to think that the call of this festivity of awakening would come to each one of us; and that the true *shakti*[3] of India's spirit, in all its multifarious variety, would at last find expression. This thought came to me because I have always believed that in such a way India would find its freedom. . . .

So, in the expectation of breathing the buoyant breezes of this new found freedom, I came home rejoicing. But what I found in Calcutta when I arrived depressed me. An oppressive atmosphere seemed to burden the land. Some outside compulsion seemed to be urging one and all to talk in the same strain, to work at the same mill. When I wanted to inquire, to discuss, my well-wishers clapped their hands over my lips saying: "not now, not now. Today, in the atmosphere of the country, there is a spirit of persecution, which is not that of armed force, but something still more alarming, because it is invisible." I found, further, that those who had their doubts as to the present activities, if they happened to whisper them out, however cautiously, however guardedly, felt some admonishing hand clutching them within. There was a newspaper which one day had the temerity to disapprove, in a feeble way, of the burning of [foreign] cloth. The very next day the editor was shaken out of his balance by the agitation of his readers. How long would it take for the fire which was burning cloth to reduce his paper to ashes? The sight that met my eye was, on the one hand, people immensely busy; on the other, intensely afraid. What I heard on every side was, that reason, and culture as well, must be closured. It was only necessary to cling to an unquestioning obedience. Obedience to whom? To some mantra, some unreasoned creed?

And why this obedience? Here again comes that same greed, our spiritual enemy. There dangles before the country the bait of getting a thing of inestimable value, dirt cheap and in double-quick time. It is like the faqir with his goldmaking trick. With such a lure men cast so readily to the winds their independent judgment and wax so mightily wroth with those who will not do likewise. So easy is it to overpower, in the name of outside freedom, the inner freedom of man. The most deplorable part of it is that so many do not even honestly believe in the hope that they swear by. "It will serve to make our countrymen do what is necessary"—say they. Evidently, according to them, the India which once declared: "In truth is victory, not in untruth"—that India would not have been fit for Swaraj. . . .

The Mahatma has won the heart of India with his love; for that we have all acknowledged his sovereignty. He has given us a vision of the shakti of truth; for that our gratitude to him is unbounded. We read about truth in books; we talk about it; but it is indeed a red-letter day when we see it face to face. Rare is the moment, in many a long year, when such good fortune happens. We can make and break Congresses every other day. It is at any time possible for us to stump the country preaching politics in English. But the golden rod which can awaken our country in Truth and Love is not a thing which can be manufactured by the nearest goldsmith. To the wielder of that rod our profound salutation! But if, having seen truth, our belief in it is not confirmed, what is the good of it all? Our mind must acknowledge the truth of the intellect, just as our heart does the truth of love. No Congress or other outside institution succeeded in touching the heart of India. It was roused only by the touch of love. Having had such a clear vision of this wonderful power of Truth, are we to cease to believe in it, just where the attainment of Swaraj is concerned? Has the truth, which was needed in the process of awakenment, to be got rid of in the process of achievement?

. . . From our master, the Mahatma—may our devotion to him

never grow less!—we must learn the truth of love in all its purity, but the science and art of building up *Swaraj* is a vast subject. Its pathways are difficult to traverse and take time. For this task, aspiration and emotion must be there, but no less must study and thought be there likewise. For it, the economist must think, the mechanic must labor, the educationist and statesman must teach and contrive. In a word, the mind of the country must exert itself in all directions. Above all, the spirit of inquiry throughout the whole country must be kept intact and untrammelled, its mind not made timid or inactive by compulsion, open or secret. . . .

Consider the burning of cloth, heaped up before the very eyes of our motherland shivering and ashamed in her nakedness. What is the nature of the call to do this? Is it not another instance of a magical formula? The question of using or refusing cloth of a particular manufacture belongs mainly to economic science. The discussion of the matter by our countrymen should have been in the language of economics. If the country has really come to such a habit of mind that precise thinking has become impossible for it, then our very first fight should be against such a fatal habit, to the temporary exclusion of all else if need be. Such a habit would clearly be the original sin from which all our ills are flowing. But far from this, we take the course of confirming ourselves in it by relying on the magical formula that foreign cloth is "impure." Thus economics is bundled out and a fictitious moral dictum dragged into its place.

Untruth is impure in any circumstances, not merely because it may cause us material loss, but even when it does not; for it makes our inner nature unclean. This is a moral law and belongs to a higher plane. But if there be anything wrong in wearing a particular kind of cloth, that would be an offense against economics, or hygiene, or aesthetics, but certainly not against morality. Some urge that any mistake which brings sorrow to body or mind is a moral wrong. To which I reply that sorrow follows in the train of every mistake. A mistake in geometry may make a road too long, or a foundation weak, or a bridge dangerous. But mathematical mistakes cannot be cured by moral maxims. If a student makes a mistake in his geometry problem and his exercise book is torn up in consequence, the problem will nevertheless remain unsolved until attacked by geometrical methods. But what if the school-master comes to the conclusion that unless the exercise books are condemned and destroyed, his boys will never realize the folly of their mistakes? If such conclusion be wellfounded, then I can only repeat that the reformation of such moral weakness of these particular boys should take precedence over all other lessons, otherwise there is no hope of their becoming men in the future.

The command to burn our foreign clothes has been laid on us. I, for one, am unable to obey it. Firstly, because I conceive it to be my very first duty to put up a valiant fight against this terrible habit of blindly obeying orders, and this fight can never be carried on by our people being driven from one injunction to another. Secondly, I feel that the clothes to be burnt are not mine, but belong to those who most sorely need them. If those who are going naked should have given us the mandate to burn, it would, at least, have been a case of self-immolation and the crime of incendiarism would not lie at our door. But how can we expiate the sin of the forcible destruction of clothes which might have gone to women whose nakedness is actually keeping them prisoners, unable to stir out of the privacy of their homes?

I have said repeatedly and must repeat once more that we cannot afford to lose our mind for the sake of any external gain. Where Mahatma Gandhi has declared war against the tyranny of the machine which is oppressing the whole world, we are all enrolled under his banner. But we must refuse to accept as our ally the illusion-haunted magic-ridden slave-mentality that is at the root of all the poverty and insult under which our country groans. Here is the enemy itself, on whose defeat alone *Swaraj* within and without can come to us.

The time, moreover, has arrived when we must think of one thing more, and that is this. The awakening of India is a part of the awakening of the world. The door of the New Age has been flung open at the trumpet blast of a great war. We have read in the Mahabharata how the day of self-revelation had to be preceded by a year of retirement. The same has happened in the world today. Nations had attained nearness to each other without being aware of it, that is to say, the outside fact was there, but it had not penetrated into the mind. At the shock of the war, the truth of it stood revealed to mankind. The foundation of modern, that is Western, civilization was shaken; and it has become evident that the convulsion is neither local nor temporary, but has traversed the whole earth and will last until the shocks between man and man, which have extended from continent to continent, can be brought to rest, and a harmony be established. . . .

THE GREAT SENTINEL
•
by M. K. Gandhi

THE BARD of Shantiniketan has contributed to the *Modern Review* a brilliant essay on the present movement. It is a series of word pictures which he alone can paint. It is an eloquent protest against authority, slave mentality or whatever description one gives of blind acceptance of a passing mania whether out of fear or hope. It is a welcome and wholesome reminder to all workers that we must not be impatient, we must not impose authority no matter how great. The poet tells us summarily to reject anything and everything that does not appeal to our reason or heart. If we would gain Swaraj, we must stand for Truth as we know it at any cost. A reformer who is enraged because his message is not accepted must retire to the forest to learn how to watch, wait and pray. With all this one must heartily agree, and the Poet deserves the thanks of his countrymen for standing up

• Published in *Young India*, October 13, 1921; reprinted with permission. Also in M. K. Gandhi, *Young India, 1919–1922* (New York: B. W. Huebsch, 1923), pp. 668-75.

for Truth and Reason. There is no doubt that our last state will be worse than our first, if we surrender our reason into somebody's keeping. And I would feel extremely sorry to discover that the country had unthinkingly and blindly followed all I had said or done. I am quite conscious of the fact that blind surrender to love is often more mischievous than a forced surrender to the lash of the tyrant. There is hope for the slave of the brute, none for that of love. Love is needed to strengthen the weak, love becomes tyrannical when it exacts obedience from an unbeliever. To mutter a *mantra* without knowing its value is unmanly. It is good, therefore, that the Poet has invited all who are slavishly mimicking the call of the *charkha* [4] boldly to declare their revolt. His essay serves as a warning to us all who in our impatience are betrayed into intolerance or even violence against those who differ from us. I regard the Poet as a sentinel warning us against the approach of enemies called Bigotry, Lethargy, Intolerance, Ignorance, Inertia, and other members of that brood.

But whilst I agree with all that the Poet has said as to the necessity of watchfulness lest we cease to think, I must not be understood to endorse the proposition that there is any such blind obedience on a large scale in the country today. I have again and again appealed to reason, and let me assure him that if happily the country has come to believe in the spinning wheel as the giver of plenty, it has done so after laborious thinking, after great hesitation. I am not sure that even now educated India has assimilated the truth underlying the *charkha*. He must not mistake the surface dirt for the substance underneath. Let him go deeper and see for himself, whether the *charkha* has been accepted from blind faith or from reasoned necessity.

I do indeed ask the poet and the page to spin the wheel as a sacrament. When there is war, the poet lays down the lyre, the lawyer his law reports, the schoolboy his books. The poet will sing the true note after the war is over, the lawyer will have occasion to go to his law books when people have time to fight among themselves. When a house is on fire, all the inmates go out, and each one takes up a bucket to quench the fire. When all about me are dying for want of food, the only occupation permissible to me is to feed the hungry. It is my conviction that India is a house on fire because its manhood is being daily scorched, it is dying of hunger because it has no work to buy food with. Khulna [5] is starving not because the people cannot work, but because they have no work. The Ceded Districts [6] are passing successively through a fourth famine. Orissa is a land suffering from chronic famines. Our cities are not India. India lives in her seven and a half lacs of villages, and the cities live upon the villages. They do not bring their wealth from other countries. The city people are brokers and commission agents for the big houses of Europe, America and Japan. The cities have cooperated with the latter in the bleeding process that has gone on for the past two hundred years. It is my belief based on experience that India is daily growing poorer. The circulation about her feet and legs has almost stopped. And if we do not take care, she will collapse altogether.

To a people famishing and idle, the only acceptable form in which God can dare appear is work and promise of food as wages. God created man to work for his food, and said that those who ate without work were thieves. Eighty per cent of India are compulsorily thieves half the year. Is it any wonder if India has become one vast prison? Hunger is the argument that is driving India to the spinning wheel. The call of the spinning wheel is the noblest of all. Because it is the call of love. And love is Swaraj. The spinning wheel will "curb the mind" when the time is spent on necessary physical labor can be said to do so. We must think of millions who are today less than animals, who are almost in a dying state. The spinning wheel is the reviving draught for the millions of our dying countrymen and countrywomen. "Why should I who have no need to work for food, spin?" may be the question asked. Because I am eating what does not belong to me. I am living on the spoliation of my countrymen. Trace the course of every piece that finds its way into your pocket, and you will realize the truth of what I write. Swaraj has no meaning for the millions if they do not know how to employ their enforced idle-

ness. The attainment of this Swaraj is possible within a short time
and it is so possible only by the revival of the spinning wheel.

I do want growth. I do want self-determination. I do want
freedom, but I want all these for the soul. I doubt if the steel
age is an advance upon the flint age. I am indifferent. It is the evolution of the soul to which the intellect and all our faculties have
to be devoted. I have no difficulty in imagining the possibility of
a man armored after the modern style making some lasting and
new discovery for mankind, but I have less difficulty in imagining
the possibility of a man having nothing but a bit of flint and a
nail for lighting his path or his matchlock ever singing new hymns
of praise and delivering to an aching world a message of peace
and good will upon earth. A plea for the spinning wheel is a plea
for recognizing the dignity of labor.

I claim that in losing the spinning wheel we lost our left lung.
We are therefore suffering from galloping consumption. The
restoration of the wheel arrests the progress of the fell disease.
There are certain things which all must do in certain climes. The
spinning wheel is the thing which all must turn in the Indian
clime for the transition stage at any rate and the vast majority
must for all time.

It was our love of foreign cloth that ousted the wheel from its
position of dignity. Therefore I consider it a sin to wear foreign
cloth. I must confess that I do not draw a sharp or any distinction between economics and ethics. Economics that hurt the
moral well-being of an individual or a nation are immoral and
therefore sinful. Thus the economics that permit one country to
prey upon another are immoral. It is sinful to buy and use articles made by sweated labor. It is sinful to eat American wheat
and let my neighbor the grain dealer starve for want of custom.
Similarly it is sinful for me to wear the latest finery of Regent
Street, when I know that if I had but worn the things woven by
the neighboring spinners and weavers, that would have clothed
me, and fed and clothed them. On the knowledge of my sin
bursting upon me, I must consign the foreign garments to the
flames and thus purify myself, and thenceforth rest content with

the rough *Khadi* made by my neighbors. On knowing that my neighbors may not, having given up the occupation, take kindly to the spinning wheel, I must take it up myself and thus make it popular.

I venture to suggest to the Poet that the clothes I ask him to burn must be and are his. If they had to his knowledge belonged to the poor or the ill-clad, he would long ago have restored to the poor what was theirs. In burning my foreign clothes I burn my shame. I must refuse to insult the naked by giving them clothes they do not need, instead of giving them work which they sorely need. I will not commit the sin of becoming their patron, but on learning that I had assisted in impoverishing them, I would give them a privileged position and give them neither crumbs nor cast off clothing, but the best of my food and clothes and associate myself with them in work.

Nor is the scheme of Non-cooperation or Swadeshi an exclusive doctrine. My modesty has prevented me from declaring from the house top that the message of Non-cooperation, Non-violence and Swadeshi is a message to the world. It must fall flat, if it does not bear fruit in the soil where it has been delivered. At the present moment India has nothing to share with the world save her degradation, pauperism and plagues. Is it her ancient Shastras that we would send to the world? Well, they are printed in many editions, and an incredulous and idolatrous world refuses to look at them, because we, the heirs and custodians, do not live them. Before, therefore, I can think of sharing with the world, I must possess. Our Non-cooperation is neither with the English nor with the West. Our Non-cooperation is with the system the English have established, with the material civilization and its attendant greed and exploitation of the weak. Our Non-cooperation is a retirement within ourselves. Our Non-cooperation is a refusal to cooperate with the English administrators on their own terms. We say to them, "Come and cooperate with us on our terms, and it will be well for us, for you and the world." We must refuse to be lifted off our feet. A drowning man cannot save others. In order to be fit to save others, we must try to save ourselves. Indian nationalism is not exclusive, nor aggressive, nor destructive. It is health-giving, religious and therefore humanitarian. India must learn to live before she can aspire to die for humanity. The mice which helplessly find themselves between the cat's teeth acquire no merit from their enforced sacrifice.

True to his poetical instinct the Poet lives for the morrow and would have us do likewise. He presents to our admiring gaze the beautiful picture of the birds early in the morning singing hymns of praise as they soar into the sky. These birds had their day's food and soared with rested wings in whose veins new blood had flown during the previous night. But I have had the pain of watching birds who for want of strength could not be coaxed even into a flutter of their wings. The human bird under the Indian sky gets up weaker than when he pretended to retire. For millions it is an eternal vigil or an eternal trance. It is an indescribably painful state which has to be experienced to be realized. I have found it impossible to sooth suffering patients with a song from Kabir.[7] The hungry millions ask for one poem—invigorating food. They cannot be given it. They must earn it. And they can earn it only by the sweat of their brow. . . .

THE TWO OUTSTANDING FIGURES
by Jawaharlal Nehru

TAGORE AND GANDHI have undoubtedly been the two outstanding and dominating figures of India in this first half of the twentieth century. It is instructive to compare and contrast them. No two persons could be so different from one another in their make-up or temperaments. Tagore, the aristocratic artist, turned

• Reprinted with permission from Jawaharlal Nehru, The Discovery of India (New York: John Day, 1946), pp. 342-43.

democrat with proletarian sympathies, represented essentially the cultural tradition of India, the tradition of accepting life in the fullness thereof and going through it with song and dance. Gandhi, more a man of the people, almost the embodiment of the Indian peasant, represented the other ancient tradition of India, that of renunciation and asceticism. And yet Tagore was primarily the man of thought, Gandhi of concentrated and ceaseless activity. Both, in their different ways, had a world outlook, and both were at the same time wholly India. They seemed to represent different but harmonious aspects of India and to complement one another.

I OWE MUCH
by M. K. Gandhi

In 1931 in Calcutta was published a beautiful "Golden Book of Tagore" in celebration of his seventieth birthday. Gandhi was one of the sponsors of this volume. His message led the pages of tributes from world figures.

In common with thousands of his countrymen I owe much to one who by his poetic genius and singular purity of life has raised India in the estimation of the world. But I owe also more. Did he not harbor in Shantiniketan the inmates of my Ashram who had preceded me from South Africa? The other ties and memories are too sacred to bear mention in a public tribute.

• Reprinted from *The Golden Book of Tagore* (Calcutta, 1931).

A MEASURE OF THEIR STATURE

by K. R. Kripalani

Tagore died in 1941. K. R. Kripalani, in an essay on the two men, gives a fitting description of their last contacts.

THEIR LAST MEETING—the most touching and beautiful of all their meetings—took place in Shantiniketan in February 1940, when "this great soul in a beggar's garb," to quote the poet's description of him, came to see him. A few months later when Tagore lay in Calcutta, hovering between life and death, Gandhi sent his personal secretary, Mahadev Desai, to see him. As Mahadev Desai handed to him Gandhi's letter, the poet's hands shook with emotion and tears trickled down his cheeks. He who never wept in sorrow wept in joy. The friendship of these two to the end, despite the many differences that seemed to divide them, will be remembered by their countrymen as an undying testimony to their greatness. Had one of them been a little less great, they would have fallen out. It was so easy to misunderstand each other, with their sensibilities and their ways of living so sharply in contrast, their fields of activity so widely separated, and each surrounded by admirers, not as tolerant and understanding as the masters. That they did not do so is a measure of their stature.

• Reprinted with permission from K. R. Kripalani, *Gandhi, Tagore and Nehru* (Bombay: Hind Kitabs, 1947), pp. 24-25.

10 THE SALT MARCH (1930)

TOWARD DANDI

by H. S. L. Polak

In the years following 1922 the nationalist movement was at a low ebb. In 1924, after his convalescence and release from prison, Gandhi conducted a dramatic twenty-one-day fast to promote Hindu-Moslem unity, but he did not consider the time ripe for a revival of civil disobedience. In 1927 the British government appointed the Simon Commission to make recommendations for further political reform in India, but as the Commission contained no Indian members it was boycotted by Indian nationalists. In 1928, in the Bardoli district near Bombay, a satyagraha campaign against a tax increase won support throughout the country and achieved its aim by non-violent means. Many in the Congress were pressing for action on a wider scale; some even advocated armed rebellion. Gandhi, however, was cautious. At his suggestion, late in 1928 the Congress resolved that unless within one year the British agreed to give India a constitution and Dominion status, a third nation-wide civil disobedience movement would be launched. When the British failed to meet its terms the Congress, in December 1929, at last announced that its goal was full inde-

• Reprinted with permission from H. S. L. Polak, *Mahatma Gandhi: The Man and His Mission* (Madras: Natesan, 8th ed., 1931[?]), pp. 106-16.

pendence. It fixed January twenty-sixth as National Independence Day, and in effect authorized Gandhi to decide the time and method of a new campaign of civil disobedience.

The manufacture of salt was a government monopoly. Accordingly Gandhi decided to inaugurate the campaign by leading a march to the sea in order to take salt illegally from its waters—an action which symbolized the Indians' refusal to recognize the authority of the government. On March 2, 1930 Gandhi warned the Viceroy, Lord Irwin, of his intentions, saying, "If my letter makes no appeal to your heart, on the eleventh day of this month I shall proceed with such co-workers of the Ashram as I can take, to disregard the provisions of the Salt Laws. I regard this tax to be the most iniquitous of all from the poor man's standpoint. As the Independence movement is essentially for the poorest in the land, the beginning will be made with this evil." The Viceroy's secretary replied: "His Excellency . . . regrets to learn that you contemplate a course of action which is clearly bound to involve violation of the law and danger to the public peace." Accordingly the famous march was begun.

TRUE TO HIS DECLARATION, just a little before daybreak on the morning of the 12th, Mahatma Gandhi with his 79 volunteers, all students of the Vidyapith,[1] left the Ashram on a campaign of civil disobedience. Their destination was the village of Dandi on the sea coast near Jalalpur[2] where Gandhi was to break the law regarding the manufacture of salt. Streams of Khaddar-clad men and women had flowed to the Ashram all night through to have a darshan[3] of Mahatmaji and witness the great march. Among those were journalists and cameramen from far and near and correspondents of some British papers as well.

"The scenes that preceded, accompanied and followed this great national event," wrote the Bombay Chronicle, "were so enthusiastic, magnificent and soul-stirring that indeed they beggar description. Never was the wave of patriotism so powerful in the hearts of mankind, as it was on this great occasion which is bound

to go down to the chapters of the history of India's national freedom as a great beginning of a Great Movement. . . ."

Mahatmaji with a gentle smile betokening his undying faith in
the justice of the cause he was pursuing and in the success of the
great campaign he had embarked upon, began at the head of the
procession to march with quick steps and unfaltering. The pace
was a trifle too fast for his health and age, wrote the correspondent:
"He was carrying a long stick in his hand obviously for support.
The whole army was marching in a perfectly disciplined manner.
The agile general in the front was indeed a source of inspiration
to all. The army passed all along the distance of ten miles up to
Aslali between the densely packed rows of people who were standing in their places for hours together, eager for the 'darshan' of
India's great General. Ahmedabad had had on the occasion one of
its hugest processions during living memory. With the possible
exception of children and decrepits, every resident of the city must
have watched the great procession which was at least two miles
in length. Those who could not find a standing place in the
streets through which the army marched had made use of house-
tops and galleries, open walls and trees and every conceivable
place they could get hold of. The whole city seemed to be enfete
on this historic occasion. The cries of 'Gandhi-ki-Jai' were rending
the skies all along the march. . . ."

As the procession marched through village after village, Mahatmaji spoke at all the halting stations, urging the people to take
to Khaddar, to stop drinking, to give up cooperation with Government and join the ranks of the Satyagrahis. At Aslali he told
his followers that he would either die on the way or else keep
away from the Ashram until Swaraj had been won. This was an
expression of despair, said his critics; while his own followers were
moved to their depths. "I have no intention of returning to the
Ashram until I succeed in getting the salt tax repealed," said Mr.
Gandhi. He exhorted villagers to take to the spinning wheel, to
look to the sanitation of the village and to treat the untouchables
with brotherly love. He urged them to join his movement to break
the salt monopoly of Government, as this would be a step forward

on the way to Swaraj. Volunteers were enrolling themselves in
the hundreds in the cause of civil disobedience and the headmen
of several villages were resigning their jobs and joining the campaign. The arrest of Mr. Gandhi was supposed to be imminent
and Mahatmaji, as might be expected, was well prepared for it
and he gave instruction that his place should be taken up by Abbas Tyabjee,[4] the aged friend, who had stood by Gandhi through
all the years of Non-cooperation. The fight threatened to be well
nigh grim; and as Sir P. C. Ray said, "Mahatma Gandhi's historic
march was like the exodus of Israelites under Moses. Until the
Seer seized the promised land, he won't turn his back." . . .

Gandhi and his party reached Dandi on the morning of the
5th April. Mrs. Sarojini Naidu had also gone there to see the
Mahatma. Interviewed by the Associated Press immediately after
his arrival at Dandi, Gandhiji said: "God be thanked for what
may be termed the happy ending of the first stage in this, for me
at least, the final struggle for freedom. I cannot withhold my
compliments from the Government for the policy of complete
non-interference adopted by them throughout the march. After
the graceless and childish performance in the matter of Mr. Val-
labhai's arrest and imprisonment and equally unprovoked arrest
and imprisonment of Mr. Sen Gupta,[5] I was wholly unprepared
for this exemplary non-interference. I am not so foolish as to imagine that the Government has suddenly lost their proved capacity for provoking popular resentment and then punishing with
frightfulness. I wish I could believe this non-interference was
due to any real change of heart or policy. The wanton disregard
shown by them to popular feeling in the Legislative Assembly
and their high-handed action leave no room for doubt that the
policy of heartless exploitation of India is to be persisted in at any
cost, and so the only interpretation I can put upon this non-interference is that the British Government, powerful though it is, is
sensitive to world opinion which will not tolerate repression of
extreme political agitation which civil disobedience undoubtedly
is, so long as disobedience remains civil and therefore necessarily
non-violent.

"It remains to be seen whether the Government will tolerate as they have tolerated the march, the actual breach of the salt laws by countless people from tomorrow. I expect extensive popular response to the resolution of the Working Committee (of the Indian National Congress). I have seen nothing to warrant the cancellation of the notice I have already issued that all Committees and organizations throughout the length and breadth of the land are free, if they are prepared to commence from tomorrow Civil Disobedience in respect of the salt laws. God willing, I expect with my companions (volunteers) to commence actual Civil Disobedience at 6:30 tomorrow morning. Sixth April has been to us since its culmination in Jallianwala massacre a day for penance and purification. We therefore commence it with prayer and fasting. I hope the whole of India will observe the National Week commencing from tomorrow in the spirit in which it was conceived. I am positive that the greater the dedication to the country's cause and the greater the purification, the speedier will be the glorious end for which the millions of India consciously or unconsciously are striving."

Gandhi's prayer on the morning of the 6th was more than usually solemn. In the course of his speech he observed that if he was arrested, they should take orders from Mr. Abbas Tyabjee and if he, too, was removed, from Mrs. Sarojini Naidu. He paid a tribute to both these leaders and asked the volunteers implicitly to obey them. Gandhiji concluded his address by asking the visitors not to offer Satyagraha that day, but to do so the next day. He considered his offer of Civil Disobedience as a great Yagna [6] and he evidently did not want demonstrations, proceeding out of motives other than spiritual, to be associated with this great movement.

Soon after prayers, Mr. Gandhi with his 84 volunteers of the Gujerat Vidyapith [7] and Saheth Punjabhai [8] of Ahmedabad, proceeded exactly at 6 in the morning for a bath in the sea. A large crowd accompanied the party. Gandhi was walking at a slow pace in grave solemnity and entered the water of the sea amidst loud cries of "Mahatma Gandhi-ki-jai."

Gandhi was leaning on Miss Abbas Tyabji's shoulder, and was accompanied by Mrs. Sarojini Naidu. Then Gandhi and his volunteers proceeded to break the salt law by picking up the salt lying on the seashore. Mrs. Sarojini Naidu hailed the Mahatma by calling him "law-breaker." No policemen appeared on the scene when Gandhi and his volunteers broke the salt law.

Immediately after breaking the salt law, Mr. Gandhi issued the following press statement: "Now that the technical or ceremonial breach of the salt law has been committed, it is now open to any one who would take the risk of prosecution under the salt law to manufacture salt wherever he wishes and wherever it is convenient. My advice is that workers should everywhere manufacture salt, and where they know how to prepare clean salt, make use of it and instruct the villagers likewise, telling the villager at the same time that he runs the risk of being prosecuted. In other words, the villagers should be fully instructed as to the incidence of the salt tax, and the manner of breaking the laws and regulations connected with it so as to have the salt tax repealed.

"It should be made absolutely clear to the villagers that the breach is open, and in no way stealthy. This condition being known, they may manufacture salt or help themselves to the salt manufactured by Nature in creeks and pits near the seashore, use it for themselves and their cattle, and sell it to those who will buy it, it being well understood that all such people are committing a breach of the salt law and running the risk of a prosecution, or even without a prosecution, are to be subjected by so-called salt officers to harassment.

"This war against the salt tax should be continued during the National Week, that is, up to the 13th April. Those who are not engaged in this sacred work should themselves do vigorous propaganda for the boycott of foreign cloth and the use of Khaddar. They should also endeavor to manufacture as much Khaddar as possible. As to this and the prohibition of liquor, I am preparing a message for the women of India who, I am becoming more and more convinced, can make a larger contribution than men towards the attainment of Independence, I feel that they will be worthier interpreters of non-violence than men, not because they are weak as men, in their arrogance, believe them to be, but because they have greater courage of the right type, and immeasurably greater spirit of self-sacrifice."

Being asked what he would do during the national week, Mr. Gandhi said, "I have a lot of work to do." He however laughingly added, "I shall encourage illicit manufacture of salt."

A PINCH OF SALT

by Louis Fischer

HAD GANDHI gone by train or automobile to make salt, the effect would have been considerable. But to walk for twenty-four days and rivet the attention of all India, to trek across a country-side saying, "Watch, I am about to give a signal to the nation," and then to pick up a pinch of salt in publicized defiance of the mighty government and thus become a criminal, that required imagination, dignity, and the sense of showmanship of a great artist. It appealed to the illiterate peasant and it appealed to a sophisticated critic and sometime fierce opponent of Gandhi's like Subhas Chandra Bose [9] who compared the Salt March to "Napoleon's march to Paris on his return from Elba."

The act performed, Gandhi withdrew from the scene. India had its cue. Gandhi had communicated with it by lifting up some grains of salt.

The next act was an insurrection without arms. Every villager on India's long seacoast went to the beach or waded into the sea with a pan to make salt. The police began mass arrests. Ramdas, third son of Gandhi, with a large group of ashramites, was ar-

• Reprinted with permission from Louis Fischer, The Life of Mahatma Gandhi (New York: Harper, 1950), pp. 268-69.

rested. Pandit Malaviya and other moderate cooperators resigned from the Legislative Assembly. The police began to use violence. Civil resisters never resisted arrest; but they resisted the confiscation of the salt they had made, and Mahadev Desai reported cases where such Indians were beaten and bitten in the fingers by constables. Congress Volunteers openly sold contraband salt in cities. Many were arrested and sentenced to short prison terms. In Delhi, a meeting of fifteen thousand persons heard Pandit Malaviya appeal to the audience to boycott foreign cloth; he himself bought some illegal salt after his speech. The police raided the Congress party headquarters in Bombay where salt was being made in pans on the roof. A crowd of sixty thousand assembled. Hundreds were handcuffed or their arms fastened with ropes and led off to jail. In Ahmedabad, ten thousand people obtained illegal salt from Congress in the first week after the act at Dandi. They paid what they could; if they had no money they got it free. The salt lifted by Gandhi from the beach was sold to a Dr. Kanuga, the highest bidder, for 1,600 rupees. Jawaharlal Nehru, the president of the Congress, was arrested in Allahabad under the Salt Acts and sentenced to six months' imprisonment. The agitation and disobedience spread to the turbulent regions of the Maharashtra and Bengal. In Calcutta, the Mayor, J. M. Sengupta, read seditious literature aloud at a public meeting and urged non-wearing of foreign textiles. He was put in prison for six months. Picketing of liquor shops and foreign cloth shops commenced throughout India. Girls and ladies from aristocratic families and from families where purdah [10] had been observed came out into the streets to demonstrate. . . .

A SPRING HAD BEEN RELEASED

by Jawaharlal Nehru

THE SIXTH of April was the first day of the National Week, which is celebrated annually in memory of the happenings in 1919, from Satyagraha Day to Jallianwala Bagh. On that day Gandhiji began the breach of the salt laws at Dandi beach, and three or four days later permission was given to all Congress organizations to do likewise and begin civil disobedience in their own areas.

It seemed as though a spring had been suddenly released; all over the country, in town and village, salt manufacture was the topic of the day, and many curious expedients were adopted to produce salt. We knew precious little about it, and so we read it up where we could and issued leaflets giving directions; we collected pots and pans and ultimately succeeded in producing some unwholesome stuff, which we waved about in triumph and often auctioned for fancy prices. It was really immaterial whether the stuff was good or bad; the main thing was to commit a breach of the obnoxious salt law, and we were successful in that, even though the quality of our salt was poor. As we saw the abounding enthusiasm of the people and the way salt-making was spreading like a prairie fire, we felt a little abashed and ashamed for having questioned the efficacy of this method when it was first proposed by Gandhiji. And we marveled at the amazing knack of the man to impress the multitude and make it act in an organized way.

• Reprinted with permission from Jawaharlal Nehru, *Toward Freedom* (New York: John Day, 1941), pp. 159-60.

ARREST AT MIDNIGHT

• by Haridas T. Muzumdar

While mass civil disobedience was being carried out through-out India, Gandhi carefully avoided participating further in the activity. He set up a temporary ashram at Camp Karadi, a mango grove midway between Dandi and the sea, from which he kept in close contact with developments throughout the country. Meanwhile he and the male members of his ashram were trying to educate nearby villagers to stop preparing an alcoholic toddy. Then, early in the morning on May 5, Gandhi was arrested.

NEAR THE COTTAGE of reeds is a plain cot out in the open, under the blue canopy of the Indian sky. Not far from the cot on one side there is a young man sleeping on the ground; on the other side of the cot is a young Indian lady (stopping over for the day) sleeping on the ground. Farther away both to the right and to the left are mango trees under which are sleeping groups of young men. Still farther away in the background is a modest school building in front of which about forty men, young and old, are sleeping. It is 12:45 A.M.

Of a sudden a tramping of feet is heard, disturbing the quiet repose of Karadi Camp. Two English officers—(1) the District Magistrate of Surat and (2) the District Superintendent of Police—and an Indian police officer, all three armed with pistols, along with thirty odd Indian policemen armed with rifles, enter the Camp through the gates in front of the school building. They make straight for the cottage of reeds and surround the cot.

• Reprinted with permission from Haridas T. Muzumdar, *Gandhi Versus the Empire* (New York: Universal Publishing Co., 1932), pp. 33-37.

Two flashlights are directed upon the face of the occupant of the cot.

The Mahatma, half-clad, weary of limb, having had less than two hours' rest, sleepily turns from one side to the other in order to dodge the dazzling light. Suddenly the words "Please wake up!" strike his ears. He is up in his bed. Gazing at the police party surrounding him, he takes in the situation all at once. He decides to break his silence.

Mahatma Gandhi: "Have you come to arrest me?"

The District Magistrate: "Yes. Your name is Mohandas Karamchand Gandhi?"

Mahatma Gandhi (getting off the bed): "Do you mind waiting until I brush my teeth and wash my face?"

The District Superintendent of Police (stiffly looking at his time-piece): "You may brush your teeth."

While the Mahatma is getting washed, a bell is rung at the school building. All the inmates of the Camp are immediately up and seen surrounding the police party. They make efforts to get inside the police cordon and after a while succeed in going near the Mahatma. They are steadfastly gazing at their beloved leader.

Mahatma Gandhi (still brushing his teeth): "Mr. District Magistrate, may I know the charge on which I am arrested? Is it Section 124-A of the Indian Penal Code?"

District Magistrate: "No, not under Section 124. I have a written order."

Mahatma Gandhi (his ablutions now finished): "Would you mind reading it to me?"

District Magistrate (with the stiff formality of which only an Englishman is capable): "Whereas the Governor-in-Council views with alarm the activities of Mohandas Karamchand Gandhi, he directs that the said Mohandas Karamchand Gandhi should be placed under restraint under Regulation XXV of 1827, and suffer imprisonment during the pleasure of the government: and that he be immediately removed to the Yeravda Central Jail."

Mahatma Gandhi (disappointed that it was not Section 124-A): "Thank you! (Turning to his grandson): Please make up my bedding. (Turning to Mr. V. G. Desai, Acting Commandant of the Non-Violent Battalion): Please take charge of the important papers from my satchels. (Turning to one of his other awestruck followers): Please get me two *taklis* (hand-spindles) and some slivers."

District Magistrate and District Superintendent of Police (in unison, their eyes fixed upon their time-pieces): "Please hurry up, please hurry up!"

It is now one o'clock. The darkness thickens.

Mahatma Gandhi (surrounded by his loyal band of Satyagrahists, i.e., Civil Resisters): "Punditji, please recite the hymn describing the qualities of a Vaishnava. [The famous hymn with which the Great March was commenced on the 12th of March, 1930, with which the violation of the Salt Act was undertaken on the 6th of April, 1930.]"

The Mahatma stands up, his eyes closed, his head bent in mute reverence, while Pundit Khare recites the hymn. At the end of the hymn Punditji leads the congregational worship in which all, including the thirty odd Indian policemen, participate. The two English officers are standing stiffly, watch in hand, during the singing of the Vaishnava hymn.

Pundit Khare (seated on the ground, mono-string musical instrument in hand): "Oh Rama! Lord of the Dynasty of Raghus! Thou, an ideal king, an ideal husband of the ideal wife Sita, Thou art verily the Redeemer of the fallen and the sinful!"

The congregation repeats this verse each time after Punditji sings it. The joyous chanting purifies the countryside—white clouds are seen hovering overhead.

District Magistrate and District Superintendent of Police (in unison, their eyes fixed upon their time-pieces, a bit nervously): "Please hurry up, please hurry up!"

One by one the Civil Resisters bow down before the Mahatma, touching his feet most reverently, and bid him farewell most tenderly and affectionately.

The young lady (touching the Mahatma's feet): "Have you any message for Kasturba?"

Mahatma Gandhi (gently patting the young lady's back): "No, I have no message for her. Tell her she is a brave girl."

The Mahatma surrenders himself into police custody. His two satchels and the small bundle of bedding are taken in charge by a police constable. The police party makes for the motor lorry. Tranquillity-incarnate, the Mahatma walks with steady steps in the direction of the gates. He is accompanied on the one side by the District Magistrate and on the other by the District Superintendent of Police—the eyes of both these officers are glued to their time-pieces. It is ten minutes past one. The policemen occupy the three police lorries. The Mahatma steps into the special lorry, casting a wistful glance at his Camp and his followers. The District Magistrate, watch in hand, gets into the same lorry. The District Superintendent of Police, watch in hand, also gets into the same lorry. And lo! the lorries are whisked away. A pall of darkness falls over the whole world.

Watches in hand, I take it, these English officers conducted the Mahatma to the railway train and helped him get into the special carriage reserved for the Gandhi party. The Gujarat Mail bound for Bombay was detained at 6:40 A.M. but for a moment at Borivli (a suburb of Bombay) where the Mahatma was made to alight. The passengers on the train paid their homage to the imprisoned Soul of India by loud shouts of "Mahatma Gandhi Ki Jai" (Victory to Mahatma Gandhi). The Mahatma was escorted to a high-powered grey car with bright pink blinds which were pulled down. The automobile with its precious cargo of barely a hundred pounds of flesh and bones arrived at its destination, the Yeravda Central Jail, Poona, at 10:30 A.M.

DHARASANA SALT RAID

• by Webb Miller

Just before Gandhi's arrest on May 5, 1930, at Karadi, near Dandi, he announced his intention of raiding the Dharasana Salt Works about 150 miles north of Bombay. With Gandhi in jail, Mrs. Sarojini Naidu—close associate of Gandhi and Indian poetess —assumed the leadership and went to the site with 2,500 volunteers. Webb Miller, well-known foreign correspondent for the United Press, heard about this projected salt raid on May 21, and wrote the following eye-witness account.

AFTER WITNESSING two serious riots at the Wadala salt pans in the suburbs of Bombay, I received on the evening of May 20, 1930, an important tip from a friendly Gandhi sympathizer. He told me they were planning the biggest demonstration yet at Dharasana, about a hundred and fifty miles north of Bombay.

"Sarojini Naidu, the famous Indian poetess, is leading a non-violent demonstration against the big salt pans near Dharasana. The nearest railway station is Dungri. It is an isolated spot and you will have to take your own food and water. You'd better telegraph Mme. Naidu to provide transportation from Dungri, otherwise you will have to walk many miles. Be sure to take an adequate supply of bottled water, because the water from native sources is unhealthy for white men."

. . . Dungri consisted of a little huddle of native huts on the dusty plain. There were no means of transportation because Mme. Naidu had not received my telegram. I could find nobody who

• Reprinted with permission from Webb Miller, *I Found No Peace* (New York: Simon and Schuster, 1936), pp. 190, 192-96.

spoke English. By repeatedly pronouncing the word "Dharasana" and pointing questioningly around the horizon, I got directions and set off across country on foot through cactus hedges, millet fields, and inch-deep dust, inquiring my way by signs.

After plodding about six miles across country lugging a pack of sandwiches and two quart bottles of water under a sun which was already blazing hot, inquiring from every native I met, I reached the assembling place of the Gandhi followers. Several long, open, thatched sheds were surrounded by high cactus thickets. The sheds were literally swarming and buzzed like a beehive with some 2,500 Congress or Gandhi men dressed in the regulation uniform of rough homespun cotton *dhotis* and triangular Gandhi caps, somewhat like American overseas soldiers' hats. They chattered excitedly and when I arrived hundreds surrounded me, with evidences of hostility at first. After they learned my identity, I was warmly welcomed by young college-educated, English-speaking men and escorted to Mme. Naidu. The famous Indian poetess, stocky, swarthy, strong-featured, barelegged, dressed in rough, dark homespun robe and sandals, welcomed me. She explained that she was busy martialing her forces for the demonstration against the salt pans and would talk with me more at length later. She was educated in England and spoke English fluently.

Mme. Naidu called for prayer before the march started and the entire assemblage knelt. She exhorted them: "Gandhi's body is in jail but his soul is with you. India's prestige is in your hands. You must not use any violence under any circumstances. You will be beaten but you must not resist; you must not even raise a hand to ward off blows." Wild, shrill cheers terminated her speech.

Slowly and in silence the throng commenced the half-mile march to the salt deposits. A few carried ropes for lassoing the barbed-wire stockade around the salt pans. About a score who were assigned to act as stretcher-bearers wore crude, hand-painted red crosses pinned to their breasts; their stretchers consisted of blankets. Manilal Gandhi, second son of Gandhi, walked among the foremost of the marchers. As the throng drew near the salt pans they commenced chanting the revolutionary slogan, "In-quilah zindabad," [11] intoning the two words over and over.

The salt deposits were surrounded by ditches filled with water and guarded by four hundred native Surat police in khaki shorts and brown turbans. Half a dozen British officials commanded them. The police carried *lathis*—five-foot clubs tipped with steel. Inside the stockade twenty-five native riflemen were drawn up.

In complete silence the Gandhi men drew up and halted a hundred yards from the stockade. A picked column advanced from the crowd, waded the ditches, and approached the barbed-wire stockade, which the Surat police surrounded, holding their clubs at the ready. Police officials ordered the marchers to disperse under a recently imposed regulation which prohibited gatherings of more than five persons in any one place. The column silently ignored the warning and slowly walked forward. I stayed with the main body about a hundred yards from the stockade.

Suddenly, at a word of command, scores of native police rushed upon the advancing marchers and rained blows on their heads with their steel-shod *lathis*. Not one of the marchers even raised an arm to fend off the blows. They went down like tenpins. From where I stood I heard the sickening whacks of the clubs on un-protected skulls. The waiting crowd of watchers groaned and sucked in their breaths in sympathetic pain at every blow.

Those struck down fell sprawling, unconscious or writhing in pain with fractured skulls or broken shoulders. In two or three minutes the ground was quilted with bodies. Great patches of blood widened on their white clothes. The survivors without breaking ranks silently and doggedly marched on until struck down. When every one of the first column had been knocked down stretcher-bearers rushed up unmolested by the police and carried off the injured to a thatched hut which had been ar-ranged as a temporary hospital.

Then another column formed while the leaders pleaded with them to retain their self-control. They marched slowly toward the police. Although every one knew that within a few minutes he would be beaten down, perhaps killed, I could detect no signs of wavering or fear. They marched steadily with heads up, without the encouragement of music or cheering or any possibility that they might escape serious injury or death. The police rushed out and methodically and mechanically beat down the second column. There was no fight, no struggle; the marchers simply walked forward until struck down. There were no outcries, only groans after they fell. There were not enough stretcher-bearers to carry off the wounded; I saw eighteen injured being carried off simultaneously, while forty-two still lay bleeding on the ground awaiting stretcher-bearers. The blankets used as stretchers were sodden with blood.

At times the spectacle of unresisting men being methodically bashed into a bloody pulp sickened me so much that I had to turn away. The western mind finds it difficult to grasp the idea of nonresistance. I felt an indefinable sense of helpless rage and loathing, almost as much against the men who were submitting unresistingly to being beaten as against the police wielding the clubs, and this despite the fact that when I came to India I sympathized with the Gandhi cause.

Several times the leaders nearly lost control of the waiting crowd. They rushed up and down, frantically pleading with and exhorting the intensely excited men to remember Gandhi's instructions. It seemed that the unarmed throng was on the verge of launching a mass attack upon the police. The British official in charge, Superintendent Robinson of Surat, sensed the imminence of an outbreak and posted his twenty-five riflemen on a little knoll ready to fire. He came to me, inquired my identity, and said: "You'd better move aside out of the line of shooting. We may be forced to open fire into the crowd." While we were talking one of the Gandhiites, a young university student, ran up to Robinson, his face contorted by rage, tore open his cotton smock, exposing his bare breast, and shrieked: "Shoot me, shoot me! Kill me, it's for my country!" The leaders managed to calm the crowd.

The Gandhi men altered their tactics, marched up in groups of twenty-five and sat on the ground near the salt pans, making no effort to draw nearer. Led by a coffee-colored Parsi sergeant of police named Antia, a hulking, ugly-looking fellow, detachments of police approached one seated group and called upon them to disperse under the non-assemblage ordinance. The Gandhi followers ignored them and refused even to glance up at the *lathis* brandished threateningly above their heads. Upon a word from Antia the beating recommenced coldly, without anger. Bodies toppled over in threes and fours, bleeding from great gashes on their scalps. Group after group walked forward, sat down, and submitted to being beaten into insensibility without raising an arm to fend off the blows.

Finally the police became enraged by the nonresistance, sharing, I suppose, the helpless rage I had already felt at the demonstrators for not fighting back. They commenced savagely kicking the seated men in the abdomen and testicles. The injured men writhed and squealed in agony, which seemed to inflame the fury of the police, and the crowd again almost broke away from their leaders. The police then began dragging the sitting men by the arms or feet, sometimes for a hundred yards, and throwing them into ditches. One was dragged to the ditch where I stood; the splash of his body doused me with muddy water. Another policeman dragged a Gandhi man to the ditch, threw him in, then belabored him over the head with his *lathi*. Hour after hour stretcher-bearers carried back a stream of inert, bleeding bodies.

I went to see Mme. Naidu, who was directing the subleaders in keeping the crowds from charging the police. While we were talking one of the British officials approached her, touched her on the arm, and said: "Sarojini Naidu, you are under arrest." She haughtily shook off his hand and said: "I'll come, but don't touch me." The crowd cheered frantically as she strode with the British officer across the open space to the barbed-wire stockade, where she was interned. Later she was sentenced to prison. Manilal Gandhi was also arrested.

In the middle of the morning V. J. Patel arrived. He had been leading the Swaraj movement since Gandhi's arrest, and had just resigned as President of the Indian Legislative Assembly in protest against the British. Scores surrounded him, knelt, and kissed his feet. He was a venerable gentleman of about sixty with white flowing beard and mustache, dressed in the usual undyed, coarse homespun smock. Sitting on the ground under a mango tree, Patel said: "All hope of reconciling India with the British Empire is lost forever. I can understand any government's taking people into custody and punishing them for breaches of the law, but I cannot understand how any government that calls itself civilized could deal as savagely and brutally with nonviolent, un-resisting men as the British have this morning."

By eleven the heat reached 116 in the shade and activities of the Gandhi volunteers subsided. I went back to the temporary hospital to examine the wounded. They lay in rows on the bare ground in the shade of an open, palm-thatched shed. I counted 320 injured, many still insensible with fractured skulls, others writhing in agony from kicks in the testicles and stomach. The Gandhi men had been able to gather only a few native doctors, who were doing the best they could with the inadequate facil-ities. Scores of the injured had received no treatment for hours and two had died. The demonstration was finished for the day on account of the heat. . . .

11 THE ROUND TABLE CONFERENCE (1931)

THE REAL CONFERENCE

by Mahadev Desai

In November 1930 the first Round Table Conference met in London to discuss a new constitution for India. Although this body contained some Indian members there were no representatives of the Congress. In January 1931 Gandhi and several other top Congress leaders were released from prison. There followed conversations between Gandhi and the Viceroy, Lord Irwin, leading to the Gandhi-Irwin agreement of March 5. Lord Irwin promised to release the other political prisoners, who numbered 100,000 or more, and Gandhi promised that the Congress would call off civil disobedience and send representatives to the second Round Table Conference, which met in London from September 14 to December 1. The conference failed to agree on a constitution, but Gandhi's stay in England did much to enlist sympathy there for the Indian cause. In fact, he regarded his unofficial contacts with the British people as "the real conference."

Gandhi gladly accepted an invitation to stay at Kingsley House,

• Reprinted with permission from C. Rajagopalachar[i] and J. C. Kumarappa, editors, The Nation's Voice (Ahmedabad: Navajivan, 1932), pp. 125-26, 220, 158-59, 197-98.

a social settlement in the London slums, and also had an office in Knightsbridge, nearer the conference headquarters. He visited many well-known personalities, including the King and Queen, Bernard Shaw, the Dean of Canterbury, Mme. Maria Montessori, Harold Laski, and General Smuts, who said of their days in South Africa, "I did not give you such a bad time as you gave me." Winston Churchill refused to see Gandhi, as did the Pope a few months later. Gandhi's relations with the press were excellent; when questioned about his habit of wearing a loincloth, he replied, "You people wear plus-fours, mine are minus fours." He made many trips outside London and addressed numerous public meetings.

Gandhi had little time for sleep in London. Here is a typical day's schedule: 1 A.M., reach Kingsley Hall; 1:45, finish the spinning quota of 160 yards of yarn; 1:50, write diary of preceding twenty-four hours; 2:00-3:45, sleep; 3:45-5:00, wash and prayer; 5:00-6:00, rest; 6:00-7:00, interview while walking; 7:00-8:00, morning ablutions and bath; 8:00-8:30, breakfast; 8:30-9:15, auto journey to office; 9:15-10:45, interviews with a journalist, an artist, a Sikh member of the Round Table Conference, and a merchant; 10:45-11:00, journey to St. James's Palace; 11 A.M. to 1 P.M., attend Round Table Conference; 1:00-2:45, speak at American journalists' luncheon; 3:00-5:30, conference with Moslems; 5:00-7:00, conference with Secretary of State for India; 7:00-7:30, return to Kingsley Hall for prayer and evening meal; 8:00-9:10, conference of temperance workers; 9:10-9:45, in transit; 9:45-12:00, conference with Nawah of Bhopal; 12:30 A.M., return to Kingsley Hall.

FRIENDS HAVE BEEN remonstrating with him against staying at this place [Kingsley Hall] so distant from the palaces and hotels. English friends have been forthcoming ready to offer their houses in the neighborhood of St. James' Palace, but Gandhiji is clear that he must not leave the home of the humble folk which has become his real home. He may have an office where he can receive and meet friends—and some Indian friends have placed their houses at his disposal for the purpose—but he cannot afford to miss the friends in the East End who meet him and bid him good morning when he is out for a walk, nor can he miss the little ones who surround him and have an occasional chat. In fact, a special meeting with these people was a thing he most enjoyed. He felt as though he was in the midst of the children of the Ashram, answering their simple but penetrating and puzzling inquiries and spreading through them his message of truth and love. "What is your language, Mr. Gandhi?" they ask, and Gandhiji takes them through the etymology of common words in English and Indian vernaculars and shows them that we are after all children of the same Father. He tells them stories of his childhood and explains how it is better by far not to hit back than to return a blow for a blow. He tells them why he wears the sort of clothes he wears and he also tells them why he lives amongst them. . . .

The child who has given Gandhiji the pet name of "Uncle Gandhi" is a boy of three in the Children's House attached to Kingsley Hall. Ever since the children saw Gandhiji, he has been in their days and their dreams. "Now, tell me, mummy, what does Gandhi eat, and why does he not wear shoes?" and so on and so forth. One day the mother said: "No, look here, you mustn't say 'Gandhi,' but 'Mr. Gandhi.' You know Mr. Gandhi is a very good man." "I am sorry, mummy," says the little tot making amends, "I will call him 'Uncle Gandhi.' " . . . So the name caught on, and on his birthday the little children sent to "Dear Uncle Gandhi" birthday presents in the shape of a toy dog and sweets, and wished "you had a birthday cake with icing and a bird on it. Please will you come here on your birthday and we will have a band and play music about 'daisy' and 'away in a manger' and light candles?"

Bernard Shaw had long been wanting to see Gandhiji, and it was not without considerable hesitation that he came. He sat with Gandhiji for close on an hour, interrogating him on a bewildering variety of topics—ethnographical, religious, social, political, and economic—and his talk was illumined by his sparkling wit and sardonic humor. "I knew something about you and felt something in you of a kindred spirit. We belong to a very small community on earth," said he. Whilst his other questions were of universal importance, he could not help asking a question about the Round Table Conference. "Does not the Round Table Conference try your patience?" he asked, and Gandhiji had to confess with sorrow: "It requires more than the patience of a Job. The whole thing is a huge camouflage and the harangues that we are treated to are meant only to mark time. Why not, I ask them, make a clean breast and announce your policy and let us make our choice? But it does not seem to be in the English political nature to do so. It must go by round about and tortuous ways!"

[Louis Fischer writes this account of their meeting: "George Bernard Shaw also paid his respects. With unusual modesty he gave the palm to Gandhi and called himself 'Mahatma Minor.' 'You and I,' he said, 'belong to a very small community on earth.' They touched on a score of subjects and Shaw's humor immensely amused 'Mahatma Major,' but it cannot be said that Gandhi liked the playwright's love of the word that shocks. Neither had Tolstoy." •

[Shaw was driven from his interview with Gandhi by the Indian journalist, T. A. Raman. When he asked Shaw for his impressions, the playwright said, "Why, that is not a man, that is a PHENOMENON. You must really give me some time to recover from the shock." ••]

Some will say the reception at Buckingham Palace was an important event. Well, with all respect to Their Majesties, I cannot say so. Do these receptions mean anything? Do Their Majesties meet people in the real sense of the term? Do they transact any business? Can they? Or is it not more or less like a pantomime show? And yet, some will say, Gandhiji went there. Why did he? If it were so meaningless, why did he not abstain from it? Shall

• Reprinted with permission from Louis Fischer, *The Life of Mahatma Gandhi* (New York: Harper, 1950), p. 282.
•• Reprinted with permission from T. A. Raman, *What Does Gandhi Want?* (London: Oxford, 1942), p. 83.

I try to give the readers an inkling of his state of mind? He described it at the Friends' meeting: "I am here," he said, "in an embarrassing position. I have come as the guest of this nation and not as the elected representative of my own nation. I must, therefore, walk warily and I cannot tell you how warily I am walking. Do you think I relished the Prime Minister's minatory speech in the Minorities Committee? I would have repudiated it there and then, but I sat mum. I came home and wrote a letter of gentle reproach. And now, this week I am faced with a moral problem. I have an invitation to attend His Majesty's reception. I am feeling so heart-sick and sore over the happenings in India that I have no heart in attending such functions, and if I had come in my own right I should not have hesitated to come to a decision. But, as I am a guest, I am hesitating; I can do nothing hastily. I have every moment to consider the morality of the thing and not the legality." And, it is the morality of the thing that decided him to go, and when he did so, he wrote a courteous letter to the Lord Chamberlain thanking him for the invitation and intimating to him that he and his companion (who had also been invited) would attend the reception in their usual dress. He usually excuses himself from all social functions, but he had to make an exception in favor of this as in some others, as he would do nothing which would be regarded in the nature of a discourtesy. He would not refrain from doing anything that might be turned against him.

[When asked once if he was sufficiently dressed for his talk with the King, Gandhi replied, "The King had enough on for both of us." •]

When we were going to Eton one of the first questions that Gandhi had asked was whether Eton was not the school where Jawaharlal [Nehru] was educated. "It was at Harrow," I said, "and not Eton," and I am not exaggerating, if I say, that part of Gandhiji's interest in the Eton visit was lost because of that knowledge. The reader will now understand why Gandhiji was

• Reprinted with permission from H. S. L. Polak, H. N. Brailsford, and Lord Pethick-Lawrence, *Mahatma Gandhi* (London: Odhams, 1949), p. 191.

looking forward to a visit to Cambridge. It is the Cambridge of Jawaharlal and Charlie Andrews, and when the latter took him out for his morning walk, Gandhiji insisted on being taken through the vast quadrangle of Trinity College where Jawaharlal' was educated. . . .

88 KNIGHTSBRIDGE, LONDON
• by Agatha Harrison

Agatha Harrison, an English Friend, was a member of the small group of interpreters of Gandhi in England which included the Henry Polaks and Horace Alexander. It became formalized as the India Conciliation Group, with Carl Heath as chairman and Miss Harrison as secretary. Miss Harrison met C. F. Andrews at the time of the Round Table Conference and they became close friends until his death in 1940. As an authority on women in industry, especially in the Orient, she visited India several times. Her description of Gandhi's "office" in London during the Round Table Conference is especially memorable.

. . . Mr. GANDHI was prevailed upon to have a *pied à terre* nearer to St. James's Palace, and 88 Knightsbridge was taken.

I do not think Mr. Gandhi was ever really happy about this arrangement. He would acknowledge its convenience, but the cost of it all was an ever-present anxiety. For you cannot be in Knightsbridge without paying its price, and this price represented to Mr. Gandhi food for starving people in India. The only time the two devoted friends, C. F. Andrews and Mr. Gandhi, had a difference of opinion in these days was over this house. Mr. An-

• Reprinted with permission from *The Christian Century*, Vol. 50, No. 1, January 4, 1933, pp. 15-17.

drews felt, naturally, that no expense should be spared to conserve the strength and time of his friend for the momentous work he was called on to do; Mr. Gandhi continued to worry about the money. He insisted on going back to Bow for his scanty hours of sleep, but at other times when the Conference was not in session, Mr. Gandhi was to be found at 88. . . .

It is almost impossible to describe our household. Perhaps the best way is to tell of some of the chief actors in that drama. First and foremost is the Mahatma.

Personally, I find it difficult to make a critical estimate of this man. For when you meet absolute honesty and directness of purpose in a tangled world, you are in the presence of something that silences criticism. I can see how difficult he makes the path of governments, for real sincerity and directness are embarrassing, and I sometimes wished he could make more allowance for this. He is the most disconcerting person to work with, but very human and lovable. How he can work in the midst of so much turmoil is amazing. He is rarely alone. The only time I saw him left by himself was after the famous session at the end of the Conference when the Prime Minister had announced the policy of the government (later incorporated in a White Paper) and Mr. Gandhi had given his serious answer foreshadowing what lay ahead. He came back to 88 immediately after, and sat by the fire spinning in silence. Watching him from the other end of the room, I was reminded of Atlas carrying an intolerable burden on frail shoulders.

The Mahatma does not believe in closed doors. The most important talks were carried on with a variety of men and women listening. Cables and letters could be seen lying about—he trusts people entirely. Just before Mr. Gandhi left for India he asked me if I would take on an impossible task—that of working as a free lance on "the mutual understanding" between our two countries. This conversation started with Mr. Gandhi, Horace Alexander and me, but soon a group of people was sitting around while arrangements, financial and otherwise, were carried on, and the

Mahatma questioned me closely on how I lived and at what cost! . . .

The picture would not be complete without mention of the two detectives attached by the government to guard the frail body of Mr. Gandhi. This particular pair are generally detailed to shadow royalty. Though accustomed to watch for the sinister side of life, their work now took a different turn. They grew to love "the little man" as they affectionately called him; he became their friend for whom they would do any service. They also lent a willing hand to the rest of us when we were extra busy.

Before Mr. Gandhi left London, when asked by a government official if there was anything more he could do for him, Mr. Gandhi requested that his two detectives might go with him as far as Brindisi. When asked why, the Mahatma replied, "Because they are part of my family." This request was granted, and they accompanied him across the continent. . . .

In the pockets of these men, going about their strange work, are the watches sent them from India with the inscription: "With love from M. K. Gandhi." What a tale these detectives could unfold if reminiscences of the doings of a criminal investigation officer were allowed to be written!

Out of all the memories that crowd these days, it is difficult to make a selection. Some stand out. The evening prayers when the room would be crowded with people eager to learn more about this man's way of life. The early mornings when Mr. Gandhi arrived, and you felt as though a torchlike "something" had come into the house. He would spring out of his car and be up in his room sitting by the fire spinning, in a flash. In every corner of the room were famous sculptors and artists trying to get a model or picture of this elusive man. Strewn around were letters and cables needing immediate attention; members of the Conference seated on the floor, anxious to get his opinion before the Conference session; men and women from all over the world waiting for a word from him; C. F. Andrews and Horace Alexander quietly working in the midst of it all; Mrs. Cheesman patiently waiting to take some important letter. And in the centre of all this the imperturbable Mahatma. Then finding it was time for the Conference, he would dart out to his car; followed by panting detectives and some of his staff clutching the famous spinning wheel and the green rush basket containing his food.

Another outstanding memory is the evening when Bishop Fisher [1] of America bridged the Atlantic by telephone from Chicago, begging the Mahatma to come to the States. Mr. Gandhi insisted on taking this call himself, though C. F. Andrews and I stood by in case he could not hear, as he so rarely uses the telephone. The press waited outside eager to catch what was said. But Mr. Gandhi soon ended this expensive conversation, for again his mind was worried about the cost, and what the money meant in terms of starving people.

There were amusing incidents. Mirabehn [2] for example, finding that someone had taken the special celery saved for Mr. Gandhi's lunch, and trying to find the culprit. They laughingly blamed C. F. Andrews for this.

Indescribable days, filled to the brim with hard work, vital interest and laughter, and a surge of people that came and went. I wish we had kept a visitors' book that there might be a record of the politicians, religious leaders, and men and women of every shade of opinion who crowded the passages of 88. Did our country realize the significance of this figure in its midst? . . .

APPEAL TO AMERICA
by M. K. Gandhi

On September 13, 1931, two days after Gandhi arrived in England, the Columbia Broadcasting System arranged for him to deliver a radio address to the American people. Gandhi did not write

• Reprinted with permission from Haridas T. Muzumdar, Gandhi Versus the Empire (New York: Universal Publishing Co., 1932), pp. 166-70.

out his speech in advance; his remarks were completely extemporaneous. He approached the microphone with curiosity and trepidation and asked, "Do I have to speak into that thing?" He was already on the air and these were the first words his listeners on the other side of the Atlantic heard. Three minutes before his time was to be up, a note was passed to him saying that his voice would be cut off in New York in three minutes. Unruffled, he began to bring his impromptu speech to a conclusion. After the engineer signaled for him to stop, he commented, "Well, that's over." These words, too, somehow were carried across the Atlantic. The American press reproduced great portions of this speech on the following day, although the British press largely ignored it.

IN MY OPINION, the Indian struggle [for freedom] bears in its consequences not only upon India [and England] but upon the whole world. It contains one-fifth of the human race. It represents one of the most ancient civilizations. It has traditions handed down from tens of thousands of years, some of which, to the astonishment of the world, remain intact. No doubt the ravages of time have affected the purity of that civilization as they have that of many other cultures and many institutions.

If India is to revive the glory of her ancient past, she can only do so when she attains her freedom. The reason for the struggle having drawn the attention of the world I know does not lie in the fact that we Indians are fighting for our liberty, but in the fact that the means adopted by us for attaining that liberty are unique and, as far as history shows us, have not been adopted by any other people of whom we have any record.

The means adopted are not violence, not bloodshed, not diplomacy as one understands it nowadays, but they are purely and simply truth and non-violence. No wonder that the attention of the world is directed toward this attempt to lead a successful bloodless revolution. Hitherto, nations have fought in the manner of the brute. They have wreaked vengeance upon those whom they have considered to be their enemies.

We find in searching national anthems adopted by great nations that they contain imprecations upon the so-called enemy. They have vowed destruction and have not hesitated to take the name of God and seek divine assistance for the destruction of the enemy. We in India have endeavored to reverse the process. We feel that the law that governs brute creation is not the law that should guide the human race. That law is inconsistent with human dignity.

I, personally, would wait, if need be, for ages rather than seek to attain the freedom of my country through bloody means. I feel in the innermost recesses of my heart, after a political experience extending over an unbroken period of close upon thirty-five years, that the world is sick unto death of blood-spilling. The world is seeking a way out, and I flatter myself with the belief that perhaps it will be the privilege of the ancient land of India to show the way out to the hungering world.

I have, therefore, no hesitation whatsoever in inviting all the great nations of the earth to give their hearty cooperation to India in her mighty struggle. It must be a sight worth contemplating and treasuring, that of millions of people giving themselves to suffering without retaliation in order that they might vindicate the dignity and honor of the nation.

I have called that suffering a process of self-purification. It is my certain conviction that no man loses his freedom except through his own weakness. I am painfully conscious of our own weaknesses. We represent in India all the principal religions of the earth, and it is a matter of deep humiliation to confess that we are a house divided against itself, that we Hindus and Mussalmans are flying at one another. It is a matter of still deeper humiliation to me that we Hindus regard several millions of our own kith and kin as too degraded even for our touch. I refer to the so-called "untouchables."

These are no small weaknesses in a nation struggling to be free. And hence you will find that in this struggle through self-purification we have assigned a foremost place to the removal of this curse of untouchability and the attainment of unity amongst all the different classes and communities of India representing the different creeds.

It is along the same lines that we seek to rid our land of the curse of drink. Happily for us, intoxicating drinks and drugs are confined to comparatively a very small number of people, largely factory hands and the like. Fortunately for us, the drink and drug curse is accepted as a curse. It is not considered to be the fashion for a man or a woman to drink or to take intoxicating drugs. All the same, it is an uphill fight that we are fighting in trying to remove this evil from our midst.

For it is a matter of regret, deep regret, for me to have to say that the existing government has made of this evil a source of very large revenue, amounting to nearly twenty-five crores of rupees [about $85,000,000]. But I am thankful to be able to say that the women of India have risen to the occasion in combatting it by peaceful means, that is, by fervent appeal to those who are given to the drink habit to give it up, and by an equally fervent appeal to the liquor dealers. A great impression has been created upon those who are addicted to these two evil habits.

I wish that it were possible for me to say that in this, at least, we were receiving the hearty cooperation of the rulers. If we could only have received that cooperation, [even] without any legislation, I dare say that we would have achieved this reform and banished intoxicating drink and drugs from our afflicted land.

There is a force which has a constructive effect and which has been put forth by the nation during this struggle. That is the great care for the semi-starved millions scattered throughout the 700,000 villages dotted over a surface of 1,900 miles long and 1,500 miles broad. It is a painful phenomenon that these simple villagers, through no fault of their own, have nearly six months in the year idleness upon their hands. The time was not very long ago when every village was self-sufficient in regard to the two primary human wants, food and clothing.

Unfortunately for us, the East India Company, by means which I would prefer not to describe, destroyed that supplementary village industry as well as the livelihood of millions of spinners who had become famous through the cunning of their deft fingers for drawing the finest thread, such as has never yet been drawn by any modern machinery. These village spinners found themselves one fine morning with their noble occupation gone. And from that day forward India has become progressively poor.

No matter what may be said to the contrary, it is a historical fact that before the advent of the East India Company, these villagers were not idle, and he who wants may see today that these villagers are idle. It, therefore, requires no great effort or learning to know that these villagers must starve if they cannot work for six months in the year.

May I not, then, on behalf of these semi-starved millions, appeal to the conscience of the world to come to the rescue of a people dying to regain its liberty?

EXCURSION TO LANCASHIRE

by Mahadev Desai

When C. F. Andrews was making preparations for Gandhi's visit to England, he wrote Gandhi that he must "meet Lancashire face to face as I myself am just going to do." Lancashire, a textile area, was in the midst of a great depression, partly because of the Indian boycott on foreign cloth. After Andrews visited Lancashire and saw the distress due to widespread unemployment, he pleaded with Gandhi to call off the boycott. Gandhi refused to do so, but promised Andrews that he would visit the Lancashire workers when he arrived in the British Isles. Gandhi made good his promise and, despite the risks involved, took the journey to Lancashire

• Reprinted with permission from C. Rajagopalachari and J. C. Kumarappa, editors, The Nation's Voice (Ahmedabad: Navajivan, 1932), pp. 207-11, 213.

IN SOME of the manufacturing areas of Lancashire the manufacturers have concentrated on cotton fabrics exclusively for export to India. "We were prepared for courtesy, which we expect from all gentlemen, we were even prepared for a little bitterness which distress and misunderstanding often create; but we found instead a warmth of affection for which we were not prepared. I shall treasure the memory of these days to the end of my earthly existence." In these words Gandhiji summed up his gratefulness for having been given the opportunity of meeting the Lancashire employers and working people. The warmth of reception could only be equalled by what Gandhiji has been familiar with in the towns and villages of India. There were no public meetings, but what was better was a heart-to-heart chat with various groups of employers and employed who placed before Gandhiji all the facts in their possession, and even at the risk of having to repeat the same reply in substance, Gandhiji met all groups and declined to interview none.

After having given all of them a patient hearing, it was no happiness to Gandhiji to tell them that he could bring them very little comfort. They had come with great expectations perhaps, but Gandhiji had, with great sorrow, to make it clear to them that he was called to undertake a task to which he and his country were unequal. "My nationalism is not so narrow that I should not feel for your distress or gloat over it. I do not want my country's happiness at the sacrifice of any other country's happiness. But whilst I see that you are hard hit, I am afraid, your distress is not largely due to India. Conditions have been bad for some years and the boycott came only as the last straw." He said at Springvale Garden Village: "There is not boycott of British cloth, as distinguished from other foreign cloth, since the 5th March when the truce was signed. As a nation we are pledged to boycott all foreign cloth, but in case of an honorable settlement between England and India, i.e., in case of a permanent peace, I should not hesitate to give preference to Lancashire cloth to all other foreign cloth, to the extent that we may need to supplement our cloth and on agreed terms. But how much relief that can give you, I do not know. You must recognize that all the markets of the world are now not open to you. What you have done, all other nations are doing today. Even Indian mills would be producing more and more cloth every day. You, surely, will not want me to restrict Indian enterprise for the sake of Lancashire."

"I am pained," he said, "at the unemployment here. But here is no starvation or semi-starvation. In India we have both. If you went to the villages of India, you would find utter despair in the eyes of the villagers, you would find half-starved skeletons, living corpses. If India could revive them by putting life and food into them in the shape of work, India would help the world. Today India is a curse. There is a party in my country which would sooner see an end to the lives of these half-starved millions in order that the rest may live. I thought of a humane method and that was to give them work with which they were familiar, which they could do in their cottages, which required no great invest-ment in implements and of which the product could be easily sold. This is a task which is worthy of the attention even of Lancashire."

"But look at these mills which were busy hives only the other day lying absolutely idle. In Blackburn, Darwen, Great Harwood and Accrington over a hundred mills have had to close down. In the Great Harwood area nothing less than 17,436 looms are idle. We took special training at College in weaving Indian textiles, we are weaving dhotis [3] exclusively for India, and why should we not make them today and bring about better relations between India and England?" said some of the employers.

"We helped India during the famine of 1897–99. We collected money for the poor and sent it to them. We have always stood for a liberal policy. Why should the boycott be directed against us?" said some of the working people. Some of them placed their individual grievances before Gandhiji. The most pathetic of them all was the following; "I am a cotton operative. I have been a weaver for 40 years and now I am without work. It is not want or distress that worries me. My estimate of myself is gone. I have fallen in my own estimate inasmuch as I am a recipient of unemployment dole. I do not think I am going to finish my life with any self-respect."

At Hayes Farm, which is a rest house in Yorkshire for the employers, and the prosperous among the employees who might care to spend a week-end there, several deputations of unemployed people waited upon Gandhiji with very nearly the same tale and the brethren in the rest house had a special service where they prayed for the will of God to prevail. It was impossible for Gandhiji to disguise his feelings. "I would be untrue to you, I would be a false friend, if I were not frank with you," said Gandhiji and poured out his heart before them for three quarters of an hour—describing how economics and ethics and politics were in his life inextricably mixed up, how he had raised the banner of truth above everything else, how he had refrained from wedding himself to the results, how he was led to place the spinning wheel before the country and how the world conditions had driven them to the present state of things. "I strove with Lord Irwin last March for the liberty to boycott liquor and foreign cloth. He suggested that I might give up this boycott for three months as a gesture and then resume it. I said I could not give it up for three minutes. You have three million unemployed, but we have nearly 300 million unemployed and underemployed for half the year. Your average unemployment dole is 70 shillings. Our average income is seven shillings and six pence a month. That operative was right in saying that he was falling in his own estimation. I do believe it is a debasing thing for a human being to remain idle and to live on doles. Whilst conducting a strike I could not brook the strikers remaining idle for a single day and got them to break stones or carry sand and work in public streets asking my own co-workers to join them in that work. Imagine, therefore, what a calamity it must be to have 300 million unemployed, several millions becoming degraded every day for want of employment, devoid of self-respect, devoid of faith in God. I dare not take before them that message of God. I may as well place before the dog over there the message of God as before those hungry millions who have no lustre in their eyes and whose only God is their bread. I can take before them a message of God only by taking the sacred message of work before them. It is good enough to talk of God whilst we are sitting here after a nice breakfast and looking forward to a nicer luncheon, but how am I to talk of God to the millions who have to go without two meals a day? To them God can only appear as bread and butter. Well, the peasants of India were getting their bread from their soil. I offered them the spinning wheel in order that they may get the butter, and if I appear today before the British public in my loin-cloth, it is because I have come as the sole representative of those half-starved, half-naked, dumb millions. . . ."

. . . The unemployed working men who saw Gandhiji were in no bitter mood. On the contrary, they asked questions about the agricultural conditions in India, why the agriculturist had no work for six months in the year, why the standard of living was so poor and so on and so forth. The question with them, as they frankly put it, was not of starvation but lowered standard of living; where they could spend a shilling they have to be satisfied with six pence, and whilst many of them can save nothing at all, many had to live on their savings. The rate of their present dole is 17/— male, 15/— female (9/— for wife if not a worker) and 2/— for each child per week. "This," said Gandhiji, "is a fortune, and for you, a resourceful race, it should not be difficult to hit upon other industries and occupations. For my starving crores, I have no other occupation. If some of you experts can find it, I am prepared to substitute it for the spinning wheel. In the meanwhile, I can hold out to you no more hope than this, that an independent India, as an equal partner of Great Britain, will give preference to Lancashire cloth, which India needs and which Lancashire alone can produce, over all foreign cloth."

Poor comfort this, but as they left I found no bitterness in them. One of them said: "Something good cannot but come out of this. And, if nothing good, no evil can come out, and good-will certainly is the immediate result. We understand each other now. It is a privilege to have seen Mr. Gandhi, a mighty force thrown up by the awakening East." Another said: "I am one of the unemployed, but if I was in India, I would say the same thing that Mr. Gandhi is saying."

TO THE PLENARY SESSION
by M. K. Gandhi

At the second Round Table Conference Gandhi was one of 112 delegates, of whom 20 represented the British government, 22 the Indian States (ruled by princes under British suzerainty), and 65 British India (provinces under direct British rule). The central issue was the Congress Party's demand for complete independence, which the British were unwilling to concede. No less difficult was the communal question, i.e., the demands of various Indian minorities—Moslems, untouchables, etc.—for special protection of their rights, which led to disagreement among the Indian delegates. Gandhi was representing the Congress, which claimed to speak for all Indians regardless of religion or caste, and he refused to countenance measures which he felt would intensify communal dissension. There were several conference committees and Gandhi spoke before those on federal structure and on minorities. During a plenary session chaired by Prime Minister J. Ramsay MacDonald, Gandhi made a historic speech which summed up his attitude, after listening to many weeks of debate, on British rule and Indian independence.

I DO NOT THINK that anything that I can say this evening can possibly influence the decision of the Cabinet. Probably the decision

• Reprinted with permission from C. Rajagopalachari and J. C. Kumarappa, editors, The Nation's Voice (Ahmedabad: Navajivan, 1932), pp. 74-8 (abridged).

has been already taken. Matters of the liberty of practically a whole Continent can hardly be decided by mere argumentation, or even negotiation. Negotiation has its purpose and has its play, but only under certain conditions. Without those conditions negotiations are a fruitless task. But I do not want to go into all these matters. I want as far as possible to confine myself within the four corners of the conditions that you, Prime Minister, read to this Conference at its opening meeting. . . .

Although you have invited the Congress, you distrust the Congress. Although you have invited the Congress, you reject its claim to represent the whole of India. Of course it is possible at this end of the world to dispute that claim, and it is not possible for me to prove this claim; but, all the same, if you find me asserting that claim, I do so because a tremendous responsibility rests upon my shoulders.

The Congress represents the spirit of rebellion. I know that the word "rebellion" must not be whispered at a Conference which has been summoned in order to arrive at an agreed solution of India's troubles through negotiation. Speaker after speaker has got up and said that India should achieve her liberty through negotiation, by argument, and that it will be the greatest glory of Great Britain if Great Britain yields to India's demands by argument. But the Congress does not hold quite that view. The Congress has an alternative which is unpleasant to you.

I heard several speakers—I have tried to follow every speaker with utmost attention and with all the respect that I could possibly give to these speakers—saying what a dire calamity it would be if India was fired with the spirit of lawlessness, rebellion, terrorism and so on. I do not pretend to have read history, but as a schoolboy I had to pass a paper in history also, and I read that the page of history is soiled red with the blood of those who have fought for freedom. I do not know an instance in which nations have attained their own without having to go through an incredible measure of travail. The dagger of the assassin, the poison bowl, the bullet of the rifleman, the spear and all these weapons and methods of destruction have been up to now used by, what

I consider, blind lovers of liberty and freedom. And the historian has not condemned them. I hold no brief for the terrorists. . . . For the sake of liberty people have fought, people have lost their lives, people have killed and have sought death at the hands of those whom they have sought to oust.

The Congress then comes upon the scene and devises a new method not known to history, namely, that of civil disobedience, and the Congress has been following up that method. But again, I am up against a stone wall and I am told that is a method that no Government in the world will tolerate. Well, of course, the Government may not tolerate, no Government has tolerated open rebellion. No Government may tolerate civil disobedience, but Governments have to succumb even to these forces, as the British Government has done before now, even as the great Dutch Government after eight years of trial had to yield to the logic of facts. General Smuts is a brave General, a great statesman, and a very hard taskmaster also, but he himself recoiled with horror from even the contemplation of doing to death innocent men and women who were merely fighting for the preservation of their self-respect. Things which he had vowed he would never yield in the year 1908, reinforced as he was by General Botha, he had to do in the year 1914, after having tried these civil resisters through and through. And in India, Lord Chelmsford had to do the same thing; the Governor of Bombay had to do the same thing in Borsad and Bardoli. I suggest to you, Prime Minister, it is too late today to resist this, and it is this thing which weighs me down, this choice that lies before them, the parting of the ways probably. I shall hope against hope, I shall strain every nerve to achieve an honorable settlement for my country, if I can do so without having to put the millions of my countrymen and countrywomen, and even children, through this ordeal of fire. It can be a matter of no joy and comfort to me to lead them again to a fight of that character, but, if a further ordeal of fire has to be our lot, I shall approach that with the greatest joy and with the greatest consolation that I was doing what I felt to be right, the country was doing what it felt to be right, and the country will have the additional satisfaction of knowing that it was not at least taking lives, it was giving lives: it was not making the British people directly suffer, it was suffering. Professor Gilbert Murray told me—I shall never forget that, I am paraphrasing his inimitable language—"Do you not consider for one moment that we Englishmen do not suffer when thousands of your countrymen suffer, that we are so heartless?" I do not think so. I do know that you will suffer; but I want you to suffer because I want to touch your hearts; and when your hearts have been touched then will come the psychological moment for negotiation. . . .

Whilst there is yet a little sand left in the glass, I want you to understand what this Congress stands for. My life is at your disposal. The lives of all the members of the Working Committee, the All-India Congress Committee, are at your disposal. But remember that you have at your disposal the lives of all these dumb millions. I do not want to sacrifice those lives if I can possibly help it. Therefore, please remember, that I will count no sacrifice too great if, by chance, I can pull through an honorable settlement. You will find me always having the greatest spirit of compromise if I can but fire you with the spirit that is working in the Congress, namely, that India must have real liberty. Call it by any name you like; a rose will smell as sweet by any other name, but it must be the rose of liberty that I want and not the artificial product. If your mind and the Congress mind, the mind of this Conference and the mind of the British people, means the same thing by the same word, then you will find the amplest room for compromise, and you will find the Congress itself always in a compromising spirit. But so long as there is not that one mind, that one definition, not one implication for the same word that you and I and we may be using, there is no compromise possible. . . .

. . . It is for friendship I crave. My business is not to throw overboard the slave-holder and tyrant. My philosophy forbids me to do so, and today the Congress has accepted that philosophy, not as a creed, as it is to me, but as a policy, because the Congress believes that is the right and the best thing for India, a nation of 350 millions, to do. . . .

But what is it that that nation does? To summarily, or at all, dismiss Englishmen? No. Its mission is today to convert Englishmen. I do not want to break the bond between England and India, but I do want to transform that bond. I want to transform that slavery into complete freedom for my country. Call it complete independence or whatever you like. I will not quarrel about that word, and even though my countrymen may dispute with me for having taken some other word, I shall be able to bear down that opposition so long as the content of the word that you may suggest to me bears the same meaning. Hence, I have times without number to urge upon your attention that the safeguards [4] that have been suggested are completely unsatisfactory. They are not in the interests of India.

. . . I will not be baffled. I shall be here as long as I am required because I do not want to revive civil disobedience. I want to turn the truce that was arrived at in Delhi into a permanent settlement. But for heaven's sake give me, a frail man 62 years gone, a little bit of a chance. Find a little corner for him and the organization that he represents. You distrust that organization though you may seemingly trust me. Not for one moment differentiate me from the organization of which I am but a drop in the ocean. I am no greater than the organization to which I belong. I am infinitely smaller than that organization; and if you find me a place, if you trust me, I invite you to trust the Congress also. Your trust in me otherwise is a broken reed. I have no authority save what I derive from the Congress. If you will work the Congress for all it is worth, then you will say goodbye to terrorism, then you will not need terrorism. Today you have to fight the school of terrorists which is there with your disciplined and organized terrorism, because you will be blind to the facts or the writing on the wall. Will you not see the writing that these terrorists are writing with their blood? Will you not see that we do not want bread made of wheat, but we want the bread of liberty; and without that liberty there are thousands today who are sworn not to give themselves peace or to give the country peace.

I urge you then to read that writing on the wall. I ask you not to try the patience of a people known to be proverbially patient. We speak of the mild Hindu, and the Musalman also by contact good or evil with the Hindu has himself become mild. And that mention of the Musalman brings me to the baffling problem of minorities. Believe me, that problem exists here, and I repeat what I used to say in India—I have not forgotten those words—that without the problem of minorities being solved there is no Swaraj for India, there is no freedom for India. I know and I realize it; and yet I came here in the hope "perchance" that I might be able to pull through a solution here. But I do not despair of some day or other finding a real and living solution in connection with the minorities problem. I repeat what I have said elsewhere that so long as the wedge in the shape of foreign rule divides community from community and class from class, there will be no real living solution, there will be no living friendship between these communities.

It will be after all and at best a paper solution. But immediately you withdraw that wedge, the domestic ties, the domestic affections, the knowledge of common birth—do you suppose that all these will count for nothing?

Were Hindus and Musalmans and Sikhs always at war with one another when there was no British rule, when there was no English face seen there? We have chapter and verse given to us by Hindu historians and by Musalman historians to say that we were living in comparative peace even then. And Hindus and Musalmans in the villages are not even today quarreling. In those days they were not known to quarrel at all. The late Maulana Muhammad Ali often used to tell me, and he was himself a bit of an historian. He said: "If God"—"Allah" as he called God— "gives me life, I propose to write the history of Musalman rule in India; and then I will show, through documents that British people have preserved, that Aurangzeb [5] was not so vile as he has been painted by the British historian; that the Mogul rule was not so bad as it has been shown to us in British history; and so on." And so have Hindu historians written. This quarrel is not old; this quarrel is coeval with this acute shame. I dare to say, it is coeval with the British advent, and immediately this relationship, the unfortunate, artificial, unnatural relationship between Great Britain and India is transformed into a natural relationship, when it becomes, if it does become, a voluntary partnership to be given up, to be dissolved at the will of either party, when it becomes that, you will find that Hindus, Musalmans, Sikhs, Europeans, Anglo-Indians, Christians, Untouchables, will all live together as one man.

. . . Last of all, my last is a pleasant task for me. This is perhaps the last time that I shall be sitting with you at negotiations. It is not that I want that. I want to sit at the same table with you in your closets and to negotiate and to plead with you and to go down on bended knees before I take the final leap and final plunge.

But whether I have the good fortune to continue to tender my cooperation or not does not depend upon me. It largely depends upon you. But it may not even depend upon you. It depends upon so many circumstances over which neither you nor we may have any control whatsoever. Then, let me perform this pleasant task of giving my thanks to all from Their Majesties down to the poorest men in the East End where I have taken up my habitation.

In that settlement, which represents the poor people of the East End of London, I have become one of them. They have accepted me as a member, and as a favored member of their family. It will be one of the richest treasures that I shall carry with me. Here, too, I have found nothing but courtesy and nothing but a genuine affection from all with whom I have come in touch. I have come in touch with so many Englishmen. It has been a priceless privilege to me. They have listened to what must have often appeared to them to be unpleasant, although it was true. Although I have often been obliged to say these things to them they have never shown the slightest impatience or irritation. It is impossible for me to forget these things. No matter what befalls me, no matter what the fortunes may be of this Round Table Conference, one thing I shall certainly carry with me, that is, that from high to low I have found nothing but the utmost courtesy and the utmost affection. I consider that it was well worth my paying this visit to England in order to find this human affection.

It has enhanced, it has deepened my irrepressible faith in human nature that although Englishmen and Englishwomen have been fed upon lies that I see so often disfiguring your press, that although in Lancashire, the Lancashire people had perhaps some reason for becoming irritated against me, I found no irritation and no resentment even in the operatives. The operatives, men and women, hugged me. They treated me as one of their own. I shall never forget that.

I am carrying with me thousands upon thousands of English friendships. I do not know them but I read that affection in their eyes as early in the morning I walk through your streets. All this hospitality, all this kindness will never be effaced from my memory, no matter what befalls my unhappy land. I thank you for your forbearance.

PART THREE 1932-1948

12
THE EPIC FAST
(1932)

GANDHI FASTS IN PRISON
by Pyarelal (Nayyar)

Gandhi returned to India from the Round Table Conference on December 28, 1931. He told a huge gathering in Bombay that "I have come back empty-handed, but I have not compromised the honor of my country." The British, intent on preventing any further civil disobedience, arrested Nehru and other Congress leaders two days before Gandhi landed. On January 4 Gandhi was arrested under a century-old regulation which provided for no trial and no fixed term of imprisonment. Once again he was confined in Yeravda prison. More than 30,000 political prisoners were incarcerated during January and February.

The new constitution proposed for India by the British specified separate elections for Hindus, Moslems, and other groups. The untouchables would vote in the Hindu elections but would also vote separately for their own representatives. Dr. B. R. Ambedkar, their leader, had advocated such a provision because he feared that otherwise his people would be swamped by the caste Hindus and would have no redress against oppression. Orthodox Hindu groups opposed separate voting for untouchables. Gandhi also op-

• Reprinted with permission from Pyarelal (Nayyar), The Epic Fast (Ahmedabad: M. M. Bhatt, 1932), pp. 40-41, 42-47, 48-49, 49-50.

posed it, but for very different reasons: he was against anything
that tended to perpetuate the line between untouchables and the
rest of the Hindu community. Accordingly, although still in
prison, he announced that he would fast "unto death" against
separate untouchable electorates.

THE FATEFUL TWENTIETH of September arrived at last. He [Gandhi]
rose early in the small hours of the morning as usual and had his
favorite "Vaishnava Jana" sung at the morning prayer, with its
haunting refrain: "He alone is the true Vaishnava, Who knows
and feels for another's woe." He had his usual meal of milk and
fruit in the morning. From 6:30 to 8:00 A.M. he had the Gita recited to him by one of his companions. At 11:30 A.M. he had his
last meal of lemon juice and honey with hot water. The fateful
hour approached. The little group prepared themselves for the ordeal by singing a beautiful song sent to Gandhiji by Shrimati
Raihanaben, the eldest daughter of Sjt. Abbas Tyabji, the Grand
Old Man of Gujarat: "O Traveller, arise, it is dawn; where is the
night that thou still sleepest?" The jail bell at last struck twelve
and with its last stroke was finally sealed a decision as fixed as the
Pole Star and as irrevocable as fate. Gandhiji's "tussle with God"
had commenced. . . .

Great anxiety was felt when Gandhiji commenced his fast
whether he would be able to stand the physical strain of it for any
length of time. For one thing, he was not the same man as he was
when he undertook his 21 days' fast at Delhi in 1924. He was
eight years older now, which means a great deal to one who is already over sixty. Moreover, it was one thing to fast at "Dilkash,"
near the Ridge, a free man, under the loving custodianship of a
Charlie Andrews and the expert care of doctors like Ansari, Jivraj
Mehta and Abdurehman, who knew his constitution and personal
habits intimately, and quite another thing to fast in a segregated
special yard in the Yeravda Prison under the surveillance of the
jail authorities, who perhaps knew how to deal with a recalcitrant
prisoner refusing to take food, but certainly had no experience of
long fasts or of fasting men of Gandhiji's type. In fairness to them

it must be admitted that so far as personal solicitude for Gandhiji was concerned they, from the very highest, left nothing to be desired. But they were handicapped by the red-tapism of jail regulations, and not even the best will in the world could take the place of specialized experience. For instance, one is amazed to learn, to mention only one instance, that till the second day of his fast Gandhiji had to walk to the office, every time that a visitor wanted to see him, instead of the visitors being taken to his bedside, and he had to move the Inspector General of Prisons in order to get the necessary change in the arrangements made.

On the morning of the 21st he was removed to a special, segregated yard. There, under the thick shade of a low mango tree, on a white iron cot on which was spread a jail mattress and a jail bedsheet, he remained for the greater part of the day. His two companions, Sardar Vallabhbhai Patel and Sjt. Mahadev Desai, were there with him. Around the cot were placed a number of chairs for visitors. Near the cot, on one side, was a stool on which was to be found a rum collection of odds and ends, books, papers, writing material, bottles of water, soda-bicarb and salt. From time to time, he would pour out some water from one of the bottles, in which he would dissolve soda and salt and sip it slowly according to need and inclination. Mrs. Naidu had been specially brought there from the female prison. When the present writer visited Gandhiji on the afternoon of the 21st, she had already constituted herself his bodyguard. She mothered him throughout the fast and stood sentry over him from morning till evening, exercising a mother's and nurse's prescriptive right to "tyrannize" over her ward and the entire household.

Gandhiji was as buoyant and cheerful as ever, and outwardly hardly betrayed any signs of a man who is racing against time and is being rushed with every second towards the abyss of the beyond. But to a close observer it did not take long to discover how fully conscious he was of the grim reality facing him. During his Delhi fast, for instance, one could not help being struck by the way in which he economized his strength. He had reduced it to a science. But now he simply did not mind. It was a limited fast then. He knew the period that he had to pull through. The present fast was going to be a "fast unto death." If he survived it, it would not be so much because of the efficacy of the medical measures that might be adopted but because God willed it. It was predominantly a spiritual wrestle in which the physical factor played only a secondary part. Although the jail authorities had allowed him to have his own nurses, one could notice that he was extremely reluctant to avail himself of their services. What mattered a few more pangs or less of physical suffering to a man who was thirsting only for the grace abounding of the Almighty, and who in any case would soon be beyond all pain? Nor could Gandhiji forget even for a moment that he was still a prisoner and that whatever facilities he was allowed were by way of a privilege. And everybody who has come in close touch with Gandhiji knows how disinclined temperamentally he is to avail himself of any special privileges of this kind. The whole of the 21st, he walked from his bed to the bathroom, every time that he had to visit it. He continued this till the afternoon of the 22nd, even though he had to take the support of his nurses. At his bath he declined to take any assistance. It was only on the 22nd, when his strength had altogether fizzled out that he resigned himself to those nursing aids with a sigh. During his Delhi fast, he used to take water with scientific precision, hourly. On the present occasion, he did it only in a haphazard way. The physical exertion as also the strain caused by speaking, induced nausea at an early stage. As the fast proceeded and the body tissue burnt away, his whole frame was racked by excruciating aches—those terrible aches which at Delhi had to be alleviated by frequent massage and shampoo and a variety of other means. But this time he was indifferent about massaging. It was only towards the close, after Mrs. Gandhi's arrival, that he agreed to have it at all, more for her than for his own satisfaction. Later on a special masseur was sent by some friends to give him the massage. This had, as it always has, a very soothing effect.

Warning signals were not, however, lacking to remind all concerned that there was a limit beyond which flesh and blood could not go. The physical exhaustion grew with every hour that passed. The voice grew feebler. Only when now and then in the course of animated discussions, his eyes shone and the face lit up that one felt the presence of an indomitable will that had remained unaffected in spite of the ravages on the body. From the 22nd onwards, he had to be removed from one place to another on a stretcher to conserve his energy.

On the 24th, Dr. Gilder [1] and Dr. Patel of Bombay after examining Gandhiji in consultation with the jail doctors opined that the margin of safety would soon be passed if unnecessary interviews and the strain of negotiations that were being carried on with him were not stopped. The blood pressure stood alarmingly high. The general condition showed distinct signs of an impending downward plunge. The report added that once the margin of safety was passed, even if the fast was broken his life would still be in danger.

An anxious consultation was held among those around Gandhiji and the jail authorities. It was impressed upon the jail authorities that Gandhiji needed constant nursing in the night time, that during his Delhi fast he had to be helped every time that he wanted even to turn his side. The Government had already intimated to Gandhiji on the 22nd that he could have his own doctors by him if he liked. But while thanking the Government for the offer, he had replied that he had full faith in the jail medical staff. They naturally felt greatly concerned. At last, it was decided, among other things, that two of his close associates should stay with him during the night time as well. This arrangement continued till the 29th evening, when all the old restrictions were reimposed upon him.

On the 26th the prognosis became alarming and Gandhiji had to be given injections of soda-bicarb dissolved in water by enema twice under the instructions of the doctors in charge. The Poet [2] had arrived from Calcutta that day. Gandhiji, who never misses an opportunity of hearing the Poet sing some of his own songs and on whom music has always a very soothing effect when he is experiencing physical suffering, suggested to Col. Doyle [3] that he should be allowed to have some music as music to him was a medical necessity. This permission was accorded to him. Again, on the evening of the 27th and the 28th, he had some of his favorite devotional hymns sung to him to the accompaniment of instrumental music by some friends who came specially from the city for the purpose.

But whilst on the physical side, Gandhiji's attitude towards the fast was characterized by utter resignation tempered with humility, on the spiritual side it was characterized by an intensity and vehemence of assault that was unprecedented.

The morning and evening prayer appointments were kept as punctiliously as ever, Gandhiji always sitting up in his bed for prayer, and the hum of the spinning wheel did not cease even for a single day during the fast. From early in the morning, as soon as the jail opened, an endless round of interviews, meetings with friends and visitors, and consultations with the members of the Conference that was deliberating outside, would commence and continue—with a brief lull at noon, when he would have bath and enema and steal a brief nap—till late in the night sometimes. To this was added the pressure of attending to his daily mail bag. Letters, telegrams, messages containing all sorts of suggestions, philosophical conundrums, and even personal requests came pouring in in increasing volume till they threatened to swamp Gandhiji's little secretariat in the Yeravda Prison. . . .

Thus it went on till the closing time for jail. At night, exhausted by the day's strain he would retire to sleep under the canopy of heaven, contemplating the various burning stars and constellations, an exercise which he extremely loves. But what his spirit was yearning to have a glimpse of from his bed of physical agony were not these outward astronomical signs but far, far beyond them the face of his Maker.

On the 22nd, Shrimati Kasturba Gandhi, whose sentence was due shortly to expire, was transferred from the Sabarmati Prison to Yeravda and permitted to attend on him. She was superb. Calm and collected as ever, she did not betray the slightest trace of agitation or grief. "Again, the same old story," she remarked as she greeted him with forced banter that could, however, hardly conceal what must have been to her a terrible ordeal of the soul. She promptly took charge of Gandhiji's little improvised nursing establishment. . . .

The 26th marked the culminating point in the inner spiritual struggle. That day, in response to a request by Mr. Laurence Houseman, the celebrated poet and dramatist, Gandhiji sent the following agonized message to be read at a special meeting in London on the 27th under the auspices of the Friends of India in celebration of his fast:

"My fast is an appeal not merely to Hindus and India in general but to British conscience, indeed, to the whole world. This distrust of and misrepresentation about a man who loves British people is an enigma to me. Since my deepest faith forbids resort to physical force, I am praying God to discover to me such final way to corporate suffering of an extreme kind and to give me strength to undergo it. When, if required, such time comes I know it will penetrate every British home. I had hoped that appeal from this fiery bed would somewhat wake up British public as it seems to have marvellously roused India. But God's will was perhaps otherwise. Wanting British sympathy and help I would value anything your meeting may do. I know I have the silent sympathy and prayer of thousands of British men and women."

A BOMBSHELL

by Jawaharlal Nehru

OUR PEACEFUL and monotonous routine in jail was suddenly upset in the middle of September 1932 by a bombshell. News

• Reprinted with permission from Jawaharlal Nehru, *Toward Freedom* (New York: John Day, 1941), pp. 236-38.

came that Gandhiji had decided to "fast unto death" in disapproval of the separate electorates given by Mr. Ramsay MacDonald's communal award to the depressed classes. What a capacity he had to give shocks to people! Suddenly all manner of ideas rushed into my head; all kinds of possibilities and contingencies rose up before me and upset my equilibrium completely. For two days I was in darkness with no light to show the way out, my heart sinking when I thought of some results of Gandhiji's action. The personal aspect was powerful enough, and I thought with anguish that I might not see him again. It was over a year ago that I had seen him last on board ship on the way to England. Was that going to be my last sight of him?

And then I felt annoyed with him for choosing a side issue for his final sacrifice. What would be the result on our freedom movement? Would not the larger issues fade into the background, for the time being at least? And, if he attained his immediate object and got a joint electorate for the depressed classes, would not that result in a reaction and a feeling that something had been achieved and nothing more need be done for a while? And was not his action a recognition, and in part an acceptance, of the communal award and the general scheme of things as sponsored by the Government? Was this consistent with non-cooperation and civil disobedience? After so much sacrifice and brave endeavor, was our movement to tail off into something insignificant?

I felt angry with him at his religious and sentimental approach to a political question, and his frequent references to God in connection with it. He even seemed to suggest that God had indicated the very date of the fast. What a terrible example to set!

If Bapu died! What would India be like then? And how would her politics run? There seemed to be a dreary and dismal future ahead, and despair seized my heart when I thought of it.

So I thought and thought, while confusion reigned in my head, with anger and hopelessness, and love for him who was the cause of this upheaval. I hardly knew what to do, and I was irritable and short-tempered with everybody, most of all with myself.

And then a strange thing happened to me. I had quite an emotional crisis, and at the end of it I felt calmer, and the future seemed not so dark. Bapu had a curious knack of doing the right thing at the psychological moment, and it might be that his action —impossible to justify as it was from my point of view—would lead to great results, not only in the narrow field in which it was confined, but in the wider aspects of our national struggle. And, even if Bapu died, our struggle for freedom would go on. So whatever happened, one had to keep ready and fit for it. Having made up my mind to face even Gandhiji's death without flinching, I felt calm and collected and ready to face the world and all it might offer.

Then came news of the tremendous upheaval all over the country, a magic wave of enthusiasm running through Hindu society, and untouchability appeared to be doomed. What a magician, I thought, was this little man sitting in Yeravda Prison, and how well he knew how to pull the strings that move people's hearts!

A telegram from him reached me. It was the first message I had received from him since my conviction, and it did me good to hear from him after that long interval. In this telegram he said: "During all these days of agony you have been before mind's eye. I am most anxious to know your opinion. You know how I value your opinion. Saw Indu [4] [and] Sarup's [5] children. Indu looked happy and in possession of more flesh. Doing very well. Wire reply. Love."

It was extraordinary, and yet it was characteristic of him, that in the agony of his fast and in the midst of his many preoccupations, he should refer to the visit of my daughter and my sister's children to him, and even mention that Indira had put on flesh! (My sister was also in prison then and all these children were at school in Poona.) He never forgets the seemingly little things in life which really mean so much.

News also came to me just then that some settlement had been reached over the electorate issue. The superintendent of the jail was good enough to allow me to send an answer to Gandhiji, and I sent him the following telegram: "Your telegram and brief news that some settlement reached filled me with relief and joy. First news of your decision to fast caused mental agony and confusion, but ultimately optimism triumphed and I regained peace of mind. No sacrifice too great for suppressed downtrodden classes. Freedom must be judged by freedom of lowest but feel danger of other issues obscuring only goal. Am unable to judge from religious viewpoint. Danger your methods being exploited by others but how can I presume to advise a magician. Love."

THE FAST IS BROKEN
by Pyarelal (Nayyar)

While Gandhi was fasting in prison, Hindu and untouchable leaders were negotiating at Birla House in Bombay. Dr. B. R. Ambedkar, the untouchable leader, called the fast "a political stunt" and demanded "my compensation" for compromises. After several bedside conferences with Gandhi, Ambedkar and the Hindu leaders, with Gandhi's assent, finally agreed on a complex formula which would eliminate a separate electorate. This was called the Yeravda Pact.

Gandhi would not end his fast until the British Government agreed to the pact. The text was cabled to London where Gandhi's friends, especially C. F. Andrews and Henry Polak, urged Prime Minister MacDonald to accept it. When the British Government cabled its acceptance, Gandhi broke his fast, which had lasted thirteen days.

THE WHOLE of the 26th was passed in anxiety and waiting in Yeravda. The Poet, who had made a hurried dash to Poona from Calcutta, visited Gandhiji at noon. The meeting was a most touching one. Without a word, he approached Gandhiji's prostrate form

• Reprinted with permission from Pyarelal (Nayyar), *The Epic Fast* (Ahmedabad: M. M. Bhatt, 1932), pp. 77-81.

and burying his face in the clothes on Gandhiji's breast, remained in that position for several minutes overcome with feeling. He had heard the news that the Cabinet had accepted the Agreement. "I have come floating on the tide of good news. I am so glad that I have come and that I have come in time," he said to Gandhiji as he recovered his voice. Then they talked intimately of several things. The Poet told Gandhiji that so far as the social side of the question of untouchability was concerned he could always be depended upon to do his bit to relieve Gandhiji's burden. He then left his bedside as the strain of conversation was proving too much for Gandhiji.

Simultaneous statements were issued in England and in India on the morning of the 26th, announcing the acceptance by the Cabinet of the Yeravda Agreement. . . . The breaking of the fast had to be postponed till Gandhiji could fully satisfy himself by studying the actual text of the Government Communique that it fulfilled the letter and spirit of his vow. At 4:15 P.M., Col. Doyle, the Inspector General of Prisons, came with the long awaited document which he personally handed over to Gandhiji. With his characteristic sense of delicacy he then left Gandhiji to enable him, as he put it, "to study and discuss the document in quiet." Sjt. C. Rajagopalachari, Sjt. Vallabhbhai Patel, Sjt. Shankerlal Banker, Pandit Hridayanath Kunzru, and a number of other friends were present. . . .

In the face of their unanimous opinion Gandhiji gave in. Calling Col. Doyle to him he said, "I have decided to break my fast. I had my misgivings, but in the face of the unanimous opinion of these friends, I do not want to take upon me the responsibility of prolonging it. But before I break my fast I want to make one thing clear. If after I break my fast all the old restrictions are reimposed on me, it will interrupt the work of reform that has been begun. I would, therefore, expect all facilities necessary for the carrying on of my untouchability work to continue, if I am to remain here." "I am not a plenipotentiary," replied Col. Doyle, "I have no power to commit myself or the Government to anything, but I shall convey your point of view in the matter to the Government tonight. And I would now like you to break your fast soon." "One thing more," he added as he warmly shook Gandhiji by the hand, "the fruit juice must be handed to you by Mrs. Gandhi." He then left him. An impressive ceremony, the like of which has perhaps never been witnessed in the history of any jail, was held at 5:15 P.M. in the Yeravda Prison. The yard was freshly sprinkled over with water, Gandhiji lay on his cot surrounded by the Poet, Shrimati Sarojini Naidu, Shrimati Vasanti Devi, Shrimati Swarup Rani Nehru,[6] Shrimati Urmila Devi, Sjt. Ambalal Sarabhai [7] and his family, Gandhiji's two companions, Sardar Vallabhbhai Patel and Sjt. Mahadev Desai. Before him were assembled a number of inmates of the Sabarmati Ashram and others, in all about 200 persons. The Poet led the prayer by singing a Bengali hymn from Gitanjali.[8] This was followed by the reciting of some Sanskrit verses by Parchure Shastri, a fellow prisoner from the leper yard of the Yeravda Prison. Then was sung, all joining, Gandhiji's favorite hymn, "The Vaishnava Jana." When it was finished, Shrimati Kasturba handed him the orange juice and Gandhiji broke his fast. Simultaneously with it, fruit and sweets were distributed to all present. Huge baskets of fruit sent by known and unknown friends had kept pouring in the whole day, in anticipation of the breaking of the fast. . . . It was a day of jubilation and union of hearts in common thanksgiving to the Almighty God in that little world in the Yeravda Prison; the milk of human kindness asserted itself and for once the woodenness of jail discipline was forgotten.

At night Gandhi dictated a statement to the press reminding the people that the breaking of the fast carried with it a sure promise of its resumption if the reform was not relentlessly pursued and achieved within a measurable period. "I had thought," the statement ran, "of laying down a period, but I feel that I may not do so without a definite call from within. The message of freedom shall penetrate every 'untouchable' home and that can only happen if reformers will cover every village." He further expressed the hope that the almost ideal solution that had been reached on the question of the Depressed Class representation would pave the way for the larger unity between the various communities and mark the dawn of a new era of mutual trust, mutual give and take, and recognition of the fundamental unity of all communities. "I am the same to the Musalman today," he declared, "that I was in 1920–22. I should be just as prepared to lay down my life as I was in Delhi to achieve organic unity and permanent peace between them and the Hindus, and I hope and pray that there will be, as a result of this upheaval, a spontaneous move in this direction, and then, surely, the other communities can no longer stand out." Proceeding, he thanked the Government and the jail staff and the medical men who had looked after him during the fast and re-iterated his assurance to the Harijans that he was wedded to the pact as a whole. . . .

WAS THE MAHATMA'S TORMENT UNNECESSARY?

by Louis Fischer

WAS the Mahatma's torment unnecessary? The answer to this question is crucial to an understanding of Gandhi's role in India's history. By the criterion of cold logic and arid legalisms, Gandhi need not have fasted to reach an agreement with Ambedkar. But Gandhi's relationship with the Indian people was not based on logic and legalism. It was a highly emotional relationship. For the Hindus, Gandhi was Mahatma, The Great Soul, a slice of God. Were they going to kill him? The moment the fast began, texts, constitutions, awards, elections, etc., lost their significance. Gandhi's life had to be saved.

From September 13th, when the fast was announced, to the

• Reprinted with permission from Louis Fischer, *The Life of Mahatma Gandhi* (New York: Harper, 1950), pp. 318-21.

afternoon of September 26th, when Gandhi drank his first orange juice, every change in Gandhi's physical condition, every word pronounced by anyone who had seen him, every journey of the least of the negotiators was broadcast to every corner of the country. A mother hovering over the crib of a tender child during a high-temperature crisis could be no more anxious than the India that watched the white cot of the sinking Mahatma. No mystic himself, Gandhi affected others mystically. They became one with him, as one as mother and babe. Reason withdrew; passionately, frantically, because the end might have come at any instant, Hindus were reacting to a single throbbing wish: The Mahatma must not die.

Gandhi had made each Hindu personally responsible for his life. On September 15th, in a statement widely disseminated, Gandhi said, "No patched-up agreement between Caste Hindus and rival Depressed Class leaders will answer the purpose. The agreement to be valid has to be real. If the Hindu mind is not yet prepared to banish untouchability root and branch it must sacrifice me without the slightest hesitation."

While the negotiators parleyed, therefore, the Hindu community—close to a quarter of a billion persons—experienced a religious-emotional upheaval. At the very beginning of the fast week, the famous Kalighat Temple of Calcutta and the Ram Mandir of Benares, citadel of Hindu orthodoxy, were thrown open to untouchables. In Delhi, Caste Hindus and Harijans demonstratively fraternized in streets and temples. In Bombay, a nationalist women's organization organized a poll in front of seven big temples. Ballot boxes, watched by volunteers, were placed outside the gates, and worshipers were asked to cast their votes on the admission of untouchables. The tally was 24,797 for, 445 against. As a result, temples in which no Harijan foot had ever trod were opened to all.

The day before the fast started, twelve temples in Allahabad were made accessible to Harijans for the first time; on the first day of the fast, some of the most sacred temples throughout the country opened their doors to untouchables. Every subsequent day, until September 26th, and then every day from the 27th to October 2nd, Gandhi's birthday, which was Anti-Untouchability Week, scores of holy places lowered the bars against Harijans. All temples in the native states of Baroda, Kashmir, Bhor, and Kolhapur canceled temple discrimination. The newspapers printed the names of the hundreds of temples that lifted the ban under the impact of Gandhi's fast.

Mrs. Swarup Rani Nehru, Jawaharlal's very orthodox mother, let it be known that she had accepted food from the hand of an untouchable. Thousands of prominent Hindu women followed her example. At the strictly Hindu Benares University, Principal Dhruva, with numerous Brahmans, dined publicly with street cleaners, cobblers, and scavengers. Similar meals were arranged in hundreds of other places.

In villages, small towns, and big cities, congregations, organizations, citizens' unions, etc., adopted resolutions promising to stop discriminating against untouchables; copies of these resolutions formed a man-high heap in Gandhi's prison yard.

Villages and small towns allowed untouchables to use water wells. Hindu pupils shared benches formerly reserved for untouchables. Roads and streets, from which they were previously excluded, were opened to Harijans.

A spirit of reform, penance, and self-purification swept the land. During the six fast days, most Hindus refrained from going to cinemas, theaters, or restaurants. Weddings were postponed.

A cold political agreement between Gandhi and Ambedkar, without a fast, would have had no such effect on the nation; it might have redressed a legal Harijan grievance, but it would have remained a dead letter as far as the Hindu's personal treatment of untouchables was concerned. Most Hindus would never have heard of it. The political pact was important only after the emotional churning which Gandhi's fast gave the country.

The fast could not kill the curse of untouchability which was more than three thousand years old. Access to a temple is not access to a good job. The Harijan remained the dregs of Indian society. Nor did segregation end when Gandhi slowly drank his orange juice.

But after the fast, untouchability forfeited its public approval; the belief in it was destroyed. A practice deeply embedded in a complicated religion full of mystic overtones and undercurrents was recognized as morally illegitimate. A taboo hallowed by custom, tradition, and ritual lost its potency. It had been socially improper to consort with Harijans; in many circles now it became socially improper not to consort with them. To practice untouchability branded one a bigot, a reactionary. Before long, marriages were taking place between Harijans and Hindus; Gandhi made a point of attending some.

Gandhi's "Epic Fast" snapped a long chain that stretched back into antiquity and had enslaved tens of millions. Some links of the chain remained. Many wounds from the chain remained. But nobody would forge new links, nobody would link the links together again. The future promised freedom.

The Yeravda Pact said, "No one shall be regarded as untouchable by reason of his birth. . . ." Orthodox Hindus, with large religious followings, signed that statement. It marked a religious reformation, a psychological revolution. Hinduism was purging itself of a millennial sickness. The mass purified itself in practice. It was good for India's moral health. The perpetuation of untouchability would have poisoned India's soul just as the retention of its economic remnants must hamper India's progress.

If Gandhi had done nothing else in his life but shatter the structure of untouchability he would have been a great social reformer. In retrospect, the wrestling with Ambedkar over seats, primaries, and referendums seems like that year's melted snow on the Himalayas. The real reform was religious and social, not political.

13 PERSONAL, NATIONAL, AND WORLD PROBLEMS

HEALTH AND DIET
by M. K. Gandhi

Gandhi's experiments with truth were not confined to the political and social sphere. Most of his life he experimented with problems of diet and other aspects of health, and his writings are full of the minutest prescriptions on health matters. One of the most interesting and frankest sequences in his writings occurs toward the end of his Autobiography, when he tells of a serious sickness and how he recovered.

IN THOSE DAYS my food principally consisted of groundnut [peanut] butter and lemons. I knew that it was possible to eat too much butter and injure one's health, and yet I allowed myself to do so. This gave me a slight attack of dysentery. I did not take serious notice of this, and went that evening to the Ashram, as was my wont every now and then. I scarcely took any medicine in those days. I thought I should get well if I skipped a meal, and indeed I felt fairly free from trouble as I omitted the morning meal next day. I knew, however, that to be entirely free I must prolong my fast and, if I ate anything at all, I should have nothing but fruit juices.

• Reprinted with permission from *Gandhi's Autobiography* (Washington: Public Affairs Press, 1948), pp. 551-54, 556-58.

297

There was some festival that day, and although I had told Kasturbai that I should have nothing for my midday meal, she tempted me and I succumbed. As I was under a vow of taking no milk or milk products, she had specially prepared for me a sweet wheaten porridge with oil added to it instead of ghee. She had reserved too a bowlful of mung [1] for me. I was fond of these things, and I readily took them, hoping that without coming to grief I should eat just enough to please Kasturbai and to satisfy my palate. But the devil had been only waiting for an opportunity. Instead of eating very little I had my fill of the meal. This was sufficient invitation to the angel of death. Within an hour the dysentery appeared in acute form.

The same evening I had to go back to Nadiad.[2] I walked with very great difficulty to the Sabarmati station, a distance of only ten furlongs. Sjt. Vallabhbhai [Patel], who joined me at Ahmedabad, saw that I was unwell, but I did not allow him to guess how unbearable the pain was.

We reached Nadiad at about ten o'clock. The Hindu Anathashram [3] where we had our headquarters was only half a mile from the station; but it was as good as ten for me. I somehow managed to reach the quarters, but the griping pain was steadily increasing. Instead of using the usual latrine which was a long way off, I asked for a commode to be placed in the adjoining room. I was ashamed to have to ask for this, but there was no escape. Sjt. Fulchand immediately procured a commode. All the friends surrounded me deeply concerned. They were all love and attention, but they could not relieve my pain. And my obstinacy added to their helplessness. I refused all medical aid. I would take no medicine, but preferred to suffer the penalty for my folly. So they looked on in helpless dismay. I must have had thirty to forty motions in twenty-hour hours. I fasted, not taking even fruit juices in the beginning. The appetite had all gone. I had thought all along that I had an iron frame, but I found that my body had now become a lump of clay. It had lost all power of resistance. Dr. Kanuga came and pleaded with me to take medicine. I declined. He offered to give me an injection. I declined that too.

My ignorance about injections was in those days quite ridiculous. I believed that an injection must be some kind of serum. Later I discovered that the injection that the doctor suggested was a vegetable substance, but the discovery was too late to be of use. The motions still continued, leaving me completely exhausted. The exhaustion brought on a delirious fever. The friends got more nervous and called in more doctors. But what could they do with a patient who would not listen to them?

Sheth Ambalal with his good wife came down to Nadiad, conferred with my co-workers and removed me with the greatest care to his Mirzapur bungalow in Ahmedabad. It was impossible for anyone to receive more loving and selfless service than I had the privilege of having during this illness. But a sort of low fever persisted, wearing away my body from day to day. I felt that the illness was bound to be prolonged and possibly fatal. Surrounded as I was with all the love and attention that could be showered on me under Sheth Ambalal's roof, I began to get restless and urged him to remove me to the Ashram. He had to yield to my importunity. . . .

I had now been trying hydropathy which gave some relief, but it was a hard job to build up the body. The many medical advisers overwhelmed me with advice, but I could not persuade myself to take anything. Two or three suggested meat broth as a way out of the milk vow, and cited authorities from Ayurveda [4] in support of their advice. One of them strongly recommended eggs. But for all of them I had but one answer—no.

For me the question of diet was not one to be determined on the authority of the Shastras. It was one interwoven with my course of life which is guided by principles no longer depending upon outside authority. I had no desire to live at the cost of them. How could I relinquish a principle in respect of myself, when I had enforced it relentlessly in·respect of my wife, children and friends?

This protracted and first long illness in my life thus afforded me a unique opportunity to examine my principles and to test them. One night I gave myself up in despair. I felt that I was at death's door. I sent word to Anasuyabehn. She ran down to the Ashram. Vallabhbhai came up with Dr. Kanuga, who felt my pulse and said, "Your pulse is quite good. I see absolutely no danger. This is a nervous breakdown due to extreme weakness." But I was far from being reassured. I passed the night without sleep.

The morning broke without death coming. But I could not get rid of the feeling that the end was near, and so I began to devote all my waking hours to listening to the Gita being read to me by the inmates of the Ashram. I was incapable of reading. I was hardly inclined to talk. The slightest talk meant a strain on the brain. All interest in living had ceased, as I have never liked to live for the sake of living. It was such an agony to live on in that helpless state, doing nothing, receiving the service of friends and co-workers, and watching the body slowly wearing away. . . .

Friends and doctors assured me that I should recuperate quicker by a change to Matheran,[5] so I went there. But the water at Matheran being very hard, it made my stay there extremely difficult. As a result of the attack of the dysentery that I had, my anal tract had become extremely tender, and owing to fissures I felt an excruciating pain at the time of evacuation, so that the very idea of eating filled me with dread. Before the week was over, I had to flee from Matheran. Shankarlal Banker now constituted himself the guardian of my health, and pressed me to consult Dr. Dalal. Dr. Dalal was called accordingly. His capacity for taking instantaneous decisions captured me.

He said: "I cannot rebuild your body unless you take milk. If in addition you would take iron and arsenic injections I would guarantee fully to renovate your constitution."

"You can give me the injections," I replied, "but milk is a different question; I have a vow against it."

"What exactly is the nature of your vow?" the doctor inquired.

I told him the whole history and the reasons behind my vow, how, since I had come to know that the cow and the buffalo were subjected to the process of *phooka*,[6] I had conceived a strong disgust for milk. Moreover, I had always held that milk is not the natural diet of man. I had therefore abjured its use altogether.

Kasturbai was standing near my bed listening all the time to this conversation.

"But surely you cannot have any objection to goat's milk then," she interposed.

The doctor too took up the strain. "If you will take goat's milk, it will be enough for me," he said.

I succumbed. My intense eagerness to take up the Satyagraha fight had created in me a strong desire to live, and so I contented myself with adhering to the letter of my vow only, and sacrificed its spirit. For although I had only the milk of the cow and the she-buffalo in mind when I took the vow, by natural implication it covered the milk of all animals. . . . Yet knowing all this I agreed to take goat's milk. The will to live proved stronger than the devotion to truth, and for once the votary of truth compromised his sacred ideal by his eagerness to take up the Satyagraha fight. The memory of this action even now rankles in my breast and fills me with remorse, and I am constantly thinking how to give up goat's milk. But I cannot yet free myself from that subtlest of temptations, the desire to serve, which still holds me.

My experiments in dietetics are dear to me as a part of my researches in Ahimsa. They give me recreation and joy. But my use of goat's milk today troubles me not from the view-point of dietetic Ahimsa so much as from that of truth, being no less than a breach of pledge. It seems to me that I understand the ideal of truth better than that of Ahimsa, and my experience tells me that, if I let go my hold of truth, I shall never be able to solve the riddle of Ahimsa. The ideal of truth requires that vows taken should be fulfilled in the spirit as well as in the letter. In the present case I killed the spirit—the soul of my vow—by adhering to its outer form only, and that is what galls me. But in spite of this clear knowledge I cannot see my way straight before me. In other words, perhaps, I have not the courage to follow the straight course. Both at bottom mean one and the same thing, for doubt is invariably the result of want or weakness of faith. "Lord, give me faith" is, therefore, my prayer day and night.

BIRTH CONTROL
• by Mahadev Desai

For many years Gandhi was deeply concerned about problems of marriage, sex, and women. In 1906, at the age of thirty-seven, he himself took the vow of continence for life. Yet even Gandhi was tempted. In Harijan for December 26, 1936 the 67-year-old Gandhi frankly wrote: "My darkest hour was when I was in Bombay a few months ago. It was the hour of my temptation. Whilst I was asleep I suddenly felt as though I wanted to see a woman. Well a man who had tried to rise superior to the instinct for nearly forty years was bound to be intensely pained when he had this frightful experience. I ultimately conquered the feeling, but I was face to face with the blackest moment of my life and if I had succumbed to it, it would have meant my absolute undoing."

Of the many interviews and writings about the problems of marriage and sex, probably none present Gandhi's viewpoint more clearly to Westerners than his interview with Margaret Sanger, the leader of the planned parenthood (birth control) movement in America. As usual, Mahadev Desai was present during the interview. His account is abridged here.

MRS. MARGARET SANGER . . . appealed to Gandhiji as a great moral teacher "to advise something practical, something that can be applied to solve the problem of too frequent child-bearing," "to give some message for those who are not yet sure but who are anxious to limit their families." . . . Mrs. Sanger approached Gan-

• Reprinted with permission from Harijan, January 25, 1936. Also in M. K. Gandhi, Self-Restraint v. Self-Indulgence (Ahmedabad: Navajivan, 1947), pp. 201-209.

dhiji in Wardha for solution of a tough problem, because, as she herself said, "there were thousands, millions, who regard your word as that of a saint." . . . Gandhiji poured his whole being into his conversation. He revealed himself inside out, giving Mrs. Sanger an intimate glimpse of his own private life . . . and said that from *him* there could be one solution and one alone. "I could not recommend the remedy of birth control to a woman who wanted my approval. I should simply say to her: 'My remedy is of no use to you! You must go to others for advice.'" Mrs. Sanger cited some hard cases. "I agree," said Gandhiji, "there are hard cases. Else birth control enthusiasts would have no case. But I would say, do devise remedies by all means, but the remedies should be other than the ones you advise. If you and I as moral reformers put our foot down on this remedy and said, 'You must fall back on other remedies,' those would surely be found." Both seemed to be agreed that woman should be emancipated, that woman should be the arbiter of her destiny.

. . . This is what he said: "My wife I made the orbit of all women. In her I studied all women. I came in contact with many European women in South Africa, and I knew practically every Indian woman there. I worked with them. I tried to show them they were not slaves either to their husbands or parents, not only in the political field but in the domestic as well. But the trouble was that some could not resist their husbands. The remedy is in the hands of women themselves. The struggle is difficult for them, and I do not blame them. I blame the men. Men have legislated against them. Man has regarded woman as his tool. She has learned to be his tool and in the end found it easy and pleasurable to be such, because when one drags another in his fall the descent is easy. . . . I have felt that during the years still left to me, if I can drive home to women's minds the truth that they are free, we will have no birth control problem in India. If they will only learn to say 'no' to their husbands when they approach them carnally, I do not suppose all husbands are brutes, and if women only know how to resist them, all will be well. I have been able to teach women who have come in contact with me how to resist their husbands. The real problem is that many do not want to resist them. . . . No resistance bordering upon bitterness will be necessary in 99 out of 100 cases. If a wife says to her husband, 'No, I do not want it,' he will make no trouble. But she hasn't been taught. Her parents in most cases won't teach her. There are some cases, I know, in which parents have appealed to their daughters' husbands not to force motherhood on their daughters. And I have come across amenable husbands too. I want woman to learn the primary right of resistance. She thinks now that she has not got it." . . .

He told her that when she went to Calcutta she would be told by those who knew what havoc contraceptives had worked among unmarried young men and women. But evidently for the purpose of the conversation, at any rate, Mrs. Sanger confined herself to propagation of knowledge of birth control among married couples only. . . .

Mrs. Sanger was thus led on to her apotheosis of "sex love," which she said "is a relationship which makes for oneness, for completeness between husband and wife and contributes to a finer understanding and a greater spiritual harmony." . . .

Gandhiji: "When both want to satisfy animal passion without having to suffer the consequences of their act it is not love, it is lust. But if love is pure, it will transcend animal passion and will regulate itself. We have not had enough education of the passions. When a husband says, 'Let us not have children, but let us have relations,' what is that but animal passion? If they do not want to have more children, they should simply refuse to unite. Love becomes lust the moment you make it a means for the satisfaction of animal needs. It is just the same with food. If food is taken only for pleasure, it is lust. You do not take chocolates for the sake of satisfying your hunger. You take them for pleasure and then ask the doctor for an antidote. Perhaps you will tell the doctor that whisky befogs your brain and he gives you an antidote. Would it not be better not to take chocolates or whisky?"

Mrs. Sanger: "No, I do not accept the analogy."

Gandhiji: "Of course you will not accept the analogy because you think this sex expression without desire for children is a need of the soul, a contention I do not endorse."

Mrs. Sanger: "Yes, sex expression is a spiritual need and I claim that the quality of this expression is more important than the result, for the quality of the relationship is there regardless of results. We all know that the great majority of children are born as an accident, without the parents having any desire for conception. Seldom are two people drawn together in the sex act by their desire to have children. . . . Do you think it possible for two people who are in love, who are happy together, to regulate their sex act only once in two years, so that relationship would only take place when they wanted a child? Do you think it possible?"

Gandhiji: "I had the honor of doing that very thing and I am not the only one."

Mrs. Sanger thought it was illogical to contend that sex union for the purpose of having children would be love, and union for the satisfaction of the sexual appetite was lust, for the same act was involved in both. Gandhiji immediately capitulated and said he was ready to describe all sexual union as partaking of the nature of lust. He made the whole thing abundantly clear by citing facts from his own life. "I know," he said, "from my own experience that as long as I looked upon my wife carnally, we had no real understanding. Our love did not reach a high plane. There was affection between us always, but we came closer and closer the more we or rather I became restrained. There never was want of restraint on the part of my wife. Very often she would show restraint, but she rarely resisted me although she showed disinclination very often. All the time I wanted carnal pleasure I could not serve her. The moment I bade goodbye to a life of carnal pleasure our whole relationship became spiritual. Lust died and love reigned instead." . . .

"Must the sexual union take place only three or four times in an entire lifetime?" she asked.

"Why should people not be taught," replied Gandhiji, "that it is immoral to have more than three or four children and that after they have had that number they should sleep separately? If they

are taught this, it would harden into custom. And if social reformers cannot impress this idea upon the people, why not a law?
If husband and wife have four children, they would have had sufficient animal enjoyment. Their love may then be lifted to a higher
plane. Their bodies have met. After they have had the children
they wanted, their love transforms itself into a spiritual relationship. If these children die and they want more, then they may
meet again. Why must people be slaves of this passion when they
are not of others? When you give them education in birth control,
you tell them it is a duty. You say to them that if they do not do
this thing, they will interrupt their spiritual evolution. You do not
even talk of regulation. After giving them education in birth control you do not say to them 'thus far and no further.' You ask
people to drink temperately, as though it were possible to remain
temperate. I know these temperate people."

And yet as Mrs. Sanger was so dreadfully in earnest Gandhiji
did mention a remedy which could conceivably appeal to him.
That method was the avoidance of sexual union during unsafe
periods, confining it to the "safe" period of about ten days during the month. That had at least an element of self-control which
had to be exercised during the unsafe period. Whether this appealed to Mrs. Sanger or not I do not know.

MRS. SANGER'S VERSION

• by Margaret Sanger

HE SPOKE fluent English in a low voice with accurate intona-
tions, never lacking for a word, and could apparently discuss any
subject near or far. Nevertheless, I felt his registering of impres-

• Reprinted with permission from Margaret Sanger, An Autobiography (New
York: W. W. Norton, 1938), pp. 470-71.

sions was blunted; while you were answering a question of his, he held to an idea or a train of thought of his own, and, as soon as you stopped, continued it as though he had not heard you. Time and again I believed he was going along with me, and then came the stone wall of religion or emotion or experience, and I could not dynamite him over this obstacle. In fact, despite his claim to open-mindedness, he was proud of not altering his opinions.

Gandhi maintained that he knew women and was in sympathetic accord with them. Personally, after listening to him for a while, I did not believe he had the faintest glimmering of the inner workings of a woman's heart or mind. He accused himself of being a brute by having desired his wife when he was younger, and classed all sex relations as debasing acts, although sometimes necessary for procreation. He agreed that no more than three or four children should be born to a family, but insisted that intercourse, therefore, should be restricted for the entire married life of the couple to three or four occasions.

I suggested that such a regimen was bound to cause psychological disturbances in both husband and wife. Furthermore, when respect and consideration and reverence were a part of the relationship I called it love, not lust, even if it found expression in sex union, with or without children.

Gandhi referred me to nature, the great director, who would solve our problems if we depended upon her, but said what we were doing was to inject man's ideas into nature.

To this I replied, "How can you differentiate? Here is cotton growing on your land and lemons also. That's nature. Would you object to dipping cotton into lemon juice and using that as a contraceptive?"

He said positively that he would. For every argument I presented he countered with "I would devise other methods," but proposed none that was not based on continence. He reiterated that women in order to control the size of their families must "resist" their husbands, in extreme cases leave them.

Those who listened to the interview declared that the Mahatma made concessions he had never made before. He himself said to me, "This has not been wasted effort. We have certainly come nearer together." Nevertheless, I knew it was futile to count on Gandhi to help the movement in India; his state of mind would not change. After reading his autobiography, I thought I saw the cause of his inhibitions. He himself had had the feeling which he termed lust, and he now hated it. It formed an emotional pivot in his brain around which centered everything having to do with sex. But there remained his kindness, his hospitality, his arrangements for your comfort, which he duplicated again and again for visitors who gave nothing, but instead received inspiration from him. And, furthermore, since humanity as a rule does little for itself and the inert mass has to be upheaved to a point where it can gain initiative, anyone who can arouse a nation of all classes and ages out of the incredible lethargy into which it has long been sunk and can stir up a people to hope is a great, even noble, person.

NON-VIOLENCE AND THE AMERICAN NEGRO

by Mahadev Desai

Gandhi was concerned with the fate of colored peoples everywhere, including the United States. Because of his color and because of what he did to lessen racism in South Africa and India, Gandhi was especially revered by large sections of the Negro population and Negro press of America. Accordingly, American Negro leaders who visited India would especially seek out Gandhi for an

• Reprinted with permission from Harijan, March 20, 1937. Also in M. K. Gandhi, Non-Violence in Peace and War (Ahmedabad: Navajivan, 1942), Vol. I, pp. 147-53.

interview. In 1937 *Dr. Channing Tobias, director of the Phelps-Stokes Fund, and Dr. Benjamin Mays, president of Morehouse College, visited Gandhi and their interviews were recorded with the help of Mahadev Desai. Three years later, some of Gandhi's techniques were adapted to the problem of lessening racism in America by a small group of University of Chicago students. This effort has since grown in several American cities and is known as the Congress of Racial Equality—CORE.*

READERS OF *Harijan* will perhaps remember how the central topic of the members of the Negro delegation who saw Gandhiji about a year ago was non-violence. Two Negro gentlemen, who came for the recent world's meeting of the committees of the Y.M.C.A., also had the same question to discuss, which shows how remarkably similar are their problems to ours! I am going to take up Dr. Tobias' questions first, though he saw Gandhiji later and on his day of silence. For the long discourse with Prof. Mays was a kind of commentary on the brief replies given in writing to Dr. Tobias. . . .

"Your doctrine of non-violence has profoundly influenced my life," said Dr. Tobias. "Do you believe in it as strongly as ever?"

"I do indeed," said Gandhiji. "My faith in it is growing."

"Negroes in U.S.A.—12 million—are struggling to obtain such fundamental rights as freedom from mob-violence, unrestricted use of the ballot, freedom from segregation, etc. Have you, out of your struggle in India, a word of advice and encouragement to give us?"

"I had to contend against some such thing, though on a much smaller scale, in South Africa. The difficulties are not yet over. All I can say is that there is no other way than the way of non-violence—a way, however, not of the weak and ignorant but of the strong and wise."

"Travancore [7] indicates that your full identification with the untouchables is bearing fruit. Do you think Travancore's example will be followed by other States in the near future?"

"I shall be surprised if it is not."

"What word shall I give my Negro brethren as to the outlook for the future?"

"With right which is on their side and the choice of non-violence as their only weapon, if they will make it such, a bright future is assured."

Prof. Mays was lucky enough to find Gandhiji free in Sevagram to give him as much time as he wanted, and in the course of the talk with him Gandhiji disclosed the secret of the conviction of a lifetime.

As the talk proceeded, one felt as though Gandhiji was giving Dr. Mays what he had seen not with any of the known senses but with a "sixth" sense. I was put in mind of Rudolf Steiner [8] who is said to have developed a second sight. . . .

"Passive resistance," said Gandhiji, "is a misnomer for non-violent resistance. It is much more active than violent resistance. It is direct, ceaseless, but three-fourths invisible and only one-fourth visible. In its visibility it seems to be ineffective, e.g., the spinning wheel which I have called the symbol of non-violence. In its visibility it appears ineffective, but it is really intensely active and most effective in ultimate result. This knowledge enables me to detect flaws in the way in which the votaries of non-violence are doing their spinning. I ask for more vigilance and more un-tiredness. Non-violence is an intensely active force when properly understood and used. A violent man's activity is most visible, while it lasts. But it is always transitory. What can be more visible than the Abyssinians done to death by Italians? There it was lesser violence pitted against much greater. But if the Abyssinians had retired from the field and allowed themselves to be slaughtered, their seeming inactivity would have been much more effective though not for the moment visible. Hitler and Mussolini on the one hand and Stalin on the other are able to show the immediate effectiveness of violence. But it will be as transitory as that of Ghenghis' [9] slaughter. But the effects of Buddha's non-violent action persist and are likely to grow with age. And the more it is practiced, the more effective and inexhaustible it becomes, and ultimately the whole world stands agape and exclaims, 'a miracle has happened.' All miracles are due to the silent and effective working of invisible forces. Non-violence is the most invisible and the most effective."

"I have no doubt in my mind about the superiority of non-violence," said Prof. Mays. "But the thing that bothers me is about its exercise on a large scale, the difficulty of so disciplining the mass mind on the point of love. It is easier to discipline individuals. What should be the strategy when they break out? Do we retreat or do we go on?"

"I have had that experience," said Gandhiji, "in the course of our movement here. People do not gain the training by preaching. Non-violence cannot be preached. It has to be practiced. . . . In violence there is nothing invisible. Non-violence, on the other hand, is three-fourths invisible, and so the effect is in the inverse ratio to its invisibility. Non-violence, when it becomes active, travels with extraordinary velocity, and then it becomes a miracle. So the mass mind is affected first unconsciously, then consciously. When it becomes consciously affected there is demonstrable victory. In my own experience, when people seemed to be weakening there was no consciousness of defeat in me. Thus I was fuller of hope in the efficacy of non-violence after the renunciation of civil disobedience in 1922, and today I continue to be in the same hopeful mood. It is not a mere emotional thing. Supposing I saw no signs of dawn coming, I should not lose faith. Everything has to come in its proper time. . . .

"But now comes your poser. There are people, you say, who do not believe in non-violence as you do. Are you to sit quiet? The friends ask: 'If not now, when will you act?' I say in reply: 'I may not succeed in my lifetime, but my faith that victory can only come through non-violence is stronger than ever.' When I spoke on the cult of the spinning wheel at Faizpur, a newspaper correspondent imputed astuteness to me. Nothing could be farther from my mind. When I came to Sevagram I was told the people might not cooperate and might even boycott me. I said: 'That may be. But this is the way non-violence works.' If I go to a village which is still farther off, the experiment may work better.

This thing has come in my search after the technique of non-violence. And each day that passes makes my faith brighter. I have come here to bring that faith to fruition and to die in the process if that is God's will. Non-violence to be worth anything has to work in the face of hostile forces. But there may be action in inaction. And action may be worse than inaction."

"Is it ever possible to administer violence in a spirit of love?"

"No. Never. I shall give you an illustration from my own experiment. A calf was lame and had developed terrible sores; he could not eat and breathed with difficulty. After three days' argument with myself and my co-workers, I put an end to its life. Now that action was non-violent because it was wholly unselfish, inasmuch as the sole purpose was to achieve the calf's relief from pain. Some people have called this an act of violence. I have called it a surgical operation. I should do exactly the same thing with my child, if he were in the same predicament. My point is that non-violence as the supreme law of our being ceases to be such the moment you talk of exceptions."

"How is a minority to act against an overwhelming majority?" asked Prof. Mays.

"I would say that a minority can do much more in the way of non-violence than a majority. I had an English friend called Symonds. He used to say: 'I am with you so long as you are in a minority. After you are a majority we are quits.' I had less diffidence in handling my minority in South Africa than I had here in handling a majority. But it would be wholly wrong for that reason to say that non-violence is a weapon of the weak. The use of non-violence requires greater bravery than that of violence. When Daniel defied the laws of the Medes and Persians, his action was non-violent."

"Should the thought of consequences that might accrue to the enemy as a result of your non-violence at all constrain you?"

"Certainly. You may have to suspend your movement as I did in South Africa when the Government was faced with the revolt of European labor. The latter asked me to make common cause with them. I said 'no.'"

"And non-violence will never rebound on you, whereas violence will be self-destroyed?" interposed the professor.

"Yes. Violence must beget violence. But let me tell you that here too my argument has been countered by a great man who said: 'Look at the history of non-violence. Jesus dies on the cross, but his followers shed blood.' This proves nothing. We have no data before us to pass judgment. We do not know the whole of the life of Jesus. The followers perhaps had not imbibed fully the message of non-violence. But I must warn you against carrying the impression with you that mine is the final word on non-violence. I know my own limitations. I am but a humble seeker after truth. And all I claim is that every experiment of mine has deepened my faith in non-violence as the greatest force at the disposal of mankind. Its use is not restricted to individuals merely, but it can be practiced on a mass scale."

TWO NEGRO VISITORS

by Mahadev Desai

About a year earlier Dr. Howard Thurman, a well-known Negro minister and writer, together with his wife, paid a visit to Gandhi. Their talk throws some further light on Gandhi's views on the American race problem.

"Is NON-VIOLENCE from your point of view a form of direct action?" inquired Dr. Thurman.

"It is not one form, it is the only form," said Gandhiji. "I do not of course confine the words 'direct action' to their technical

• Reprinted with permission from *Harijan*, March 14, 1936. Also in M. K. Gandhi, *Non-Violence in Peace and War* (Ahmedabad: Navajivan, 1942), Vol. I, pp. 131-34.

meaning. But without a direct active expression of it, non-violence to my mind is meaningless. It is the greatest and the activist force in the world. One cannot be passively non-violent. In fact 'non-violence' is a term I had to coin in order to bring out the root meaning of Ahimsa. In spite of the negative particle 'non,' it is no negative force. Superficially we are surrounded in life by strife and bloodshed, life living upon life. But some great seer, who ages ago penetrated the centre of truth, said: It is not through strife and violence but through non-violence that man can fulfil his destiny and his duty to his fellow creatures. It is a force which is more positive than electricity, and more powerful than even ether. At the centre of non-violence is a force which is self-acting. Ahimsa means 'love' in the Pauline sense, and yet something more than the 'love' defined by St. Paul, although I know St. Paul's beautiful definition is good enough for all practical purposes. Ahimsa includes the whole creation, and not only human. Besides 'love' in the English language has other connotations, and so I was compelled to use the negative word. But it does not, as I have told you, express a negative force, but a force superior to all the forces put together. One person who can express Ahimsa in life exercises a force superior to all the forces of brutality."

Q. "And is it possible for any individual to achieve this?"

Gandhiji: "Certainly. If there was any exclusiveness about it, I should reject it at once."

Q. "Is any idea of possession foreign to it?"

Gandhiji: "Yes. It possesses nothing, therefore it possesses everything."

Q. "Is it possible for a single human being to resist the persistent invasion of the quality successfully?"

Gandhiji: "It is possible. Perhaps your question is more universal than you mean. Isn't it possible, you mean to ask, for one single Indian, for instance, to resist the exploitation of 300 million Indians? Or do you mean the onslaught of the whole world against a single individual personality?"

Dr. Thurman: "Yes, that is one-half of the question. I wanted to know if one man can hold the whole violence at bay."

Gandhiji: "If he cannot, you must take it that he is not a true representative of Ahimsa. Supposing I cannot produce a single instance in life of a man who truly converted his adversary, I would then say that it is because no one had yet been found to express Ahimsa in its fulness."

Q. "Then it overrides all other forces?"

Gandhiji: "Yes, it is the only true force in life."

"Forgive now the weakness of this question," said Dr. Thurman, who was absolutely absorbed in the discussion. "Forgive the weakness, but may I ask how are we to train individuals or communities in this difficult art?"

Gandhiji: "There is no royal road, except through living the creed in your life which must be a living sermon. Of course, the expression in one's own life presupposes great study, tremendous perseverance, and thorough cleansing of one's self of all the impurities. If for mastering of the physical sciences you have to devote a whole lifetime, how many lifetimes may be needed for mastering the greatest spiritual force that mankind has known? But why worry even if it means several lifetimes? For, if this is the only permanent thing in life, if this is the only thing that counts, then whatever effort you bestow on mastering it is well spent. Seek ye first the Kingdom of Heaven and everything else shall be added unto you. The Kingdom of Heaven is Ahimsa."

Mrs. Thurman had restrained herself until now. But she could not go away without asking the question with which, she knew, she would be confronted any day. "How am I to act, supposing my own brother was lynched before my very eyes?"

"There is such a thing as self-immolation," said Gandhiji. "Supposing I was a Negro, and my sister was ravished by a white or lynched by a whole community, what would be my duty?—I ask myself. And the answer comes to me: I must not wish ill to these, but neither must I cooperate with them. It may be that ordinarily I depend on the lynching community for my livelihood. I refuse to cooperate with them, refuse even to touch the food that comes from them, and I refuse to cooperate with even my brother Negroes who tolerate the wrong. That is the self-immolation I mean.

I have often in my life resorted to the plan. Of course a mechanical act of starvation will mean nothing. One's faith must remain undimmed whilst life ebbs out minute by minute. But I am a very poor specimen of the practice of non-violence, and my answer may not convince you. But I am striving very hard, and even if I do not succeed fully in this life, my faith will not diminish."

Mrs. Thurman is a soulful singer, and Dr. Thurman would not think of going away without leaving with us something to treasure in our memory. We sat enraptured as she gave us the two famous Negro spirituals—"Were you there, when they crucified my Lord" and "We are climbing Jacob's ladder"—which last suited the guests and hosts equally, as it gave expression to the deep-seated hope and aspiration in the breast of every oppressed community to climb higher and higher until the goal was won.

And now came the parting. "We want you to come to America," said the guests with an insistence, the depth of love behind which could be measured as Mrs. Thurman reinforced the request with these words: "We want you not for White America, but for the Negroes; we have many a problem that cries for solution, and we need you badly."

"How I wish I could," said Gandhiji. "But I would have nothing to give you unless I had given an ocular demonstration here of all that I have been saying. I must make good the message here before I bring it to you. I do not say that I am defeated, but I have still to perfect myself. You may be sure that the moment I feel the call within me I shall not hesitate."

Dr. Thurman explained that the Negroes were ready to receive the message. "Much of the peculiar background of our own life in America is our own interpretation of the Christian religion. When one goes through the pages of the hundreds of Negro spirituals, striking things are brought to my mind which remind me of all that you have told us today."

"Well," said Gandhiji, bidding good-bye to them, "if it comes true, it may be through the Negroes that the unadulterated message of non-violence will be delivered to the world."

ZIONISM AND ANTI-SEMITISM

by M. K. Gandhi

Gandhi had some close Jewish friends, especially in South Africa. There three of his closest Western co-workers were of Jewish ancestry: Henry S. L. Polak, Herman Kallenbach, and his secretary, Sonya Schlesin. Later, in 1939, Kallenbach paid a visit to Gandhi and lived with him at the Sevagram ashram. With the rise of Hitler and anti-Semitism in Germany, Gandhi felt compelled to denounce this aspect of racism, which he felt was akin to the kind of religious and racial discrimination he had fought all his life. He did not, however, regard Zionism as the right answer to the Jewish problem.

SEVERAL LETTERS have been received by me asking me to declare my views about the Arab-Jew question in Palestine and the persecution of the Jews in Germany. It is not without hesitation that I venture to offer my views on this very difficult question.

My sympathies are all with the Jews. I have known them intimately in South Africa. Some of them became lifelong companions. Through these friends I came to learn much of their age-long persecution. They have been the untouchables of Christianity. The parallel between their treatment by Christians and the treatment of untouchables by Hindus is very close. Religious sanction has been invoked in both cases for the justification of the inhuman treatment meted out to them. Apart from the friendships, therefore, there is the more common universal reason for my sympathy for the Jews.

• Reprinted with permission from *Harijan*, November 26, 1938. Also in M. K. Gandhi, *Non-Violence in Peace and War* (Ahmedabad: Navajivan, 1942), Vol. I, pp. 183-88.

But my sympathy does not blind me to the requirements of justice. The cry for the national home for the Jews does not make much appeal to me. The sanction for it is sought in the Bible and the tenacity with which the Jews have hankered after return to Palestine. Why should they not, like other peoples of the earth, make that country their home where they are born and where they earn their livelihood?

Palestine belongs to the Arabs in the same sense that England belongs to the English or France to the French. It is wrong and inhuman to impose the Jews on the Arabs. What is going on in Palestine today cannot be justified by any moral code of conduct. The mandates have no sanction but that of the last war. Surely it would be a crime against humanity to reduce the proud Arabs so that Palestine can be restored to the Jews partly or wholly as their national home.

The nobler course would be to insist on a just treatment of the Jews wherever they are born and bred. The Jews born in France are French in precisely the same sense that Christians born in France are French. If the Jews have no home but Palestine, will they relish the idea of being forced to leave the other parts of the world in which they are settled? Or do they want a double home where they can remain at will? This cry for the national home affords a colorable justification for the German expulsion of the Jews.

But the German persecution of the Jews seems to have no parallel in history. The tyrants of old never went so mad as Hitler seems to have gone. And he is doing it with religious zeal. For, he is propounding a new religion of exclusive and militant nationalism in the name of which any inhumanity becomes an act of humanity to be rewarded here and hereafter. The crime of an obviously mad but intrepid youth is being visited upon his whole race with unbelievable ferocity. If there ever could be a justifiable war in the name of and for humanity, a war against Germany, to prevent the wanton persecution of a whole race, would be completely justified. But I do not believe in any war. A discussion of the pros and cons of such a war is, therefore, outside my horizon or province.

But if there can be no war against Germany, even for such a crime as is being committed against the Jews, surely there can be no alliance with Germany. How can there be alliance between a nation which claims to stand for justice and democracy and one which is the declared enemy of both? Or is England drifting towards armed dictatorship and all it means?

Germany is showing to the world how efficiently violence can be worked when it is not hampered by any hypocrisy or weakness masquerading as humanitarianism. It is also showing how hideous, terrible and terrifying it looks in its nakedness.

Can the Jews resist this organized and shameless persecution? Is there a way to preserve their self-respect, and not to feel helpless, neglected and forlorn? I submit there is. No person who has faith in a living God need feel helpless or forlorn. Jehovah of the Jews is a God more personal than the God of the Christians, the Mussalmans or the Hindus, though as a matter of fact, in essence, He is common to all and one without a second and beyond description. But as the Jews attribute personality to God and believe that He rules every action of theirs, they ought not to feel helpless. If I were a Jew and were born in Germany and earned my livelihood there, I would claim Germany as my home even as the tallest gentile German might, and challenge him to shoot me or cast me in the dungeon; I would refuse to be expelled or to submit to discriminating treatment. And for doing this I should not wait for the fellow Jews to join me in civil resistance, but would have confidence that in the end the rest were bound to follow my example. If one Jew or all the Jews were to accept the prescription here offered, he or they cannot be worse off than now. And suffering voluntarily undergone will bring them an inner strength and joy which no number of resolutions of sympathy passed in the world outside Germany can. Indeed, even if Britain, France and America were to declare hostilities against Germany, they can bring no inner joy, no inner strength. The calculated violence of Hitler may even result in a general massacre of the Jews by way of his first answer to the declaration of such hostilities. But if the Jewish mind could be prepared for voluntary suffering, even the massacre

I have imaged could be turned into a day of thanksgiving and joy
that Jehovah had wrought deliverance of the race even at the hands
of the tyrant. For to the God-fearing, death has no terror. It is a
joyful sleep to be followed by a waking that would be all the more
refreshing for the long sleep.

It is hardly necessary for me to point out that it is easier for the
Jews than for the Czechs to follow my prescription. And they have
in the Indian Satyagraha campaign in South Africa an exact parallel. There the Indians occupied precisely the same place that the
Jews occupy in Germany. The persecutions had also a religious
tinge. President Kruger used to say that the white Christians were
the chosen of God and Indians were inferior beings created to
serve the whites. A fundamental clause in the Transvaal constitution was that there should be no equality between the whites and
colored races including Asiatics. There too the Indians were consigned to ghettos described as locations. The other disabilities were
almost of the same type as those of the Jews in Germany. The Indians, a mere handful, resorted to Satyagraha without any backing
from the world outside or the Indian Government. Indeed the
British officials tried to dissuade the satyagrahis from their contemplated step. World opinion and the Indian Government came to
their aid after eight years of fighting. And that too was by way of
diplomatic pressure, not of a threat of war.

But the Jews of Germany can offer Satyagraha under infinitely
better auspices than the Indians of South Africa. The Jews are a
compact, homogeneous community in Germany. They are far more
gifted than the Indians of South Africa. And they have organized
world opinion behind them. I am convinced that, if someone with
courage and vision can arise among them to lead them in non-violent action, the winter of their despair can in the twinkling of an
eye be turned into the summer of hope. And what has today become a degrading man-hunt can be turned into a calm and determined stand offered by unarmed men and women possessing the
strength of suffering given to them by Jehovah. It will be then a
truly religious resistance offered against the godless fury of a de-
humanized man. The German Jews will score a lasting victory over

the German gentiles in the sense that they will have converted the latter to an appreciation of human dignity. They will have rendered service to fellow-Germans and proved their title to be the real Germans as against those who are today dragging, however unknowingly, the German name into the mire.

And now a word to the Jews in Palestine. I have no doubt that they are going about in the wrong way. The Palestine of the Biblical conception is not a geographical tract. It is in their hearts. But if they must look to the Palestine of geography as their national home, it is wrong to enter it under the shadow of the British gun. A religious act cannot be performed with the aid of the bayonet or the bomb. They can settle in Palestine only by the goodwill of the Arabs. They should seek to convert the Arab heart. The same God rules the Arab heart who rules the Jewish heart. They can offer Satyagraha in front of the Arabs and offer themselves to be shot or thrown into the Dead Sea without raising a little finger against them. They will find the world opinion in their favor in their religious aspiration. There are hundreds of ways of reasoning with the Arabs, if they will only discard the help of the British bayonet. As it is, they are co-sharers with the British in despoiling a people who have done no wrong to them.

I am not defending the Arab excesses. I wish they had chosen the way of non-violence in resisting what they rightly regard as an unwarrantable encroachment upon their country. But according to the accepted canons of right and wrong, nothing can be said against the Arab resistance in the face of overwhelming odds.

Let the Jews who claim to be the chosen race prove their title by choosing the way of non-violence for vindicating their position on earth. Every country is their home including Palestine not by aggression but by loving service. A Jewish friend has sent me a book called *The Jewish Contribution to Civilization* by Cecil Roth. It gives a record of what the Jews have done to enrich the world's literature, art, music, drama, science, medicine, agriculture, etc. Given the will, the Jew can refuse to be treated as the outcaste of the West, to be despised or patronized. He can command the attention and respect of the world by being man, the chosen creation of God, instead of being man who is fast sinking to the brute and forsaken by God. They can add to their many contributions the surpassing contribution of non-violent action.

QUESTIONS ON THE JEWS
• by M. K. Gandhi

FRIENDS have sent me two newspaper cuttings criticizing my appeal to the Jews. The two critics suggest that in presenting non-violence to the Jews as a remedy against the wrong done to them I have suggested nothing new, and that they have been practicing non-violence for the past two thousand years. Obviously, so far as these critics are concerned, I did not make my meaning clear. The Jews, so far as I know, have never practiced non-violence as an article of faith or even as a deliberate policy. Indeed, it is a stigma against them that their ancestors crucified Jesus. Are they not supposed to believe in eye for an eye and tooth for a tooth? Have they no violence in their hearts for their oppressors? Do they not want the so-called democratic powers to punish Germany for her persecution and to deliver them from oppression? If they do, there is no non-violence in their hearts. Their non-violence, if it may be so called, is of the helpless and the weak.

What I have pleaded for is renunciation of violence of the heart and consequent active exercise of the force generated by the great renunciation. One of the critics says that favorable public opinion is necessary for the working of non-violence. The writer is evidently thinking of passive resistance conceived as a weapon of the weak. I have drawn a distinction between passive resistance of the

• Reprinted with permission from *Harijan*, December 17, 1938. Also in M. K. Gandhi, *Non-Violence in Peace and War* (Ahmedabad: Navajivan, 1942), Vol. I, pp. 191-93.

weak and active non-violent resistance of the strong. The latter can and does work in the teeth of the fiercest opposition. But it ends in evoking the widest public sympathy. Sufferings of the non-violent have been known to melt the stoniest hearts. I make bold to say that, if the Jews can summon to their aid the soul power that comes only from non-violence, Herr Hitler will bow before the courage which he has never yet experienced in any large measure in his dealings with men, and which, when it is exhibited, he will own is infinitely superior to that shown by his best storm troopers. The exhibition of such courage is only possible for those who have a living faith in the God of Truth and Non-violence, i.e., Love. . . .

REPLY TO JEWISH FRIENDS
• by M. K. Gandhi

I HAVE two letters from Jewish friends protesting against a remark of mine in a dialogue reported in *Harijan* over the Jewish question. Here is one of the letters:

"My attention has been called to a paragraph in *Harijan* of December 24th, 1938, in which you are reported to have said that 'The Jews called down upon the Germans the curses of mankind, and they wanted America and England to fight Germany on their behalf.' I can hardly doubt that you have been misreported, for there is nothing that could possibly justify such a statement. But as the paragraph much distressed me, I should be glad to receive from you a word of reassurance."

I am sorry to say that I cannot give the reassurance required. For I did make the remark put into my mouth by Shri Pyarelal.

• Reprinted with permission from *Harijan*, February 18, 1939. Also in M. K. Gandhi, *Non-Violence in Peace and War* (Ahmedabad: Navajivan, 1942), Vol. I, pp. 229-30.

Hardly a paper comes to me from the West which does not describe the agony of the Jews who demand retribution by the democratic powers for German atrocities. Nor do I see anything wrong in the attitude. The Jews are not angels. My point was that they were not non-violent in the sense meant by me. Their non-violence had and has no love in it. It is passive. They do not resist because they know that they cannot resist with any degree of success. In their place, unless there were active non-violence in me, I should certainly call down upon my persecutors the curses of Heaven. It is not contended by my correspondents that the German Jews do not want the big powers like England, America, and France to prevent the atrocities, if need be, even by war against Germany. I happen to have a Jewish friend [10] living with me. He has an intellectual belief in non-violence. But he says he cannot pray for Hitler. He is so full of anger over the German atrocities that he cannot speak of them with restraint. I do not quarrel with him over his anger. He wants to be non-violent, but the sufferings of fellow-Jews are too much for him to bear. What is true of him is true of thousands of Jews who have no thought even of "loving the enemy." With them, as with millions, "revenge is sweet, to forgive is divine."

JEWS AND PALESTINE

by M. K. Gandhi

HITHERTO I have refrained practically from saying anything public regarding the Jew-Arab controversy. I have done so for good reasons. That does not mean any want of interest in the question,

• Reprinted with permission from Harijan, July 21, 1946. Also in M. K. Gandhi, Non-Violence in Peace and War (Ahmedabad: Navajivan, 1949), Vol. II, pp. 122-23.

but it does mean that I do not consider myself sufficiently equipped with knowledge of the purpose. For the same reason I have tried to evade many world events. Without airing my views on them, I have enough irons in the fire. But four lines of a news-paper column [11] have done the trick and evoked a letter from a friend who has sent me a cutting which I would have missed but for the friend drawing my attention to it. It is true that I did say some such thing in the course of a long conversation with Mr. Louis Fischer [12] on the subject. I do believe that the Jews have been cruelly wronged by the world. "Ghetto" is, so far as I am aware, the name given to Jewish locations in many parts of Europe. But for their heartless persecution, probably no question of return to Palestine would ever have arisen. The world should have been their home, if only for the sake of their distinguished contribution to it.

But, in my opinion, they have erred grievously in seeking to impose themselves on Palestine with the aid of America and Britain and now with the aid of naked terrorism. Their citizenship of the world should have and would have made them honored guests of any country. Their thrift, their varied talent, their great industry should have made them welcome anywhere. It is a blot on the Christian world that they have been singled out, owing to a wrong reading of the New Testament, for prejudice against them. "If an individual Jew does a wrong, the whole Jewish world is to blame for it." If an individual Jew like Einstein makes a great discovery or another composes unsurpassable music, the merit goes to the authors and not to the community to which they belong.

No wonder that my sympathy goes out to the Jews in their unenviably sad plight. But one would have thought, adversity would teach them lessons of peace. Why should they depend upon American money or British arms for forcing themselves on an unwelcome land? Why should they resort to terrorism to make good their forcible landing in Palestine? If they were to adopt the matchless weapon of non-violence whose use their best prophets have taught and which Jesus the Jew who gladly wore the crown of thorns bequeathed to a groaning world, their case would be the world's, and I have no doubt that among the many things that the Jews have given to the world, this would be the best and the brightest. It is twice blessed. It will make them happy and rich in the true sense of the word and it will be a soothing balm to the aching world.

SOCIALISM AND COMMUNISM
• by Pyarelal (Nayyar)

Gandhi never visited Soviet Russia and never had close contact with organized Communism in India. While in detention in the Aga Khan Palace during World War II he finally read Karl Marx's Das Kapital and, according to Pyarelal, "went through some of the other writings of Marx as also of Engels, Lenin and Stalin [and] some books about the Reds in China." From time to time Gandhi answered specific questions about socialism and Communism. His discussion of the subject with the American writer, Louis Fischer, in July 1948 was fortunately recorded by Pyarelal.

"WHILST I HAVE the greatest admiration for the self-denial and spirit of sacrifice of our Socialist friends," said Gandhiji, "I have never concealed the sharp difference between their method and mine. They frankly believe in violence and all that is in its bosom. I believe in non-violence through and through."

That turned the discussion on to socialism. "You are a socialist and so are they," interpolated Fischer.

Gandhiji: "I am, they are not. I was a socialist before many of them were born. I carried conviction to a rabid socialist in Johan-

• Reprinted with permission from K. G. Mashruwala, *Gandhi and Marx* (Ahmedabad: Navajivan, 1951), pp. 109-10.

nesburg, but that is neither here nor there. My claim will live when their socialism is dead."

"What do you mean by your socialism?"

"My socialism means 'even unto this last.' I do not want to rise on the ashes of the blind, the deaf and the dumb. In their socialism, probably these have no place. Their one aim is material progress. For instance, America aims at having a car for every citizen. I do not. I want freedom for full expression of my personality. I must be free to build a staircase to Sirius if I want to. That does not mean that I want to do any such thing. Under the other socialism, there is no individual freedom. You own nothing, not even your body."

"Yes, but there are variations. My socialism in its modified form means that the State does not own everything. It does in Russia. There you certainly do not own your body even. You may be arrested at any time, though you may have committed no crime. They may send you wherever they like."

"Does not, under your socialism, the State own your children and educate them in any way it likes?"

"All States do that. America does it."

"Then America is not very different from Russia."

"You really object to dictatorship."

[Gandhi] "But socialism is dictatorship or else arm-chair philosophy. I call myself a Communist also."

"O, don't. It is terrible for you to call yourself a Communist. I want what you want, what Jaiprakash [13] and the Socialists want: a free world. But the Communists don't. They want a system which enslaves the body and the mind."

"Would you say that of Marx?"

"The Communists have corrupted the Marxist teaching to suit their purpose."

"What about Lenin?"

"Lenin started it. Stalin has since completed it. When the Communists come to you, they want to get into the Congress and control the Congress and use it for their own ends."

[Gandhi] "So do the Socialists. My communism is not very

different from socialism. It is a harmonious blending of the two. Communism, as I have understood it, is a natural corollary of socialism."

"Yes, you are right. There was a time when the two could not be distinguished. But today Socialists are very different from Communists."

"You mean to say, you do not want communism of Stalin's type."

"But the Indian Communists want communism of the Stalin type in India and want to use your name for that purpose."

"They won't succeed."

FORMULA FOR COMMUNISTS
by M. K. Gandhi

Q. How CAN WE COUNTERACT the activities of the Communists, who are openly opposing the Congress?

A. The Communists seem to have made trouble-shooting their profession. I have friends among them. Some of them are like sons to me. But it seems they do not make any distinction between fair and foul, truth and falsehood. They deny the charge. But their reported acts seem to sustain it. Moreover, they seem to take their instructions from Russia, whom they regard as their spiritual home rather than India. I cannot countenance this dependence on an outside power. I have even said that we should not depend even on Russian wheat in our present food crisis. We must have the ability and courage to subsist on what our soil can give us rather than depend on foreign charity. Otherwise, we shall

• Reprinted with permission from Harijan, October 6, 1946. Also in M. K. Gandhi, Towards Non-Violent Socialism (Ahmedabad: Navajivan, 1951), p. 159.

not deserve to exist as an independent country. The same applies to foreign ideologies. I would accept them only to the extent that I can assimilate them and adapt them to the Indian scene. But I must refuse to go under them. My formula for the Communists, therefore, is that I would prefer to die at their hands, but I will not retaliate.

MARX AND GANDHI

by Vinoba Bhave

Gandhi's "socialism" had more in common with the Christian socialism of the West than with the doctrines of Communism. What it might mean in practice is illustrated in the work of Vinoba Bhave, a follower of Gandhi. After Gandhi's death Bhave traveled widely in India seeking, with considerable success, to persuade landlords voluntarily to turn over their land to poor peasants. This "Bhoodan" movement was endorsed by Jayaprakash Narayan, leader of the Indian Socialist Party, who wrote in 1953: "Gandhism does not concentrate on the capture of power, nor depend on the power of the State, but goes to the people and helps them to effect the revolution in their lives and consequently revolution in the life of the community. . . . Socialism wishes to advance by setting class against class, Gandhism by cutting across classes. . . . " [14] *The movement founded by Bhave has done much to counteract Communism in India.*

WHATEVER INTEREST the world may or may not take in the comparative study of Gandhi and Marx, in our own country at least, it has become a subject of everyday discussion among the educated.

• Reprinted with permission from K. G. Mashruwala, *Gandhi and Marx* (Ahmedabad: Navajivan, 1951), pp. 16-17, 20-21.

Every discourser attempts to weigh and measure them up according to his capacity. If the Gandhian thought shows up a halo of spirituality around it, Communism has at its back the support of a scientific terminology. Having proved its worth by securing Swaraj for us, Gandhism may no longer be dubbed visionary and impracticable. And Communism, too, has for the moment proved its virility by rejuvenating the hoary old China. This tempts some workers to seek a reconciliation of the two systems, and has led to the enunciation of formulae like, "Gandhism is Communism minus violence." The fact of the matter is that these two ideologies are irreconcilable; the differences between them are fundamental. . . .

They say that Valmiki wrote the Ramayana long before the birth of Rama, and Rama conformed to every word of it during his earthly career and, so, had also no occasion to worry himself about using his own judgment in order to take a decision. He had just to consult the book and act accordingly. Since the consequences had also been predicted, he was not worried about the results also. So, too, is the case with the Communists. Lenin acted as Marx had prescribed; we, too, (according to them) have merely to follow him and straightway reach our goal. If at times there appears a discrepancy between the words of Marx and the actions of Lenin, the pandits of Communism have of course to labor a little to prove that there is no real discrepancy. This is not very difficult. For, it is a well-known maxim of interpretation that a smriti-text (rule) must conform to a shruti-text (law). And, hence, if a rule is clear, then one need only so interpret the law that the former is justified! Do that and you get the "line clear"!

It is quite otherwise with the Gandhian ideology. If Communism is a solid and imposing structure of granite, Gandhism is an ever-changing amoeba. If we examine Gandhiji's ideas we will find them always growing. If his later pronouncements contradict his earlier ones, he would ask us not to worry about reconciling the two, but to accept the later and reject the earlier and proceed further. Even in his major fights, he had no premeditated plans, no technique, no ordered arrangement, etc. Since he used to say, "One step is enough for me," why should the Lord show him two? And, what was the amount of authority to be attached even to his latest utterances? His answer was, "Do not be author-ity-bound. Use your own talent. You might ask me while I am available. Thereafter every one is free to think and decide for him-self." That is why there is no unanimity of ideas even among his closest followers. . . .

14 WORLD WAR II (1938-1946)

IF I WERE A CZECH
by M. K. Gandhi

*Although Gandhi was a world figure, he was never as inti-
mately connected with or informed about world events as some
of his contemporaries in India and other countries. With the rise
of Hitler, however, and the foreshadowing of a second World
War, Gandhi was more often called upon to comment on world
events. Gandhi did not oppose the first World War, but after that
he increasingly took the pacifist viewpoint in international affairs.
This attitude toward war and aggression is reflected in his message
to the people of Czechoslovakia, written just after the Munich
settlement.*

IF I HAVE CALLED the arrangement with Herr Hitler "peace without honor," it was not to cast any reflection on British or French
statesmen. I have no doubt that Mr. Chamberlain [1] could not
think of anything better. He knew his nation's limitations. He
wanted to avoid war, if it could be avoided at all. Short of going
to war, he pulled his full weight in favor of the Czechs. That it

---

• Reprinted with permission from *Harijan*, October 15, 1938. Also in M. K.
Gandhi, *Non-Violence in Peace and War* (Ahmedabad: Navajivan, 1942),
Vol. I, pp. 174-77.

could not save honor was no fault of his. It would be so every time there is a struggle with Herr Hitler or Signor Mussolini.

It cannot be otherwise. Democracy dreads to spill blood. The philosophy for which the two dictators stand calls it cowardice to shrink from carnage. They exhaust the resources of poetic art in order to glorify organized murder. There is no humbug about their word or deed. They are ever ready for war. There is nobody in Germany or Italy to cross their path. Their word is law.

It is different with Mr. Chamberlain or M. Daladier.[2] They have their Parliaments and Chambers to please. They have parties to confer with. They cannot maintain themselves on a perpetual war footing, if their language is to have a democratic accent about it.

Science of war leads one to dictatorship pure and simple. Science of non-violence can alone lead one to pure democracy. England, France and America have to make their choice. That is the challenge of the two dictators.

Russia is out of the picture just now. Russia has a dictator who dreams of peace and thinks he will wade in it through a sea of blood. No one can say what Russian dictatorship will mean to the world.

It was necessary to give this introduction to what I want to say to the Czechs and through them to all those nationalities which are called "small" or "weak." I want to speak to the Czechs because their plight moved me to the point of physical and mental distress, and I felt that it would be cowardice on my part not to share with them the thoughts that were welling up within me. It is clear that the small nations must either come or be ready to come under the protection of the dictators or be a constant menace to the peace of Europe. In spite of all the goodwill in the world England and France cannot save them. Their intervention can only mean bloodshed and destruction such as has never been seen before. If I were a Czech, therefore, I would free these two nations from the obligation to defend my country. And yet I must live. I would not be a vassal to any nation or body. I must have absolute independence or perish. To seek to win in a clash of arms would be pure bravado. Not so, if in defying the might of one who would deprive me of my independence I refuse to obey his will and perish unarmed in the attempt. In so doing, though I lose the body, I save my soul, i.e., my honor.

This inglorious peace should be my opportunity. I must live down the humiliation and gain real independence.

But says a comforter, "Hitler knows no pity. Your spiritual effort will avail nothing before him."

My answer is: "You may be right. History has no record of a nation having adopted non-violent resistance. If Hitler is unaffected by my suffering, it does not matter. For I shall have lost nothing of worth. My honor is the only thing worth preserving. That is independent of Hitler's pity. But as a believer in non-violence I may not limit its possibilities. Hitherto he and his likes have built upon their invariable experience that men yield to force. Unarmed men, women and children offering non-violent resistance without any bitterness in them will be a novel experience for them. Who can dare say it is not in their nature to respond to the higher and finer forces? They have the same soul that I have."

But says another comforter, "What you say is all right for you. But how do you expect your people to respond to the novel call? They are trained to fight. In personal bravery they are second to none in the world. For you now to ask them to throw away their arms and be trained for non-violent resistance seems to me to be a vain attempt."

"You may be right. But I have a call I must answer. I must deliver my message to my people. This humiliation has sunk too deep in me to remain without an outlet. I, at least, must act up to the light that has dawned on me."

This is how I should, I believe, act if I was a Czech. When I first launched out on Satyagraha I had no companion. We were 13,000 men, women and children against a whole nation capable of crushing the existence out of us. I did not know who would listen to me. It all came as in a flash. All the 13,000 did not fight.

Many fell back. But the honor of the nation was saved. New history was written by the South African Satyagraha.

A more apposite instance, perhaps, is that of Khansaheb Abdul Ghaffar Khan, the servant of God as he calls himself, the pride of Afghan as the Pathans delight to call him. He is sitting in front of me as I pen these lines. He has made several thousands of his people throw down their arms. He thinks he has imbibed the lesson of non-violence. He is not sure of his people. I reproduce below the pledge that his soldiers of peace make. I have come to the Frontier Province, or rather he has brought me, to see with my own eyes what his men here are doing. I can say in advance and at once that these men know very little of non-violence. All the treasure they have on earth is their faith in their leader. I do not cite these soldiers of peace as at all a finished illustration. I cite them as an honest attempt being made by a soldier to convert fellow soldiers to the ways of peace. I can testify that it is an honest attempt, and whether in the end it succeeds or fails, it will have its lessons for satyagrahis of the future. My purpose will be fulfilled, if I succeed in reaching these men's hearts and making them see that, if their non-violence does not make them feel much braver than the possession of arms and the ability to use them, they must give up their non-violence, which is another name for cowardice, and resume their arms which there is nothing but their own will to prevent them from taking back.

I present Dr. Benes [3] with a weapon not of the weak but of the brave. There is no bravery greater than a resolute refusal to bend the knee to an earthly power, no matter how great, and that without bitterness of spirit and in the fullness of faith that the spirit alone lives, nothing else does.

THE KHUDAI KHIDMATGAR'S [4] PLEDGE

The following is a free translation of the pledge which every Khudai Khidmatgar signs before enrolment:

In presence of God I solemnly affirm that:

1. I hereby honestly and sincerely offer myself for enrolment as a **Khudai Khidmatgar.**

2. I shall be ever ready to sacrifice personal comfort, property, and even life itself to serve the nation and for the attainment of my country's freedom.

3. I shall not participate in factions, nor pick up a quarrel with or bear enmity towards anybody. I shall always protect the oppressed against the tyranny of the oppressor.

4. I shall not become member of any other organization, and shall not furnish security or tender apology in the course of the non-violent fight.

5. I shall always obey every legitimate order of my superior officers.

6. I shall always live up to the principle of non-violence.

7. I shall serve all humanity equally. The chief objects of my life shall be attainment of complete independence and religious freedom.

8. I shall always observe truth and purity in all my actions.

9. I shall expect no remuneration for my services.

10. All my services shall be dedicated to God; they shall not be for attaining rank or for show.

HOW TO COMBAT HITLERISM
by M. K. Gandhi

Although Gandhi developed the technique of satyagraha during his early residence in South Africa, he continually tried to perfect it and adapt it to new uses. With the rise of Hitlerism, he suggested how it could be used to defeat Hitlerism on an international scale.

• Reprinted with permission from *Harijan*, June 22, 1940. Also in M. K. Gandhi, *Non-Violence in Peace and War* (Ahmedabad: Navajivan, 1942), Vol. I, pp. 310-12.

WHATEVER HITLER may ultimately prove to be, we know what Hitlerism has come to mean. It means naked, ruthless force reduced to an exact science and worked with scientific precision. In its effect it becomes almost irresistible.

In the early days of Satyagraha when it was still known as passive resistance, "The Star" of Johannesburg, stirred by the sight of a handful of Indians, wholly unarmed and incapable of organized violence even if they wished it, pitting themselves against an overwhelmingly armed government, had a cartoon in which the latter was depicted as a steam-roller representing irresistible force, and passive resistance was depicted as an elephant unmoved and comfortably planting himself in his seat. This was marked immovable force. The cartoonist had a true insight into the duel between the irresistible and the immovable forces. It was then a stalemate. The sequel we know. What was depicted and appeared to be irresistible was successfully resisted by the immovable force of Satyagraha— call it suffering without retaliation.

What became true then can be equally true now. Hitlerism will never be defeated by counter-Hitlerism. It can only breed superior Hitlerism raised to nth degree. What is going on before our eyes is a demonstration of the futility of violence as also of Hitlerism.

Let me explain what I mean by failure of Hitlerism. It has robbed the small nations of their liberty. It has compelled France to sue for peace. Probably by the time this is in print Britain will have decided upon her course. The fall of France is enough for my argument. I think French statesmen have shown rare courage in bowing to the inevitable and refusing to be party to senseless mutual slaughter. There can be no sense in France coming out victorious if the stake is in truth lost. The cause of liberty becomes a mockery, if the price to be paid is wholesale destruction of those who are to enjoy liberty. It then becomes an inglorious satiation of ambition. The bravery of the French soldier is world-known. But let the world know also the greater bravery of the French statesmen in suing for peace. I have assumed that the French statesmen have taken the step in a perfectly honorable manner as behooves true soldiers. Let me hope that Herr Hitler will impose no humiliating terms but show that, though he can fight without mercy, he can at least conclude peace not without mercy.

But to resume the thread of the argument. What will Hitler do with his victory? Can he digest so much power? Personally he will go as empty-handed as his not very remote predecessor Alexander. For the Germans he will have left not the pleasure of owning a mighty empire but the burden of sustaining its crushing weight. For they will not be able to hold all the conquered nations in perpetual subjection. And I doubt if the Germans of future generations will entertain unadulterated pride in the deeds for which Hitlerism will be deemed responsible. They will honor Herr Hitler as a genius, as a brave man, a matchless organizer, and much more. But I should hope that the Germans of the future will have learnt the art of discrimination even about their heroes. Anyway I think it will be allowed that all the blood that has been spilled by Hitler has added not a millionth part of an inch to the world's moral stature.

As against this imagine the state of Europe today if the Czechs, the Poles, the Norwegians, the French and the English had all said to Hitler: "You need not make your scientific preparation for destruction. We will meet your violence with non-violence. You will, therefore, be able to destroy our non-violent army without tanks, battleships and airships." It may be retorted that the only difference would be that Hitler would have got without fighting what he has gained after a bloody fight. Exactly. The history of Europe would then have been written differently. Possession might (but only might) have been then taken under non-violent resistance, as it has been taken now after perpetration of untold barbarities. Under non-violence only those would have been killed who had trained themselves to be killed, if need be, but without killing anyone and without bearing malice towards anybody. I dare say that in that case Europe would have added several inches to its moral stature. And in the end I expect it is the moral worth that will count. All else is dross.

I have written these lines for the European Powers. But they are meant for ourselves. If my argument has gone home, is it not time for us to declare our changeless faith in non-violence of the strong and say we do not seek to defend our liberty with the force of arms, but we will defend it with the force of non-violence?

HITLERISM AND AERIAL WARFARE
• by M. K. Gandhi

The critics of Gandhi's method of satyagraha admit that it might be useful in person-to-person situations, but not in modern warfare, where, through mechanization, there is a high degree of impersonalization. Gandhi denied this in several editorials written on this problem.

How CAN NON-VIOLENCE combat aerial warfare, seeing that there are no personal contacts? The reply to this is that behind the death-dealing bomb there is the human hand that releases it, and behind that still is the human heart that sets the hand in motion. And at the back of the policy of terrorism is the assumption that terrorism if applied in a sufficient measure will produce the desired result, namely, bend the adversary to the tyrant's will. But supposing a people make up their mind that they will never do the tyrant's will, nor retaliate with the tyrant's own methods, the tyrant will not find it worth his while to go on with his terrorism. If sufficient food is given to the tyrant, a time will come when he will have had more than surfeit. If all the mice in the world held conference together and resolved that they would no more fear the cat but all run into her mouth, the mice would live. I have

• Reprinted with permission from *Harijan*, December 24, 1938. Also in M. K. Gandhi, *For Pacifists* (Ahmedabad: Navajivan, 1949), pp. 64-66.

actually seen a cat play with a mouse. She did not kill it outright but held it between her jaws, then released it, and again pounced upon it as soon as it made an effort to escape. In the end the mouse died out of sheer fright. The cat would have derived no sport, if the mouse had not tried to run away. I learnt the lesson on non-violence from my wife, when I tried to bend her to my will. Her determined resistance to my will on the one hand, and her quiet submission to the suffering my stupidity involved on the other, ultimately made me ashamed of myself and cured me of my stupidity in thinking that I was born to rule over her, and in the end she became my teacher in non-violence. And what I did in South Africa was but an extension of the rule of Satyagraha which she unwillingly practiced in her own person.

But one of the visitors objected: "You do not know Hitler and Mussolini. They are incapable of any kind of moral response. They have no conscience, and they have made themselves impervious to world opinion. Would it not be playing into the hands of these dictators, if, for instance, the Czechs, following your advice, confronted them with non-violence? Seeing that dictatorships are unmoral by definition, would the law of moral conversion hold good in their case?"

"Your argument," replied Gandhiji, "presupposes that the dictators like Mussolini or Hitler are beyond redemption. But belief in non-violence is based on the assumption that human nature in its essence is one and therefore unfailingly responds to the advances of love. It should be remembered that they have up to now always found ready response to the violence that they have used. Within their experience, they have not come across organized non-violent resistance on an appreciable scale, if at all. Therefore it is not only highly likely, but I hold it to be inevitable, that they would recognize the superiority of non-violent resistance over any display of violence that they may be capable of putting forth. Moreover the non-violent technique that I have presented to the Czechs does not depend for its success on the goodwill of the dictators, for a non-violent resister depends upon the unfailing assistance of God which sustains him throughout difficulties which would otherwise be considered insurmountable. His faith makes him indomitable."

The visitor retorted that these dictators wisely refrain from using force, but simply take possession of what they want. In the circumstances what can non-violent resisters do?

"Suppose," replied Gandhiji, "they come and occupy mines, factories and all sources of natural wealth belonging to the Czechs, then the following results can take place: (1) The Czechs may be annihilated for disobedience to orders. That would be a glorious victory for the Czechs and the beginning of the fall of Germany. (2) The Czechs might become demoralized in the presence of overwhelming force. This is a result common in all struggles. But if demoralization does take place, it would not be on account of non-violence, but it would be due to absence or inadequacy of non-violence. (3) The third thing that can take place is that Germany might use her new possessions for occupation by her surplus population. This, again, could not be avoided by offering violent resistance, for we have assumed that violent resistance is out of the question. Thus non-violent resistance is the best method under all conceivable circumstances."

QUALIFICATIONS OF A PEACE BRIGADE

by M. K. Gandhi

SOMETIME AGO I suggested the formation of a peace brigade whose members would risk their lives in dealing with riots, especially communal. The idea was that this brigade should substitute [for]

• Reprinted with permission from Harijan, June 18, 1938. Also in M. K. Gandhi, Non-Violence in Peace and War (Ahmedabad: Navajivan, 1942), Vol. I, pp. 166-68.

the police and even the military. This reads ambitious. The achievement may prove impossible. Yet, if the Congress is to succeed in its non-violent struggle, it must develop the power to deal peacefully with such situations. Communal riots are engineered by politically-minded men. Many of those who take part in them are under the influence of the latter. Surely it should not be beyond the wit of Congressmen to devise a method or methods of avoiding ugly communal situations by peaceful means. I say this irrespective of whether there is or there is not a communal pact. It cannot be that any party seeks to force a pact by violent means. Even if such a pact were a possibility, it would not be worth the paper on which it might be written. For behind such a pact there will be no common understanding. What is more, even after a fact is arrived at, it would be too much to expect that there would never be any communal riots.

Let us, therefore, see what qualifications a member of the contemplated peace brigade should possess.

1. He or she must have a living faith in non-violence. This is impossible without a living faith in God. A non-violent man can do nothing save by the power and grace of God. Without it he won't have the courage to die without anger, without fear and without retaliation. Such courage comes from the belief that God sits in the hearts of all, and that there should be no fear in the presence of God. The knowledge of the omnipresence of God also means respect for the lives of even those who may be called opponents or goondas. This contemplated intervention is a process of stilling the fury of man when the brute in him gets the mastery over him.

2. This messenger of peace must have equal regard for all the principal religions of the earth. Thus, if he is a Hindu, he will respect the other faiths current in India. He must, therefore, possess a knowledge of the general principles of the different faiths professed in the country.

3. Generally speaking this work of peace can only be done by local men in their own localities.

4. The work can be done singly or in groups. Therefore no one

need wait for companions. Nevertheless one would naturally seek companions in one's own locality and form a local brigade.

5. This messenger of peace will cultivate, through personal service, contacts with the people in his locality or chosen circle, so that when he appears to deal with ugly situations, he does not descend upon the members of a riotous assembly as an utter stranger liable to be looked upon as a suspect or an unwelcome visitor.

6. Needless to say, a peace-bringer must have a character beyond reproach and must be known for his strict impartiality.

7. Generally there are previous warnings of coming storms. If these are known, the peace brigade will not wait till the conflagration breaks out, but will try to handle the situation in anticipation.

8. Whilst, if the movement spreads, it might be well if there are some whole-time workers it is not absolutely necessary that there should be. The idea is to have as many good and true men and women as possible. These can be had only if volunteers are drawn from those who are engaged in various walks of life but have leisure enough to cultivate friendly relations with the people living in their circle and otherwise possess the qualifications required of a member of the peace brigade.

9. There should be a distinctive dress worn by the members of the contemplated brigade so that in the course of time they will be recognized without the slightest difficulty.

These are but general suggestions. Each centre can work out its own constitution on the basis here suggested.

Lest false hopes may be raised, I must warn workers against entering the hope that I can play any active part in the formation of peace brigades. I have not the health, energy or time for it. I find it hard enough to cope with tasks I dare not shirk. I can only guide and make suggestions through correspondence or these columns. Therefore let those who appreciate the idea and feel they have the ability, take the initiative themselves. I know that the proposed brigade has great possibilities, and that the idea behind it is quite capable of being worked out in practice.

TO EVERY BRITON

by M. K. Gandhi

The following article was published early in July 1940, when Allied fortunes were at their lowest ebb. France had fallen and Britain faced the imminent threat of a Nazi invasion. Meanwhile many Indian nationalists were torn between their sympathy for Britain in her fight against Hitler and their determination to win freedom for their own country from British rule. To Gandhi, all war was wrong, and suddenly it "came to him like a flash" to appeal to the British to adopt the method of non-violence.[5]

IN 1896 I addressed an appeal to every Briton in South Africa on behalf of my countrymen who had gone there as laborers or traders and their assistants. It had its effect. However important it was from my viewpoint, the cause which I pleaded then was insignificant compared with the cause which prompts this appeal. I appeal to every Briton, wherever he may be now, to accept the method of non-violence instead of that of war, for the adjustment of relations between nations and other matters. Your statesmen have declared that this is a war on behalf of democracy. There are many other reasons given in justification. You know them all by heart. I suggest that, at the end of the war, whichever way it ends, there will be no democracy left to represent democracy. This war has descended upon mankind as a curse and a warning. It is a curse inasmuch as it is brutalizing man on a scale hitherto unknown. All distinctions between combatants and non-combatants have been abolished. No one and nothing is to be spared. Lying has been reduced to an art. Britain was to defend small nationalities.

• Reprinted with permission from *Harijan*, July 6, 1940. Also in M. K. Gandhi, *Non-Violence in Peace and War* (Ahmedabad: Navajivan, 1942), Vol. I, pp. 318-21.

One by one they have vanished, at least for the time being. It is also a warning. It is a warning that, if nobody reads the writing on the wall, man will be reduced to the state of the beast, whom he is shaming by his manners. I read the writing when the hostilities broke out. But I had not the courage to say the word. God has given me the courage to say it before it is too late.

I appeal for cessation of hostilities, not because you are too exhausted to fight, but because war is bad in essence. You want to kill Nazism. You will never kill it by its indifferent adoption. Your soldiers are doing the same work of destruction as the Germans. The only difference is that perhaps yours are not as thorough as the Germans. If that be so, yours will soon acquire the same thoroughness as theirs, if not much greater. On no other condition can you win the war. In other words, you will have to be more ruthless than the Nazis. No cause, however just, can warrant the indiscriminate slaughter that is going on minute by minute. I suggest that a cause that demands the inhumanities that are being perpetrated today cannot be called just.

I do not want Britain to be defeated, nor do I want her to be victorious in a trial of brute strength, whether expressed through the muscle or the brain. Your muscular bravery is an established fact. Need you demonstrate that your brain is also as unrivalled in destructive power as your muscle? I hope you do not wish to enter into such an undignified competition with the Nazis. I venture to present you with a nobler and braver way, worthy of the bravest soldier. I want you to fight Nazism without arms, or, if I am to retain the military terminology, with non-violent arms. I would like you to lay down the arms you have as being useless for saving you or humanity. You will invite Herr Hitler and Signor Mussolini to take what they want of the countries you call your possessions. Let them take possession of your beautiful island, with your many beautiful buildings. You will give all these but neither your souls, nor your minds. If these gentlemen choose to occupy your homes, you will vacate them. If they do not give you free passage out, you will allow yourself man, woman and child, to be slaughtered, but you will refuse to owe allegiance to them.

This process or method, which I have called non-violent non-cooperation, is not without considerable success in its use in India. Your representatives in India may deny my claim. If they do, I shall feel sorry for them. They may tell you that our non-cooperation was not wholly non-violent, that it was born of hatred. If they give that testimony, I will not deny it. Had it been wholly non-violent, if all the non-cooperators had been filled with good-will towards you, I make bold to say that you who are India's masters would have become her pupils and, with much greater skill than we have, perfected this matchless weapon and met the German and Italian friends' menace with it. Indeed the history of Europe during the past few months would then have been written differently. Europe would have been spared seas of innocent blood, the rape of so many small nations, and the orgy of hatred.

This is no appeal made by a man who does not know his business. I have been practicing with scientific precision non-violence and its possibilities for an unbroken period of over fifty years. I have applied it in every walk of life, domestic, institutional, economic and political. I know of no single case in which it has failed. Where it has seemed sometimes to have failed, I have ascribed it to my imperfections. I claim no perfection for myself. But I do claim to be a passionate seeker after Truth, which is but another name for God. In the course of that search the discovery of non-violence came to me. Its spread is my life mission. I have no interest in living except for the prosecution of that mission.

I claim to have been a lifelong and wholly disinterested friend of the British people. At one time I used to be also a lover of your empire. I thought that it was doing good to India. When I saw that in the nature of things it could do no good, I used, and am still using, the non-violent method to fight imperialism. Whatever the ultimate fate of my country, my love for you remains, and will remain, undiminished. My non-violence demands universal love, and you are not a small part of it. It is that love which has prompted my appeal to you.

May God give power to every word of mine. In His name I began to write this, and in His name I close it. May your statesmen have the wisdom and courage to respond to my appeal. I am telling His Excellency, the Viceroy, that my services are at the disposal of His Majesty's Government, should they consider them of any practical use in advancing the object of my appeal.

GANDHI AND KAGAWA

by Mahadev Desai

In 1939 Gandhi was visited by Dr. Toyohiko Kagawa, the eminent Japanese Christian, social worker, and leader of the cooperative movement. At this time Europe was still at peace but Japan had been fighting China since 1937.

GANDHIJI . . . went straight to the question on which he wanted to hear firsthand from Dr. Kagawa. "What is the feeling of people in Japan about the war?"

"I am rather a heretic in Japan," said Dr. Kagawa. "Rather than I express my views, I would like to learn from you what you would do if you were in my position."

"It would be presumptuous for me to express my views."

"No, I would like very much to know what you would do."

"I would declare my heresies and be shot. I would put the cooperatives and all your work in one scale, and put the honor of your nation in the other, and if you found that the honor was being sold, I should ask you to declare your views against Japan and in so doing make Japan live through your death. But, for this, inner conviction is necessary. I do not know that I should be able to do all that I have said if I were in your position, but I must give you my opinion since you have asked for it."

• Reprinted with permission from *Harijan*, January 21, 1939. Also in M. K. Gandhi, *Non-Violence in Peace and War* (Ahmedabad: Navajivan, 1942), Vol. I, pp. 207-208.

"The conviction is there. But friends have been asking me to desist."

"Well, don't listen to friends when the Friend inside you says, 'Do this.' And friends, however good, can sometimes well deceive us. They cannot argue otherwise. They would ask you to live and do your work. The same appeal was made to me when I took the decision to go to jail. But I did not listen to friends, with the result that I found the glow of freedom when I was confined within the four solid walls of prison. I was inside a dark cell, but I felt that I could see everything from within those walls, and nothing from outside."

Dr. Kagawa seemed to shrink from continuing this discussion. There was indeed no room for it. The conviction was there, but it could fructify only in its proper time. So he switched on again to his theme of cooperation: "Have you some irrigation cooperatives in India?" But Gandhiji was full of other things.

"I do not think so," Gandhiji replied. "Of course you have all these things. You have done marvellous things, and we have many things to learn from you. But how can we understand this swallowing alive of China, drugging her with poison, and so many other horrid things that I read about in a book called "What War Means" [6] which Pandit Jawaharlal has given me? And then your great poet calls it a war of humanity and a blessing to China!"

ATOMIC WARFARE
by M. K. Gandhi

THERE HAVE BEEN cataclysmic changes in the world. Do I still adhere to my faith in truth and non-violence? Has not the

• Reprinted with permission from Harijan, February 10, 1946. Also in M. K. Gandhi, Non-Violence in Peace and War (Ahmedabad: Navajivan, 1949), Vol. II, p. 94.

atom bomb exploded that faith? Not only has it not done so but it has clearly demonstrated to me that the twins constitute the mightiest force in the world. Before it the atom bomb is of no effect. The two opposing forces are wholly different in kind, the one moral and spiritual, the other physical and material. The one is infinitely superior to the other which by its very nature has an end. The force of the spirit is ever progressive and endless. Its full expression makes it unconquerable in the world. In saying this I know that I have said nothing new. I merely bear witness to the fact. What is more, that force resides in everybody, man, woman, and child, irrespective of the color of the skin. Only in many it lies dormant, but it is capable of being awakened by judicious training.

It is further to be observed that without the recognition of this truth and due effort to realize it, there is no escape from self-destruction. The remedy lies in every individual training himself for self-expression in every walk of life, irrespective of response by the neighbors.

THE ATOM BOMB, AMERICA AND JAPAN
by M. K. Gandhi

IT HAS BEEN SUGGESTED by American friends that the atom bomb will bring in Ahimsa (non-violence) as nothing else can. It will, if it is meant that its destructive power will so disgust the world that it will turn it away from violence for the time being. This is very like a man glutting himself with dainties to the point

• Reprinted with permission from *Harijan*, July 7, 1946. Also in M. K. Gandhi, *For Pacifists* (Ahmedabad: Navajivan, 1949), pp. 83-84.

of nausea and turning away from them only to return with redoubled zeal after the effect of nausea is well over. Precisely in the
same manner will the world return to violence with renewed zeal
after the effect of disgust is worn out.

So far as I can see, the atomic bomb has deadened the finest
feeling that has sustained mankind for ages. There used to be the
so-called laws of war which made it tolerable. Now we know the
naked truth. War knows no law except that of might. The atom
bomb brought an empty victory to the allied arms but it resulted for
the time being in destroying the soul of Japan. What has happened
to the soul of the destroying nation is yet too early to see. Forces
of nature act in a mysterious manner. We can but solve the mys-
tery by deducing the unknown result from the known results of
similar events. A slaveholder cannot hold a slave without putting
himself or his deputy in the cage holding the slave. Let no one
run away with the idea that I wish to put in a defense of Japanese
misdeeds in pursuance of Japan's unworthy ambition. The difference was only one of degree. I assume that Japan's greed was more
unworthy. But the greater unworthiness conferred no right on the
less unworthy of destroying without mercy men, women and children of Japan in a particular area.

The moral to be legitimately drawn from the supreme tragedy
of the bomb is that it will not be destroyed by counter-bombs
even as violence cannot be by counter-violence. Mankind has to
get out of violence only through non-violence. Hatred can be overcome only by love. Counter-hatred only increases the surface as
well as the depth of hatred. I am aware that I am repeating what
I have many times stated before and practiced to the best of my
ability and capacity. What I first stated was itself nothing new.
It was as old as the hills. Only I recited no copy-book maxim but
definitely announced what I believed in every fibre of my being.
Sixty years of practice in various walks of life has only enriched the
belief which experience of friends has fortified. It is however the
central truth by which one can stand alone without flinching. I believe in what Max Müller [7] said years ago, namely that truth
needed to be repeated as long as there were men who disbelieved it.

INDIA AND THE WAR

LETTER TO CHIANG KAI-SHEK

by M. K. Gandhi

At the beginning of World War II Great Britain declared, without consulting the Indians, that India was at war. The next day Gandhi told the Viceroy, Lord Linlithgow, that he would not embarrass the British government, but he would not participate in the war effort. The Indian National Congress, on the other hand, was prepared to support the war effort on certain conditions, arguing that India could fight wholeheartedly only if she were defending her own freedom. On September 14, 1939 the Congress Working Committee issued a manifesto indicating that "a free and democratic India will gladly associate herself with other free nations for mutual defense against aggression." This offer was repeated—against Gandhi's advice—in July 1940, after the fall of France. When it was rejected by the British, the Congress turned for leadership to Gandhi, who decided on a limited form of civil disobedience in which certain Congress leaders, including Nehru and Patel, defied the ban on propaganda against the war and were promptly arrested.

After Pearl Harbor India itself was in danger. With the Japa-

• Reprinted with permission from M. K. Gandhi, *Non-Violence in Peace and War* (Ahmedabad: Navajivan, 1942), Vol. I, pp. 456-59.

nese advancing in Burma and the Germans in North Africa, there
was talk of a possible junction of their forces in India. At this
point, in March 1942, the British government sent Sir Stafford
Cripps to India with a set of proposals. These promised Dominion
status after the war and left the door open for a separate Moslem
state as demanded by the Moslem League; during the war, representatives of the principal Indian parties would share in the government of India. After extended discussion the proposals were
rejected by all the major Indian parties.

In 1941 Chiang Kai-shek had made representations to President
Roosevelt and to the British government on behalf of Indian independence. (Ironically, in 1951, Gandhi's heir, Nehru, made representations to President Truman to recognize Mao Tse-tung, and
not Chiang, as the ruler of China.) In February 1942 Chiang visited India to seek Indian support for the war against Japan. Gandhi
journeyed to Calcutta especially to see him, and spent several
hours talking with the Generalissimo and his wife. Nehru and
Mahadev Desai were also present. Some months later, in June,
Gandhi sent Chiang a letter which summarized his attitude toward China and his attitude as an Indian toward the war against
Japan.

Sevagram
June 14, 1942

DEAR GENERALISSIMO,

I can never forget the five hours' close contact I had with you
and your noble wife in Calcutta. I had always felt drawn towards
you in your fight for freedom, and that contact and our conversation brought China and her problem still nearer to me. Long ago,
between 1905 and 1913, when I was in South Africa, I was in constant touch with the small Chinese colony in Johannesburg. I
knew them first as clients and then as comrades in the Indian passive resistance struggle in South Africa. I came in touch with them
in Mauritius [1] also. I learnt then to admire their thrift, industry,
resourcefulness and internal unity. Later in India I had a very fine
Chinese friend living with me for a few years and we all learnt to
like him.

I have thus felt greatly attracted towards your great country and, in common with my countrymen, our sympathy has gone out to you in your terrible struggle. Our mutual friend, Jawaharlal Nehru, whose love of China is only excelled, if at all, by his love of his own country, has kept us in intimate touch with the developments of the Chinese struggle.

Because of this feeling I have towards China and my earnest desire that our two great countries should come closer to one another and cooperate to their mutual advantage, I am anxious to explain to you that my appeal to the British Power to withdraw from India is not meant in any shape or form to weaken India's defense against the Japanese or embarrass you in your struggle. India must not submit to any aggressor or invader and must resist him. I would not be guilty of purchasing the freedom of my country at the cost of your country's freedom. That problem does not arise before me as I am clear that India cannot gain her freedom in this way, and a Japanese domination of either India or China would be equally injurious to the other country and to world peace. That domination must therefore be prevented and I should like India to play her natural and rightful part in this.

I feel India cannot do so while she is in bondage. India has been a helpless witness of the withdrawals from Malaya, Singapore and Burma. We must learn the lesson from these tragic events and prevent by all means at our disposal a repetition of what befell these unfortunate countries. But unless we are free, we can do nothing to prevent it, and the same process might well occur again, crippling India and China disastrously. I do not want a repetition of this tragic tale of woe.

Our proffered help has repeatedly been rejected by the British Government and the recent failure of the Cripps mission has left a deep wound which is still running. Out of that anguish has come the cry for immediate withdrawal of British Power so that India can look after herself and help China to the best of her ability.

I have told you of my faith in non-violence and my belief in the effectiveness of this method if the whole nation could turn to it. That faith in it is as firm as ever. But I realize that India today as a whole has not that faith and belief, and the government in free India would be formed from the various elements composing the nation.

Today the whole of India is impotent and feels frustrated. The Indian army consists largely of people who have joined up because of economic pressure. They have no feeling of a cause to fight for, and in no sense are they a national army. Those of us who would fight for a cause, for India and China, with armed forces or with non-violence, cannot, under the foreign heel, function as they want to. And yet our people know for certain that India free can play even a decisive part not only on her own behalf, but also on behalf of China and world peace. Many like me feel that it is not proper or manly to remain in this helpless state and allow events to overwhelm us when a way to effective action can be opened to us. They feel, therefore, that every possible effort should be made to ensure independence and that freedom of action which is so urgently needed. This is the origin of my appeal to the British Power to end immediately the unnatural connection between Britain and India.

Unless we make the effort there is grave danger of public feeling in India going into wrong and harmful channels. There is every likelihood of subterranean sympathy for Japan growing simply in order to weaken and oust British authority in India. This feeling may take the place of robust confidence in our ability never to look to outsiders for help in winning our freedom. We have to learn self-reliance and develop the strength to work out our own salvation. This is only possible if we make a determined effort to free ourselves from bondage. That freedom has become a present necessity to enable us to take our due place among the free nations of the world.

To make it perfectly clear that we want to prevent in every way Japanese aggression, I would personally agree, that the Allied Powers might, under treaty with us, keep their armed forces in India and use the country as a base for operation against the threatened Japanese attack.

I need hardly give you my assurance that, as the author of the

new move in India, I shall take no hasty action. And whatever
action I may recommend will be governed by the consideration
that it should not injure China, or encourage Japanese aggression
in India or China. I am trying to enlist world opinion in favor of
a proposition which to me appears self-proved and which must
lead to the strengthening of India's and China's defense. I am
also educating public opinion in India and conferring with my
colleagues. Needless to say, any movement against the British Government with which I may be connected will be essentially non-
violent. I am straining every nerve to avoid a conflict with British
authority. But if in the vindication of the freedom which has become an immediate desideratum, this becomes inevitable, I shall
not hesitate to run any risk however great.

Very soon you will have completed five years of war against Japanese aggression and invasion and all the sorrow and misery that
these have brought to China. My heart goes out to the people of
China in deep sympathy and in admiration for their heroic struggle
and endless sacrifices in the cause of their country's freedom and
integrity against tremendous odds. I am convinced that this hero-
ism and sacrifice cannot be in vain; they must bear fruit. To you,
to Madame Chiang and to the great people of China, I send my
earnest and sincere wishes for your success. I look forward to the
day when a free India and a free China will cooperate together
in friendship and brotherhood for their own good and for the
good of Asia and the world.

In anticipation of your permission, I am taking the liberty of
publishing this letter in *Harijan*.

Yours sincerely,

M. K. Gandhi

LETTER TO FRANKLIN D. ROOSEVELT

by M. K. Gandhi

After the United States entered the war the American government was concerned about the status of India. President Roosevelt tried tactfully, though with little success, to persuade Prime Minister Churchill to adopt a more liberal attitude toward the claims of Indian nationalists. In April 1942, when the Cripps mission was in India, Roosevelt urged Harry Hopkins, then with Churchill in England, to do everything possible to prevent a breakdown of the British-Indian negotiations. Roosevelt also sent Churchill the following cable: "I am unable regretfully to agree with the point of view you express in your message to me that the American public believes that negotiations have failed on general broad lines. The general impression here is quite the contrary. The almost universal feeling is that the deadlock has been due to the unwillingness of the British government to concede the right of self-government to the Indian people notwithstanding the Indians' willingness to entrust technical military and naval defense control to the competent British authorities. American public opinion cannot understand why, if the British government is willing to permit component parts of India to secede from the British Empire after the war, it is not willing to permit them during the war to enjoy what is tantamount to self-government."

In the spring of 1942 Louis Fischer, American journalist and later a biographer of Gandhi, visited Gandhi for a week at his ashram at Sevagram. After Fischer left Sevagram for New Delhi,

• Reprinted with permission from Louis Fischer, The Life of Mahatma Gandhi (New York: Harper, 1950), pp. 539-40.

he received a letter from Gandhi to transmit to President Roosevelt. Gandhi wrote Fischer, "*if it does not commend itself to you, you may tear it to pieces.*"

Sevagram via Wardha (India)
July 1, 1942

DEAR FRIEND,

I twice missed coming to your great country. I have the privilege of having numerous friends there both known and unknown to me. Many of my countrymen have received and are still receiving higher education in America. I know too that several have taken shelter there. I have profited greatly by the writings of Thoreau and Emerson. I say this to tell you how much I am connected with your country. Of Great Britain I need say nothing beyond mentioning that in spite of my intense dislike of British rule, I have numerous friends in England whom I love as dearly as my own people. I had my legal education there. I have therefore nothing but good wishes for your country and Great Britain. You will therefore accept my word that my present proposal, that the British should unreservedly and without reference to the wishes of the people of India immediately withdraw their rule, is prompted by the friendliest intention. I would like to turn into good will the ill will which, whatever may be said to the contrary, exists in India towards Great Britain and thus enable the millions of India to play their part in the present war.

My personal position is clear. I hate all war. If, therefore, I could persuade my countrymen, they would make a most effective and decisive contribution in favor of an honorable peace. But I know that all of us have not a living faith in non-violence. Under foreign rule, however, we can make no effective contribution of any kind in this war, except as helots.

The policy of the Indian National Congress, largely guided by me, has been one of non-embarrassment to Britain, consistently with the honorable working of the Congress, admittedly the largest political organization of the longest standing in India. The British policy as exposed by the Cripps mission and rejected by almost all parties has opened our eyes and has driven me to the proposal I have made. I hold that the full acceptance of my proposal and that only can put the Allied cause on an unassailable basis. I venture to think that the Allied declaration that the Allies are fighting to make the world safe for the freedom of the individual and for democracy sounds hollow, so long as India and for that matter Africa are exploited by Great Britain, and America has the Negro problem in her own home. But in order to avoid all complications, in my proposal I have confined myself only to India. If India becomes free the rest must follow, if it does not happen simultaneously.

In order to make my proposal fool-proof I have suggested that if the Allies think it necessary they may keep their troops, at their own expense, in India, not for keeping internal order but for preventing Japanese aggression and defending China. So far as India is concerned, she must become free even as America and Great Britain are. The Allied troops will remain in India during the war under treaty with the free India govt. that may be formed by the people of India without any outside interference, direct or indirect.

It is on behalf of this proposal that I write this to enlist your active sympathy.

I hope that it would commend itself to you.

Mr. Louis Fischer is carrying this letter to you.

If there is any obscurity in my letter, you will have but to send me word and I shall try to clear it.

I hope finally that you will not resent this letter as an intrusion but take it as an approach from a friend and well wisher of the Allies.

I remain
yours sincerely,
M. K. Gandhi

GANDHI'S CORRESPONDENCE WITH LORD LINLITHGOW

by M. K. Gandhi and Lord Linlithgow

Following the failure of the Cripps mission, the Congress, on August 8, 1942, adopted its famous "Quit India" resolution calling for an immediate end of British rule but offering to fight on the Allied side under a provisional national government. If this offer were rejected, the Congress authorized a mass civil disobedience movement under Gandhi's leadership. On August 8 Gandhi, Nehru, and other Congress leaders were arrested. Gandhi was taken to the palace of the Aga Khan at Yeravda, near Poona. The next day Mrs. Gandhi was arrested and joined him at the palace. Soon afterward, civil disturbances broke out in India with many instances of violence and sabotage. Gandhi then engaged in a long correspondence (greatly abridged here) with the Viceroy, Lord Linlithgow, in which each sought to blame the other party for the disturbances. No agreement between Britain and India was possible until after the war.

The Aga Khan's Palace,
Yeravda, 14-8-'42

DEAR LORD LINLITHGOW,

The Government of India were wrong in precipitating the crisis. The Government resolution justifying the step is full of distortions and misrepresentations. That you had the approval of your Indian "colleagues" can have no significance, except this

• Reprinted with permission from *Gandhiji's Correspondence with the Government, 1942–44* (Ahmedabad: Navajivan, 1945), pp. 15-16, 19-20, 21, 23-27, 29-33, 38-39, 41, 55.

that in India you can always command such services. That co-operation is an additional justification for the demand of withdrawal irrespective of what people and parties may say.

The Government of India should have waited at least till the time that I inaugurated mass action. I had publicly stated that I fully contemplated sending you a letter before taking concrete action. It was to be an appeal to you for an impartial examination of the Congress case. As you know the Congress has readily filled in every omission that has been discovered in the conception of its demand. So would I have dealt with every deficiency if you had given me the opportunity. The precipitate action of the Government leads one to think that they were afraid that the extreme caution and gradualness with which the Congress was moving towards direct action, might make world opinion veer round to the Congress as it had already begun doing, and expose the hollowness of grounds for the Government rejection of the Congress demand. They should surely have waited for an authentic report of my speeches on Friday and on Saturday night after the passing of the resolution by the A.I.C.C.[2] You would have found in them that I would not hastily begin action. You should have taken advantage of the interval foreshadowed in them and explored every possibility of satisfying the Congress demand. . . .

One thing more. The declared cause is common between the Government of India and us. To put it in the most concrete terms, it is the protection of the freedom of China and Russia. The Government of India think that freedom of India is not necesssary for winning the cause. I think exactly the opposite. I have taken Jawaharlal Nehru as my measuring rod. His personal contacts make him feel much more the misery of the impending ruin of China and Russia than I can, and may I say than you can. In his misery he tried to forget his old quarrel with imperialism. He dreads much more than I do the success of Nazism and Fascism. I argued with him for days together. He fought against my position with a passion which I have no words to describe. But the logic of facts overwhelmed him. He yielded when he saw clearly that without the freedom of India that of the other two was in great jeopardy. Surely you are wrong in having imprisoned such a powerful friend and ally.

If notwithstanding the common cause, the Government's answer to the Congress demand is hasty repression, they will not wonder if I draw the inference that it was not so much the Allied cause that weighed with the British Government, as the unexpressed determination to cling to the possession of India as an indispensable part of imperial policy. This determination led to the rejection of the Congress demand and precipitated repression.

The present mutual slaughter on a scale never before known to history is suffocating enough. But the slaughter of truth accompanying the butchery and enforced by the falsity of which the resolution is reeking adds strength to the Congress position.

It causes me deep pain to have to send you this letter. But however much I dislike your action, I remain the same friend you have known me. I would still plead for a reconsideration of the Government of India's whole policy. Do not disregard this pleading of one who claims to be a sincere friend of the British people.

Heaven guide you!

I am,
Yours sincerely,
M. K. Gandhi

The Viceroy's House, New Delhi,
22nd August, 1942

DEAR MR. GANDHI,

Thank you very much for your letter dated the 14th August, which reached me only a day or two ago.

I have read, I need not say, what you have been good enough to say in your letter with very close attention, and I have given full weight to your views. But I fear in the result that it would not be possible for me either to accept the criticisms which you advance of the resolution of the Governor-General-in-Council, or your request that the whole policy of the Government of India should be reconsidered.

Yours sincerely,
Linlithgow

M. K. Gandhi, Esq.

Personal

Detention Camp,
New Year's Eve, 1942

DEAR LORD LINLITHGOW,

This is a very personal letter. Contrary to the Biblical injunction I have allowed many suns to set on a quarrel I have harbored against you. But I must not allow the old year to expire without disburdening myself of what is rankling in my breast against you. I have thought we were friends and should still love to think so. However what has happened since the 9th of August last makes me wonder whether you still regard me as a friend. I have perhaps not come in such close touch with any occupant of your gadi ³ as with you.

Your arrest of me, the communique you issued thereafter, your reply to Rajaji and the reasons given therefor, Mr. Amery's ⁴ attack on me, and much else I can catalogue go to show that at some stage or other you must have suspected my bona fides. Mention of other Congressmen in the same connection is by the way. I seem to be the fons et origo of all the evil imputed to the Congress. If I have not ceased to be your friend why did you not, before taking drastic action, send for me, tell me of your suspicions and make yourself sure of your facts?

I am quite capable of seeing myself as others see me. But in this case I have failed hopelessly. I find that all the statements made about me in Government quarters in this connection contain palpable departures from truth.

I have so much fallen from grace that I could not establish

contact with a dying friend. I mean Prof. Bhansali who is fasting in regard to the Chimur affair ! ! ! [5]

And I am expected to condemn the so-called violence of some people reputed to be Congressmen, although I have no data for such condemnation save the heavily censored reports of newspapers. I must own that I thoroughly distrust those reports. I could write much more, but I must not lengthen my tale of woe. I am sure, what I have said is enough to enable you to fill in details.

You know I returned to India from South Africa at the end of 1914 with a mission which came to me in 1906, namely, to spread truth and non-violence among mankind in the place of violence and falsehood in all walks of life. The law of Satyagraha knows no defeat. Prison is one of the many ways of spreading the message. But it has its limits. You have placed me in a palace where every reasonable creature comfort is ensured. I have freely partaken of the latter purely as a matter of duty, never as a pleasure, in the hope that some day those who have the power will realize that they have wronged innocent men. I had given myself six months. The period is drawing to a close. So is my patience. The law of Satyagraha as I know it prescribes a remedy in such moments of trial. In a sentence it is, 'Crucify the flesh by fasting.' That same law forbids its use except as a last resort. I do not want to use it if I can avoid it.

This is a way to avoid it. Convince me of my error or errors, and I shall make ample amends. You can send for me or send someone who knows your mind and can carry conviction. There are many other ways if you have the will.

May I expect an early reply?

May the New Year bring peace to us all!

I am,
Your sincere friend,
M. K. Gandhi

Personal   The Viceroy's House,
                                    New Delhi, 13th Jan., 1943

DEAR MR. GANDHI,

Thank you for your personal letter of December 31st, which I have just received. I fully accept its personal character, and I welcome its frankness. And my reply will be, as you would wish it to be, as frank and as entirely personal as your letter itself.

I was glad to have your letter, for, to be as open with you as our previous relations justify, I have been profoundly depressed during recent months first by the policy that was adopted by the Congress in August, secondly, because while that policy gave rise, as it was obvious it must, throughout the country to violence and crime (I say nothing of the risks to India from outside aggression) no word of condemnation for that violence and crime should have come from you, or from the Working Committee. When you were first at Poona I knew that you were not receiving newspapers, and I accepted that as explaining your silence. When arrangements were made that you and the Working Committee should have such newspapers as you desired I felt certain that the details those newspapers contained of what was happening would shock and distress you as much as it has us all, and that you would be anxious to make your condemnation of it categorical and widely known. But that was not the case; and it has been a real disappointment to me, all the more when I think of these murders, the burning alive of police officials, the wrecking of trains, the destruction of property, the misleading of these young students, which has done so much harm to India's good name, and to the Congress Party. You may take it from me that the newspaper accounts you mention are well founded—I only wish they were not, for the story is a bad one. I well know the immense weight of your great authority in the Congrss movement and with the Party and those who follow its lead, and I wish I could feel, again speaking very frankly, that a heavy responsibility did not rest on you. (And unhappily, while the initial responsibility rests with the leaders, others have to bear the consequences, whether as law breakers, with the results that that involves, or as the victims.)

But if I am right in reading your letter to mean that in the light of what has happened you wish now to retrace your steps and dissociate yourself from the policy of last summer, you have only to let me know and I will at once consider the matter further. And if I have failed to understand your object, you must not hesitate to let me know without delay in what respect I have done so, and tell me what positive suggestion you wish to put to me. You know me well enough after these many years to believe that I shall be only too concerned to read with the same close attention as ever any message which I receive from you, to give it the fullest weight and approach it with the deepest anxiety to understand your feelings and your motives.

Yours sincerely,
Linlithgow

Personal   Detention Camp,
19-1-'43

DEAR LORD LINLITHGOW,

I received your kind letter of 13th instant yesterday at 2:30 P.M. I had almost despaired of ever hearing from you. Please excuse my impatience.

Your letter gladdens me to find that I have not lost caste with you.

My letter of 31st December was a growl against you. Yours is a counter-growl. It means that you maintain that you were right in arresting me and you were sorry for the omissions of which, in your opinion, I was guilty.

The inference you draw from my letter is, I am afraid, not

correct. I have read my letter in the light of your interpretation, but have failed to find your meaning in it. I wanted to fast and should still want to if nothing comes out of our correspondence and I have to be a helpless witness to what is going on in the country including the privations of the millions owing to the universal scarcity stalking the land. . . .

I am,

Your sincere friend,

M. K. Gandhi

Personal   The Viceroy's House,

New Delhi, 25th Jan., 1943

DEAR MR. GANDHI,

Many thanks for your personal letter of the 19th January, which I have just received, and which I need not say I have read with close care and attention. But I am still, I fear, rather in the dark. I made clear to you in my last letter that, however reluctantly, the course of events, and my familiarity with what has been taking place, has left me no choice but to regard the Congress movement, and you as its authorized and fully empowered spokesman at the time of the decision of last August, as responsible for the sad campaign of violence and crime, and revolutionary activity which has done so much harm, and so much injury to India's credit, since last August. I note what you say about non-violence. I am very glad to read your unequivocal condemnation of violence, and I am well aware of the importance which you have given to that article of your creed in the past. But the events of these last months, and even the events that are happening today, show that it has not met with the full support of certain at any rate of your followers, and the mere fact that they may have fallen short of an ideal which you have advocated is no answer to the relations of those who have lost their lives, and to those themselves who have lost their property or suffered severe injury as a result of violent activities on the part of Congress and its supporters. And I cannot I fear accept as an answer your suggestion that "the whole blame" has been laid by you yourself at the door of the Government of India. We are dealing with facts in this matter, and they have to be faced. And while, as I made clear in my last letter, I am very anxious to have from you anything that you may have to say or any specific proposition that you may have to make, the position remains that it is not the Government of India, but Congress and yourself that are on their justification in this matter. . . .

Yours sincerely,
Linlithgow

M. K. Gandhi, Esq.

Detention Camp,
29th January, 1943

DEAR LORD LINLITHGOW,

I must thank you warmly for your prompt reply to my letter of 19th instant.

I wish I could agree with you that your letter is clear. I am sure you do not wish to imply by clearness simply that you hold a particular opinion strongly. I have pleaded and would continue to plead till the last breath that you should at least make an attempt to convince me of the validity of the opinion you hold, that the August resolution of the Congress is responsible for the popular violence that broke out on the 9th August last and after, even though it broke out after the wholesale arrests of principal Congress workers. Was not the drastic and unwarranted action of the Government responsible for the reported violence? You have not even said what part of the August resolution is bad or offensive in your opinion. That resolution is in no way a retraction by the Congress of its policy of non-violence. It is definitely against Fascism in every shape or form. It tenders co-operation in war effort under circumstances which alone can make effective and nation-wide co-operation possible. . . .

If then I cannot get soothing balm for my pain, I must resort to the law prescribed for Satyagrahis, namely, a fast according to capacity. I must commence after the early morning breakfast of the 9th February, a fast for twenty-one days ending on the morning of the 2nd March. Usually, during my fasts, I take water with the addition of salts. But nowadays, my system refuses water. This time therefore I propose to add juices of citrus fruits to make water drinkable. For, my wish is not to fast unto death, but to survive the ordeal, if God so wills. The fast can be ended sooner by the Government giving the needed relief.

I am not marking this letter personal, as I did the two previous ones. They were in no way confidential. They were mere personal appeals.

I am,
Your sincere friend,
M. K. Gandhi

The Viceroy's House,
New Delhi,
5th February, 1943

DEAR MR. GANDHI,

Many thanks for your letter of 29th January which I have just received. I have read it, as always, with great care and with every anxiety to follow your mind and to do full justice to your argument. But I fear that my view of the responsibility of Congress and of yourself personally for the lamentable disorders of last autumn remains unchanged. . . .

Let me in conclusion say how greatly I regret, having regard to your health and age, the decision that you tell me that you now have in your mind to take. I hope and pray that wiser counsels may yet prevail with you. But the decision whether or not to undertake a fast with its attendent risks is clearly one that must be taken by you alone and the responsibility for which and for its consequences must rest on you alone. I trust sincerely that in the light of what I have said you may think better of your resolution and I would welcome a decision on your part to think better of it, not only because of my own natural reluctance to see you wilfully risk your life, but because I regard the use of a fast for political purposes as a form of political blackmail (himsa) for which there can be no moral justification, and understood from your own previous writings that this was also your view.

Yours sincerely,
Linlithgow

M. K. Gandhi, Esq.

Detention Camp,
7-2-'43

DEAR LORD LINLITHGOW,

I have to thank you for your long reply dated 5th instant to my letter of 29th January last.

I would take your last point first, namely, the contemplated fast which begins on 9th instant. Your letter, from a Satyagrahi's stand-point, is an invitation to fast. No doubt the responsibility for the step and its consequences will be solely mine. You have allowed an expression to slip from your pen for which I was unprepared. In the concluding sentence of the second paragraph your describe the step as an attempt "to find an easy way out." That you, as a friend, can impute such a base and cowardly motive to me passes comprehension. You have also described it as "a form of political blackmail," and you quote my previous writings on the subject against me. I abide by my writings. I hold that there is nothing inconsistent in them with the contemplated step. I wonder whether you have yourself read those writings. . . .

I have not attempted an exhaustive reply to the views and statements attributed to me. This is not the place nor the time for such reply. I have only picked out those things which in my opinion demanded an immediate answer. You have left me no loophole for escaping the ordeal I have set before for myself. I begin it on 9th instant with the clearest possible conscience. Despite your description of it as "a form of political blackmail," it is on my part meant to be an appeal to the Highest Tribunal for justice which I have failed to secure from you. If I do not survive the ordeal I shall go to the Judgment Seat with the fullest faith in my innocence. Posterity will judge between you as representative of an all-powerful Government and me as a humble man who had tried to serve his country and humanity through it. . . .

> I am,
> Your sincere friend,
> M. K. Gandhi

Gandhi carried out his fast, beginning on February 10, 1943. The British had offered to release him from prison for the duration of the fast but he declined. Later, when Lord Linlithgow was about to leave India, Gandhi wrote to him again.

> Detention Camp,
> 27-9-1943

DEAR LORD LINLITHGOW,

On the eve of your departure from India I would like to send you a word.

Of all the high functionaries I have had the honor of knowing none has been the cause of such deep sorrow to me as you have been. It has cut me to the quick to have to think of you as having countenanced untruth, and that regarding one whom you at one time considered as your friend. I hope and pray that God will some day put it into your heart to realize that you, a representative of a great nation, had been led into a grievous error.

With good wishes,

I still remain,
Your friend,
M. K. Gandhi

Personal

Viceroy's Camp, India,
(Simla), 7th October, 1943

DEAR MR. GANDHI,

I have received your letter of 27th September. I am indeed sorry that your feelings about any deeds or words of mine should be as you describe. But I must be allowed, as gently as I may, to make plain to you that I am quite unable to accept your interpretation of the events in question.

As for the corrective virtues of time and reflection evidently they are ubiquitous in their operation, and wisely to be rejected by no man.

I am sincerely,
Linlithgow

M. K. Gandhi, Esq.

TO EVERY JAPANESE

• by M. K. Gandhi

A minority among the Indian nationalists, including the prominent Congress leader, Subhas Chandra Bose, was prepared

• Reprinted with permission from *Harijan*, July 26, 1942. Also in M. K. Gandhi, *Non-Violence in Peace and War* (Ahmedabad: Navajivan, 1942), Vol. I, pp. 459-63.

to help Japan and Germany against Britain in order to hasten
the independence of India. Gandhi rejected this position. The
following article, written in July 1942, shows his attitude toward
Japanese militarism and his determination to resist Japanese imperialism no less than British.

I MUST CONFESS at the outset that, though I have no ill-will against
you, I intensely dislike your attack upon China. From your lofty
height you have descended to imperial ambition. You will fail to
realize that ambition and may become the authors of the dis-
memberment of Asia, thus unwittingly preventing world federation
and brotherhood without which there can be no hope for humanity.

Ever since I was a lad of eighteen studying in London over
fifty years ago, I learnt, through the writings of the late Sir Edwin
Arnold,[6] to prize the many excellent qualities of your nation. I
was thrilled when in South Africa I learnt of your brilliant victory
over Russian arms. After my return to India from South Africa in
1915, I came in close touch with Japanese monks who lived as
members of our Ashram from time to time. One of them became a
valuable member of the Ashram in Sevagram, and his application
to duty, his dignified bearing, his unfailing devotion to daily worship, affability, unruffledness under varying circumstances, and his
natural smile which was positive evidence of his inner peace had
endeared him to all of us. And now that owing to your declaration
of war against Great Britain he has been taken away from us, we
miss him as a dear co-worker. He has left behind him as a memory
his daily prayer and his little drum, to the accompaniment of
which we open our morning and evening prayers.

In the background of these pleasant recollections I grieve deeply
as I contemplate what appears to me to be your unprovoked
attack against China and, if reports are to be believed, your merci-
less devastation of that great and ancient land.

It was a worthy ambition of yours to take equal rank with the
Great Powers of the world. Your aggression against China and

your alliance with the Axis Powers was surely an unwarranted excess of that ambition.

I should have thought that you would be proud of the fact that that great and ancient people, whose old classical literature you have adopted as your own, are your neighbors. Your understanding of one another's history, tradition, literature should bind you as friends rather than make you the enemies you are today.

If I was a free man, and if you allowed me to come to your country, frail though I am, I would not mind risking my health, maybe my life, to come to your country to plead with you to desist from the wrong you are doing to China and the world and therefore to yourself.

But I enjoy no such freedom. And we are in the unique position of having to resist an imperialism that we detest no less than yours and Nazism. Our resistance to it does not mean harm to the British people. We seek to convert them. Ours is an unarmed revolt against British rule. An important party in the country is engaged in a deadly but friendly quarrel with the foreign rulers.

But in this they need no aid from foreign Powers. You have been gravely misinformed, as I know you are, that we have chosen this particular moment to embarrass the Allies when your attack against India is imminent. If we wanted to turn Britain's difficulty into our opportunity we should have done it as soon as the war broke out nearly three years ago.

Our movement demanding the withdrawal of the British Power from India should in no way be misunderstood. In fact, if we are to believe your reported anxiety for the independence of India, a recognition of that independence by Britain should leave you no excuse for any attack on India. Moreover the reported profession sorts ill with your ruthless aggression against China.

I would ask you to make no mistake about the fact that you will be sadly disillusioned if you believe that you will receive a willing welcome from India. The end and aim of the movement for British withdrawal is to prepare India, by making her free for resisting all militarist and imperialist ambition, whether it is called British Imperialism, German Nazism, or your pattern. If we do not, we shall have been ignoble spectators of the militarization of the world in spite of our belief that in non-violence we have the only solvent of the militarist spirit and ambition. . . .

To Britain and the Allies we have appealed in the name of justice, in proof of their professions, and in their own self-interest. To you I appeal in the name of humanity. It is a marvel to me that you do not see that ruthless warfare is nobody's monopoly. If not the Allies some other Power will certainly improve upon your method and beat you with your own weapon. Even if you win you will leave no legacy to your people of which they would feel proud. They cannot take pride in a recital of cruel deeds however skillfully achieved.

Even if you win it will not prove that you were in the right, it will only prove that your power of destruction was greater. This applies obviously to the Allies too, unless they perform now the just and righteous act of freeing India as an earnest and promise of similarly freeing all other subject peoples in Asia and Africa.

Our appeal to Britain is coupled with the offer of Free India's willingness to let the Allies retain their troops in India. The offer is made in order to prove that we do not in any way mean to harm the Allied cause, and in order to prevent you from being misled into feeling that you have but to step into the country that Britain has vacated. Needless to repeat that if you cherish any such idea and will carry it out, we will not fail in resisting you with all the might that our country can muster. I address this appeal to you in the hope that our movement may even influence you and your partners in the right direction and deflect you and them from the course which is bound to end in your moral ruin and the reduction of human beings to robots.

The hope of your response to my appeal is much fainter than that of response from Britain. I know that the British are not devoid of a sense of justice and they know me. I do not know you enough to be able to judge. All I have read tells me that you listen to no appeal but to the sword. How I wish that you are cruelly misrepresented and that I shall touch the right chord in your heart! Anyway I have an undying faith in the responsiveness of human nature. On the strength of that faith I have conceived the impending movement in India, and it is that faith which has prompted this appeal to you.

HOW TO MEET A JAPANESE INVASION

• by Mirabehn and M. K. Gandhi

In 1942 the Japanese occupied Burma and it was feared that they would soon land on the coast of India. At Gandhi's suggestion one of his trusted co-workers, Miss Madeleine Slade, went to Orissa, a province on India's east coast, to prepare the people for non-violent resistance to the invaders. Her report on the situation and Gandhi's advice are given below. (The expected invasion did not materialize, although later, in 1944, the Japanese did invade the province of Assam by land, but were repulsed.)

Miss Slade, the daughter of a British admiral, first heard about Gandhi from Romain Rolland. After reading Romain's biography of Gandhi she decided to devote her life to him and spent a year in preparation for entering his ashram, during which she practiced spinning. On November 7, 1925 she reached the Sabarmati ashram, near Ahmedabad, and fell on her knees at Gandhi's feet. "He lifted me up," she wrote later, "and taking me in his arms said, 'You shall be my daughter.' And so it has been from that day." Gandhi gave her the name "Mira" and she has been usually known in India as Mirabehn. She was associated with Gandhi for almost twenty-three years, and was imprisoned with him. When she was not with him they corresponded frequently, and in 1949 Miss Slade published part of this correspondence.

• Reprinted with permission from *Gandhi's Letters to a Disciple* (New York: Harper, London: Victor Gollancz, 1950), pp. 210-15.

REPORT BY MIRA

WE MAY TAKE IT that the Japanese will land somewhere along the Orissa coast. Probably there will be no bombing or firing at the time of landing, as there are no defense measures on the coast. From the coast they will advance rapidly across the flat dry rice fields, where the only obstructions are rivers and ditches, now mostly dry and nowhere unfordable. As far as we are able to make out there will be no serious attempt to hold the Japanese advance until the hilly and wooded regions of the Orissa States are reached. The army of defense, whatever it is, is reported to be hidden in the jungle of these parts. It is likely to make a desperate attempt to defend the Jamshedpur [7] road, but the chances of its being successful must be very small. That means we may expect a battle to be fought in the northwest of Orissa, after which the Japanese army will pass on into Bihar. At that time the Japanese are not likely to be broadly distributed over the country, but concentrated on their lines of communication between the sea and their advancing army. The British administration will have previously disappeared from the scene.

The problem before us is, in the event of these things happening, how are we to act?

The Japanese armies will rush over the fields and through the villages, not as avowed enemies of the population, but as chasers and destroyers of the British and American war effort. The population in its turn, is vague in its feelings. The strongest feeling is fear and distrust of the British, which is growing day by day on account of the treatment they are receiving. Anything that is not British is therefore something welcome. Here is a funny example. The villagers in some parts say—"Oh, the aeroplanes that make a great noise are British, but there are silent planes also, and they are Mahatma's planes." I think the only thing possible for these simple, innocent people to learn is the attitude of neutrality, for it is, in reality, the only position that can be made logical to them. The British not only leave them to their fate without even instructing them in self-protection from bombing, etc., but they issue such orders as will, if obeyed, kill them before the day of battle comes. How then can they be ready enthusiastically to obstruct the Japanese who are chasing this detested Raj,[8] especially when the Japanese are saying, "It is not you we have come to fight." But I have found the villagers ready to take up the position of neutrality. That is to say, they would leave the Japanese to pass over their fields and villages, and try as far as possible not to come in contact with them. They would hide their foodstuffs and money, and decline to serve the Japanese. But even that much resistance would be difficult to obtain in some parts, the dislike of the British Raj being so great, that anything anti-British will be welcomed with open arms. I feel we have got to try and gauge the maximum resistance which the average inhabitants may be expected to put up and maintain, and make that our definite stand. A steady, long sustained stand, though not cent per cent resistance, will be more effective in the long run than a stiff stand, which quickly breaks.

This maximum sustainable stand which we may expect from the average people is probably:

1. To resist firmly, and mostly non-violently, the commandeering by the Japanese of any land, houses, or movable property.
2. To render no forced labor to the Japanese.
3. Not to take up any sort of administrative service under the Japanese.

(This may be hard to control in connection with some types of city people, Government opportunists and Indians brought in from other parts.)

4. To buy nothing from the Japanese.
5. To refuse their currency and any effort on their part at setting up a Raj.

(Lack of workers and lack of time make it very hard, but we have to strive to stem the tide.)

Now as to certain difficulties and questions which arise:

1. The Japanese may offer to pay for labor, food and materials in British currency notes. Should the people refuse to sell for good prices or work for a good wage? For long sustained resistance over many months it may be difficult to prevent this. So long as they refuse to buy or take "service," the exploitation danger is kept off.

2. What should be done about the rebuilding of bridges, canals, etc. which the British will have blown up? We shall also need the bridges and canals. Should we, therefore, set our hands to their rebuilding, even if it means working side by side with the Japanese, or should we retire on the approach of Japanese bridge builders?

3. If Indian soldiers, who were taken prisoners in Singapore and Burma, land with the Japanese invading army, what should be our attitude towards them? Should we treat them with the same aloofness as we are to show the Japanese or should we not try to win them over to our way of thinking?

4. After the exodus (before the approaching Japanese) of the British Raj, what shall we do about currency?

5. After battles have been fought and the Japanese armies will have advanced, the battlefield will be left strewn with dead and wounded. I think we must unhesitatingly work side by side with the Japanese in burning and burying the dead and picking up and serving the wounded? The Japanese are likely to attend to the lightly wounded of their own men and take prisoner the lightly wounded of their enemy, but the rest would probably be left, and it will be our sacred duty to attend to them. For this we are from now planning the training of volunteers under the guidance of local doctors. Their services can also be used in case of internal disturbances, epidemics, etc.

6. Besides dead and wounded on the battlefield, a certain amount of rifles, revolvers and other small arms are likely to be left lying about unpicked up by the Japanese. If we do

not make a point of collecting these things they are likely to fall into the hands of robbers, thieves and other bad characters, who always come down like hawks to loot a battlefield. In an unarmed country like India this would lead to much trouble. In the event of our collecting such arms and ammunition, what should we do with them? My instinct is to take them out to sea and drop them in the ocean. Please tell us what you advise.

GANDHI'S REPLY

Sevagram,
Via Wardha, C. P.
31-5-'42

CHI. MIRA,

I have your very complete and illuminating letter. The report of the interview [9] is perfect, your answers were straight, unequivocal and courageous. I have no criticism to make. I can only say, "Go on as you are doing." I can quite clearly see that you have gone to the right place at the right time. I therefore need do nothing more than come straight to your questions which are all good and relevant.

1. I think we must tell the people what they should do. They will act according to their capacity. If we begin to judge their capacity and give directions accordingly our directions will be halting and even compromising which we should never do. You therefore read my instructions in that light. Remember that our attitude is that of complete non-cooperation with Japanese army, therefore we may not help them in any way, nor may we profit by any dealings with them. Therefore we cannot sell anything to them. If people are not able to face the Japanese army, they will do as armed soldiers do, i.e., retire when they are overwhelmed. And if they do so the question of having any dealings with Japanese does not and should not arise. If, however, the people have not the courage to resist Japanese unto death and not the courage and capacity to evacuate the portion invaded by the Japanese, they will do the best they can in the light of instructions. One

thing they should never do—to yield willing submission to the Japanese. That will be a cowardly act, and unworthy of freedom-loving people. They must not escape from one fire only to fall into another and probably more terrible. Their attitude therefore must always be of resistance to the Japanese. No question, therefore, arises of accepting British currency notes or Japanese coins. They will handle nothing from Japanese hands. So far as dealings with our own people are concerned they will either resort to barter or make use of such British currency that they have, in the hope that the National Government that may take the place of the British Government will take up from the people all the British currency in accordance with its capacity.

2. Question about cooperation in bridge-building is covered by the above. There can be no question of this cooperation.

3. If Indian soldiers come in contact with our people, we must fraternize with them if they are well disposed, and invite them, if they can, to join the nation. Probably they have been brought under promise that they will deliver the country from foreign yoke. There will be no foreign yoke and they will be expected to befriend people and obey National Government that might have been set up in place of British Government. If the British have retired in an orderly manner leaving things in Indian hands, the whole thing can work splendidly and it might even be made diffi-cult for Japanese to settle down in India or any part of it in peace, because they will have to deal with a population which will be sullen and resistant. It is difficult to say what can happen. It is enough if people are trained to cultivate the power of resistance, no matter which power is operating—the Japanese or the British.

4. Covered by (1) above.

5. The occasion may not come, but if it does, cooperation will be permissible and even necessary.

6. Your answer about the arms found on the wayside is most tempting and perfectly logical. It may be followed but I would not rule out the idea of worthy people finding them and storing them in a safe place if they can. If it is impossible to store them and keep them from mischievous people yours is an ideal plan.

16 WESTERN FRIENDS

A VISIT FROM GANDHI

•

by Romain Rolland

Romain Rolland was a professor of art at the Sorbonne who produced many critical and historical works, including the romance of Jean-Christophe (1904–12), which brought him worldwide fame. During World War I he was a pacifist and, because of his beliefs, he was persona non grata with most of his countrymen. He therefore lived in Switzerland for many years, returning to France in 1938. He died in 1944.

In 1924 Rolland published a small volume entitled Mahatma Gandhi. This was translated into English and had a wide sale in several languages. It was one of the earliest biographies of Gandhi and the first to be widely circulated in the Western world. Rolland and Gandhi never met until 1931, although they had many friends in common, including Rabindranath Tagore, C. F. Andrews, and Madeleine Slade.

• Reprinted with permission from *The Nation* (New York), February 10, 1932, Vol. 134, pp. 167-68. Rolland wrote this letter to an American friend who, without his permission, published it. Rolland wrote to Gandhi apologizing for its publication. Gandhi wrote of it to Mira as follows: "Give my love to the Rollands and tell them I simply enjoyed that letter to the American friend. Surely there was nothing wrong about it. And how can there be anything wrong in an honest expression of opinion?"

381

When Gandhi journeyed to London in the autumn of 1931 to attend the Round Table Conference, he was met at Marseilles by Mlle. Madeleine Rolland, sister of Rolland. After the conclusion of the conference in December 1931 Gandhi arranged to spend a few days with Rolland near Villeneuve, Switzerland, at the end of Lake Leman. Afterwards, in an article for Young India describing his European sojourn, Gandhi wrote, "Last, but not least, was my pilgrimage to Romain Rolland, the sage of Villeneuve. Could I have left India just to visit him and his inseparable sister, Madeleine, his interpreter and friend, I would have undertaken the voyage."

After Gandhi's visit, Rolland wrote a short description of the visit in a letter to a friend. After Gandhi's death, Madame Rolland released a fuller description of the visit as found in Rolland's Journal.

How I should have liked to have you here during the visit of the Indians! They stayed five days—from Sunday night until Friday afternoon, the eleventh—at the Villa Lionette. The little man, bespectacled and toothless, was wrapped in his white burnoose, but his legs thin as a heron's stilts, were bare. His shaven head with its few coarse hairs was uncovered and wet with rain. He came to me with a dry laugh, his mouth open, like a good dog panting, and flinging an arm around me leaned his cheek against my shoulder. I felt his grizzled head against my cheek. It was, I amuse myself thinking, the kiss of St. Dominic and St. Francis.

Then came Mira [Miss Slade], proud of figure and with the stately bearing of a Demeter, and finally three Indians, one a young son of Gandhi, Devadas, with a round and happy face. He is gentle, and but little aware of the grandeur of his name. The others were secretaries—disciples—two young men of rare qualities of heart and mind: Mahadev Desai and Pyarelal.

As I had contrived shortly beforehand to get a severe cold on my chest, it was to my house and to the chamber on the second floor where I sleep at Villa Olga—you will remember it—that Gandhi came each morning for long conversations. My sister in-

terpreted, with the assistance of Mira, and I had also a Russian
friend and secretary, Miss Kondacheff, who took notes on our
discussions. Some good photographs by Schlemmer, our neighbor
from Montreux, recorded the aspect of our interviews.

Evenings, at seven o'clock, prayers were held in the first floor
salon. With lights lowered, the Indians seated on the carpet, and
the little assembly of the faithful grouped about, there was a suite
of three beautiful chants—the first an extract from the *Gita*, the
second an ancient hymn on the Sanskrit texts which Gandhi had
translated, and the third a canticle of Rama and Sita, intoned by
the warm, grave voice of Mira.

Gandhi held other prayers at three o'clock in the morning, for
which, in London, he used to wake his harassed staff, although he
had not retired until one. This little man, so frail in appearance,
is tireless, and fatigue is a word which does not exist in his vocabu-
lary. He could calmly answer for hours the heckling of a crowd,
as he did at Lausanne and Geneva, without a muscle of his face
twitching. Seated on a table, motionless, his voice always clear and
calm, he replied to his adversaries open or masked—and they
were not lacking at Geneva—giving them rude truths which left
them silenced and suffocated.

The Roman bourgeoisie, militarist and nationalist, who had at
first received him with crafty looks, quivered with rage when he
left. I believe that if his stay had lasted any longer the public
meetings would have been forbidden. He pronounced himself as
unequivocally as possible on the double question of national
armaments and the conflict between capital and labor. I was
largely responsible for steering him on this latter course.

His mind proceeds through successive experiments into action
and he follows a straight line, but he never stops, and one would
risk error in attempting to judge him by what he said ten years
ago, because his thought is in constant evolution. I will give you
a little example of it that is characteristic.

He was asked at Lausanne to define what he understood by
God. He explained how, among the noblest attributes which the
Hindu scriptures ascribed to God, he had in his youth chosen

the word "truth" as most truly defining the essential element. He had then said, "God is Truth." "But," he added, "two years ago I advanced another step. I now say, 'Truth is God.' For even the atheists do not doubt the necessity for the power of truth. In their passion for discovering the truth, the atheists have not hesitated to deny the existence of God, and, from their point of view, they are right." You will understand from this single trait the boldness and independence of this religious spirit from the Orient. I noted in him traits similar to Vivekananda.

And yet not a single political ruse catches him unprepared. And his own politics are to say everything that he thinks to everybody, not concealing a thing.

On the last evening, after the prayers, Gandhi asked me to play him a little of Beethoven. (He does not know Beethoven, but he knows that Beethoven has been the intermediary between Mira and me, and consequently between Mira and himself, and that, in the final count, it is to Beethoven that the gratitude of us all must go.) I played him the *Andante* of the Fifth Symphony. To that I added *Les Champs Elysées* of Gluck—the page for the orchestra and the air for the flute.

He is very sensitive to the religious chants of his country, which somewhat resemble the most beautiful of our Gregorian melodies, and he has worked to assemble them. We also exchanged our ideas on art, from which he does not separate his conception of truth, nor from his conception of truth that of joy, which he thinks truth should bring. But it follows of itself that for this heroic nature joy does not come without effort, nor even life itself without hardship. "The seeker after truth hath a heart tender as the lotus, and hard as granite."

Here, my dear friend, are a few hints of those days of ours together on which I have taken much more detailed notes. What I do not dwell on to you is the hurricane of intruders, loiterers, and half-wits which this visit loosed on our two villas. No, the telephone never ceased ringing; photographers in ambuscades let fly their fusillades from behind every bush. The milkmen's syndicate at Leman informed me that during all the time of this sojourn with me of the "King of India" they intended to assume complete responsibility for his "victualling." We received letters from "Sons of God." Some Italians wrote to the Mahatma beseeching him to indicate for them the ten lucky numbers for the next drawing of the weekly national lottery!

My sister, having survived, has gone to take ten days' rest at a cure in Zurich. She returns tomorrow. For my part, I have entirely lost the gift of sleep. If you find it, send it to me by registered mail!

FROM ROLLAND'S JOURNAL
by Romain Rolland

... THE NEXT DAY, Monday, is Gandhi's "day of silence." He does not speak, but he listens. As he said once laughingly, it is the best opportunity to impose upon him all things one wants him to hear. He must hear without replying (though he does not forbid himself certain brief written answers). Precisely at 10 A.M. he arrives. His irregular chuckle announces him as he ascends the stairs; and I seat him in a big folding arm chair next to my table, upon which I rest my elbows and from my swivel chair I lean towards him. Immediately he pulls his naked feet from his sandals, and, enveloped in his cloak, he folds his legs under him. He wears big bifocal glasses which allow him to see far and near. His complexion is tanned, but sunburned rather than dark. The profile of his skull is elongated, and this impression is accentuated by the absence of front teeth which renders his mouth ratlike—his fairly

• Reprinted with permission from Rolland's Journal; published under the title "Les Propos de Gandhi à Romain Rolland" in *Le Figaro Littéraire* (Paris), February 7, 1948, pp. 1, 4. Copyright by Mme. Romain Rolland and translated for this anthology by Michael Kay.

big lower lip protruding and the upper lip bearing a grey, sparse moustache. The nose is straight, rather deep-set, flattened at the end with two wide nostrils. The ears stand out. The forehead is wide and well built; it is deeply wrinkled when he speaks; but the cheeks and the rest of the face, substantially strong, do not show the web of wrinkles of our European faces. This first impression of frailty is deceiving: the man is solid. His big, thin hands which clutch his cloak over his arms are all bones, veins and salient, swollen muscles. They betray to me by their continuous quiverings (and by those, which one may guess, of his feet under the cloak) the nervousness of so calm a man yet always master of himself. . . .

Tuesday, the 8th, at half-past nine, the interview with Gandhi is resumed. He wants first of all to deal with the Italian question. He says that he has been invited to Italy by consul Scarpa, a man of culture, who is acquainted with Hindus and has interests in India. Scarpa has a good reputation in India. This reputation is based on his alleged sympathy for the national cause. But Gandhi is suspicious. He thinks that Scarpa's aims are purely selfish. Already in India, Gandhi received an invitation to visit Italy. . . . I wish to go there, to see Mussolini, declares Gandhi. My desire is to see people; to bring them the mission of peace. That they should not accept it does not concern me, and it will not deter me. And I want to see the Pope who sent me a good message; if I see him, I could handle better the Indian Roman Catholics; and I shall see their chief as I see Moslem chiefs. . . .

Gandhi: I must take literally what Scarpa tells me (that he is not acting on Government's behalf but on his own). I shall accept the thing (Scarpa's invitation to speak. . . .). But I shall impose the condition that I choose freely the subject.

Rolland: Then you must demand that foreign reporters be present to take down what you say. Though these foreigners might also be fascists. . . . It is very difficult to be sure that what you will say will not be concealed or distorted.

Gandhi: It is against my nature to prearrange.

Rolland: A vacuum will be created around you; you will be secluded; you will be surrounded only by fascists. . . .

Gandhi: I realize this; but this will not prevent me from breaking through the cordon. My condition will be that I must speak freely and not about neutral subjects; I shall say what I think. This is how I feel. I cannot act otherwise; but I have received the invitation and I think that I shall be able to speak even in this atmosphere.

Rolland: A good impression is impossible for it will be impossible for you to be in touch with the right people. You will be only with the chosen accomplices of the regime. . . . Where, when, and how would you see other people? They will think that you came to pay homage to the oppressor.

Gandhi: Tell me, then, your final opinion as to my stop-over in Rome.

Rolland: I would impose conditions. Otherwise, I am afraid you would be the victim of a fraud. Over there you must not mince matters; no softness or courtesy. To whatever you say they would all answer: Yes, yes. (Like Mussolini answering Tagore who was saying that violence horrified him: Me, too. . . .) and they would all think the opposite. . . .

Rolland: Among men, cruelties and offences are sometimes caused by a morbid, pathological state of mind. In all societies people exist who are harmful and really should be treated. What attitude should the followers of non-violence adopt in respect to these sick, insane people so as to protect society from them? How to act in this instance without violence?

Gandhi: I would keep them under restraint. And I would not call it violence. If my brother were to lose his mind, I would handcuff him to prevent him from causing harm; but I would not use violence against him for there is no reason to do so. And my brother would not feel either that violence is employed. On the contrary, when he comes to his senses, he will thank me for having restrained him. I must not take into account his resistance during his period of insanity, for my action must be inspired by unadulterated love. My action is without any hidden selfishness; it is not even to protect myself from him. I know that while handcuffing him, I run the risk of being struck by him; but I shall not care. I tie his hands so that he can regain his mental balance. If I tie them, it is not to save myself; if he wounds me while I am saving him, I shall let him. I would act in the same manner towards the partially-insane of whom you speak. I would put them in sick bays, not guarded by harsh jailers but surrounded by care. I would have them treated by specialists who have studied their sicknesses and the ways of curing them. I would go deeper and determine the causes. It is the present society which gives birth to the criminals of this type. To my mind the root of the problem is the race for profits, competition and forced equalization. This is why I would reorganize society. I would commission experts to discover the special and ulterior causes. And then research would go on in the treatment not only of mentally sick criminals but also of all kinds of crimes. . . .

IMPRESSIONS OF GANDHI
by C. F. Andrews

Of all the Westerners who were friends of Gandhi, none was closer to him for a longer period than C. F. Andrews, the missionary. In 1904 Andrews left England to teach at a Christian college in Delhi. He participated in Indian life more than most Englishmen. When in 1913 the tension over Indians in South Africa was at a climax, he volunteered to go to South Africa to

• Reprinted with permission from S. Radhakrishnan, editor, *Mahatma Gandhi: Essays and Reflections on His Life and Work* (London: Allen and Unwin, 2nd ed., 1949), pp. 48-53.

help the cause of the Indians. Gokhale, the Indian leader and friend of Gandhi, bade him go to South Africa with another young Englishman, William W. Pearson.[1] They were met at the quay in Durban, Natal, by Henry Polak, Herman Kallenbach, and Gandhi. Andrews, when introduced to Gandhi, bent swiftly down and touched Gandhi's feet.

Andrews participated in the negotiations of the Indians with the South African government. He and Gandhi remained friends for the next thirty-six years, and in 1924 Gandhi said of him, "We are as blood-brothers." It is said that Andrews was the only person who in later years called Gandhi "Mohan"—for Mohandas. Andrews was on equally intimate terms with Rabindranath Tagore. He spent his whole life aiding Indians the world over—in Fiji, South America, and South Africa. His extensive travels and his work are described in the biography, Charles Freer Andrews, by Benarsidas Chaturvedi and Marjorie Sykes.

Andrews was the foremost Western interpreter of Gandhi, especially through the three volumes which he edited: Mahatma Gandhi's Ideas, Mahatma Gandhi: His Own Story, and Mahatma Gandhi At Work: His Own Story Continued. He also wrote many articles about Gandhi. One of the last of these was for a volume of essays and reflections on Gandhi's work presented to Gandhi on his seventieth birthday in 1939.

LET US now turn to the human side. Here there are touches which are very tender and lovable, and these should always be placed side by side with the austerity. . . .

Many years ago I had been deeply impressed by the insight of the great writer Romain Rolland, who had described Mahatma Gandhi as the "St. Paul of our own days." This seemed to me to contain an important truth; for Gandhi, like Paul, comes clearly under the category of the twice-born among men of religion. He experienced at a special moment in his life that tremendous convulsion of the human spirit, which we call "conversion." In his early days he had followed a career at the Bar as a lawyer with great ardor. Success had been a main ambition—success in his profession; success in life as a man; and deeper down in his heart, success as a national leader.

He had gone out to South Africa on a business visit to act as a lawyer in an important trial, wherein two Indian merchants were engaged in litigation. Hitherto, he had only a distant knowledge of the color bar and had never considered what it might mean to himself if he was personally attacked and insulted. But as he journeyed from Durban and reached Maritzburg this dreadful experience came to him suddenly in all its cruel nakedness. He was thrown out of his compartment by the railway official, though he carried a first-class ticket; and the mail train went on without him. It was late at night and he was in an utterly strange railway station, knowing no one. There, all night long, as he sat shivering with cold, after enduring this insult, he wrestled within himself, whether to take the next steamer back to India, or to go through to the bitter end, suffering what his own people had to suffer. Before the morning the light came to his soul. He determined by God's grace to play the man. More humiliations were soon to be heaped upon him of the same character and in South Africa he was never without them. But he had put his hand to the plough and he would never turn back.

I heard him tell the story of that night to Dr. Mott [2] last November. He made clear, as he told it, that this was the turning-point from which his own new life began.

There are other qualities in Mahatma Gandhi that have their counterpart in the rugged figure of the Apostle Paul—a faith in God that will never allow him to yield to man; a sense of the black horror of sin, especially sins of the flesh; a severity towards those whom he loves most dearly, lest they should fall short of his own earnest longing for them, and yet withal a pathetic tenderness of heart which makes him long for a touch of human sympathy whenever he is misunderstood.

There is also something more in him which comes near to St. Francis of Assisi, for Gandhi also has taken Poverty as his bride. He might truly be called to-day "the Little Poor Man of Segaon." For he lives there, among the depressed and poor villagers, sharing their burdens with them. On two occasions I have seen him when this likeness to St. Francis became luminously clear to me.

The former of these was in the still afterglow of a dark evening twilight at the Ashram (retreat) called Phoenix, near Durban. The strain of a long day of unwearied ministry among the poor was over, and Mahatma Gandhi was seated under the open sky, tired almost beyond human endurance, but even at such a time he nursed a sick child on his lap who clung to him with a pathetic affection. A Zulu girl from the school on the Hill beyond the Ashram was seated there also. He asked me to sing "Lead, Kindly Light" as the darkness grew deeper and deeper. Even then, though he was much younger, his frail body was worn with suffering that could never be laid aside even for a moment: yet his spirit within was radiant when the hymn broke the silence, with its solemn close,

> And with the morn those angel faces smile,
> Which I have loved long since and lost awhile.

I can remember how we all sat in silence when the hymn was finished, and how he then repeated to himself those two lines which I have quoted. The other scene was in Orissa, near to the place where I am now writing. He had been very near death; for a sudden and complete exhaustion had come over him and his blood pressure had mounted perilously high. On receiving a telegram, I had traveled all through the night to be at his side. When I reached him he lay there facing the sunrise, after a restless night. A man from one of the lowest grades of the untouchables suddenly drew near to him in supplication just as we began our talk. In a moment his own sickness seemed to have vanished and his whole heart was torn with agony by the cruel humiliation which had reduced the man who prostrated himself before us almost to a sub-human level. . . .

ANDREWS ON HIS DEATH-BED

by Benarsidas Chaturvedi and Marjorie Sykes

WHEN [Andrews] was examined in the Presidency General Hospital at Calcutta [3] it was feared that a major operation might prove necessary, and a smaller interim operation had to be performed at once. Recovery was very slow; speech and writing were difficult for weeks, and decision about the major operation was postponed. Friends surrounded him as he lay in hospital; after a time he could dictate, slowly but quite clearly and coherently, letters to dear ones, messages of love and requests for prayer.

Mahatma Gandhi came down to Calcutta and paid a long visit to the hospital; Charlie looked at his friend with deep affection. "Swaraj is coming, Mohan," he whispered. "Both Englishmen and Indians can make it come if they will. Do you know? I am quite reconciled to my illness. I think it was God's blessing in disguise. . . ."

. . . Later, when the critical operation had been decided upon, Gandhi sent him a brief telegram of love and blessing. Andrews read it, and sat on for a while in silence. "I have no anxiety now," he said at last. "Once when Bapu was fasting I begged him to consult a doctor and he answered, 'Charlie, don't you believe in God?' I am thinking of that great Doctor today. Whatever He does will be right for me and good for India and the world."

Yet he desired to live, and had not grown weary of service.

After the second operation he was rarely fully conscious; but when he opened his eyes and saw one whom he loved by his bedside, the beautiful smile lit up his face. . . . On the fourth day he was sinking, and he died in the very early hours of Friday, April 5th.

• Reprinted with permission from Benarsidas Chaturvedi and Marjorie Sykes, *Charles Freer Andrews* (New York: Harper, 1950), pp. 316-18.

THE LEGACY LEFT BY ANDREWS
by M. K. Gandhi

AT THE PRESENT MOMENT [4] I do not wish to think of English misdeeds. They will be forgotten but not one of the heroic deeds of Andrews will be forgotten so long as India and England live. . . . It is possible, quite possible, for the best Englishmen and the best Indians to meet together and never to separate till they have evolved a formula acceptable to both. The legacy left by Andrews is worth the effort. .

MY GANDHI
by John Haynes Holmes

Dr. John Haynes Holmes, minister of the Community Church in New York City from 1919 to 1949, was the original interpreter of Gandhi to America. C. F. Andrews, the greatest interpreter of Gandhi to the whole Western world, wrote that Dr. Holmes was "the very first to make the name of Gandhi known and loved in America. What Romain Rolland has done in Europe, he himself has accomplished in the New World." Dr. Holmes first told the

• Reprinted with permission from C. F. Andrews, editor, *Mahatma Gandhi's Ideas* (London: Allen and Unwin, 1949), p. 13.
•• Reprinted with permission from John Haynes Holmes, *My Gandhi* (New York: Harper, 1953), pp. 13-14, 27-30, 34, 38-41, 111, 113-14, 115-16, 123-25.

story of his discovery of Gandhi in a sermon entitled "The Christ of Today," which was widely distributed in America and also reprinted in India. As editor of the magazine Unity in the 1920s and 1930s he wrote frequently on Gandhi. Gandhi's autobiography was first published in America in this magazine, in serial form. Dr. Holmes made a great collection of books by and about Gandhi, which has now been deposited in the Harvard University Library. In 1953 he wrote an intimate account of his experiences with the Mahatma in a volume called My Gandhi.

I WAS ONE among a multitude of persons who were blessed with Gandhi's friendship. I corresponded with him on casual occasions, and on two or three of the great crises of his career. I met and talked with him, first, in London in 1931, and again in New Delhi in 1947, thus seeing him against a background of my Western and his Eastern civilization. Through long periods of time and at great distances, I carried Gandhi in my heart, and grew to love him as my own. All this is too scant to constitute a chapter in the Mahatma's life. But it is a part of the record, and is so set down.

Some will complain that my contact with Gandhi, while pleasant, was none the less quite unimportant. I do not complain at this complaint, as I never tried to make this relationship with the Mahatma important, nor myself important for having had it. But there is an importance which attaches to anything that has to do with a really great man. And there is a duty which imposes itself upon anybody who has touched greatness to share with the world the privilege which he has had. . . .

Gandhi came into my life. At the moment I most needed him, I discovered that there was such a man. He was living in the faith that I had sought. He was making it work and proving it right. He was everything I believed but hardly dared to hope. He was a dream come true.

I have already stated that, so far as I can remember, I had never in my life up to that time heard Gandhi's name. But here it was, Mohandas Karamchand Gandhi, spread like a banner on Gilbert Murray's pages in the Hibbert Journal. I know I had never heard

the story of the exploits of this extraordinary man in the rebellion
of his fellow countrymen in South Africa, which he had so patiently and bravely led against the prejudice of the people and the
oppression of the government. But here was the outline of it in a
few vivid words set down in Professor Murray's article on conscientious objection to participation in war. Gandhi! Why did I not
know this name? Gandhi! Who was this man, and what did he
look like? GANDHI! How had he gotten into South Africa? How
had he organized his nonviolent resistance campaign against the
inequity and injustice which ground the coolie Indians into the
dust of the white man's rule? Above all, by what miracle had this
one man sustained the fight for twenty years, without violence or
bloodshed, and at last carried it through to victory? There was
little in what Professor Murray had written to satisfy my curiosity.
But this little was quite enough to prod me wide awake, and to
shake me, like a midnight earthquake, to the very foundations of
my being. I lived the experience of John Keats when he first read
Chapman's Homer, and wrote his immortal confession,

> Then felt I like some watcher of the skies
> When a new planet swims into his ken.

. . . I left the library that afternoon in a daze of wonder and excitement. I must learn about this man whom I had so unexpectedly discovered. I must get information to dispel my ignorance.
But my quest proved to be difficult. People in general and scholars
in particular seemed to know as little about this Indian in South
Africa as I did. For Gandhi had not broken into the magic circle
of the public press. He had not yet attracted the attention of
journalists who hold the key to the closed door of contemporary
knowledge. There was material, of course, published in South
Africa, but this was mostly inaccessible in America. Not until I
went to England in 1922 did I lay hold on some of this material,
and have the great good fortune to meet Mr. Henry S. L. Polak,
early associate of Gandhi, who was the first to write of him. My
search, however, proved to be mostly an experience of frustration.
But all the while, in my early bafflement and occasional despair,

I felt within me the ever-deepening conviction that I was on the right track. This Gandhi was a great and wonderful man. Where was there anybody to match him in our troubled and wicked world? Did he not hold in his heart the secret of man's deliverance from the evils, mostly of man's own choosing, which were now besetting him and threatening to destroy him? Must he not be proclaimed at once as a world leader, the compeer of the greatest men of our own or any other time?

The more I thought of it, the more this conviction grew upon me. It was under its impress—an intuition of the soul rather than any persuasion of the mind—that I climbed tremulously into my pulpit on Sunday morning, April 10, 1922, to preach to my people on the subject, "Who Is the Greatest Man in the World?" and to answer my own question, M. K. Gandhi, of India. The audacity of this declaration, in the light of what was known, and not known, at that time about Gandhi here in our western world, seems now incredible. A great audience had gathered, for the subject of my discourse was a riddle which titillated the public imagination. Interest was keen, as the war had brought many men to the conspicuous attention of mankind, and people wanted to know which one I would choose to be supreme. But all was confusion when I named Gandhi, for few had ever heard of this Indian, knew even that he was an Indian, and fewer still knew anything about his career. This confusion is the explanation of the fact that my sermon did not carry very far in the public prints. Newspapers are not expected to present dictionaries and encyclopedias with their news reports. But by some strange miracle of fortune, the sermon found its way to India—first, the story that I had declared Gandhi to be "the greatest man in the world," and later the full text of what I had said to justify this judgment. This was widely published, even in the native press, and everywhere stirred interest and acclaim. The Indians knew Gandhi, and already reverenced him. And here was evidence that the West was discovering him, and recognizing and welcoming his work for the liberation of his people. Everything that has happened since that date, now over thirty years ago, every word spoken and deed done

by Gandhi, his life, his death, the applause of men, all have con-
spired, as it were, to confirm my original pronouncement. And
today the whole world accepts all that I dared, at that early hour,
to declare. Nay more, far more! For Gandhi is today listed among
the immortals. His people name him with Buddha, and so enroll
him in the pantheon of the spirit. . . .

It was Saturday, the 12th of September, 1931—a cold, rainy, and
dismal day. I was in London, to meet Gandhi. "Charlie" Andrews, beloved of Gandhi through many years, had sent me word
that the Mahatma was landing that very morning at Folkestone,
and would I come and join the little group of friends who would
be there on the pier to meet and greet him on his arrival. Gandhi's
mission in England, as all the world knew, was to attend the impending sessions of the famous Round Table Conference on
Indian affairs. . . .

In a few moments, which seemed like hours, we were aboard
the ship, and I was standing at the door of Gandhi's cabin, awaiting my turn to be received. It was here I had my first glimpse of
the Mahatma.

He was sitting cross-legged upon his berth, engaged in earnest
conversation with Reginald Reynolds, who was a member of the
Quaker group which had been appointed to welcome Gandhi in
the name of the English Friends. His head and shoulders were
bent forward in a listening attitude, so that I could not see his
face. A naked arm, long and lean and wiry, reached out of the
shawl, flung lightly about his shoulders, and took a paper from
Reginald's hand. There was a quick interchange of words, a flit-
ting smile, and the conference was over.

It was now my turn. I stepped into the little cabin. Instantly,
when Gandhi saw me, he jumped to his feet, and with the lithe
quick step of a schoolboy, came forward to greet me. I cannot
now seem to remember whether or not he gave me the familiar
Hindu salutation. But I felt his hands take mine with a grasp as
firm as that of an athlete.

"I wish you might have met me at Marseilles," he said, referring to his landing at the French port, and taking a train north to the Channel and Folkestone.

I replied that I was afraid that I would be in the way—that I was always reluctant to intrude upon busy and important people. Whereupon he rebuked me gently, and invited me to be with him in London. Then the conversation drifted, as conversations have a way of doing on such occasions, to other and more general themes. I do not recall particularly what was said. I was too excited and confused to make note of Gandhi's remarks. But I shall never forget those bright eyes shining through his spectacles, his voice so clear and yet so gentle, his whole presence so simple and yet so strong. We had only a few precious moments together—others were pressing upon us and clamoring for attention. So I withdrew and contented myself with watching this man whose spirit had reached me, years before, across the continents and seas of half the world.

I have often been asked to describe my initial impression of Gandhi. I do not find this question hard to answer. It centered, first of all, in my somewhat amusing recognition of the fact that he looked exactly like the photographs and cartoons that I had seen of him in recent years. In one way, this was inevitable, so distinctive were the characteristics of his personality. In another way, this was remarkable, so difficult was it to get Gandhi before a camera or drawing board. I suppose I have seen hundreds of his pictures, but I find it hard to remember one for which the Mahatma had made a deliberate pose. In an interview with him at New Delhi, on my visit to India in 1947–1948, I was accompanied by my son. I asked if the latter could "snap" us as we talked. Gandhi smiled, said that he was used to these "instruments of torture," and went right on in his conversation with me, as though nothing else were going on at all. Gandhi had no time, least of all any interest, in posing for pictures. So photograph and drawings were, in a very special sense of the word, mere glimpses of a man in action. And here he was, precisely the man I had seen so many times in the newspaper or on the screen. As I watched the scene in the crowded cabin of the ship, I felt as though I were looking at mute representations of the Mahatma suddenly come to life.

My second and strangely simultaneous impression was of the infinite grace and charm of Gandhi, who, in his physical appearance, was so awkward. Thus, everybody who entered this little room in which we stood, was, in one way or another, under strain, and thus uneasy. The officials present were anxious that there should be no error or mischance in the proceedings of the occasion. Journalists were eager to get their stories, photographers their pictures, each one his own and thus original. Friends were embarrassed by the difficulties of getting at their beloved Mahatma, and paying him the attention and protection which a tired man would welcome. Some few persons, like myself, were frankly frightened—this stupendous personal experience was too much for our equanimity and courage! But all these varied reactions speedily vanished, like the morning mist, before Gandhi's easy grace. What we saw at the start was the physical appearance of one of the world's great figures. But this almost instantly passed into the spiritual presence of a loving and infinitely lovable man. What we felt, in the first few moments, was reverence and awe, but this was immediately caught up and absorbed by his simplicity, innocence, and charm. Gandhi's attitude had all the naturalness and spontaneity of a little child. There was in him and about him not an iota of self-consciousness—no pose, pretentiousness, or pride. In no time at all, Gandhi had us all laughing, as completely at our ease as though we had known one another and him for years. If, in this world of varied personalities, there is a single man even half as charming, and thus as irresistible, as Gandhi, I have not seen him. . . .

I last saw Gandhi on my visit to India in 1947–1948. I went to the Far East, on appointment by an American foundation, to lecture at Indian colleges and universities. When the invitation was received and accepted, and plans for distant traveling were under way, I wrote to the Mahatma about my journey, and asked if I could come and see him. He answered promptly and as follows:

"You have given me not only exciting but welcome news. The news appears to be almost too good to be true, and I am not going to believe it in its entirety unless you are physically in India."

. . . It was under such conditions as these, marking a supreme crisis in his life and India, that Gandhi, in the kindliness of his spirit, arranged an appointment on the very day of my arrival, at the precise hour of four o'clock in the afternoon. On the very tick of this hour, for I remembered Gandhi's extreme emphasis on punctuality, I was at Birla House. The door from the street was wide open, and I entered without ceremony, or any particular attention on the part of several secretaries or attendants who were moving about, and of one or two native newspapermen who were squatting on the threshold. Everything was easy and informal and marvelously quiet. But I soon found I was expected, and was taken without a moment's delay to Gandhi's room at the far end of the hallway on the main floor.

Gandhi was sitting cross-legged upon his linen-covered cushions placed comfortably upon the floor. He had given instructions that I should not be asked to remove my shoes, according to custom, since I would be more at my ease if I did not think of them at all. On seeing me, he extended his right hand, in smiling welcome, and seized my hand in the warm clasp which was the familiar gesture of my country and not of his. Then, without a word, he beckoned me to a chair placed close in front of him, and asked me to sit down. . . .

One thought smote me with astonishment on this visit, and has lingered with me since. I refer to the fact that, as I looked upon Gandhi in New Delhi, I seemed to see the same man I had earlier seen in London in 1931. Seventeen years had passed since that first meeting, and they had apparently not touched the Mahatma at all. Oh yes—his hair had whitened, and retreated farther back from the broad and open brow. But I could see no wrinkles, nor looseness of the flesh. He walked more slowly, with a step which had lost its quick and lithe response. But his strength was quite unexhausted, as witness his pilgrimage into Bengal, to stay the uprisings and the violent fighting in that unhappy region. Cer-

tainly he appeared the same, apart from unimportant aspects of
face and body. As I talked with him, I could feel that it was only
the day before that I had been with him at Kingsley Hall, and
that all the years between had been rolled back and were now as
though they had never been. Here was a man who had mastered
the regimen of life—had broken the barriers of the flesh, and entered already into the pure realm of the spirit. Gandhi had been
quoted as promising his disciples that he would live to be a hundred and twenty-five years old. I had taken this to be an expansive
statement of the Mahatma's continuing good health, already extraordinary for a man of seventy-eight living constantly in the
midst of alarms. What was my astonishment when I heard one of
the outstanding public leaders of India, governor of a great province, a man of high intelligence and unimpeachable character,
declare in all seriousness that he believed that, barring accidents,
Gandhi would survive to precisely that great age. Having seen
Gandhi, who was I to doubt? . . .

My last meeting with Gandhi was brief, hurried, unsatisfactory, and yet to me a benediction. . . . Quickly, as though under
inspiration, I decided to go to Birla House, and wait there until
there came some happy interval when I might see the Mahatma
if only for a moment snatched between two interviews. In the
blazing heat of early afternoon, I made my way to the house, and
entered without interference or even inquiry. Fortune was with
me, for who was this coming down the hall but Mirabehn. I told
her at once of my predicament, that I was leaving and must see
Gandhi, and besought her help. She smiled assurance, placed me
in a small reception room, and went off to make inquiries. She
was soon returned with the message that Gandhiji was sleeping—
his regular afternoon nap. But he was due to awaken at any moment, and I could then see him at once.

We sat together and talked—some fifteen minutes, perhaps.
Then came the summons, and I was in Gandhiji's presence again.
It was all very simple and unimportant. I told him I must say
good-by—explained the long journey before me. I might be back,
and then again I might not. I shall not forget how Gandhiji took

my hand and, with his old smile of loving-kindness, made me promise that I would come again. I said, Yes—if circumstances did not forbid. Which is just what circumstances did in this case! I did not see him again. This was my last farewell. . . .

I often wonder that there was so little anticipation of Gandhi's death. When people in dismay of the future would say to me that anything might happen in India today, the final disaster waiting upon any chance event, I would say, "What, for example?" And they would say, "Why, Nehru might be shot," or "Gandhi might die of some latest fast." But I do not recall ever hearing anybody suggest that Gandhi might be shot, or otherwise assassinated. His sanctity had won immunity from violence! No hand could or would be raised against him. But it was just this which shook the world, like some cosmic earthquake, when Gandhi died.

It was a few minutes after nine o'clock, on the morning of Friday, January 30, 1948. I had returned from India and was in my study, examining the mail. Suddenly there came a sharp ringing of the telephone, and the voice of one excitedly declaring that Gandhi was dead. At first I could not seem to understand. Gandhi dead? I telephoned the information bureau of the New York Times and made inquiry. The answer came back crisp and clear. "Yes, Gandhi is dead. He was shot last evening." "But is he dead," I asked again, finding it impossible to believe that the Mahatma could die. The reply was definite and unhesitating. Gandhi was dead!

I stood as though in a daze, unable even to think. I seemed paralyzed, and did not move. Slowly, like coming out of the ether on an operating table, I recovered consciousness. I spoke to my secretary. I thought of my wife. I ran to her in an agony of spirit. Then, when I saw her and heard her speak as though from a great distance, a strange thing happened. I began to cry, and found, to my amazement and alarm, that I could not stop. . . .

17 HOME AND FAMILY

AT SEVAGRAM
by Mahadev Desai

*Gandhi's Boswell was Mahadev Desai, who first became asso-
ciated with him in 1917, when he volunteered to work as a teacher
in the villages of Champaran. For more than twenty-four years he
was Gandhi's personal secretary and chronicler. He lived with
Gandhi, toured with him, and went to prison with him. It was
in detention at the Aga Khan Palace in 1942 that Desai died of a
heart attack in the presence of Gandhi. Desai wrote several books
about Gandhi as well as numerous descriptions of Gandhi's interviews with the great and the unknown.*

. . . NURSING THOSE who are ailing mentally and physically has
been a passion with him throughout his life. But for his fundamental objection to vivisection, he might have been a physician
and a surgeon.

But though he chose law as his profession and then public life
claimed the bulk of his time, the passion has remained and developed from what it once was—a hobby—to a sort of spiritual need.

In one of his most intimate articles recently written in Gujarati,

• Reprinted with permission from D. G. Tendulkar et al., editors, *Gandhiji:
His Life and Work* (Bombay: Karnatak, 1944), pp. 247-51, 256-59.

he wrote, "I needed the solitude of Sevagram. It has been my experience that I can draw my inspiration only from my natural setting—the surroundings in which I live. Since the discovery of Satyagraha I have been fixing up my abode in what are called ashrams and pursuing my sadhana [1] there. But Sevagram I have hesitated to call by the name of ashram. I had originally thought of living and working there in solitude.

"But in spite of myself the place has developed into an ashram without any rules and regulations. It is growing and new huts are springing up. Today it has become a hospital. In jest I have called it a 'Home for the Invalids.' I am physically and even mentally an invalid and I have collected about myself a crowd of invalids.

"I have even likened it to a lunatic asylum—by no means an inappropriate comparison. Surely swaraj through the spinning wheel can be the proposition only of a lunatic. But luckily lunatics are unaware of their lunacy. And so I regard myself as sane."

Well, it is these ailing and the infirm and the so-called lunatics that give him his inspiration. When we are away from headquarters the letters to be placed on the top of the day's post must be from these. His most concentrated work, his most important talk or interview, may be interrupted by anyone seeking his advice about the diet, bath and treatment of these patients.

Curiously enough, everyone knows his weakness in the matter, and so only with one or two rare exceptions has the Working Committee met outside Wardha. The formal meetings have been held in Wardha but the informal and more important ones have been held in the little mud hut where Gandhiji dwells, the smallest and yet the neatest little tenement in the colony.

It is there that men like Lord Lothian [2] and Sir Stafford Cripps have had talks with him. There is no furniture but the Sevagram-made palm-leaf mats spread on the floor, a stool being sometimes provided for those who cannot manage to sit cross-legged.

Though the absence of furniture leaves enough floor-space, we are sometimes hard put to it when there are deputations of ten to fifteen people wanting to interview him. The walls are decorated with palm trees in clay relief done by Mirabehn, for whom the hut was originally made, but whose gipsy blood will not allow her to stay in one hut for any length of time. . . .

There are two classes of people, says Karel Capek;[3] one class loves to collect odds and ends until their abode is littered with them, the other class will have as few things for themselves as they possibly can. Gandhiji combines in himself both the types, having the fewest possible needs and yet collecting all kinds of odds and ends.

Even like his memory, which retains the essentials and rejects the unessentials, his odds and ends, which you find collected in the hut, have their uses for him, and the moment he needs a nail or a pin or some cardboard or an envelope made by the hand from waste-paper, his finger unerringly falls on the proper place.

But to turn to the mud hut, whatever the number of visitors and whatever the time, the little hut remains the scene of Gandhiji's various activities from morning until night. At 11 o'clock every day it is turned into a dining room, for Gandhiji's instructions regarding the diet of the patients are final, in spite of their general treatment being in charge of Dr. Sushila Nayyar.

So the patients—among whom have been distinguished people like Jairamdas Doulatram, member of the Working Committee[4] —have their meals served before Gandhiji, who looks into every little detail.

Within an hour after this the hut becomes office with the day's post and newspapers, and after he has heard the main items or cast his eye over the post, it becomes his siesta-room, the time being utilized by his many helpers too for the same purpose.

Then writing or the giving of interviews begins, sometimes these taking place as he is lying on his back with a mud poultice on his abdomen. This is part of his permanent treatment for blood pressure—not prescribed by any doctors but by himself.

In the hot season a mud-bandage on the head is an additional item, and to wondering visitors he often delights in describing the wonderful properties of mother earth: "That is why, instead of treading upon it, I have it on my head and on my abdomen."

Then comes spinning, almost always being accompanied by the giving of interviews. But sometimes one finds him engrossed in examining the details of the latest model of charkha and making suggestions to the designer.

Perhaps very few people know that it was Gandhiji who, by numerous experiments in Yeravda Prison, perfected the portable spinning wheel which was originally designed by a Surat friend called Vimawala. It is therefore that the perfected wheel goes by the name of "Yeravda Charkha," even as the pact that was sealed with a fast in the same prison goes by the name of the Yeravda Pact.

But I have digressed. At five o'clock goes the bell for the final meal of the day and the patients foregather in the hut, which has again become the dining room. Babu Rajendra Prasad who with his inseparable companion asthma is always a patient, often turns up with tough questions on the day's business and stays to have his meal with the patients.

The dinner over, the hut is deserted by the many occupants who go out for their evening constitutional. And after evening prayers the hut is converted, along with a little verandah attached to it, into a bed-room.

The morning and the evening constitutionals are as much part of Gandhiji's regular routine as the prayers. Plenty of business is transacted during these walks—details about the kitchen, or the crops, or the latest born calf in the dairy being discussed with those in charge of them. Many of the workers in Wardha, in charge of the tannery or the Village Industries Association, do not ask for separate time for themselves but simply walk out with Gandhiji to finish their business.

Often enough interviews of a serious nature do take place on these walks, but when there is no such interviewer, the day's fatigue is lightened by Gandhiji chatting away and amusing himself with the tiny tots who accompany him. . . .

With the introduction of the Wardha Scheme of Education the Aryanayakams [5] who were in Wardha were attracted to Sevagram and started the experiment in its proper environment.

With the growing population and the milk-needs of the patients came into being the dairy, with someone to take charge of it.

All the milk, butter and other milk products needed for the colony are produced on the premises, and so too the vegetables and part of the cereals. That necessarily means a herd of cattle, not to mention the goats.

So it is the *sanyasi's* [6] story over again. The *sanyasi* had a cat, a cow was needed to give it milk, then someone to take care of the cow, and so on. And I have little doubt that even if Gandhiji were to retire to the Himalayas, the *sanyasi's* story would be repeated there in all its vivid detail.

But how did the "menagerie," the name which Sardar Vallabhbhai often gives to the *ashram*, come into being? In a word, I can say that it sprang out of Gandhiji's loyalty to his co-workers and his weakness for birds of the same feather. However radical he may be he is conservative in his tastes and attachment to friends and co-workers. Old co-workers gravitate towards him and he gravitates towards them!

At the head of the queer crowd is Bhansali, as unlike the rest as anything could be. Once a professor in the Gujarat Vidyapith, and then a jail-bird, he ultimately turned recluse, went to the length of fasting for weeks, and ultimately betook himself to the forest, where he wandered for years without a shred of cloth on him. He took a vow of silence for several years, sewed up his lips with a copper-ring, and lived on raw wheat flour and *neem* [7] leaves.

Once during his wanderings he stumbled upon Gandhiji and stayed. Gandhiji gently nursed him back to ordinary life, and the man who questioned the necessity for work, and hated it as a kind of bondage, now puts in about seventeen hours of it every day. He cards his cotton, spins for eight to ten hours and teaches for seven hours. He not only speaks now—but fills the *ashram* and its neighborhood with roars of laughter. He is now civilized to the extent of wrapping a piece of cloth round his waist, but has no weakness for the belongings to which ordinary human beings are slaves.

In a place infested with scorpions and poisonous snakes he moves about without a lantern and without shoes, believing that these creatures of God are no less his brothers than the human beings among whom he lives. He often harks back to his life of fiery penance and comes in with a request to Gandhiji for permission to hang down a well head-over-heels! But, thank God, he accepts Gandhiji's discipline.

There is among us a Japanese sadhu (monk) who works like a horse and lives like a hermit, doing all the hard chores of the ashram and going about merrily beating his drum early every morning and evening, filling the air with his chanting of Om Namyo Hom Renge Kyom.[8] He is, of course, pro-Japanese and believes that Japan is out to serve and civilize China. But I do not believe there is an iota of truth in the charge some people have levelled at him of being a Government spy. If he is a spy, spies must be most amiable specimens of humanity and I should like to be one. To my mind he lives up to the gospel of ahimsa better than any one of us not excluding Gandhiji.

Among the patients there is a leper. He was a political jail-bird with us in Yeravda and got leprosy there, or had it diagnosed there, I forget which. He is a profound Sanskrit scholar and talks with you in Sanskrit, making you feel as though it was as easy as your mother tongue. After having wandered for years as a castaway, having even gone on an indefinite fast out of loathing for the fell disease which is now in a considerably advanced stage, he rolled in here one fine morning, saying he wanted to lay his bones here, that he knew he would have shelter here and would not go if he was turned out.

"How can I say 'no' to you?" said Gandhiji. "If I harbor a son-in-law suffering from tuberculosis, why should I not harbor you? There is Ba to look after him. Of Valji Desai [9] everyone is fond and I am sure he would be taken care of. But who will look after you if I don't? I shall build you a hut right near my hut, and you make the place your abode. Even if no one remains here you at least shall stay."

An addition to this mosaic, Maurice Frydman, a mechanical

genius whose restless spirit has now brought him here. He belongs to the nation which is reduced to ashes by Germany and has in him the fire that is hidden under the cinders.

He might have made a pile in Mysore as an engineer, but he came under the influence of Ramana Maharshi,[10] became a sanyasi—Bharatanand is his new name—worked in Aundh,[11] and has now come here. His inventive genius is ever active and why should it not be? President Mosciki of Poland had scores of inventions to his credit, and so many has Bharatanand—in a way more unique than others, for he swears by the gospel of a handicraft civilization based on non-violence.

There are many others whom I would fain mention, but these specimens should suffice. There is always a floating population, and like Gandhiji's own hut Kasturba's hut too has the elasticity of accommodating as many as may be necessary. Women guests she has to take in, but sometimes she has inconvenient guests too. . . .

"Quite a motley crowd that," some one will exclaim. They have not only their idiosyncracies, but their angularities and weaknesses too. But their love for Gandhiji and his work is a common bond that binds them. And with a will and a cheer they cook their own food, wash their own clothes, clean their own latrines, and so on.

In their midst Gandhiji lives and works, beginning his day at three o'clock in the morning, never missing his prayers or spinning, more regular than any one else, and turning out more work than most public men I know—though he describes himself as physically and mentally an invalid.

With its mud and bamboo houses built without much of a plan, without any guest house and without anything like the art that lends charm to many other institutions, the Sevagram *ashram* still attracts the attention of numerous visitors and even workers. . . .

But what about the work for which Gandhiji made the irrevocable decision to come and settle down in a village which was chosen because it was most difficult to tackle? Has he been able to do it justice? Is the village changed for the better after three-and-a-half years of Gandhiji's stay?

I confess the answer cannot be given in a resounding affirmative. All we have been able to do is to give a fair number of people employment on a meagre wage, we have given a fairly bad blow to untouchability, we have introduced a few spinning wheels in the village and interested the children in our work and the Basic system of education, and we have given medical aid to many of them.

But there is a hiatus between the villagers and us. There is yet no living link between us. We have our morning and evening prayers, but they touch not these simple folks.

Maybe we have, with the best wishes in the world, not succeeded in coming down to their level and becoming one with them. Like Basic Education the passion to revive the village has come rather late in Gandhiji's life, when he has preoccupations which leave him no time and energy to tackle the life problem of the village as he would like to do.

And not the least handicap is the gathering about him of people like the present writer, each good in his or her own way, but not fit to bear or even to share the burdens he has taken upon himself. . . .

THE DEATH OF KASTURBA

• by Devadas Gandhi

Kasturba was born in the same year as Gandhi—1869. Their betrothal occurred in their seventh year, although their actual wedding did not take place until 1882. They were married for

• Reprinted with permission from R. K. Prabhu, editor, *Sati Kasturba* (Bombay: Hind Kitabs, 1944), pp. 43-46.

sixty-two years and had four sons—Harilal (1888), Manilal (1892), Ramdas (1897), and Devadas (1900). Gandhi, however, took a vow of continence in 1906 and they never lived together as man and wife after that time.

Kasturba went to South Africa with her husband and took part in the satyagraha struggles there, saying, "If you can endure hardships and so can my boys, why cannot I? I am bound to join the struggle." She went to London with Gandhi in 1914 and back in India was the "presiding deity" of the ashram near Ahmedabad. In 1922, when Gandhi was arrested and sentenced to prison, she issued a stirring message to the nation. It was she who faced the agony of Gandhi's several fasts. In 1932 she spent six weeks in prison. Six weeks after being released, she was again sentenced to six months' rigorous imprisonment.

Kasturba was again imprisoned without trial in 1939, in her native Rajkot, but was released with other political prisoners an hour after Gandhi broke his fast. Her last arrest took place in Bombay on August 9, 1942. Her husband had been arrested early that morning and she announced that she would speak to the meeting which Gandhi was to have addressed that evening. Two police officers asked Kasturba if she was determined to address the meeting; if so they had orders to arrest her. "Yes," she replied emphatically. Accordingly she was arrested and confined, with Gandhi, in the Aga Khan Palace at Poona.

In March 1943 a government communiqué indicated that Kasturba had suffered two heart attacks while in detention. Her health was a matter of serious concern after that time and on February 20, 1944 the government announced that "Mrs. Gandhi's condition has been deteriorating for some days past and is now very grave." She died on February 22 and her youngest son, Devadas, wrote a description of her last hours.

SHE NEVER completely lost consciousness till the last moment. When the Government communiqué on Sunday (Feb. 20) pronounced her condition to be grave, she was still hoping against hope to survive the latest phase of her illness. The kidneys had failed to function during the last few days due to the feeble action of the heart and this was complicated by apical pneumonia without fever. The blood pressure had come down to 75/52. The doctors had given up the struggle. When I reached her on Monday evening she was in distress which only the devoted nursing of her fellow-detainees could superficially relieve. It was against medical expectation that she survived the night. That was the last night of her earthly existence, every second of which she received the ministrations of all her companions and Gandhiji. In a semi-conscious state she would answer questions in monosyllables or by gently shaking her head. Once when Gandhiji came near her she raised her hand and asked "who is it?" and then seemed greatly comforted when he attended to her for nearly an hour. Beside her he looked several years younger, although his hands shook. The scene reminded me of the incident in South Africa nearly 32 years ago when mother had just emerged a complete physical wreck from a course of three months' imprisonment there. A European acquaintance meeting both my parents at a railway station said, "Mr. Gandhi, is this your mother?" In the morning she looked worse but peaceful. On Monday she had clung to a lingering hope. On Tuesday she seemed to be resigned. The mind was at peace and clearer in spite of the gathering effects of uraemia. She had refused all medicine and even water since Monday. But she opened her mouth wide for a drop of Ganges water at midday on Tuesday. It comforted her for a while.

Then at about 3 P.M. she sent for me and told me that she was going. "I must go some day, why not today?" she pleaded. I, the last child she had given birth to, was evidently holding her. But with this remark and other tender and sweet words, in the presence of all others, she tore herself away from me. Never did her articulation sound clearer, or her words appear choicer to me. Almost immediately after this she joined her hands together, sat up unaided and with her head bowed low she prayed for several minutes in the loudest tone she could manage.

"God my Refuge, Thy Mercy I crave."

That is how I would translate into English the winged words

which went up from her again and again. When I left the room to dry my tears, penicillin had just arrived in the verandah of the Aga Khan's Palace. The doctors had little desire to try it. Pneumonia was only a contributory factor. The final failure of the kidneys would not have been relieved by the penicillin. And besides it was too late. Yet, this wonder-drug for pneumonia was being mechanically got ready. At about 5 o'clock I gathered courage to face mother again. Now she smiled. It was the smile which has spoiled me these 43 years. But it was also a dying mother's last pensive smile to cheer her son. My mother was intensely human. On her behalf I crave the forgiveness of all those who have come into close contact with her, for the extra share of affection she reserved for me. God surely will condone the frailties of one who otherwise lent glamor to His creation. This smile, however, revived my interest in penicillin and I thought it my duty to pursue the matter with the doctors. They were willing to try it but offered little hope of success.

When Gandhiji came to know that I had approved the idea of giving painful injections to mother he sacrificed his evening walk in the garden to reason with me. "You can't cure your mother now, no matter what wonder-drugs you may muster. I will yield to you if you insist. But you are hopelessly wrong. She has refused all medicines and water these two days. She is in God's hands now. You may interfere, if you wish to, but I advise against the course you are adopting. And remember you are seeking to cause physical pain by an injection every four or six hours to a dying mother."

It was not for me to argue. The doctors felt most relieved.

Just when this sweetest of all wrangles I have ever had with my father was over, word came that mother had called out for him. He immediately took over from those who were giving her restful support. He leaned her against his shoulder and tried to give her what comfort he could. As I stood in front watching along with ten others I saw that the shadow on mother's face had deepened; but she spoke and moved her arms about for fuller comfort. . . .

Then in the twinkling of an eye the collapse came. Tears rolled down from several eyes while Gandhiji forced back his. The entire group stood in a semi-circle and chanted the favorite prayer which they had been used to say so long in her company. Within two minutes she was still. . . .

KASTURBA'S CREMATION
• by R. K. Prabhu

KASTURBA'S BODY was cremated at 10:40 A.M. on the 23rd. Her last rites were performed by her youngest son, Devadas Gandhi. Over a hundred persons, relatives and friends of the Gandhi family, were present at the ceremony.

Dressed in a white khaddar *sari* and covered with an orange-colored khaddar sheet with *kumkum* (vermillion) anointed on her forehead, Kasturba looked as though she was having a peaceful sleep. Decked with flowers the bier was carried by her sons and relatives from the Palace to the place of cremation, 100 yards away from the building.

The Brahmin priest who officiated at the funeral ceremony of the late Mahadev Desai officiated at this ceremony also. The ceremony itself was a short and simple one.

Swami Anand, Sjt. Kanu Gandhi, Mahatma Gandhi's grand-nephew, Mr. Shantikumar Morarji,[12] Mr. Kamalanarayan Bajaj and other friends who were present on the occasion arranged the funeral pyre.

As Kasturba's body was lifted from the bier and placed on the pyre, Mahatma Gandhi was visibly moved and with his shawl he was seen wiping his eyes. Excepting for this moment of sentiment, Mahatma Gandhi remained cool throughout and showed no signs

• Reprinted with permission from R. K. Prabhu, editor, *Sati Kasturba* (Bombay: Hind Kitabs, 1944), pp. 47-50.

of emotion or excitement. All the time he was seen talking to the visitors.

After the preliminary rites of cremation had been performed and the body placed on the pyre, Mahatma Gandhi beckoned to the priest to allow him to conduct a brief service. Recitations from the Koran, the Bhagavadgita and the Bible were made, and some of the members of the ashram sang in chorus a few *bhajans.* Dr. M. D. D. Gilder recited a passage from the Zoroastrian sacred texts while Mirabehn recited a Psalm.

The services over, Mahatma Gandhi directed the priest to continue the ceremony and himself stood leaning on his staff. Sandalwood was piled on the body and ghee was poured. Devadas Gandhi with fire in hand went round the body three times and, amidst cries of "Govinda, Govinda, Govinda",[13] lit the funeral pyre.

The "Sanchayan"[14] ceremony of Kasturba's ashes was performed in the Aga Khan Palace on Feb. 25. Gandhiji, his sons Harilal, Ramdas and Devadas, and other inmates of the Palace were present on the occasion.

Devadas writes: "I am on my way to Allahabad, as I write these lines, with her remains which will be consigned to the Ganges on Monday. These consist of a literal handful of tiny motherly bones. They were collected on Friday by the inmates of the camp with due ritual from the ashes of the pyre. They were then laid out on a banana leaf and after being decorated with flowers and vermillion and incense and after a consecration ceremony they were prepared for the last journey. I am thus travelling in the company of my mother but after tomorrow I know I shall never travel with her again. It was Gandhiji's clear decision that this ceremony of immersion in the confluence of the two great rivers be performed. 'What crores of Hindus do as a sacrament is what will please your mother,' he said to me. The decision was reinforced by a telegram from the revered Pandit Malaviyaji expressing a wish that this should be done. The bulk of the ashes were, according to custom, consigned in the river Indrayani near Poona. . . . For me and the little company which visited the riverside before sunrise on Friday morning it was a solemn and uplifting ceremony. A small quantity of ashes collected on the second day after the cremation has been preserved in the detention camp and these include the five glass bangles which formed part of the funeral pyre and were subsequently found intact and unbroken.

"I ought to add a word as to how Gandhiji has stood this ordeal. He was looking obviously fagged. He grieves over this tragic gap which has come into his life, for she in large measure was responsible for what he is today. But he maintains a philosophic calm and keeps his emotions under the control expected of him. The atmosphere around him was one of sadness without gloom and when my brother and I parted company with the camp on Friday he cracked his customary jokes as a substitute for tears. His health, I believe, is good."

18 COMMUNAL TENSIONS (1944–1947)

THE GANDHI-JINNAH CORRESPONDENCE

• by M. K. Gandhi and M. A. Jinnah

Conflict between Hindus and Moslems was long a major stumbling-block in the path of Indian independence, as well as a threat to internal peace in India. Throughout his life Gandhi worked assiduously for peaceful cooperation between the Hindu and Moslem communities.

After the failure of the Cripps mission, the Congress "Quit India" resolution, and Gandhi's imprisonment (August 1942), a political deadlock ensued. The Moslem League continued to demand a separate Moslem state—Pakistan, claiming that as the Moslems were in a minority they would be oppressed by the Hindu majority in a free India. The Congress insisted on a united India although it was willing to give certain guarantees to safeguard Moslem rights. Chakravarti Rajagopalachari, a prominent Congress leader, tried to break the deadlock by arranging a compromise, but without success.

In May 1943 while still in prison, Gandhi wrote to Mohammed

• Reprinted with permission from *Gandhi-Jinnah Talks* (New Delhi: Hindustan Times, 1944), pp. 69-70, 76, 3-6, 25-26, 40-41.

Ali Jinnah, leader of the Moslem League, suggesting a meeting between them, but the British authorities refused to forward the letter. In May 1944 Gandhi was released from prison on medical grounds. In July he repeated his invitation to Jinnah, which was accepted, and the two men met in Bombay from September 9 to 27. Jinnah was a well-to-do lawyer, proud, shrewd, able, and ambitious, who had once been a member of the Congress but subsequently devoted himself to the Moslem cause and often criticized Gandhi. Although Gandhi was personally opposed to the partition of India, he proposed an agreement on the basis of a formula devised by Rajagopalachari, which provided that the Congress and the Moslem League would cooperate to attain independence under a provisional government, after which the question of partition would be decided by a plebiscite in the districts having a Moslem majority. Jinnah took his stand on the Lahore Resolution, adopted by the Moslem League in 1940, which demanded independence for the Moslem-majority areas without mention of a plebiscite. Jinnah also insisted that Gandhi must speak in the name of the Congress; Gandhi said he had no authority to do this but he would recommend that the Congress accept any agreement reached between him and Jinnah. Finally, to Gandhi the attainment of independence for all Indians from British rule was the most urgent issue, while to Jinnah the creation of Pakistan was the paramount consideration. The conversations eventually ended without an agreement, and the correspondence between Gandhi and Jinnah before and during their talks was made public. There were twenty-four letters, amounting to some 15,000 words, from which extracts are given below. The first is Gandhi's letter written to Jinnah from prison.

Detention Camp, May 4, 1943

DEAR QAID-I-AZAM,[1]

When sometime after my incarceration Government asked me for a list of newspapers I would like to have, I included *Dawn*[2] in my list. I have been receiving it with more or less regularity. Whenever it comes to me I read it carefully. I have followed the proceedings of the League as reported in the *Dawn* columns. I noted your invitation to me to write to you. Hence this letter.

I welcome your invitation. I suggest our meeting face to face rather than talking through correspondence. But I am in your hands.

I hope that this letter will be sent to you and if you agree to my proposal, the Government will let you visit me.

One thing I had better mention. There seems to be an "if" about your invitation. Do you say I should write only if I have changed my heart? God alone knows men's hearts.

I would like you to take me as I am.

Why should not both you and I approach the great question of communal unity as men determined on finding a common solution and work together to make our solution acceptable to all who are concerned with it or interested in it?

Yours sincerely,
M. K. Gandhi

The following press communiqué was issued by the Government of India on May 26, 1943, announcing their decision not to forward Mahatma Gandhi's letter to Mr. Jinnah.

THE GOVERNMENT of India have received a request from Mr. Gandhi to forward a short letter from himself to Mr. Jinnah expressing a wish to meet him. In accordance with their known policy in regard to correspondence or interviews with Mr. Gandhi, the Government of India have decided that this letter cannot be forwarded and have so informed Mr. Gandhi and Mr. Jinnah. They are not prepared to give facilities for political correspondence or contact to a person detained for promoting an illegal mass movement which he has not disavowed and thus gravely embarrassing India's war effort at a critical time. It rests with Mr. Gandhi to satisfy the Government of India that he can safely be allowed once more to participate in the public affairs of the country, and until he does so the disabilities from which he suffers are of his own choice.

After leaving prison Gandhi wrote to Jinnah as follows:

Dilkusha (Panchgani), July 17, 1944

BROTHER JINNAH,

There was a time when I was able to induce you to speak in the mother tongue.³ Today I venture to write to you in the mother tongue. I have already suggested a meeting between you and me in my invitation issued from jail. I have not yet written to you since my release. Today I am impelled to do so. Let us meet whenever you wish. Do not regard me as an enemy of Islam or of Indian Muslims. I have always been a servant and friend to you and to mankind. Do not disappoint me.

Your brother,
M. K. Gandhi

H. B. "Queen Elizabeth,"
Srinagar (Kashmir), July 24, 1944

DEAR MR. GANDHI,

I received your letter dated July 17 here on July 22 and I thank you for it.

I shall be glad to receive you at my house in Bombay on my return which will probably be about the middle of August. By that time I hope that you will have recuperated your health fully and will be returning to Bombay. I would like to say nothing more till we meet.

I am very pleased to read in the Press that you are making very good progress, and I hope that you will soon be all right.

Yours sincerely,
M. A. Jinnah

Fourteen interviews took place between Gandhi and Jinnah at Bombay. The following letters were exchanged after their first talk.

September 10, 1944

DEAR MR. GANDHI,

With reference to our talk yesterday (September 9), I understood from you that you had come to discuss the Hindu-Muslim settlement with me in your individual capacity, and not in any representative character or capacity, on behalf of the Hindus or the Congress; nor had you any authority to do so. I naturally pointed out to you that there must be some one on the other side with authority holding a representative status with whom I can negotiate and, if possible, come to a settlement of the Hindu-Muslim question, and that for the position you had adopted there was no precedent, and that this raises great difficulties in my way.

As you know, I can only speak on behalf of Muslim India and the All-India Muslim League, as the President of the organization which I represent, and as such I am subject to and governed by its constitution, rules and regulations. I think you realize and will admit that a settlement of the Hindu-Muslim question is the foremost and major hurdle, and unless the representatives of these two nations put their heads together, how is one to make any headway with it?

Nevertheless, I explained to you the Lahore resolution [4] of March, 1940, and tried to persuade you to accept the basic and fundamental principles embodied in it, but you not only refused to consider it but emphasized your opposition to the basis indicated in that resolution, and remarked that there was "an ocean between you and me," and when I asked you what is then the alternative you suggest, you put forward a formula [5] of Mr. Rajagopalachari approved by you. We discussed it, and as various matters were vague and nebulous, and some required clarification, I wanted to have a clear idea of what it really meant and what were its implications, and asked you for explanations and clarification regarding the proposals embodied in that formula. . . .

These are some of the important points that occur to me for the moment, which require explanation and clarification, and I hope that you will let me have full details about the various points that I have raised, in order that I may be better able to understand and judge your proposals before I can deal with them satisfactorily.

Yours sincerely,

M. A. Jinnah

September 11, 1944

DEAR QAID-I-AZAM,

I received your letter yesterday at 3:30 P.M. I was in the midst of appointments. I hasten to reply at the earliest opportunity.

I have said in my letter to you, it is implied in the Rajaji [6] formula and I have stated publicly that I have approached you as an individual. My life mission has been Hindu-Muslim unity which I want for its own sake but which is not to be achieved without the foreign ruling Power being ousted. Hence the first condition of the exercise of the right of self-determination is achieving Independence by the joint action of all the parties and groups composing India. If such joint action is unfortunately impossible, then too I must fight with the assistance of such elements as can be brought together.

I am glad, therefore, that you did not break off our talks when I refused to assume or accept representative capacity. Of course, I am pledged to use all the influence I may have with the Congress to ratify my agreement with you. May I remind you that the Rajaji formula was designed in the first instance for your acceptance and submission thereafter to the League?

It is true that I said an ocean separated you and me in outlook. But that had no reference to the Lahore resolution of the League. The Lahore resolution is indefinite. Rajaji has taken from it the substance and given it a shape. . . .

Yours sincerely,

M. K. Gandhi

The following letters were exchanged when the talks were nearing a breakdown.

September 23, 1944

DEAR QAID-I-AZAM,

Last evening's talk has left a bad taste in the mouth. Our talks and our correspondence seem to run in parallel lines and never touch one another. We reached the breaking point last evening but, thank God, we were unwilling to part. We resumed discussion and suspended it in order to allow me to keep my time for the evening public prayer.

In order that all possible chance of making any mistake in a matter of this great importance may be removed, I would like you to give me in writing what precisely on your part you would want me to put my signature to.

I adhere to my suggestion that we may call in some outside assistance to help us at this stage.

Yours sincerely,
M. K. Gandhi

September 23, 1944

DEAR MR. GANDHI,

I am in receipt of your letter of September 23. May I refer you to my letter of today's date which I sent you in reply to yours of September 22? I have nothing new or fresh to add, but I may say that it is not a case of your being asked to put your signature as representing anybody till you clothe yourself with representative capacity and are vested with authority. We stand by, as I have already said, the basic and fundamental principles embodied in the Lahore resolution of March 1940. I appeal to you once more to revise your policy and program, as the future of this subcontinent and the welfare of the peoples of India demand that you should face realities.

Yours sincerely,
M. A. Jinnah

The following statement was handed to the press by Jinnah, along with the text of the correspondence, on the evening of September 27.

MR. GANDHI from the very commencement of our talks made it clear that he had approached me in his individual capacity and that he represented no one but himself. However, he assured me that he was really open to conviction and conversion to the Muslim League Lahore resolution of March 1940.

Without prejudice to my objection that in order to reach any settlement, negotiations can only be carried on properly when the other side is also fully represented and vested with authority, in deference to Mr. Gandhi's wishes I agreed to the task of persuading and converting him to the fundamentals of the Lahore resolution.

I have placed before him everything and every aspect of the Muslim point of view in the course of our prolonged talks and correspondence, and we discussed all the pros and cons generally, and I regret to say that I have failed in my task of converting Mr. Gandhi.

We have, therefore, decided to release to the Press the correspondence that has passed between us.

Nevertheless, we hope that the public will not feel embittered, and we trust that this is not the final end of our effort.

On the evening of September 27 Gandhi addressed the audience after the public prayers. It was reported in the third person as follows:

SPEAKING in Gujarati, he said he was not addressing them in Hindustani as before because he wanted his words to go straight to the hearts of the audience most of whom were Gujaratis. He had particularly the women in mind who were not accustomed to Hindustani speech.

He had told them that when the talks were over he would let them know the result. That stage had been reached the day before but as copies of the correspondence were not ready its actual release had to be postponed till that day. Authorized copies of the correspondence had now been sent to the Press with a prefatory statement by the Qaid-i-Azam.

Hitherto he had told them that he was not without hope with regard to the outcome of the talks. He had to confesss that the result that he was hoping for had not materialized. But he had no sense of disappointment or despondency. He was convinced that even out of that breakdown good would result.

Although the Qaid-i-Azam and he had known each other fairly well in public life before, they had never come into such close personal contact. Their conversations were carried out with friendliness and cordiality. He wanted all the communities to cultivate the same spirit of friendliness and cordiality in their relations with one another. They should try to convert one another through it.

They might ask, why was it then that he and the Qaid-i-Azam had failed to convert each other? His reply was that he had tried his level best to go as far as he could to meet the Qaid-i-Azam's viewpoint. He had taken incalculable pains to understand him and to make himself understood. But he had failed.

He had placed before Qaid-i-Azam Rajaji's formula but that did not commend itself to him. He had thereupon put forth another proposal of his own in its place but even that had failed to secure Jinnah Saheb's approval. In the same way, Jinnah Saheb's proposal had failed to commend itself to him. If either of them had been weak, they would have possibly come to some sort of agreement but as responsible men they could not afford to be weak. A helmsman had to be firm and unwavering or else the ship would founder upon the rocks. Each one of them had tried to convince the other. It was possible that both of them might be in the wrong. But so long as each felt himself to be in the right he could not let go his hold.

The news of the breakdown he knew would cause grief to the friends of India and might give cause for jubilation to their enemies. He drew their attention to the last sentence in their statement in which he had said that it was not the final end of their effort.

Although they had been unable to appreciate each other's viewpoint, the public could help them to do so. They should not lose heart. If there was any one who had reason to feel disappointed it was he. He had knocked at the Qaid-i-Azam's door. But as he had already observed there was no despondency in him. It was not for a votary of truth and non-violence to feel despondent if his effort at times failed to yield the result aimed at. Failure should only serve as spur to further effort. God alone knew what was best for them. It was not for them to question God's ways. Therefore, instead of feeling despondent they should regard the breakdown as a challenge to their faith and as an incentive for greater effort for establishing true unity among the various communities.

COMMUNAL RIOTS IN BENGAL

Immediately after Japan's surrender Prime Minister Clement R. Attlee announced that Great Britain favored early self-government for India. Soon afterward elections were held for the central and provincial legislatures, and the Indian National Congress and the Moslem League emerged as the two principal parties. Lord Wavell, the Viceroy, wanted to convene a constitutional convention for all India, but Jinnah held out for a separate state of Pakistan. A British Cabinet Mission was sent to India to consult with Indian leaders and work out the details of the transfer of power. Its report, released on May 16, 1946, called for a united federal India whose constitution would be drafted by a national assembly elected by members of the provincial legislatures. The plan provided for an interim government, but the Congress and the Moslem League could not agree on its composition. Jinnah wanted the right to veto the appointment of any Moslem member of the provisional cabinet, which the Congress would not accept. Finally, on August 12, 1946, Nehru was asked by the Viceroy to form a government. He offered to include five members chosen by Jinnah, but the latter refused, and the government was formed with two Moslem members not affiliated with the Moslem League. In protest, Jinnah proclaimed August 16 as Direct Action Day, and at least 5,000 were killed in the ensuing riots in Calcutta. Nehru took office as Prime Minister of India on September 2. Jinnah proclaimed it a day of mourning. Gandhi, heavy at heart, said, "We are not yet in the midst of civil war, but we are nearing it."

Communal violence spread to many parts of the country, especially Bengal and the Punjab. Sometimes Hindus were the victims, sometimes Moslems. In October there were specially horrible attacks by Moslems on Hindus in Noakhali in eastern Bengal.

Gandhi resolved to leave Delhi and journey to Noakhali. He toured Noakhali—in the relatively inaccessible delta of the Ganges and the Brahmaputra rivers—from November 7, 1946 to March 2, 1947, trying to stem the tide of fear and violence.

In these days Gandhi no longer had time to write long editorials for Harijan. Paragraphs of his addresses at prayer meetings were, however, reported in Harijan along with descriptive material contributed by members of his party.

· As GANDHIJI sat listening to the stories that came from Bengal, his mind was made up. "If I leave Delhi," he remarked, "it will not be in order to return to Sevagram but only to go to Bengal. Else, I would stay here and stew in my own juice. He consulted two

· Reprinted with permission from Harijan, October 27, 1946. Also in M. K. Gandhi, Communal Unity (Ahmedabad: Navajivan, 1949), p. 383.

friends from Bengal that evening about it. "Allow us to go there first and report," said they. "Give us a chance to do our bit and then, if necessary, you can come." Gandhiji agreed.

• The week's events were not calculated to lift the darkness that had descended on Gandhiji's spirits. . . . "I am trying to take my bearings, to see where I stand," he casually remarked the other day in the course of a conversation. He has since been pouring out his anguish in a series of prayer gathering addresses. There was first the flood havoc in Assam.[7] Thousands had been rendered homeless, property worth lakhs had been destroyed and many lives lost. That was an act of God. But far worse than the news from Assam was the fact that an orgy of madness had seized a section of humanity in Bengal. Man had sunk lower than the brute. Reports were coming through that the Hindus, who are a very small minority there, were being attacked by Mussalmans. Ever since he had heard of the happenings in Noakhali he had been furiously thinking as to what his own duty was. God would show him the way. He knew that his stock had gone down with the people so far as the teaching of non-violence was concerned. They still showered affection upon him. He appreciated their affection and felt thankful for it. But the only way in which he could express his thanks and appreciation was to place before them and through them the world the truth which God had vouchsafed to him and to the pursuit of which his whole life was devoted, even at the risk of forfeiting their affection and regard. At the moment, he felt prompted to tell them that it would be wrong on the part of the Hindus to think in terms of reprisals for what had happened in Noakhali and elsewhere in East Bengal. Non-violence was the creed of the Congress. It had brought them to their present strength. But it would be counted only as a coward's expedient if its use was to be limited only against the British power which was strong and while violence was to be freely used against our own

• Written in New Delhi on October 18. Reprinted with permission from *Harijan*, October 27, 1946. Also in M. K. Gandhi, *Communal Unity* (Ahmedabad: Navajivan, 1949), pp. 386-87.

brethren. He refused to believe that they could ever adopt that as their creed. Although the Congress had an overwhelming majority of the Hindus on its membership rolls, he maintained that it was by no means a Hindu organization and that it belonged equally to all communities. He had told Acharya Kripalani,[8] who had succeeded Pandit Nehru in the Presidentship of the Congress, that it was going to prove no feather-bed for him. If the Chief Minister of the Cabinet had to wear a crown of thorns the Congress President would have to lie on a bed of thorns. The late Sir Syed Ahmed had called Hindus and Mussalmans the two eyes of India. The Congress President could not possibly discriminate between the two. He was pledged to equally serve both. He, the speaker, had therefore asked him to proceed on a mission of peace to East Bengal to teach people the art of dying without killing. It should be his privilege to demonstrate it by his personal example. He was going there with his wife not to protect one party but to stop the fratricide which threatened to overwhelm India. It was a good beginning for Acharya Kripalani and his wife. Shri Sarat Babu, the brother of the late Subhas Babu,[9] was going with them. He knew no barriers of caste or creed.

The fair name of Bengal was being tarnished—Bengal that had given them so much. Bengal, the home of Gurudev [10] whose bhajan they had just heard sung. That hymn asked God to make the devotee wide-hearted and fearless. It was with that hymn on their lips that they were going and it was the audience's duty to wish them every success.

· "Why do you want to go to Noakhali? You did not go to Bombay, Ahmedabad or Chhapra, where things have happened that are infinitely worse than Noakhali. Would not your going there only add to the existing tension?" Was it because in these places it was the Muslims who had been the sufferers that he did not go there and would go to Noakhali because the sufferers there were

· Written in Sodepur on November 1. Reprinted with permission from *Harijan*, November 10, 1946. Also in M. K. Gandhi, *Communal Unity* (Ahmedabad: Navajivan, 1949), pp. 408-409.

Hindus? he was asked by a Muslim friend the other day. Gandhiji's reply was that he made no distinction between a Hindu and a Muslim. He would certainly have gone straight to any of the places mentioned by the friend, if anything approaching what had happened at Noakhali had happened there and if he felt that he could do nothing without being on the spot. It was the cry of outraged womanhood that had peremptorily called him to Noakhali. He felt he would find his bearings only on seeing things for himself at Noakhali. His technique of non-violence was on trial. It remained to be seen how it would answer in the face of the present crisis. If it had no validity it were better that he himself should declare his insolvency. He was not going to leave Bengal until the last embers of the trouble were stamped out. "I may stay on here for a whole year or more. If necessary, I will die here. But I will not acquiesce to failure. If the only effect of my presence in the flesh is to make people look up to me in hope and expectation which I can do nothing to vindicate, it would be far better that my eyes were closed in death." He had mentally prepared himself, he added, for abstention from the Congress session, if necessary. He had similarly disengaged himself mentally from all his responsibilities in respect of Sevagram and Uruli [11]—his latest love.

But with all his impatience to get to Noakhali he had to announce on the fourth day at the prayer gathering that he would not be able to leave for Noakhali on the next day as he had intended to. The Prime Minister had sent him word that the train for him could not be arranged so soon. He hoped to leave on Saturday or Sunday. In the meantime he would try to render whatever service he could to the Metropolis.

• At Goalando, Gandhiji took steamer and steaming down the Padma 80 miles reached Chandpur at evening. Chandpur, the native place of that superoctogenarian Congressman, the late Babu Hardayal Nag, called up poignant memories. Two deputations, one

• Written in Chaumuhani, November 10. Reprinted with permission from *Harijan*, November 2, 1946. Also in M. K. Gandhi, *Communal Unity* (Ahmedabad: Navajivan, 1949), pp. 421-24.

of Muslim Leaguers and the other of Hindus, met Gandhiji here. At 2 p.m. the party reached Chaumuhani where Gandhiji has fixed up his headquarters for the present.

At Laksham there is a refugees' camp. And it was to the refugees that Gandhiji's words were addressed through the crowd that had assembled at the platform to hear him and have his darshan. "I have not come on a whirlwind propaganda visit. I have come to stay here with you as one of you. I have no provincialism in me. I claim to be an Indian and therefore a Bengali even as I am a Gujarati. I have vowed to myself that I will stay on here and die here if necessary, but I will not leave Bengal till the hatchet is finally buried and even a solitary Hindu girl is not afraid to move freely about in the midst of Mussalmans. . . ."

Chaumuhani was normally a population of not more than 5,000. But at the evening prayer gathering that was held here in the compound of the Hindu Vidya Mandir [12] on the first day of Gandhiji's arrival, there was a gathering of not less than 15,000. Large numbers had come from places around about Chaumuhani. About eighty per cent of these were Muslims. The town itself has remained free from the worst communal excesses, but round about it the whole area has been ablaze. Speaking after the prayer Gandhiji poured out his soul to the gathering, particularly to the Muslim section, for over twenty minutes. . . . He had come to them in sadness. What sin had Mother India committed that her children, Hindus and Muslims, were quarreling with each other? He had learnt that no Hindu woman was safe today in some parts of East Bengal. Ever since he had come to Bengal, he was hearing awful tales of Muslim atrocities. Saheed Saheb, their Prime Minister, and Shamsuddin Saheb had admitted that there was some truth in the reports that one heard.

"I have not come to excite the Hindus to fight the Mussalmans. I have no enemies. I have fought the British all my life. Yet they are my friends. I have never wished them ill."

He heard of forcible conversions, forcible feeding of beef, abductions and forcible marriages, not to talk about murders, arson and loot. They had broken idols. The Muslims did not worship them nor did he. But why should they interfere with those who wished to worship them? These incidents are a blot on the name of Islam. "I have studied the *Koran*. The very word Islam means peace. The Muslim greeting 'Saloam Alaikum' [13] is the same for all whether Hindus or Muslims, or any other. Nowhere does Islam allow such things as had happened in Noakhali and Tipperah." Saheed Saheb and all the ministers and League leaders who met him in Calcutta had condemned such acts unequivocally. "The Muslims are in such overwhelming majority in East Bengal that I expect them to constitute themselves the guardians of the small Hindu minority. They should tell Hindu women that while they are there, no one dare cast an evil eye on them. . . .

· Early in the morning on Wednesday last Gandhiji announced to his party an important decision. He had decided to disperse his party detailing each member, including the ladies, to settle down in one affected village and make himself or herself hostage of the safety and security of the Hindu minority of that village. They must be pledged to protect with their lives, if necessary, the Hindu population of that village. His decision was not binding on any one of his party, he said. Those who wanted to, were free to go away and take up any of his other constructive activities. "Those who have ill-will against the Mussalmans or Islam in their hearts or cannot curb their indignation at what has happened should stay away. They will only misrepresent me by working under this plan."

So far as he was concerned, he added that his decision was final and irrevocable and left no room for discussion. He was going to bury himself in East Bengal until such time that the Hindus and Mussalmans learnt to live together in harmony and peace. He would deprive himself of the services of all his companions and fend for himself with whatever assistance he could command locally.

· Written in Kazirkhil, November 16. Reprinted with permission from *Harijan*, November 24, 1946. Also in M. K. Gandhi, *Communal Unity* (Ahmedabad: Navajivan, 1949), pp. 425-28.

• On the eve of his departure for Shrirampur Gandhiji issued the following statement to the Press:

I find myself in the midst of exaggeration and falsity. I am unable to discover the truth. There is terrible mutual distrust. Oldest friendships have snapped. Truth and *ahimsa* by which I swear, and which have to my knowledge sustained me for sixty years, seem to fail to show the attributes I have ascribed to them.

To test them, or better, to test myself, I am going to a village called Shrirampur, cutting myself away from those who have been with me all these years, and who have made life easy for me. I am taking Prof. Nirmal Kumar Bose [14] as my Bengali teacher and interpreter and Shri Parsuram, who has been my most devoted, selfless and silent stenographer.

The other workers, whom I have brought with me will each distribute themselves in other villages of Noakhali to do the work of peace, if it is at all possible, between the two communities. They are, unfortunately, all non-Bengalis except little Abha.[15] They will, therefore, be accompanied by one Bengali worker each as teacher and interpreter, even like Prof. N. K. Bose will be to me.

Distribution work and selection work will be done by Shri Satish Chandra Dasgupta of the Khadi Pratishthan.[16] My ideal is to live in a local Muslim League family, but I see that I must not wait for that happy day. I must meanwhile establish such contacts with the Muslims as I can in their own villages. My suggestion to the League ministers is that they should give me one honest and brave Muslim to accompany one equally honest and brave Hindu for each affected village. They should guarantee at the cost of their lives if need be, the safety of the returning Hindu refugees. I am sorry to have to confess that without some such thing it seems difficult to induce them to return to their villages.

From all accounts received by me, life is not as yet smooth and safe for the minority community in the villages. They, therefore,

• Released in Kazirkhil, November 20. Reprinted with permission from *Harijan*, December 1, 1946. Also in M. K. Gandhi, *Communal Unity* (Ahmedabad: Navajivan, 1949), pp. 432-33.

prefer to live as exiles from their own homes, crops, plantations, and surroundings, and live on inadequate and ill-balanced doles.

Many friends from outside Bengal have written to me to allow them to come for peace work, but I have strongly dissuaded them from coming. I would love to let them come if and when I see light through this impenetrable darkness.

In the meantime, both Pyarelal and I have decided to suspend all other activities in the shape of correspondence, including the heavy work of the *Harijan* and the allied weeklies. I have asked Shri Kishorlal, Shri Kakasaheb, Shri Vinoba [17] and Shri Narhari Parikh to edit the weeklies jointly and severally. Pyarelal and I may, if our work permits, send stray contributions from our respective villages. Correspondence will be attended to from Sevagram.

How long this suspense will last is more than I can say. This much, however, I can. I do not propose to leave East Bengal till I am satisfied that mutual trust has been established between the two communities and the two have resumed the even tenor of their life in their villages. Without this there is neither Pakistan nor Hindustan—only slavery awaits India, torn asunder by mutual strife and engrossed in barbarity.

No one need at present be disturbed about my low diet. . . . I resumed goat's milk from yesterday and propose to revert to normal diet as early as the system permits. The future is in God's keeping.

· Emerald green fields of paddy [18] meet the eye just now in Noakhali District wherever you go. There has been a bumper crop this year such as has not been known for the last twelve years. But nature's bounty has been more than offset by the sadistic cruelty of man. The crop is in ear and about to ripen but a number of those who sowed them are not there to reap or garner. Some have been killed. Others have fled for safety to various refugee camps. . . .

On the 8th instant Gandhiji accompanied by the Parliamentary

· Written in Kazirkhil on November 17. Reprinted with permission from *Harijan*, December 1, 1946. Also in M. K. Gandhi, *Communal Unity* (Ahmedabad: Navajivan, 1949), pp. 434-38.

Secretaries Janab Nasrullah Saheb and Abdur Rashid Saheb, Mr. McInerny the District Magistrate and the Superintendent of Police, Noakhali, motored from Chaumuhani to the village of Gopairbag. Here, buried deep in the midst of thick groves of slender arecanut and cocoa-nut palms whose tall tops seemed to meet overhead, are scattered five clusters of huts occupied by Hindu families, in the midst of nearly fifty times that number of Muslim families. One of these is a Patwari's [19] house. Silken plantain leaves spread out in graceful arches under a sapphire blue sky. The loveliness of nature was spread all around. The air was delightfully fresh and cool. But the human scene that met the eye froze one's blood. There had been murder and arson. The place of worship had been desecrated. The corpses of slaughtered men were piled up in a heap in one corner of the courtyard and burnt. Charred remains of what was once flesh and blood bore witness to the grim tragedy. There were blood stains on the doorsteps of some of the houses. The kutcha [20] floors in many houses had been dug up presumably in search of hidden cash or jewels. The odor of death still hung over the place. It was a picture of desolation. Three girls had been abducted from the house, two of whom were still missing. . . .

The 11th was Gandhiji's day of silence. All the same he visited the villages Noakhola, Sonachak and Khilpara, all in the Lakhimpur Thana. The journey was partly by motor and partly by boats which were punted with difficulty in khals [21] that were choked with thickly tangled masses of water hyacinth. At Noakhola eight people were said to have been murdered including a schoolboy of 15. Four skulls and charred remains of the bones were scattered all over the place. The houses had almost all been burnt down. In the house where the boy was murdered his school books and freshly written exercise books were strewn over the floor. The betelnut and cocoa-nut trees surrounding the houses were scorched. Those that were not killed or did not run away were said to have been converted including a deaf-mute who by piteous signs showed the tuft of hair in a piece of cloth which had been removed from his head and to which he still clung. The few women that remained were all weeping and wailing in a heart-rending manner.

At Sonachak the place of worship had been desecrated and set fire to. Broken images lay on footpaths and in the debris inside the ruined temple. In this village too the same piteous weeping and wailing of women met Gandhiji. . . .

· The following is the text of Gandhiji's speech delivered in Hindustani at the prayer meeting at Dattapara on the evening of the 10th November:

Whether you believe me or not, I want to assure you that I am a servant of both the Hindus and the Mussalmans. I have not come here to fight Pakistan. If India is destined to be partitioned, I cannot prevent it. But I wish to tell you that Pakistan cannot be established by force. In the *bhajan* that was just sung the poet has likened God to the philosopher's stone. The proverbial philosopher's stone is said to turn iron into gold. That is not always desirable. For instance, if all the rails of the railway track were turned into gold by the touch of the stone, the trains would not be able to run over them. But the touch of God purifies the soul. That is always desirable.

That philosopher's stone is within us all. All that I wish to tell my Muslim brethren is that, whether they live as one people or two, they should live as friends with the Hindus. If they do not wish to do so, they should say so plainly. I would in that case confess myself defeated. The refugees cannot stay on as refugees for ever. The Government cannot go on feeding them. And what sort of feed are they getting? Less than half the daily ration of cereals to keep an able-bodied man alive, no fish, no vegetables, nor anything else to supplement it. It is not possible for them to exist like this for any length of time. If, therefore, the Muslims do not want them back in their villages, they must go elsewhere.

But even if every Hindu of East Bengal went away, I will still continue to live amidst the Muslims of East Bengal and eat what they give me and what I consider lawful for me to partake of. I

· Written in Kazirkhil, November 16. Reprinted with permission from *Harijan*, December 1, 1946. Also in M. K. Gandhi, *Communal Unity* (Ahmedabad: Navajivan, 1949), pp. 450-51.

will not bring my food from outside. I do not need fish or flesh. All that I need is a little fruit, vegetables and some goat's milk. As far as goat's milk and cereals are concerned, I would take them again only when it pleases God that I should do so. I have given them up and would not resume them till the Hindus were really penitent of what they had done in Bihar.

For a thousand Hindus to surround a hundred Mussalmans or for a thousand Mussalmans to surround a hundred Hindus and oppress them is not bravery but cowardice. A fair fight means even numbers and previous notice. That does not mean that I approve of their fighting. It has been said that the Hindus and Muslims cannot stay together as friends or cooperate with each other. No one can make me believe that, but if that is your belief, you should say so. I would in that case not ask the Hindus to return to their homes. They would leave East Bengal and it would be a shame for both the Mussalmans and the Hindus. If, on the other hand, you want the Hindus to stay in your midst, you should tell them that they need not look to the military for protection but to their Muslim brethren instead. Their daughters and sisters and mothers are your own daughters, sisters and mothers and you should protect them with your lives. I addressed them in the refugee camp yesterday. The District Magistrate Mr. McInerny told them that all mankind being descended from Adam and Eve, they were all members of one family—relatives, whatever their race or religion. So they should live together as relatives.

One man is said to have returned to his village last evening after the prayer meeting. He found his house surrounded by Muslims. They would not let him take his property. How can I, under these circumstances (if they are true), ask anyone to go back? You should ponder over what I have said and let me know what you really wish. I shall advise the Hindus accordingly.

I am told and I believe that there are many good Muslims who would welcome the Hindus back but the goondas [22] stand in the way. I wish to tell you that if the good Muslims spoke out with one voice and acted according to their professions, the so-called goondas would become ineffective and would mend their ways.

· Gandhiji's "one night one village tour" commenced on Tuesday morning (7th January) when he left Chandipur for village Masimpur about two miles from there.

"During my journey I will eat whatever I get, and am even prepared to go without milk," said he to one interviewer.

Gandhiji is prepared to live any kind of rough life during his "pilgrimage." He will dispense with all secretarial work during his "one village one day" journey. He would not have any interviewers during his journey. He will spend most of his time in meeting Hindus and Muslims, visiting houses destroyed and gathering social and economic facts about the villagers. Wherever he goes he would ask all to live in peace and fear none in this world except God. He would ask them to reorganize and spend their time in village reconstruction and constructive work. During his journey he will meet deputations of Muslims, Hindus and women separately.

He will have very few bags with him. His narrow blanket, bed and a few other necessaries of daily life, his box charkha will be with him, and also a few of his favorite books including the Gita, the Koran, and the Bible. His only walk-hour companion is his walking stick.

In this way Gandhiji will walk from village to village every day without spending more than one night in one village. . . .

VIOLENCE IN CALCUTTA
·· by M. K. Gandhi

Because of even worse communal rioting in Bihar, Gandhi left Noakhali in March 1947 and toured the province of Bihar,

· Reprinted with permission from Harijan, January 26, 1947. Also in M. K. Gandhi, Communal Unity (Ahmedabad: Navajivan, 1949), p. 500.
·· Reprinted with permission from Harijan, September 14, 1947. Also in M. K. Gandhi, Communal Unity (Ahmedabad: Navajivan, 1949), pp. 739-42.

where a Hindu majority was persecuting a Moslem minority. Shortly before Gandhi went to Bihar, Prime Minister Attlee announced that Britain would leave India "not later than June 1948" and he appointed Lord Mountbatten as the last Viceroy of India. The new Viceroy summoned Gandhi and other Indian leaders, including Jinnah, to meet with him in New Delhi and Gandhi left Bihar to attend these conferences.

Gandhi stayed in Delhi two weeks, returned to Bihar, and was asked to return to Delhi to participate in the decision of the Congress Working Committee on whether or not to accept the partitioning of the nation—Pakistan. The Congress committee reluctantly agreed to Pakistan, but Gandhi was opposed to the vivisection of his country. Gandhi returned to Bihar via Calcutta determined more than ever to stop the communal riots and thus demonstrate that Pakistan was unnecessary.

On August 15, 1947—the day Britain withdrew from India— Gandhi was in Calcutta, saddened by the turn of events which had divided the country and led to fratricidal strife. The disturbances had continued for a year after the Direct Action day proclaimed by Jinnah in August 1946. Gandhi had come to Calcutta to help quell the rioting there, and on August 31 he himself narrowly escaped injury in an incident which he described in a statement to the press the next day.

I REGRET to have to report to you that last night some young men brought to the compound a bandaged man. He was said to have been attacked by some Muslims. The Prime Minister had him examined and the report was that he had no marks of stabbing, which he was said to have received. The seriousness of the injury, however, is not the chief point. What I want to emphasize is that these young men tried to become judges and executioners.

This was about 10 P.M. Calcutta time. They began to shout at the top of their voices. My sleep was disturbed but I tried to lie quiet, not knowing what was happening. I heard the window panes being smashed. I had lying on either side of me two very brave girls. They would not sleep but without my knowledge, for my eyes were closed, they went among the small crowd and tried to pacify them. Thank God, the crowd did not do any harm to them. The old Muslim lady in the house endearingly called Bi Amma and a young Muslim stood near my matting, I suppose, to protect me from harm.

The noise continued to swell. Some had entered the central hall, and began to knock open the many doors. I felt that I must get up and face the angry crowd. I stood at the threshold of one of the doors. Friendly faces surrounded me and would not let me move forward. My vow of silence admitted of my breaking it on such occasions and I broke it and began to appeal to the angry young men to be quiet. I asked the Bengali granddaughter-in-law to translate my few words into Bengali. All to no purpose. Their ears were closed against reason.

I clasped my hands in the Hindu fashion doing nothing. More window panes began to crack. The friendly ones in the crowd tried to pacify the crowd. There were police officers. Be it said to their credit that they did not try to exercise authority. They too clasped their hands in appeal. A lathi blow missed me and everybody around me. A brick aimed at me hurt a Muslim friend standing by. The two girls would not leave me and held on to me to the last. Meanwhile the Police Superintendent and his officers came in. They too did not use force. They appealed to me to retire. Then there was a chance of their stilling the young men. After a time the crowd melted.

What happened outside the compound gate I do not know except that the police had to use tear gas to disperse the crowd. Meanwhile, Dr. P. C. Ghosh,[23] Annada Babu [24] and Dr. Nripen [25] walked in and after some discussion left. Happily, Shaheed Saheb [26] had gone home to prepare for tomorrow's proposed departure for Noakhali. In view of the above ugly incident, which no one could tell where it would lead to, I could not think of leaving Calcutta for Noakhali.

What is the lesson of the incident? It is clear to me that if India is to retain her dearly-won independence all men and women must completely forget lynch law. What was attempted was an indifferent imitation of it. If Muslims misbehaved, the complainants could, if they would not go to the Ministers, certainly go to me or my friend, Shaheed Saheb. The same thing applies to Muslim complainants. There is no way of keeping the peace in Calcutta or elsewhere if the elementary rule of civilized society is not observed. Let them not think of the savagery of the Punjab or outside India. The recognition of the golden rule of never taking the law into one's own hands has no exceptions.

My secretary, Dev Prakash, in Patna, wires: "Public agitated Punjab happenings. Feel statement necessary impressing duty of public and the Press." Shri Dev Prakash is never unduly agitated. There must be some unguarded word by the Press. If that is so, at this time when we are sitting on a powder magazine, the Fourth Estate has to be extra-wise and reticent. Unscrupulousness will act as a lighted match. I hope every editor and reporter will realize his duty to the full.

One thing I must mention. I have an urgent message calling me to the Punjab. I hear all kinds of rumors about recrudescence of trouble in Calcutta. I hope they are exaggerated, if not quite baseless. The citizens of Calcutta have to reassure me that there would be nothing in Calcutta and that peace, once restored, will not be broken.

From the very first day of peace, that is August 14th last, I have been saying that the peace might only be a temporary lull. There was no miracle. Will the foreboding prove true and will Calcutta again lapse into the law of the jungle? Let us hope not, let us pray to the Almighty that He will touch our hearts and ward off the recurrence of insanity.

Since the foregoing was written, i.e., about 4 o'clock, during silence, I have come to know fairly well the details of what has happened in various parts of the city. Some of the places which were safe till yesterday have suddenly become unsafe. Several deaths have taken place. I saw two bodies of very poor Muslims. I saw also some wretched-looking Muslims being carted away to a place of safety. I quite see that last night's incidents so fully described above, pale into insignificance before this flare-up. Nothing that I may do in the way of going about in the open conflagration could possibly arrest it.

I have told the friends who saw me in the evening what their duty is. What part am I to play in order to stop it? The Sikhs and the Hindus must not forget what the East Punjab has done during these few days. Now the Muslims in the West Punjab have begun the mad career. It is said that the Sikhs and the Hindus are enraged over the Punjab happenings.

I have adverted above to an urgent call for me to go to the Punjab. But now that the Calcutta bubble seems to have burst, with what face can I go to the Punjab? The weapon which has hitherto proved infallible for me is fasting. To put in an appearance before a yelling crowd does not always work. It certainly did not last night. What my word in person cannot do, my fast may. It may touch the hearts of all the warring elements in the Punjab, if it does in Calcutta. I therefore, begin fasting from 8:15 tonight to end only if and when sanity returns to Calcutta. I shall, as usual, permit myself to add salt and soda bicarb to the water I may wish to drink during the fast.

If the people of Calcutta wish me to proceed to the Punjab and help the people there, they have to enable me to break the fast as early as may be.

FAST IN CALCUTTA

• by Pyarelal (Nayyar)

ALTHOUGH CALCUTTA was apparently in an ecstasy of communal amity, Gandhiji's mind, uncannily sensitive to the hidden

• Written in Calcutta and Dacca, September 5-6, 1947. Reprinted with permission from Harijan, September 14, 1947. Also in M. K. Gandhi, Communal Unity (Ahmedabad: Navajivan, 1949), pp. 742-50.

lie in the soul, was anything but restful. After some hesitation he decided to go to Noakhali in spite of the alarming news which continued to pour from the Punjab. "Shall I start tomorrow morning or the day after tomorrow?" he asked those around him and the latter day was fixed for departure. That evening, He who keeps watch when humanity's vision fails, gave the warning signal. "My resolve to go to Noakhali has collapsed after this evening's happenings," he said that night. "I cannot go to Noakhali or for that matter anywhere when Calcutta is in flames. Today's incident to me is a sign and a warning from God. Tell the people of Noakhali that if my colleagues for any reason cannot be there, they will find me, surely, in their midst."

And then casually he hinted that if the conflagration spread, he would have no alternative but to fast. "Have I not often said that there is yet another fast in store for me?" The next day was his day of silence. Ugly news continued to pour in. Several deputations waited on him in the course of the day to consult him as to what they should do to quench the fire. "Go in the midst of the rioters and prevent them from indulging in madness or get killed in the attempt. But do not come back alive to report failure. The situation calls for sacrifice on the part of top rankers. So far the unknown, nameless rank and file alone have been the victims of the holocaust with the one exception of the late Ganesh Shankar Vidyarthi.[27] That is not enough."

Even as he uttered these words, he was cogitating within himself, as to where he came into the picture which he was presenting to them. For he added, "Of course, I cannot do today what I have told them to do. I will not be permitted to. I saw that yesterday. Everybody will protect me from harm if I went in the midst of the maddened crowd. I may drop down from sheer physical exhaustion—that is nothing. It won't do for a soldier to be exhausted in the midst of battle." But inaction in a crisis is not in Gandhiji's nature. When a dear old friend saw him that night his mind was already made up. "You don't expect me to approve of your proposed step," remarked the friend with his usual affectionate banter as he perused Gandhiji's statement setting forth his reasons for going on a fast which the latter had kept ready against his arrival. Together they took stock of the situation thrashing out the question in the minutest detail.

"Can you fast against the *goondas?*" argued the friend.

"The conflagration has been caused not by the *goondas* but by those who have become *goondas*. It is we who make *goondas*. Without our sympathy and passive support, the *goondas* would have no legs to stand upon. I want to touch the hearts of those who are behind the *goondas*."

"But must you launch your fast at this stage?" finally argued the friend. "Why not wait and watch a little?"

To this Gandhiji's reply was that the fast had to be now or never. "It would be too late afterwards. The minority Muslims cannot be left in a perilous state. My fast has to be preventive if it is to be any good."

"I know I shall be able to tackle the Punjab too if I can control Calcutta," he continued. "But if I falter now, the conflagration may spread, and soon, I can see clearly, two or three Powers will be upon us and thus will end our short-lived dream of independence."

"But supposing you die, the conflagration would be worse," argued the friend.

"At least I won't be there to witness it. I shall have done my bit. More is not given a man to do," replied Gandhiji.

The friend capitulated. . . .

This was on Monday night. Two days later a prominent member of the Calcutta Muslim League waited on him to plead with him to give up the fast. "Your very presence in our midst is an asset to us. It is the guarantee of our safety. Do not deprive us of it," he added.

"My presence did not check the rowdies the other day. My word seemed to have lost all efficacy so far as they were concerned. My fast will now be broken only when the conflagration ends and the pristine peace of the last fifteen days returns. If the Muslims really love me and regard me as an asset, they can demonstrate their faith by refusing to give way to the instinct of revenge and

retaliation even if the whole of Calcutta goes mad. In the meantime, my ordeal must continue."

The friend retired with a heavy heart. Added Gandhiji after
he had left, "Let the evil-doers desist from evil, not to save my
life, but as a result of a true heart change. Let all understand
that a make-believe peace cannot satisfy me. I do not want a
temporary lull to be followed by a worse conflagration. In that
event I shall have to go on an unconditional fast unto death."

Then the miracle happened. As the leaden hours crept by and
drop by drop strength ebbed out of the frail little man on the
fasting bed, it caused a deep churning up in the hearts of all concerned, bringing the hidden lie to the surface. People came to
Gandhiji and confessed to him what they would not have uttered
to any living ear. Hindus and Muslims combined in an all-out
effort to save the precious life that was being offered as ransom for
disrupted peace between brother and brother. Mixed processions,
consisting of all communities, issued forth and paraded through
the affected parts of the city to restore communal harmony. A
group of about fifty people, credited with the power to control the
turbulent elements in the city, saw Gandhiji on the fourth instant and gave an undertaking that they would immediately bring
the troublemakers under check. They told Gandhiji that they had
already traced and put under restraint the ringleaders who had organized the rowdyism in his camp on Sunday last, including the
person who had hurled the stick that had narrowly missed hit-
ting him. They would all surrender themselves to him and take
whatever punishment might be meted out to them. Would not
Gandhiji on the strength of that assurance now break his fast,
so that they might be able to go to work unburdened by the oppression of the fast? they asked. If not, what was his condition
for breaking the fast? In reply Gandhiji told them that he would
break his fast only when they could assure him that there would
never again be recrudescence of communal madness in the city
even though the whole of West Bengal and, for that matter,
India might go forth into a blaze and the Muslims themselves
would come and tell him that they now felt safe and secure and,

therefore, he need not further prolong his fast. He did not expect, he proceeded to explain, to be able to control all the *goondas* in the city, though he would love to, as he had not the requisite degree of purity, detachment and steadfastness of mind. But if he could not even make them purge themselves of the communal virus, he would feel that life was not worth living and he would not care to prolong it. They had referred to the oppression of his fast. He could not understand that. Why should they have a feeling of oppression if what they had told him came right from their hearts? If a single step is taken under pressure of the fast, not from conviction, it would cause oppression, but there should be no oppression if there was complete cooperation between the head and the heart. "The function of my fast is to purify, to release our energies by overcoming our inertia and mental sluggishness, not to paralyze us or to render us inactive."

"My fast isolates the forces of evil; the moment they are isolated they die, for evil by itself has no legs to stand upon. I expect you therefore," he concluded, "to work with even greater vigor under the instigation of my fast, not to feel its oppression."

The deputation went back realizing that it was not fair to ask him to give up his fast unless they could deliver the goods. Later in the afternoon a number of those who had led the disturbances in his camp on Sunday night came to him and made their surrender with what to all intents appeared to be genuine contrition.

That evening, another deputation of prominent citizens of Calcutta representing all communities, including Shaheed Saheb, Shri N. C. Chatterjee [28] and Sardar Niranjan Singh Talib,[29] waited on him. They told him that they had been to all the affected parts of the city and there was quiet everywhere. They had every reason to hope that there would be no recrudescence of trouble which was not communal really but was the work of the *goondas*. They requested him to break his fast. Gandhiji mildly rebuked them for the habit of taking refuge behind moral alibis by blaming it all on the *goondas*. . . .

Taking up next their request to break his fast, he asked them two straight questions. Could they in all sincerity assure him that there would never be any more recrudescence of communal madness in Calcutta? Could they say that there was a genuine change of heart among the citizens of Calcutta so that they would no longer foster or tolerate communal frenzy? They should let him continue his fast if they could not give him that guarantee for, in the event of the present communal outbreak being followed by another, he would have to undertake an irrevocable fast unto death. "But supposing there is another communal outbreak in spite of your assurances, since you are not omniscient," he resumed, "would you give your word of honor that you would in that event suffer to the uttermost before a hair of the minority community is injured, that you would die in the attempt to put out the conflagration but not return alive to report failure? And I want this from you in writing." If they could give that guarantee, he would break his fast. "But mind you," he added, "my blood will be upon your head if you say one thing and mean another; rather than thoughtlessly hurry, let me prolong my fast a little longer. It will not hurt me. When a man fasts it is not the gallons of water he drinks that sustains him, but God."

He spoke with deep passion. A pin-drop silence followed. Shaheed Saheb broke the ice. Gandhiji had said that he would break the fast when Calcutta would return to sanity. That condition had been fulfilled. Was he not imposing fresh conditions by asking them to sign that declaration? To this "legal argument" Gandhiji replied that there was no fresh condition imposed. All that was already implied in the original terms of the fast. "What I have spoken now is only a home truth to make you know what is what. If there is complete accord between your conviction and feeling, there should be no difficulty in signing that declaration. It is the acid test of your sincerity and courage of conviction. If, however, you sign it merely to keep me alive, you will be encompassing my death."

Everybody realized the solemnity of the warning. Rajaji and Acharya Kripalani, who had arrived during the latter part of the discussion, proposed that they might leave Gandhiji alone a little while and retire to the adjoining room to confer together. Shaheed Saheb endorsed the suggestion. They were about to retire when an appeal signed by about 40 representatives of the Hindus and Mussalmans, residents of Narkel Danga, Sitlatala, Manicktola, and Kankirgathi areas [30] was brought in. In their appeal, the signatories swore that they would not allow any untoward event or incident in that locality which was the worst affected during the previous riots and earnestly prayed to Gandhiji to break his fast. "It may also be reported," continued the signatories, "that no incident occurred in this mixed area since 14th of August 1947." "So our effort has not been in vain," remarked Shaheed Saheb, as he read out the appeal. "Yes, the leaven is at work," Gandhiji added.

Shaheed Saheb resumed, "Now that even the Muslims have joined in the appeal, won't you break your fast? This shows that they have fully accepted your peace mission although they are the aggrieved party in the present riots. It is all the more strange because at one time they looked upon you as their arch enemy. But their hearts have been so touched by the services you have rendered them that today they acclaim you as their friend and helper."

It was a graceful thing, gracefully uttered. Rajaji, not to be beaten in a tournament of chivalry, quickly added, "If I may vary the language, I would say that he is safer today in the hands of the Muslims than in those of the Hindus."

Gandhiji followed with interest this contest of chivalry and picked out for his comments only the portion of Shaheed Saheb's remarks in which he had referred to the Muslims as the aggrieved party. He did not like the "aggrieved party" language. "Do not think of Muslims as the aggrieved party," he remarked. "The essence of our present peace mission is that we are to forget the past. I do not want the Muslims to feel that in West Bengal they are the underdog. Unless we can forget the distinction, we will not have done solid work."

They then all retired to the next room and Gandhiji who had

an attack of weakness and nausea during the latter part of the talk was left alone to rest.

In the deliberations that took place in the adjoining room Shaheed Saheb was cautious and circumspect, which only showed his sincerity and sense of responsibility. Acharya Kripalani was cynical and full of sardonic humor as ever; Rajaji, tactful and persuasive and full of practical wisdom, concealing his emotion under a mask of ratiocination. The discussion was brief but unhurried. Rajaji dictated the draft of the pledge which was signed by Shri N. C. Chatterjee first, then by Shri Deven Mukerjee [31] followed by Shaheed Saheb Suhrawardy, Shri R. K. Jaidka,[32] and Sardar Niranjan Singh Talib to be followed later by others. A car load of hand grenades and arms had in the meantime arrived to be surrendered to Gandhiji as a token of repentance on the part of those who had taken part in the savagery of reprisals and counter-reprisals. Without any loss of time the signatories then returned to Gandhiji with the document.

"But sir, is it any good my signing this document?" remarked Shaheed Saheb to Gandhiji. "I may any time be called to Pakistan and then what happens to my pledge?"

"You must in that event have confidence that those whom you leave behind will deliver the goods," replied Gandhiji. "Moreover, you can come back."

"I have no desire to hoodwink you and I never will do so deliberately," remarked Shaheed Saheb in reply, explaining his extreme cautiousness, which Gandhiji greatly appreciated.

"Well, I will break this fast now," said Gandhiji at last, "and leave for the Punjab tomorrow. I shall now go there with far greater strength and confidence than I could have three days back."

Shaheed Saheb interposed, "You cannot leave tomorrow. Your presence is necessary here at least for a couple of days yet to consolidate the peace." Others supported him. They did not tell him what was uppermost in their minds besides, that they were deeply concerned at his undertaking a railway journey in his present state of health. The unruly crowds in Bihar and all along the line would tear him to pieces in their blind adoration.

So, Saturday was provisionally fixed for his departure.

Dr. Dinshah Mehta [33] had in the meantime hurried away to get orange juice ready. Before breaking the fast Gandhiji according to his usual practice, had prayer recited.

> "When life is dry and parched up,
> Descend Thou in a shower of mercy. . . ."

followed by Ramadhun [34] filled the air.

19 LAST DAYS (1948)

THE LAST FAST

by Louis Fischer

The communal disturbances which attended the partition of India into two nations cost something like half a million lives. About twelve million people became homeless refugees as Hindus fled from Pakistan to India and Moslems fled from India to Pakistan. Gandhi traveled about the country doing what he could to stem the tide.

Early in September 1947 Gandhi left Calcutta and returned to Delhi. Customarily he stayed at the untouchables' quarters at Kingsway, but these were occupied by refugees from the Punjab. He was, therefore, asked to stay at Birla House. Here he held long conferences with the leaders of the government and also with the leaders of various organizations whom Gandhi called his Constructive Workers. Each evening he led a prayer meeting on the grounds of Birla House, after which he would talk to the people. Also he toured Delhi and its environs to help quell the riots. The continuing tension between Hindus and Moslems agonized him.

• Reprinted with permission from Louis Fischer, The Life of Mahatma Gandhi (New York: Harper, 1950), pp. 494-99.

451

Hence, on January 13, 1948—several months after his seventy-eighth birthday—he began his last fast.

ON JANUARY 13, 1948, Mahatma Gandhi commenced his last fast. It engraved an image of goodness on India's brain.

The killings in Delhi had ceased. Gandhi's presence in the city had produced its effect. But he was still in "agony." "It is intolerable to me," he said, "that a person like Dr. Zakir Hussain,[1] for instance, or for that matter Shaheed Suhrawardy [the ex-prime minister of Bengal] should not be able to move about in Delhi as freely and with as much safety as I myself." Gandhi wanted to go to Pakistan to help the Hindus and Sikhs there, but how could he when the Moslems of Delhi had not obtained full redress? "I felt helpless," he said. "I have never put up with helplessness in all my life."

He therefore fasted; it was an "all-in fast," to death. "It came to me in a flash." He had not consulted Nehru or Patel or his doctors. To the charge that he had acted impatiently when the situation was improving, he replied that he had waited patiently since the riots started a year ago; the spirit of interreligious killing was still abroad in the land. "It was only when in terms of human effort I had exhausted all resources . . . that I put my head on God's lap. . . . God sent me the fast. . . . Let our sole prayer be that God may vouchsafe me strength of spirit during the fast that the temptation to live may not lead me into a hasty or premature termination of the fast."

The fast, Gandhi declared on the first day, was directed to "the conscience of all," to the Hindus and Moslems in the Indian Union and to the Moslems of Pakistan. "If all or any one of the groups respond fully, I know the miracle will be achieved. For instance, if the Sikhs respond to my appeal as one man I shall be wholly satisfied." He would go and live among the Sikhs of the Punjab.

"We are steadily losing hold on Delhi," Gandhi asserted; he feared a recrudescence of violence in the capital, and "if Delhi goes, India goes, and with that the last hope of world peace."

Hindus had been murdered in Karachi, the capital of Pakistan, and elsewhere in the Moslem Dominion. With his fingertips, the Mahatma sensed the danger of a new wave of riots. In Delhi refugees were ejecting Moslems from their homes, and demands had been heard to banish all the Moslem inhabitants of the city. "There is storm within the breast," Gandhi said; "it may burst forth any day."

He had brooded over the situation for three days without telling anybody. When at last he decided to fast "it made me happy." He felt happy for the first time in months.

He knew he might die, "but death for me would be a glorious deliverance rather than that I should be a helpless witness to the destruction of India, Hinduism, Sikhism, and Islam." His friends, he announced, must not rush to Birla House to try to dissuade him. Nor must they be anxious. "I am in God's hands." Instead of worrying about him they should "turn the searchlight inward; this is essentially a testing time for all of us."

The first day of the fast he walked to the evening prayer meeting and conducted the services as usual. "A fast weakens nobody during the first twenty-four hours after a meal," he told the congregation with a smile. A written question passed to him on the platform asked who was to blame for the fast. No one, he replied, "but if the Hindus and Sikhs insist on turning out the Moslems of Delhi they will betray India and their religions; and it hurts me." Some taunted him, he said, with fasting for the sake of the Moslems. They were right. "All my life I have stood, as everyone should stand, for minorities and those in need. . . .

"I expect a thorough cleansing of hearts," he declared. It did not matter what the Moslems in Pakistan were doing. Hindus and Sikhs should remember Tagore's favorite song: "If no one responds to your call, Walk alone, Walk alone."

He would break his fast when Delhi became peaceful "in the real sense of the term."

The second day of the fast the doctors told Gandhi not to go to prayers, so he dictated a message to be read to the congregation. But then he decided to attend and addressed the worshipers after the hymns and holy scriptures had been chanted. He had been deluged with messages, he said. The most pleasant was from Mrdulla Sarabhai [2] in Lahore, Pakistan. She wired that his Moslem friends, including some in the Moslem League and Pakistan government were anxious for his safety and asked what they should do.

His answer was: "The fast is a process of self-purification and is intended to invite all who are in sympathy with the mission of the fast to take part in the process of self-purification. . . . Supposing there is a wave of self-purification throughout both parts of India. Pakistan will become *pak*, pure. . . . Such a Pakistan can never die. Then, and only then, shall I repent that I ever called partition a sin, as I am afraid I must hold today. . . ."

"I have not the slightest desire that the fast should be ended as soon as possible," he assured the congregation. "It matters little if the ecstatic wishes of a fool like me are never realized and the fast is never broken. I am content to wait as long as it may be necessary, but it will hurt me to think that people have acted merely to save my life."

In this fast Gandhi did not wish to be examined by the physicians. "I have thrown myself on God," he told them. But Dr. Gilder, the heart specialist of Bombay, said the doctors wished to issue daily bulletins and could not tell the truth unless they examined him. That convinced the Mahatma and he relented. Dr. Sushila Nayyar told him there were acetone bodies in his urine.

"That is because I haven't enough faith," Gandhi said.

"But this is a chemical," she protested.

He looked at her with a faraway look and said, "How little science knows. There is more in life than science, and there is more in God than in chemistry."

He could not drink water; it caused nausea. He refused to add some drops of citrus juice or honey to the water to prevent nausea. The kidneys were functioning poorly. He had lost much strength; his weight dropped two pounds each day.

The third day he submitted to a high colonic irrigation. At 2:30 in the morning he awoke and asked for a hot bath. In the tub he dictated a statement to Pyarelal asking the Indian Union government to pay the government of Pakistan 550,000,000 rupees, or approximately $180,000,000. This was Pakistan's share in the assets of pre-partition India; the New Delhi authorities had delayed payment, and Gandhi was demanding immediate transfer of the money. Having dictated the memorandum, he felt giddy and Pyarelal lifted him out of the water and sat him in a chair. The Mahatma's weight was down to 107 pounds, his blood pressure 140:98.

The Indian Union government paid out the money.

That day, Gandhi occupied a cot which stood in an enclosed porch at the side of Birla House. Most of the time he lay in a crouched position, like an embryo, with his knees pulled up toward his stomach and his fists under his chest. The body and head were completely covered with a white khadi cloth which framed the face. His eyes were closed and he appeared to be asleep or half conscious. An endless queue filed past at a distance of ten feet. Indians and foreigners in the line were moved to pity as they observed him; many wept and murmured a prayer, and touched their palms together in a greeting which he did not see. Acute pain was written on his face. Yet even in sleep or semi-consciousness, the suffering seemed to be sublimated; it was suffering dulled by the exhilaration of faith, suffering moderated by an awareness of service. His inner being knew that he was making a contribution to peace and he was therefore at peace with himself.

Before prayers at 5 P.M. he was fully awake but he could not walk to the prayer ground, and arrangements were made for him to speak from his bed into a microphone connected with a loudspeaker at the prayer ground and with the All-India Radio which would broadcast his remarks throughout the country.

"Do not bother about what others are doing," he said in a weak voice. "Each of us should turn the searchlight inward and purify his or her heart as much as possible. I am convinced that if you purify yourselves sufficiently you will help India and shorten the period of my fast. . . . You should think how best to improve yourselves and work for the good of the country. . . . No one can escape death. Then why be afraid of it? In fact, death is a friend who brings deliverance from suffering."

He could speak no further. The rest of his message was read for him. Journalists had submitted questions to him, and he was answering them orally.

"Why have you undertaken a fast when there was no disturbance of any kind in any part of the Indian Dominion?"

"What was it if not a disturbing disturbance," he replied, "for a crowd to make an organized and a determined effort to take forcible possession of Moslem houses? The disturbance was such that the police had reluctantly to resort to tear gas and even a little shooting, if only overhead, before the crowd dispersed. It would have been foolish for me to wait till the last Moslem had been turned out of Delhi by subtle, undemonstrative methods which I would describe as killing by inches." . . .

The fourth day, Gandhi's pulse was irregular. . . . He insisted on addressing the prayer meeting by microphone for two minutes. This was followed by the reading of a statement which he had dictated earlier. The government of the India Union was paying Pakistan 550,000,000 rupees. This, Gandhi hoped, would lead to an honorable settlement of the Kashmir question and all outstanding differences between the two Dominions. "Friendship should replace the present enmity. . . . What will be Pakistan's counter-gesture?"

January 17th, Gandhi's weight was stabilized at 107 pounds. He was accumulating water apparently from the irrigations. He suffered nausea and was restless. But for hours he rested quietly or slept. Nehru came and cried. Gandhi sent Pyarelal into the city to ascertain whether it was safe for Moslems to return. Hundreds of telegrams arrived from princes, from Moslems in Pakistan, from every corner of India. Gandhi felt gratified, but his written statement that day was a warning: "Neither the Rajas nor Maharajas nor the Hindus or Sikhs or any others will serve themselves or India as a whole if at this, what is to me sacred juncture they mislead me with a view to terminating my fast. They should know that I never feel so happy as when I am fasting for the spirit. This fast has brought me higher happiness than hitherto. No one need disturb this happy state unless he can honestly claim that in his journey he has turned deliberately from Satan toward God."

January 18th, Gandhi felt better. He permitted some light massage. His weight remained at 107 pounds.

Ever since 11 A.M. on the 13th when Gandhi commenced to fast, committees representing numerous communities, organizations, and refugee groups in Delhi had been meeting in the house of Dr. Rajendra Prasad, the new Congress president, in an effort to establish real peace among divergent elements. It was not a matter of obtaining signatures to a document. That would not satisfy Gandhi. They must make concrete pledges which they knew their followers would carry out. If the pledges were broken Gandhi could easily and quickly ascertain the fact, and then he would fast irrevocably to death. Conscious of the responsibility, some representatives hesitated and went away to consult their conscience and subordinates. . . .

BREAKING THE FAST

by Pyarelal (Nayyar)

THE FEVERISH ANXIETY into which the whole city of Delhi and the country at large had been plunged was terminated when Gandhiji broke his fast at Birla House, New Delhi, today [January 18, 1948] at 12:45 P.M. with due solemnity. Earlier in the day, representatives of all the important groups and organizations in the city, including representatives of the refugees and from the three worst affected parts of the city, namely, Karol Bagh, Sabzimandi and Paharganj, had assembled under the chairmanship of Dr.

• Reprinted with permission from M. K. Gandhi, *Communal Unity* (Ahmedabad: Navajivan, 1949), pp. 948-54.

Rajendraprasad [3] at the latter's residence and put their signatures to a seven-point declaration covering the conditions laid down by Gandhiji for breaking his fast. The document was recorded in both the Persian and Devanagari scripts at Gandhiji's special insistence. At the meeting were also present Maulana Azadsaheb and Major General Shah Nawazkhan.[4] Delhi Muslims were represented by Maulanas Hifzur Rahman and Ahmed Saeed of the Jamiat-ul-Ulema [5] and Maulana Habib-ur-Rahman. Goswami Shri Ganesh Datt, Shri Basantlal and Shri Narain Das represented the Rashtriya Sevak Sangh [6] and the Hindu Mahasabha.[7] There were too the representatives of the various Sikh organizations. They then all repaired (numbering over 100) to Birla House, where they assembled in Gandhiji's room, to request him to break the fast. Maulanasaheb and Pandit Jawaharlalji [Nehru] had arrived there already and Janab Zahid Hussainsaheb, the Pakistan's High Commissioner came in a little later.

Dr. Rajendraprasad opened the proceedings by narrating to Gandhiji how they had all assembled on the previous night at the former's residence and after full discussion decided to sign the declaration then and there. But as representatives of some organizations were not present in that meeting, they felt that they should not go to Gandhiji immediately with the signed document but wait till the remaining signatures were obtained. They had accordingly met again in the morning when all those who were absent during the previous night's meeting came and gave their signatures. . . . As the President of the Congress, Dr. Rajendraprasad said that he had signed the document in view of the guarantee which they had all jointly and severally given. Janab Khurshid, the Chief Commissioner, and Shri Randhawa, Deputy Commissioner of Delhi, who were present, had signed the document on behalf of the administration. It had been decided to set up a number of committees to implement the pledge. Dr. Rajendraprasad hoped that Gandhiji would now terminate his fast.

Shri Deshabandhu Gupta,[8] speaking next, described some touching scenes of fraternization between the Hindus and Muslims which he had witnessed when a procession of about 150 Muslims was taken out that morning in Sabzimandi and was received with ovation and offered fruit and refreshments by the Hindu inhabitants of that locality.

Gandhiji replying said that what they had told him had touched him deeply. They had given him all that he had asked for. But if their words meant that they held themselves responsible for communal peace in Delhi only and what happened in other places was no concern of theirs, then their guarantee was nothing worth and he would feel and they too would one day realize that it was a great blunder on his part to have given up his fast. . . . Delhi was the heart of the Indian Dominion and they (the representatives gathered there) were the cream of Delhi. If they could not make the whole of India realize that the Hindus, Sikhs and Muslims were all brothers, it would bode ill for the future of both the Dominions. What would happen to Hindustan if they quarrelled with one another?

Here Gandhiji broke down owing to overwhelming feeling as he explained on resumption. What he had said was repeated aloud by me and partly by Dr. Sushila Nayyar.

Resuming his remarks after the interval, Gandhiji again appealed to them to search well their hearts so that they might not take any step which they would have to regret afterwards. The occasion demanded of them bravery of the highest order. They should clearly realize the implications of their pledge. It was nothing less than that what they had achieved in Delhi had to be realized in the whole of India. That did not mean that the ideal could be realized in a day. But it did mean that whilst in the past they had turned their face towards Satan, they had now resolved to turn it Godward. If, in their hearts, they did not accept what he had placed before them or if they had made up their minds that it was beyond them, they should plainly tell him so.

There could be nothing more wrong on their part, continued Gandhiji, then to hold that Hindustan belonged only to the Hindus and the Muslims could have no place in it or on the reverse that Pakistan belonged to the Muslims only and the Hindus and Sikhs could have no place in it. He wanted the refugees to understand that if they set things right in Delhi, as he had suggested, that was the only way to set things right in Pakistan too. He reminded them that he was not a man to shirk another fast, should he afterwards discover that he had been deceived or had deceived himself into breaking it prematurely. They should, therefore, act with circumspection and cent per cent sincerity. He invited the representatives of Mussalmans who had been meeting him frequently to tell him whether they were satisfied that the conditions in Delhi were now such as to warrant breaking the fast on his part.

Addressing next a few words to the Muslims especially, he asked if there was any ground for the suspicion that the Muslims did not regard India as their country. They lived in it in the midst of the Hindus because they could not help it, but one day they had to part company. He hoped that that suspicion was baseless. Similarly, if there was a Hindu who regarded the Muslims as yavanas [9] or asuras [10] incapable of realizing God, he was guilty of the worst blasphemy, which could possibly have no room in the covenant which they had signed.

He then referred to a book which a Muslim friend had lovingly presented him at Patna. In the book the writer had propounded that according to the Koran, Kafirs (i.e. Hindus) were worse than poisonous reptiles and fit only to be exterminated. Not only was there no sin in using every conceivable variety of force or fraud to compass that end, it was meritorious in the eyes of God. He was sure that no God-fearing Muslims could subscribe to or even secretly sympathize with that creed. . . .

Concluding, Gandhiji remarked that if they fully accepted the implications of their pledge, they should release him from Delhi so that he might be free to go to Pakistan. In his absence they should welcome such refugees from Pakistan as might want to return to their homes. The latter were none too happy over there just as the Hindus in the Indian Dominion were none too happy to lose large numbers of Muslim artisans and craftsmen. It was not easy to reproduce in a day traditional skill that had been acquired through generations. It was a loss on both sides which no sane people would like willingly to perpetuate.

Gandhiji ended by once more asking them to turn the search-light inward and not to deceive themselves or others by asking him to give up his fast, if what he had said did not find a responsive echo in their hearts.

Maulanasaheb Abul Kalam Azad, being next asked to say something, remarked that so far as the guarantee of communal peace was concerned it could be given only by the representatives of the citizens of Delhi. He, however, did not want to leave unchallenged the Muslim friends' observation to which Gandhiji had referred, as it referred to the teachings of Islam. He quoted a verse from the Koran which was to the effect that all mankind are brethren, irrespective of their race or religion. The remarks to which Gandhiji had referred were abhorrent to the teachings of Islam. They were only indicative of the insanity that had of late seized some sections of the people.

He was followed by Maulana Hifzur-Rahmansaheb, who categorically repudiated the allegation that his co-religionists did not regard India as their country which claimed their full and undivided allegiance, but only as a place where they were forced to live by expediency and by the compulsion of circumstances. Their thirty years' unbroken record of service of the nationalist cause gave the lie to that charge. They regarded it as an insult to their nationalism to be asked to reiterate their loyalty to India. He recalled how during the recent disturbances at one stage their Congress friends and colleagues had offered to provide a safe asylum to them outside Delhi as they were not sure that they would be able to give them adquate protection in Delhi. But they had declined that offer and had preferred to stay in and go about the city without any police escort, trusting to God alone. . . .

Describing next the change that had come over the city as a result of Gandhiji's fast, he said that they regarded it as a happy augury and a presage of things to come. They were satisfied that the tide had definitely turned and was now fast flowing in the direction of communal harmony and peace when previously bitterness and hatred ran riot. Now that the administration had underwritten the assurances given by the representatives of the people they were satisfied that they would be implemented, though it might take some time. He, therefore, joined Dr. Rajendraprasad in his appeal that Gandhiji should break the fast.

After Shri Ganesh Datt had on behalf of the Hindu Mahasabha and the R. S. S. reiterated that appeal, Janab Zahid Hussainsaheb addressed a few words to Gandhiji. He was there, he said, to convey to Gandhiji how deeply concerned the people in Pakistan were about him and how they were daily inundating him with anxious inquiries about his (Gandhiji's) health. It was their heart's desire that circumstances might soon prevail which would enable him to break the fast. If there was anything that he could fittingly do towards that end he was ready and so were the people of Pakistan.

Janab Zahid Hussainsaheb was followed by Janab Khurshid and Shri Randhawa who on behalf of the administration reiterated the assurance that all the conditions mentioned in the citizens' pledge would be duly implemented, and no effort would be spared to restore to the Indian capital its glorious old tradition of communal harmony and peace.

Sardar Harbans Singh endorsed on behalf of the Sikhs what his predecessors had said. Gandhiji then expressed his readiness to break the fast, which was done with the usual ceremony of prayer at which texts from the Japanese, Muslim and Parsi scriptures were recited followed by the mantra:

> "Lead me from untruth to truth,
> From darkness to light,
> From death to immortality."

A Hindustani hymn and the Christian hymn, "When I Survey the Wondrous Cross," were then sung by the girl inmates of the Ashram followed by Ramadhun. [11] The glass of fruit juice was handed by Maulanasaheb and Gandhiji broke the fast after fruit was distributed to and partaken by all present.

THE TASK AHEAD
by M. K. Gandhi

Speaking on the microphone from his bed, after breaking the fast, Gandhi said that he had earlier dictated a message for the prayer audience, which was then read.

I EMBARKED on the fast in the name of Truth whose familiar name is God. Without living Truth God is nowhere. In the name of God we have indulged in lies, massacres of people without caring whether they were innocent or guilty, men or women, children or infants. We have indulged in abductions, forcible conversions and we have done all this shamelessly. I am not aware if anybody has done these things in the name of Truth. With that same name on my lips I have broken the fast. The agony of our people was unbearable. Rashtrapati [12] Dr. Rajendrababu brought over a hundred people representing the Hindus, Muslims, Sikhs, representatives of the Hindu Mahasabha, the Rashtriya Swayam Sevak Sangh and representatives of refugees from the Punjab, the Frontier Province and Sind. . . . Dr. Rajendrababu read a document in Hindustani signed by these representatives, asking me not to put any further strain on them and end the agony by breaking the fast. Telegrams after telegrams have come from Pakistan and the Indian Union urging me to do the same. I could not resist the counsel of all these friends. I could not disbelieve their pledge that come what may, there would be complete friendship between the Hindus, Muslims, Sikhs, Christians, Parsis, and Jews, a friendship not to be broken. To break the friendship would be to break the nation.

As I write, comforting telegrams are deluging me. How I wish that God will keep me fit enough and sane enough to render the

• Reprinted with permission from *Harijan*, January 25, 1948. Also in M. K. Gandhi, *Communal Unity* (Ahmedabad: Navajivan, 1949), pp. 944-45.

service of humanity that lies in front of me! If the solemn pledge made today is fulfilled, I assure you that it will revive with redoubled force my intense wish and prayer before God that I should be enabled to live the full span of life doing service of humanity till the last moment. That span according to learned opinion is at least one hundred twenty-five years, some say one hundred thirty-three. The letter of my vow has been fulfilled early beyond expectation, through the great goodwill of all the citizens of Delhi, including the Hindu Mahasabha leaders and the Rashtriya Sevak Sangh. The result could not be otherwise when I find that thousands of refugees and others have been fasting since yesterday. Signed assurances of heart friendship have been pouring in upon me from thousands. Telegraphic blessings have come from all over the world. Can there be a better sign of God's hand in this act of mine? But beyond the letter of fulfilment of my solemn vow lies its spirit without which the letter killeth. The spirit of the vow is sincere friendship between the Hindus, Muslims and Sikhs of the Union and a similar friendship in Pakistan. If the first is assured, the second must follow, as sure as day follows night. If there is darkness in the Union, it would be folly to expect light in Pakistan. But if the night in the Union is dispelled beyond the shadow of a doubt, it cannot be otherwise in Pakistan, nor are signs wanting in that direction. Numerous messages have come from Pakistan, not one of dissent. May God, who is Truth, guide us as He has visibly guided us during all these six days.

BOMB AT PRAYERS
• by M. K. Gandhi

For several days after the end of his fast Gandhi was weak and had to be carried to the prayer grounds. On January 20, in

• Reprinted with permission from M. K. Gandhi, *Delhi Diary* (Ahmedabad: Navajivan, 1948), pp. 365-67.

his talk after prayers, he said he was sorry to hear that an official of the Hindu Mahasabha had repudiated the pledge of communal peace. If only the inhabitants of Delhi and the refugees in the capital would remain steadfast and not be swayed by happenings elsewhere, they would save India and also Pakistan. He said the least he expected them to do was not to take the law into their own hands and commit inhuman acts. They and their newspapers were never tired of condemning as barbarous the acts of those Americans who lynched Negroes. Were similar acts on their part any less barbarous?

During the question period, an explosion was heard. Gandhi minimized it by asserting, "Don't worry about it. Listen to me." Only later did he learn that a bomb had been thrown at him from the garden wall.

SPEAKING AFTER PRAYERS on Wednesday evening, Gandhiji referred to the previous day's bomb explosion. . . . He had been receiving anxious inquiries and praise for being unruffled at the accident. He thought that it was military practice and therefore nothing to worry about. He had not realized till after the prayers that it was a bomb explosion and that the bomb was meant against him. God only knew how he would have behaved in front of a bomb aimed at him and exploding. Therefore, he deserved no praise. He would deserve a certificate only if he fell as a result of such an explosion and yet retained a smile on his face and no malice against the doer. What he wanted to say was that no one should look down upon the misguided youth [13] who had thrown the bomb. He probably looked upon Gandhiji as an enemy of Hinduism. After all, had not the Gita said that whenever there was an evil-minded person damaging religion, God sent some one to put an end to his life? That celebrated verse had a special meaning. The youth should realize that those who differed from him were not necessarily evil. The evil had no life apart from the toleration of good people. No one should believe that he or she was so perfect that he or she was sent by God to punish the evil-doers, as the accused seemed to flatter himself he was.

He (Gandhiji) had heard that the youth had without permission occupied a masjid [14] for lack of other accommodation and now that the police were getting all mosques evacuated, he resented the act. It was a wrong thing on his part to have occupied the masjid in the first place and it was doubly wrong to defy the authorities, who asked him to vacate it.

To those who were at the back of the youth, he would appeal to desist from such activity. That was not the only way to save Hinduism. Hinduism could be saved only by Gandhiji's method. Gandhiji had practiced Hinduism from early childhood. His nurse had taught him to invoke Rama when he feared evil spirits. Later on he had come in contact with Christians, Muslims and others and, after making a fair study of other religions, had stuck to Hinduism. He was as firm in his faith today as in his early childhood. He believed God would make him an instrument of saving the religion that he loved, cherished and practiced. In any case, one had to have constant practice and acquaintance with the fundamentals of religion before being qualified for becoming God's instrument.

Continuing Gandhiji said that some Sikh friends came and said that he (Gandhiji) should not think that the Sikhs had anything to do with the deed. He knew that the youth was not a Sikh. But what did it matter whether he was a Sikh or a Hindu or a Muslim? He wished well to all perpetrators. He had told the Inspector General of Police also not to harass him in any way. They should try to win him over and convert him to right thinking and doing. He hoped that the youth and his guides would realize their error. For, it was a wrong done to Hinduism and the country. At the same time Gandhiji warned his hearers against being angry with the accused. He did not know that he was doing anything wrong. They should pity him. If they harbored resentment against Gandhiji's fast and had still pledged themselves to maintain peace in order to save an old servant of the nation, the guilt was theirs, not that of the young man who had thrown the bomb. If, on the other hand, they had signed the Peace Pledge whole-heartedly, persons like the young man were ultimately bound to come to their way of thinking.

Gandhiji said that he expected the audience to go on with the prayers in spite of bomb explosions or a shower of bullets. He was glad to learn that a poor unlettered woman was the cause of the arrest of the miscreant. If the heart was sound, if there was right thought, lack of letters was not of any consequence. He congratulated the unlettered sister on her simple bravery. . . .

INTO A THIRD WORLD WAR
by Vincent Sheean

During the final week of his life Gandhi gave interviews to several Americans, among them Vincent Sheean, the American writer, who conferred with him at Birla House on January 27 and 28.

IT WAS a small rectangular room with glass doors or French windows on one side, where the steps were, and long windows on the other two. The fourth wall was the wall of Birla House, against which this room was as a sort of annex, but an almost transparent annex: curious persons were peering through the windows or doors at all times and the Mahatma, through long training, did not even notice.

As I came in he was walking up and down on a rectangular blue carpet which covered less than half the floor. This, and his white pallet in the corner, made the only furniture of the room. In the corner at the right were three or four of "the girls": granddaughters, grandnieces, seated on the floor and talking in whispers.

• Reprinted with permission from Vincent Sheean, *Lead, Kindly Light* (New York: Random House, 1949), pp. 182-84, 185-88, 189, 191.

I began by saying that I wanted to make a rather extensive study of his system of thought and action. (I think I actually said "Good evening, sir," at the outset.) He said: "Yes, Pandit Nehru told me." He paused and looked up at me with a curious birdlike motion (I was much taller). "Pandit Nehru did not tell me," he said, "whether you wished to see me *absolutely* alone." The delicate emphasis on *absolutely* was full of meaning; I knew quite well that Mr. Gandhi never saw anybody "absolutely" alone.

"No, sir," I said. "I make no conditions."

"Very well," he said. "Would you like to walk or to sit?"

"Whatever you wish," I said. "Perhaps you are tired after the meeting . . .?"

"On the contrary," he said with a sort of gentle decision (oddly, I can still hear this phrase when some more important ones are preserved only by written notes). "At this hour I prefer to walk a little."

We walked up and down the blue carpet. . . . I was also aware that his swift steps up and down the carpet were much more numerous than mine. For me walking up and down that carpet was hardly walking at all; in three steps I had reached the end of it and turned back with him.

"Then you would not object," he went on, "if some notes were taken . . . ?" He motioned with his hand toward Mr. Pyarelal, who was keeping pace with him on the other side.

"No, sir," I said. "On the contrary. . . ."

"They might even be useful?" He finished the sentence for me on a rising note, with a curious half-smile.

"I have been reading your edition of the Gita," I said, "and my questions are based on that."

He smiled and exclaimed something ("*Acha, Acha!*" I believe, conveying assent). I went on:

"I propose to begin with action and the fruits of action."

He stopped still in his walk and looked up at me with his head slightly on one side. This is the characteristic motion I have called birdlike. He then straightened his head and pointed a long finger at the carpet.

"Let me get one thing clear," he said. "I have typhoid fever. Doctors are sent for and by means of injections of sulpha drugs or something of the kind they save my life. This, however, proves nothing. It might be that it would be more valuable to humanity for me to die."

He stopped again for a few seconds; we were both standing still now. The moment was of tremendous importance.

"Is that quite clear?" he asked, looking at me with his head up. "If it is not, I will repeat it."

This was the nearest thing to asperity—a very gentle kind of asperity—in the whole conversation.

"No, sir," I said. "I think I understand it."

We resumed the walk.

"What I wish to ask is this: how can a righteous battle produce a catastrophic result?" I said. "The battle is righteous in the terms of the Gita. The result is a disaster. How can this be?"

"Because of the means used," he said. "Means are not to be distinguished from ends. If violent means are used there will be a bad result."

"Is this true at all times and places?" I asked.

"I say so," he said with his curious lisp, and rather shyly, too, as if he had never gone quite so far before (as indeed he had not). Then he produced a statement which was much bolder.

"As I read the Gita, even the first chapter, the battlefield of Kurukshetra [15] is in the heart of man. I must tell you that orthodox scholars have criticized my interpretation of the Gita as being unduly influenced by the Sermon on the Mount."

He took a few more steps and then made a really defiant profession of faith.

"There is one learned book in existence," he said, "which supports my interpretation of the Gita. But even if there were no such book, and even if it could be proved that my interpretation was wrong, I would still believe it."

I was so taken aback by this certainty that I could not get out another question for the moment. Gandhi smiled and said: "Now I think we might sit down. Shall we?" . . .

After a considerable amplification of these ideas of means and ends, action and the fruits of action, I came to the specific case I had in mind all the time, which was our war against Hitlerism. The instance was my own—he may have had some other instance in mind—but I had avoided mentioning it before because I wanted to get the principles straight to begin with.

I told him that I was thinking of our war, which, in my view, had been a righteous battle.

"I knew some of the leaders on our side," I told him. He nodded his head slowly, accepting by that nod both Roosevelt and Churchill as being righteous in intention. (I did not mention their names; he knew.)

"How can such a truly righteous battle as our fight against the evil of Fascism produce the result which now faces us?"

That was my question as my diary records it on the following day. (Even this may not be quite accurate; the memory even from one day to the next can hardly be literal.)

With great sadness, leaning toward me and speaking almost in a whisper (so gentle was his voice) he said that our ends may have been good but our means were bad, and that this was not the way of truth. Then he made a few direct remarks which I remember verbatim (I can hear them now).

"You cannot destroy a great nation like Germany," he said.

"I know it, sir," I replied. "It is madness to try."

"You cannot destroy the spirit of Japan."

"I know it, sir."

"You are heading straight into a third world war."

It was just here, I think, that I returned to my main subject. (The possibility of a third world war was not included.)

"Those who govern us are obviously concerned with the fruits of action rather than with the truth of action," I said. "How, then, are we to be well governed?"

"You must give up the worship of Mammon," he said.

(Here, I believe, he was speaking of America, whereas by "we" I had meant all the people everywhere.)

He proceeded to outline a theory of representative democracy in characteristic terms, using the first person generically.

"I am ten million people," he said. "I send into government certain men to represent me. They may be corrupted. If they are corrupted I will recall them. I cannot recall myself."

He paused and leaned forward in a way which I could only regard as a little mysterious. (These movements forward and back, with the putting on and taking off of his spectacles, are beyond description; they indicate in retrospect that he was almost as tense by this time in his contemplation of the questions as I was.)

"Have nothing to do with power," he said, again as a sort of aside from the main discussion.

"Do you mean that power corrupts?" I asked him. (I was quoting Lord Acton, I suppose, but did not think it necessary to say so.)

He leaned back on the cushion with a sigh and said: "Yes, I am afraid I do mean that power corrupts." Then he sat up again and resumed his discourse:

"I have five constructive institutions. In all of these five constructive institutions I have constantly told the workers to have nothing to do with power. I do not send them to Parliament. They are to educate and guide those who vote, so that they may do so well."

(The five constructive institutions to which he referred were undoubtedly the organizations he had founded for village women, cottage industries, the All-India Spinners' Association, and the like.) . . .

I then asked him, on impulse, how he could explain how quite different persons, such as Bernard Shaw, for example, could get at the same disciplinary resolutions without religion. The sentence was so phrased that "disciplinary resolutions" came at the end of it, and before I had pronounced the words Mahatmaji caught me up with his sudden smile and the substitute word "conclusions." I let that pass, although I had meant chiefly vegetarianism, abstinence from stimulants, self-control in general, and not anything

quite so large as "conclusions." I then added: "Unless you say that
Mr. Shaw is himself religious."

The Mahatma, still smiling almost playfully at the thought, said
with his slow, careful enunciation:

"I was just about to say that it would be difficult for anybody to
say that Bernard Shaw had no religion. In everything of his that
I have read there has been a religious center."

I think it was at this point that he said to me: "You would be
astonished if you knew how few books I have read." This was a
sort of aside, almost in an undertone, and I answered in the same
way: "I don't see what difference the number makes if they were
good ones." . . .

He himself spoke of the failure of the United Nations—which
was one of the reasons that had brought me to him—and I said:
"I have hoped in the past year that perhaps you could be persuaded to come to Lake Success and talk to the United Nations.
Then they would be forced to listen."

He laughed; the idea seemed to him funny for a moment. He
then said, more seriously: "Perhaps, if I were spared for more
years of service. . . ." It sounded as if he did not regard this as
probable, and we dropped the subject. . . .

At about this point we all looked at our watches—that is, Mr.
Gandhi, Mr. Pyarelal and I. Almost a full hour had passed, and I
realized that there must be many people waiting for appointments. I said: "I'm afraid . . ."

Gandhi, looking at that enormous and very cheap watch he
wore in his shawl—the kind that was called a "turnip" in America
when I was young—said: "Well, this is more than I had bar-
gained for. Do you want to come back again tomorrow?"

"Whenever I can, whenever you have time for me," I said,
rising from the floor. He looked up at me and smiled.

"You can come every day," he said. "You can move into the
house if you like. I will find the time somehow. But in a few days
I hope to go to Wardha, and perhaps it is better if you come to
Wardha."

"At what hour shall I come tomorrow?" I asked.

"At this hour," he said, "after the prayer-meeting."

"I'll come to the prayer-meeting," I said.

This made him laugh.

"Come to the prayer-meeting!" he said, with an almost disembodied gayety. "And consider that a standing invitation!"

As I said: "Thank you, sir," he added very gently, in a voice that would have melted the heart of an enemy (and I was no enemy): "If there is no time, will you understand?" . . .

DEATH BEFORE PRAYERS

by Louis Fischer

On Friday, January 30, Gandhi was assassinated on his way to the prayer ground.

AT 4:30 P.M., Abha [16] brought in the last meal he was ever to eat; it consisted of goat's milk, cooked and raw vegetables, oranges, and a concoction of ginger, sour lemons, and strained butter with juice of aloe. Sitting on the floor of his room in the rear of Birla House in New Delhi, Gandhi ate, and talked with Sardar Vallabhbhai Patel, Deputy Prime Minister of the new government of independent India. Maniben, Patel's daughter and secretary, was also present. The conversation was important. There had been rumors of differences between Patel and Prime Minister Jawaharlal Nehru. This problem, like so many others, had been dropped into the Mahatma's lap.

Abha, alone with Gandhi and the Patels, hesitated to interrupt. But she knew Gandhi's attachment to punctuality. Finally, therefore, she picked up the Mahatma's nickel-plated watch and showed

• Reprinted with permission from Louis Fischer, The Life of Mahatma Gandhi (New York: Harper, 1950), pp. 3-4.

it to him. "I must tear myself away," Gandhi remarked, and so saying he rose, went to the adjoining bathroom, and then started toward the prayer ground in the large park to the left of the house. Abha, the young wife of Kanu Gandhi, grandson of the Mahatma's cousin, and Manu, the granddaughter of another cousin, accompanied him; he leaned his forearms on their shoulders. "My walking sticks," he called them.

During the daily two-minute promenade through the long, red-sandstone colonnade that led to the prayer ground, Gandhi relaxed and joked. Now, he mentioned the carrot juice Abha had given him that morning.

"So you are serving me cattle fare," he said and laughed.

"Ba used to call it horse fare," Abha replied. Ba was Gandhi's deceased wife.

"Isn't it grand of me," Gandhi bantered, "to relish what no one else wants?"

"Bapu (father)," said Abha, "your watch must be feeling very neglected. You would not look at it today."

"Why should I, since you are my timekeepers?" Gandhi retorted.

"But you don't look at the timekeepers," Manu noted. Gandhi laughed again.

By this time he was walking on the grass near the prayer ground. A congregation of about five hundred had assembled for the regular evening devotions. "I am late by ten minutes," Gandhi mused aloud. "I hate being late. I should be here at the stroke of five."

He quickly cleared the five low steps up to the level of the prayer ground. It was only a few yards now to the wooden platform on which he sat during services. Most of the people rose; many edged forward; some helped to clear a lane for him; those who were nearest bowed low to his feet. Gandhi removed his arms from the shoulders of Abha and Manu and touched his palms together in the traditional Hindu greeting.

Just then, a man [17] elbowed his way out of the congregation into the lane. He looked as if he wished to prostrate himself in the customary obeisance of the devout. But since they were late, Manu tried to stop him and caught hold of his hand. He pushed her away so that she fell and, planting himself about two feet in front of Gandhi, fired three shots from a small automatic pistol.

As the first bullet struck, Gandhi's foot, which was in motion, descended to the ground, but he remained standing. The second bullet struck; blood began to stain Gandhi's white clothes. His face turned ashen pale. His hands, which had been in the touch-palm position, descended slowly, and one arm remained momentarily on Abha's neck.

Gandhi murmured, "Hey, Rama (Oh, God)." A third shot rang out. The limp body settled to the ground. His spectacles dropped to the earth. The leather sandals slipped from his feet.

Abha and Manu lifted Gandhi's head, and tender hands raised him from the ground and carried him into his room in Birla House. The eyes were half closed and he seemed to show signs of life. Sardar Patel, who had just left the Mahatma, was back at Gandhi's side; he felt the pulse and thought he detected a faint beat. Someone searched frantically in a medicine chest for adrenalin but found none.

An alert spectator fetched Dr. D. P. Bhargava. He arrived ten minutes after the shooting. "Nothing on earth could have saved him," Dr. Bhargava reports. "He had been dead for ten minutes."

A SON'S LAST VIGIL

by Devadas Gandhi

Devadas, Gandhi's fourth son, was managing editor of the Hindustan Times in New Delhi. Consequently he saw his father often during the final months when Gandhi was living at Birla House in New Delhi. He was not with him at the assassination, however, but arrived half an hour later. The following speech by Devadas Gandhi was broadcast to the nation on February 5, 1948.

I SPEAK as an orphan impelled to share in this special and direct way my grief and thoughts with fellow-orphans. The darkness that has descended upon us draws no distinctions and I know that it is not my exclusive experience to feel suddenly blinded, both physically and metaphorically, since the evening of Friday last.

During the past few months that he was in Delhi, it was a privilege of my three-year-old boy to be lovingly fondled by Bapu. I was a complete back number and once recently he told me that he missed Gopu more than me whenever we failed to turn up at Birla House. The little urchin now draws renewed tears from our eyes when he pouts his lips in imitation of the way his grand-

• Reprinted with permission from *Homage to Mahatma Gandhi* (New Delhi: Ministry of Information and Broadcasting, 1948), pp. 32-36.

father greeted him. And yet Gandhiji's interest in the narrow domestic circle was of the meagrest, and I had long ceased to look upon him as my father in any possessive sense. He was to me a saint as much as to any of you who listen to me and I feel and see the void exactly as you do.

I, therefore, view the disaster with the detachment of one living in the North Pole and having ties neither of blood nor of race with the Great One of whose loss we are as yet but dimly aware.

When I got there nearly 30 minutes after he expired, his body was still warm. His skin was always tender and smooth to the touch and naturally beautiful. As I gently pressed the arm with both my hands, there seemed nothing the matter. But there was no pulse. He lay in his usual sleeping posture on his low bed, his head resting on Ava's [18] lap. Sardar Patel and Pandit Nehru sat near him in silence and many others sobbed as they tried to chant hymns. I was late. I pleaded in Father's ear for pardon, but in vain. So often had he forgiven my little lapses in the past that I fondly hoped he would relent this last time and give me just one look. But his lips were tightly sealed and his eyes closed in eternal repose. There was a calm determination about the expression which seemed to say firmly but without reproach to a habitually unpunctual son: "I shall not be disturbed now."

We kept vigil the whole of that night. So serene was the face and so mellow the halo of divine light that surrounded the body that it seemed almost sacrilegious to grieve or to fear death— "the incomparable friend" whom Bapu beckoned, as it would now appear from the statement with which he commenced his fast on January 13.

The most unbearably poignant moment for all of us was when we unwrapped the shawls which covered him and in which he had proceeded to the prayer meeting and when we removed the clothes to bathe the body in fulfilment of the religious rite. Always tidy to perfection in his scanty dress, he was even more so that day. The outer shawl had on it the dust and the tiny blades of grass from the lawn of the prayer ground where he had been struck down. We folded it gently as I was taking care not to shake off the dust or the grass. The empty shell of one of the bullets was found in the folds of the shawl, which shows that the shots were fired at less than point-blank range. The little piece of linen with which he covered the chest and shoulders had huge patches of the blood that had flowed. When all the clothes were off save the classic loin cloth and he was in view as the "naked faqir" we all knew, we could contain ourselves no longer. Those knees, those hands, with the fingers in characteristic pose, those feet were all there intact. How difficult it was to resist suggestions to have the body embalmed! Hindu sentiment would not allow it and Bapu would never forgive us if we agreed. . . .

We sat in the tragic room round Father that night. I prayerfully, but childishly, hoped that the flesh would triumph over the three ghastly bullet wounds and that life would somehow return before sunrise; then as time went inexorably on and nothing on earth would disturb his slumber, I began to wish that the sun would never rise. But the flowers had to come in and we started to decorate the body for the final journey. I asked for the chest to be left bare. No soldier ever had a finer chest than Bapu's. Then we sat round him chanting the hymns and scriptural texts that he liked most. The crowds kept coming the whole night and in the early morning he made his last collection for the Harijan Fund as coins and notes mixed with flowers were showered by people filing past. The Diplomatic Corps with their ladies and staff did reverent obeisance. It was far from formal. They were saying goodbye to one they had met before and knew so well.

The previous night I had had one of those rarest of rare experiences, that of being alone with Bapu for a moment. It was my customary call at 9:30. He was in bed but was just finishing giving instructions to one of the inmates of the ashram about catching an early train to Wardha. I stepped in and was greeted by "What news?" That was his way always of reminding me that I was a newspaperman. It carried a caution well understood by me. Hardly ever did he keep anything from me. He always gave me the quintessence of anything I asked about. Sometimes he did it on his own. But generally he disclosed things to me when I wished to know, on the supposition that I would ask only if absolutely necessary and that too for a purpose which had nothing to do with news in the newspaper sense. He trusted me in these matters as he would himself. I naturally had no news to give. So I asked: "How does the ship of State fare?" "I am sure," he said, "the little differences will vanish." "But," he added, "things may have to await my return from Wardha. That won't be long. The Government is composed of patriots and no one will do anything that is in conflict with the interests of the country. I am sure that they must hold together at all costs and they will. There is no difference of substance."

There was more conversation on the same lines and I would have invited the usual "crowd" even at that hour, had I tarried. So, preparing to leave, I said: "Bapu, will you sleep now?" "No, there is no hurry. You may talk for some time longer if you like." As I have just said, the permission to continue conversation could not be renewed the next day.

A few days earlier, when taking my leave at night, I said I was taking Pyarelal to dine with me. "Oh, yes, of course. But do you ever think of inviting me?" he said laughing heartily, as he always did.

I do not agree that the future is dark. Who but a prophet can speak with confidence of the future? The present is admittedly dark. But the future should be bright if we work for the ideals for which Bapu lived and died. I am, therefore, not gloomy. Bapu would be entitled to call us greedy if we wished him to live in our midst for ever. We are now thrown on our own resources and must depend on our own enterprise. I would not waste time or emotion in fruitless sorrow over God's will. Bapu himself is in bliss. We no longer have his physical presence. But his spirit will guide and help us. In his daily discourses of the past four months we have a set of balanced instructions which say almost everything that he would have had to say. We can, if we wish, quarrel and fall out. But, on the other hand, with a little effort at cohesion we may dissipate the dark clouds to find round the corner a glorious dawn.

"RAM, RAM"

by Margaret Bourke-White

Margaret Bourke-White, the American photographer, interviewed Gandhi on January 30. "Only a few hours later," she wrote, "this man who believed that even the atom bomb should be met with nonviolence was struck down by revolver bullets. . . ." Hearing the news, she hastened to Birla House, where Gandhi was staying.

I WAS ONLY a few blocks away when the assassin's bullet was fired. Friends ran to find me, and in a few minutes I was back in Albuquerque Road trying to make my way through the gate. Word-of-mouth news travels with lightning swiftness in India, and thousands of people were already pressing toward the scene of the tragedy.

The crush around Birla House was so great I could hardly reach the door, but once I was there the guards recognized me and slipped me through. In the next moment I was inside the room where Gandhi, dead less than an hour, lay on a mattress in the corner on the floor. His head was cradled lovingly in the lap of Brij Krishan, his secretary. The devoted little grandnieces and granddaughters-in-law who had always surrounded him in life clustered around now as he lay in his last sleep.

Already his face was changed. It had lost that taut look—glowing brown skin stretched tightly over lean bones—which used to give him, even in sleep, an expression of such extraordinary alertness. I remembered how we had been allowed to receive his darshan while he slept, during the exhausting days of his fast,

• Reprinted with permission from Margaret Bourke-White, *Halfway to Freedom* (New York: Simon and Schuster, 1949), pp. 234-37.

and the joyful moment when he had broken his fast in this very room. I had stood on this very spot, and watched him smile up from the same mattress, while he blessed the orange slices and people shared in "God's gift." Then the people in this room were laughing and crying with joy. Now they were silent and stunned. Few people even wept.

The only sound was the endless chanting of the Gita by the women followers, who sat along the edge of the mattress and swayed to the rhythmic recitation of the "Song of God." They were singing the final cantos, always sung at the death of a Hindu; for Gandhi these verses had special appropriateness. The Gita tells how the warrior hero Arjuna, perplexed by the distressing knowledge that brothers and blood relatives fight against one another, lays down his bow. And Lord Krishna teaches him the virtue of performing the right action and leaving the consequences to God —for everything comes from God and everything returns to God.

The women kneeling along the mattress were chanting the name of God now, singing "Ram, Ram" and beating their hands softly to the rhythm of the prayer. Suddenly into the numbness of that grief-filled room came the incongruous tinkle of broken glass. The glass doors and windows were giving way from the pressure of the crowds outside, straining wildly for one last look at their Mahatma, one last darshan, even in death. . . .

I slipped away from the wordless tragedy in that little room and pressed through the sorrowing crowds to the garden path where Gandhiji had met his end. Already a radiance hung over the spot. Someone had marked the place with a candle and its beam was steady and golden in the black Indian night. The place was marked off with a humble little line of sticks, simply laid out in a triangular shape on the ground, and a large and very ordinary-looking tin can—about the size of a large jam tin—had been set down to encircle the precise spot where he fell. Kneeling around it were men and women of all religions—just as Gandhiji would have had it. United in deepest sorrow, they were reverently scooping up into their handkerchiefs small handfuls of the bloodstained earth to carry away and preserve.

Then a new current developed in the crowd, and I was swept along with it to the front of the house, where I found Nehru was speaking. Once more he had climbed up on the gate of Birla House to address the people. Illuminated by a street lamp, he stood there, his face ashen gray and his features drawn with pain and shock. "Mahatmaji is gone," he was saying. "And the great light is extinguished. Darkness of sorrow and distress surrounds us all. I have no doubt he will continue to guide us from the borders of the Great Beyond. But we shall never be able to get that solace which we got by running up to him for advice in every difficulty." At this point Jawaharlal Nehru, who of all Indian leaders had probably depended the most on Gandhiji for strength and solace in difficulties, broke down and wept openly, and the mourning thousands wept with him. Then he made a supreme effort to speak his final sentence. "We can best serve the spirit of Bapu by dedicating ourselves to the ideals for which he lived and the cause for which he died."

All through that terrible night people gathered in hushed groups in the streets of New and Old Delhi. . . .

By dawn the lawns and gardens of Birla House and all surrounding houses, Albuquerque Road and all streets leading into it, were flooded with people. By the tens of thousands they swirled through the Birla gates, until they crushed in an indivisible mass against the house. And still they came, beating against the walls of the house in surging waves of mourning humanity. I doubt that there has ever been a scene like it; certainly there has been none in my experience. The house, with its rising terraces, was like a rocky island holding its precious burden high above this sea of grief. Laid out on the roof of a terrace was the figure of Gandhi, tranquil and serene, where all could see and receive his last darshan.

A MILLION AND A HALF MARCHED

by Louis Fischer

Following Hindu custom, Gandhi was cremated the day after he died, on a funeral pyre on the banks of the Jumna river. The funeral procession is thus described by Louis Fischer.

DURING THE NIGHT the chassis of a Dodge fifteen-hundredweight army weapon-carrier had been replaced by a new superstructure with a raised floor so that all spectators could see the body in the open coffin. Two hundred men of the Indian Army, Navy, and Air Force drew the vehicle by four stout ropes. The motor was not used. Non-commissioned officer Naik Ram Chand sat at the steering wheel. Nehru, Patel, several other leaders, and several of Gandhi's young associates rode on the carrier.

The cortege, two miles long, left Birla House on Albuquerque Road in New Delhi at 11:45 A.M., and, moving forward inch by inch through dense masses of humanity, reached the Jumna River, five and a half miles away, at 4:20 P.M. A million and a half marched and a further million watched. Branches of New Delhi's splendid shade trees bent under the weight of persons who had climbed upon them to get a better view. The base of the big white monument of King George V, which stands in the middle of a broad pond, was covered with hundreds of Indians who had waded through the water.

Now and then the voices of Hindus, Moslems, Sikhs, Parsis, and Anglo-Indians mingled in loud shouts of "*Mahatma Gandhi ki jai* (Long Live Mahatma Gandhi)." At intervals the multitude

• Reprinted with permission from Louis Fischer, *The Life of Mahatma Gandhi* (New York: Harper, 1950), pp. 6-8.

broke into sacred chants. Three Dakota aircraft flew over the procession, dipped in salute, and showered countless rose petals.

Four thousand soldiers, a thousand airmen, a thousand policemen, and a hundred sailors, in varied and varicolored uniforms
and headdress, marched before and after the bier. Prominent
among them were mounted lancers bearing aloft red and white
pennants—the bodyguard of Governor-General Lord Mountbatten.
Armored cars, police, and soldiers were present to maintain order.
In charge of the death parade was Major General Roy Bucher, an
Englishman chosen by the Indian government to be the first
commander-in-chief of its army.

By the holy waters of the Jumna, close to a million people had
stood and sat from early morning waiting for the cortege to arrive
at the cremation grounds. The predominant color was white, the
white of women's saris and men's garments, caps, and turbans.

Several hundred feet from the river, at Rajghat, stood a fresh
funeral pyre made of stone, brick, and earth; it was about two
feet high and eight feet square. Long thin sandalwood logs sprinkled with incense had been stacked on it. Gandhi's body was laid
on the pyre with the head to the north and the feet to the south.
In this position Buddha had met his end.

At 4:45 P.M., Ramdas set fire to his father's funeral pyre. The
logs burst into flame. A groan went up from the vast assemblage.
Women wailed. With elemental force the crowd surged toward
the fire and broke through the military cordon. But in a moment
the people seemed to realize what they were doing and dug in
their bare toes and prevented an accident.

The logs crackled and seethed and the flames united in a single
fire. Now there was silence. . . . Gandhi's body was being reduced
to cinders and ashes.

The pyre burned for fourteen hours. All the while prayers were
sung; the entire text of the *Gita* was read. Twenty-seven hours
later, when the last embers had grown cold, priests, officials,
friends, and relatives held a special service in the guarded wire
enclosure around the pyre and collected the ashes and the splin-
ters of bone that had defeated the fire. The ashes were tenderly

scooped into a homespun cotton bag. A bullet was found in the ashes. The bones were sprinkled with water from the Jumna and deposited in a copper urn. Ramdas placed a garland of fragrant flowers around the neck of the urn, set it in a wicker basket filled with rose petals, and, pressing it to his breast, carried it back to Birla House. . . .

"MAHATMA GANDHI KI-JAI!"

by Vincent Sheean

After Gandhi's cremation, there were thirteen days of mourning as prescribed for orthodox Hindus of his caste. On February 12, 1948—the thirteenth day—his ashes were distributed to the seven sacred rivers of India and elsewhere. The chief immersion ceremony took place at Allahabad, at the confluence of the Ganges, Jumna, and Saraswati rivers.

THE SPECIAL TRAIN which was to carry the Mahatma's ashes to the confluence of the rivers was made up of third-class carriages, all swept and garnished but otherwise no different from the ordinary carriages used by the Indian poor. The difference was that on this train each place was reserved, with tickets which had been given out by Ramdas Gandhi the evening before, and the unimaginable overcrowding which is the chief characteristic of Indian third-class carriages was avoided. In the center of the train one carriage had been arranged as a sort of catafalque, with a platform or table covered with marigolds in the middle, on which the urn with Gandhiji's ashes would rest. This carriage containing the ashes was brightly lighted throughout the journey, so that any who beheld

• Reprinted with permission from Vincent Sheean, *Lead, Kindly Light* (New York: Random House, 1949), pp. 219-22.

it, even by chance, could receive the darshan of that mighty
spirit. . . .

The long journey of the train across the central plain of India
was an evidence—if any were needed—of how every inhabitant,
whatever his condition, felt this loss. I quote from my diary as
written in Benares on Friday, the 13th:

"Wherever the train stopped, and in a great many places where
it did not stop, crowds of people had assembled for darshan. In
many towns the behavior was impressively solemn. In empty fields,
at small villages and at crossroads it was even more impressive to
see the peasants standing with their hands joined in the attitude
of prayer (this has become also an attitude of ordinary salutation)
as the train passed. The terrific demonstration was at Cawnpore,
which we reached at about five o'clock on Wednesday evening.
An immense multitude, said to have been at least half a million,
had gathered there, in and around the railroad station and along
the tracks into and out of the town. We stayed in Cawnpore Station two hours for the darshan and then had to leave before more
than a proportion of the people had obtained it. As we pulled out,
the excitement of the people could no longer be contained and
their instinct moved them to cries of "*Mahatma Gandhi ki-jai!*"
(Victory, or Triumph, to Mahatma Gandhi!) which was what
they used to cry out to him in life. I thought this very thrilling,
especially as it rose to a great height as we slowly pulled out of
the city. . . .

"Bonfires and torches burned along our way during the night
until we reached Rasulabad (how Muslim all these names are!)
where we stopped for the night. In the morning at seven we resumed the journey and reached Allahabad at 9 A.M. (Thursday).
Nehru, Mrs. Naidu, Pandit Pant,[1] Patel and other dignitaries were
there on the platform to receive the ashes. We then started the
long march to the Sangam, the confluence of the rivers. I don't
know how many miles it was but I felt exhausted at the end. . . .
By the Christian cathedral a choir sang 'Lead, Kindly Light.' Our
procession was completely enclosed by lines of infantry soldiers,

but children and other determined persons succeeded in infiltrating and joining the march."

That march was a long, dusty and (in the end) sweltering pilgrimage. An assemblage of people which may indeed have formed the greatest single crowd ever known had converged upon Allahabad. Hundreds of thousands had already been there for the religious fair (the "miniature" or at least minor replica of the great twelve-year fair called the Kumbh Mela which the Mahatma had so disliked in 1915). They had remained for the immersion of their Father's ashes, and millions had joined them. The whole crowd, from Allahabad station to the confluence of the sacred rivers, about seven miles away (as I later learned), was said to have numbered four million, the greater part of which had assembled in a dense mass on the great plain. . . .

The procession was preceded by the great white catafalque, covered with flowers, in the center of which Gandhiji's ashes had been placed. Accompanying the ashes on this vehicle were Mr. Nehru, Mr. Patel and other high officers of the government. The diary continues:

"As we came over a ridge and saw the Ganges and Jumna flowing together (having passed through a long stretch of tents and bazaars of the Kumbh Mela) the sight was indescribable: all that space was filled with people, the greatest concourse of people I have ever seen. . . ."

THE LIGHT HAS GONE OUT

• by Jawaharlal Nehru

The news of Gandhi's assassination was conveyed to the nation by Prime Minister Nehru, who spoke extemporaneously over

• Reprinted with permission from *Homage to Mahatma Gandhi* (New Delhi: Ministry of Information and Broadcasting, 1948), pp. 9-10.

the *All-India Radio*. He was followed by Sardar Vallabhbhai Patel, Deputy Prime Minister, also a long-time associate of Gandhi.

The Indian government received more than 3,000 messages from foreign countries expressing condolences on the death of Gandhi. Among those who paid tribute were King George VI, President Harry S. Truman, Prime Minister Clement Attlee, Mohammed Ali Jinnah, Mrs. Eleanor Roosevelt, General Douglas MacArthur, Albert Einstein, Andrei Gromyko, Pearl Buck, and Mary McLeod Bethune. The Indian Ministry of Information declared, "Perhaps no man in recorded history received such spontaneous tributes of universal praise, reverence and love as did Mahatma Gandhi at his death."

FRIENDS AND COMRADES, the light has gone out of our lives and there is darkness everywhere. I do not know what to tell you and how to say it. Our beloved leader Bapu as we called him, the father of the nation, is no more. Perhaps I am wrong to say that. Nevertheless, we will not see him again as we have seen him for these many years. We will not run to him for advice and seek solace from him and that is a terrible blow not to me only but to millions and millions in this country, and it is a little difficult to soften the blow by any other advice that I or anyone else can give you.

The light has gone out, I said, and yet I was wrong. For the light that shone in this country was no ordinary light. The light that has illumined this country for these many years will illumine this country for many more years and a thousand years later that light will still be seen in this country and the world will see it and it will give solace to innumerable hearts. For that light represented something more than the immediate present; it represented the living truth . . . the eternal truths, reminding us of the right path, drawing us from error, taking this ancient country to freedom.

All this has happened when there was so much more for him to do. We could never think that he was unnecessary or that he had done his task. But now, particularly, when we are faced with so many difficulties, his not being with us is a blow most terrible to bear.

A madman has put an end to his life, for I can only call him mad who did it, and yet there has been enough of poison spread in this country during the past years and months and this poison has had effect on people's minds. We must face this poison, we must root out this poison and we must face all the perils that encompass us and face them not madly or badly but rather in the way that our beloved teacher taught us to face them. The first thing to remember now is that no one of us dare misbehave because we are angry. We have to behave like strong and determined people, determined to face all the perils that surround us, determined to carry out the mandate that our great teacher and our great leader has given us, remembering always that if, as I believe, his spirit looks upon us and sees us, nothing would displease his soul so much as to see that we have indulged in any small behavior or any violence.

So we must not do that. But that does not mean that we should be weak but rather that we should in strength and in unity face all the troubles that are in front of us. We must hold together and all our petty troubles and difficulties and conflicts must be ended in the face of this great disaster. A great disaster is a symbol to us to remember all the big things of life and forget the small things, of which we have thought too much. . . .

Tomorrow should be a day of fasting and prayer for all of us. . . . And while we pray, the greatest prayer that we can offer is to take a pledge to dedicate ourselves to the truth and to the cause for which this great countryman of ours lived and for which he has died. . . .

HOMAGE FROM PATEL

by Vallabhbhai Patel

JUST NOW my dear brother, Pandit Jawaharlal Nehru, has spoken to you. My heart is aching. What shall I say to you? My tongue is tied. This is a day of sorrow, shame and agony for India. . . .

Friends, the occasion demands not anger, but earnest heart-searching from us all. If we give vent to our understandable anger, it would mean that we have forgotten our beloved master's teachings so soon after his death. And let me say, we haltingly followed our master even in his lifetime. Therefore, I beseech you all in humility to stand firm and together, unshaken by violent impulses of the moment. This is a time of severest trial for us all. We have to prove worthy of our great master. A very heavy responsibility rests on us all now. So heavy a responsibility that it might even break many of us. Indeed Gandhiji was a pillar of strength and a source of inspiration to the nation. And in his death, we who were his closest associates have suffered an irreparable loss. Gandhiji is gone, but Gandhiji will live in our hearts for ever. . . .

I am sure Gandhiji's supreme sacrifice will wake up the conscience of our countrymen and evoke a higher response in the heart of every Indian. I hope and pray that it may be given to us to complete Gandhiji's mission. At this solemn moment, no one of us can afford to waver or lose his or her heart. Let us all stand united and bravely face the national disaster that has overtaken us. Let us solemnly pledge ourselves afresh to Gandhiji's teachings and ideals.

• Reprinted with permission from *Homage to Mahatma Gandhi* (New Delhi: Ministry of Information and Broadcasting, 1948), pp. 11-12.

HOMAGE FROM MIRABEHN
by Mirabehn

The following article was written for the press a few days after Gandhi's death.

FOR ME there were only two, God and Bapu. And now they have become one!

When I heard the news something deep, deep down within me opened—the door to the imprisoned soul—and Bapu's spirit entered there. From that moment a new sense of the eternal abides with me.

Though Bapu's beloved physical presence is no longer with us, yet his sacred spirit is even nearer. Sometimes Bapu had said to me, "When the body is no more there will not be separation, but I shall be nearer to you. The body is a hindrance." I listened in faith. Now I know, through experience, the divine truth of these words.

Did Bapu know what was coming? One evening in December, shortly before I left Delhi for Rishikesh, I said to him, "Bapu, in March, when the cow-sheds are built and the work is organized, is there just a possibility that you might find time to come for the opening ceremony and give your blessings to the poor suffering Indian cow?" "Don't think of my coming," Bapu replied —and then, as if half speaking to himself, he added, "What is the good of counting on a corpse?" The words were so terrible that I repeated them to nobody, but put them away silently in my heart, with a prayer to God. The fast came and went, and I hoped the meaning of the reference had passed with it. But the reference was prophetic, and the prophecy has been fulfilled.

• Reprinted with permission from *Gandhi's Letters to a Disciple* (New York: Harper, London: Victor Gollancz, 1950), pp. 230-31.

That fateful evening, as I sat upright and motionless in meditation, I felt a shudder of anguish passing round the whole world. Again the blood of an *avatar*[2] had flowed for the salvation of mankind, and the earth moaned with the weight and horror of a deadly sin.

That sin is not of one man, it is the Sin which floods the whole world from age to age, and which nothing but the crucifixion of God's beloved can stem.

Now must we move heaven and earth to fulfil the task which Bapu has left us. Bapu lived and died for us all—every man, woman and child. He lived, working unceasingly, and died a martyr's death, that we might be turned from the evil path of hatred, greed, violence and untruth. If we are to atone for our sins, and serve Bapu's sacred cause, communalism in every form must go, and many other things as well. Black marketing, corruption, favoritism, jealousies, rivalries and a host of other dark manifestations of untruth and violence. These must be tackled with a firm will and unfaltering hand. Bapu was full of love and gentleness, but in his fight with evil he was relentless.

Bapu could fight the evil without because he had mastered the evil within. May God so purify us that we may become worthy of the mighty task before us.

A GLORY DEPARTED

•

by Jawaharlal Nehru

Jawaharlal Nehru first met Gandhi at the convention of the Indian National Congress in Lucknow in December 1916. Nehru was then twenty-seven years old and Gandhi, his South African experiences behind him, was forty-seven. Three years later, when

• Reprinted with permission from Jawaharlal Nehru, *Nehru on Gandhi* (New York: John Day, 1948), pp. 129-34.

Gandhi announced the civil disobedience against the Rowlatt Act, Nehru was "afire with enthusiasm and wanted to join the Satyagraha campaign immediately." But Nehru's father—the prominent lawyer, Pandit Motilal Nehru—was "dead against this new idea." The more the father thought about it, the less he liked it. Motilal summoned Gandhi to Allahabad and they had long talks, as a result of which Gandhi advised Jawaharlal not to do anything which might upset his father.

The action of the British in 1919 had a profound effect on the elder Nehru. "His whole legal and constitutional foundations were shaken by them, and his mind was gradually prepared for that change which was to come a year later." Motilal abandoned his lucrative law practice and became a complete non-cooperator. Soon both father and son were close associates of Gandhi, and both were sentenced to prison. Of those early years, Nehru later wrote, "Gandhiji himself was a very difficult person to understand; sometimes his language was almost incomprehensible to an average modern. But we felt that we knew him quite well enough to realize that he was a great and unique man and a glorious leader, and, having put our faith in him, we gave him an almost blank check, for the time being at least. Often we discussed his fads and peculiarities among ourselves and said, half-humorously, that when Swaraj came these fads must not be encouraged."

In 1924 Gandhi presided over the meetings of the Indian National Congress at Belgaum and, at his insistence, Nehru was re-elected working secretary of the Congress. In January 1931 Gandhi, Nehru, and other Congress leaders were discharged from prison. Because Motilal Nehru was ailing, the members of the Working Committee of the Congress made for Allahabad, where they met next door to the Nehru house. Gandhi visited often with Motilal and once the latter said to Gandhi, "I am going soon, Mahatmaji, and I shall not be here to see Swaraj. But I know that you have won it and will soon have it." He died a few days later and Gandhi spoke to the multitude assembled on the banks of the Ganges after his body was cremated. Nehru acknowledged "above all, the wonderfully soothing and healing presence of Gandhiji that helped my mother and all of us to face that crisis in our lives."

Gandhi and Nehru were co-workers for almost three decades. Once Nehru wrote, "To me, personally, Gandhiji had always shown extraordinary kindness and consideration, and my father's death had brought him particularly near to me." Yet there arose, from time to time, sharp differences between teacher and disciple —differences over religion, economics, and political strategy.

At the time of Gandhi's death Nehru was Prime Minister of the newly independent Indian nation, of which Gandhi was the founder and elder statesman. The following address (abridged) was delivered in the Indian Parliament on February 2, 1948.

I HAVE A SENSE of utter shame both as an individual and as head of the government of India that we should have failed to protect the greatest treasure we possessed. It is our failure, as it has been our failure in the past many months, to give protection to many an innocent man, woman, and child. It may be that that burden and task was too great for us or for any government; nevertheless, it is a failure, and today the fact that this mighty person, whom we honored and loved beyond measure, has gone because we could not give him adequate protection is shame for all of us. It is shame to me as an Indian that an Indian should have raised his hand against him, it is shame to me as a Hindu that a Hindu should have done this deed and done it to the greatest Indian of the day and the greatest Hindu of the age.

We praise people in well-chosen words and we have some kind of measure for greatness. How shall we praise him and how shall we measure him, because he was not of the common clay that all of us are made of? He came, lived a fairly long span of life, and has passed away. No words of praise of ours in this house are needed, for he has had greater praise in his life than any living man in history and during these two or three days since his death he has had the homage of the world. What can we add to that? How can we praise him?—how can we who have been children of his, and perhaps more intimately children of his than the children of his body, for we have all been in some greater or smaller measure the children of his spirit, unworthy as we were?

A glory has departed and the sun that warmed and brightened our lives has set and we shiver in the cold and dark. Yet he would not have us feel this way after all that glory that we saw, for all these years that man with divine fire changed us also, and, such as we are, we have been molded by him during these years and out of that divine fire many of us also took a small spark which strengthened and made us work to some extent on the lines that he fashioned. . . . He spread out over India, not in palaces only or in select places or in assemblies, but in every hamlet and hut of the lowly and of those who suffer. He lives in the hearts of millions and he will live for immemorial ages. . . .

We mourn him, we shall always mourn him, because we are human and cannot forget our valued master; but I know that he would not like us to mourn him. No tears came to his eyes when his dearest and closest went away, only the firm resolve to persevere, to serve the great cause that he had chosen. So he would chide us if we merely mourn. That is a poor way of doing homage to him. The only way is to express our determination, to pledge ourselves anew, to conduct ourselves so and to dedicate ourselves to the great task which he undertook and which he accomplished to such a large extent. So we have to work, we have to labor, we have to sacrifice, and thus prove to some extent at least worthy followers of his. . . .

He has gone, and all over India there is a feeling of having been left desolate and forlorn. All of us sense that feeling and I do not know when we shall be able to get rid of it. And yet, together with that feeling, there is also a feeling of proud thanksgiving that it has been given to us of this generation to be associated with this mighty person. In the ages to come, centuries and maybe millenniums after us, people will think of this generation when this man of God trod the earth, and will think of us who, however small, could also follow his path and probably tread on that holy ground where his feet had been. Let us be worthy of him, let us always be so.

VICTORY TO MAHATMA GANDHI
by Jawaharlal Nehru

*The following address (abridged) was delivered on February
12, 1948, on the occasion of the immersion of Gandhi's ashes in
the sacred rivers of India.*

. . . LET US, standing here on the banks of the Ganges, search
our own hearts and ask ourselves the question: How far have we
followed the path shown to us by Gandhiji and how far have we
tried to live in peace and co-operation with others? If even now we
follow the right path, it will be well with us and well with our
country.

Our country gave birth to a mighty one and he shone like a
beacon not only for India but for the whole world. And yet he was
done to death by one of our own brothers and compatriots. How
did this happen? You might think that it was an act of madness,
but that does not explain this tragedy. It could only occur because
the seed for it was sown in the poison of hatred and enmity that
spread throughout the country and affected so many of our people.
Out of that seed grew this poisonous plant. It is the duty of all
of us to fight this poison of hatred and ill will. If we have learned
anything from Gandhiji, we must bear no ill will or enmity
towards any person. The individual is not our enemy. It is the
poison within him that we fight and which we must put an
end to. . . .

He brought us to freedom and the world marvelled at the way
he did it. But at the very moment of gaining our freedom we forgot the lesson of the Master. A wave of frenzy and fanaticism

• Reprinted with permission from Jawaharlal Nehru, *Nehru on Gandhi* (New
York: John Day, 1948), pp. 141-46.

overtook our people and we disgraced the fair name of India. Many of our youth were misled and took to wrong paths. Are we to drive them away and crush them? They are our own people and we have to win them over and mold them and train them to right thought and action.

The communal poison, which has brought disaster upon us, will put an end to our freedom also if we are not vigilant and if we do not take action in time. It was to awaken us to this impending danger that Gandhiji undertook his last fast two or three weeks ago. His self-crucifixion roused the nation's conscience and we pledged before him to behave better. It was only then that he broke his fast. . . .

Democracy demands discipline, tolerance and mutual regard. Freedom demands respect for the freedom of others. In a democracy changes are made by mutual discussion and persuasion and not by violent means. If a Government has not got popular support, another government takes its place which commands that popular support. It is only small groups, who know that they cannot get sufficient popular support, that resort to methods of violence, imagining in their folly that they can gain their ends in this way. This is not only utterly wrong but it is also utterly foolish. For the reaction to the violence of the minority, which seeks to coerce the majority, is to provoke the majority into violence against them.

This great tragedy has happened because many persons, including some in high places, have poisoned the atmosphere of this country of ours. It is the duty of the government as well as the people to root out this poison. We have had our lesson at a terrible cost. Is there anyone among us now who will not pledge himself after Gandhiji's death to fulfil his mission—a mission for which the greatest man of our country, the greatest man in the world, has laid down his life? . . .

How often we have shouted "Mahatma Gandhi Ki Jai"—"Victory to Mahatma Gandhi." . . . Throughout his life he thought of India in terms of the poor and the oppressed and the downtrodden. To raise them and free them was the mission of his life.

He adopted their ways of life and dress so that none in the country may feel lowly. Victory to him was the growth of freedom of these people.

What kind of triumph did Gandhiji wish for us? Not the triumph for which most people and countries strive through violence, fraud, treachery and evil means. That kind of victory is not stable. For the foundations of a lasting victory can only be laid on the rock of truth. Gandhiji gave us a new method of struggle and political warfare and a new kind of diplomacy. He demonstrated the efficacy of truth and goodwill and non-violence in politics. He taught us to respect and cooperate with every Indian as a man and as a fellow-citizen, irrespective of his political belief or religious creed. We all belong to Mother India and have to live and die here. We all are equal partners in the freedom that we have won. Everyone of our three or four hundred million people must have an equal right to the opportunities and blessings that free India has to offer. It was not for a few privileged persons that Gandhiji strove for and died for. We have to strive for the same ideal and in the same way. Then only shall we be worthy to say "Mahatma Gandhi Ki Jai."

NOTES

1. A small peninsula in western India, northwest of Bombay, divided into a number of small states.

2. The chief minister of the state.

3. The ruler.

4. A period of four months. A vow of fasting and semi-fasting during the four months of the rains. The period is a sort of long Lent.

5. A fast in which the daily quantity of food is increased or diminished according to the moon's waxing or waning.

6. Gandhi no doubt refers here to the occasion when, with his father on his death-bed, he left him and went to his wife's room in a moment of "animal passion." On his return, he found his father had died. Cf. his Autobiography, p. 45.

7. A Gujarati poet who lived in the first half of the nineteenth century; he was a disciple of Sahajananda, founder of the Swaminarayan sect.

8. The seven steps a Hindu bride and bridegroom walk together, making at the same time promises of mutual fidelity and devotion, after which the marriage becomes irrevocable.

9. A preparation of wheat which the pair partake of together after the completion of the ceremony.

10. A Hindu sect worshiping Vishnu as the supreme God.

11. A Vaishnava temple.

12. The name of God.

13. The sacred epic of north India.

14. A recitation of sacred texts asking for the protection of Rama.

15. "The Great God"—a name of Siva.

16. Tulsidas (1532–1623), a poet, author of a Hindi version of the Ramayana.

17. Bhagavad Gita, part of the national epic, Mahabharata.

18. Eleventh day of the bright and the dark half of a lunar month.

19. Laws of Manu, a Hindu law-giver. They have the sanction of religion. This is an ancient religious code upholding the caste system and containing accounts of creation.

20. Non-violence.

21. Dalpatram Shulka, one of the four Indians in London to whom he had notes of introduction.

22. He was admitted as a student of the Inner Temple on November 6, 1888.

23. Theosophy is a combination of occult, Indian, and modern spiritualism founded by Madame Helena P. Blavatsky.

24. A seventeenth-century Gujarati poet.

25. I.e., Mohammed.

26. Charles Bradlaugh (1833–1891), English freethinker and politician.

27. A barrister or counselor at law who passed his law examinations in India.

28. The solicitor under English practice does not have the right to plead in a superior court.

29. A Moslem sect, comprising mostly the mercantile community in Bombay, Kathiawar, etc.

CHAPTER 2

1. A Bombay jeweler and poet to whom Gandhi looked in this period for advice.

2. Edward Maitland (1824–1897), an English humanitarian and writer on vegetarianism and anti-vivisection.

3. Gandhi read Count Leo Tolstoy's *The Kingdom of God Is Within You* and said that it gave his conviction of *satyagraha* "a permanent form." In 1909 he wrote a long letter to Tolstoy, who noted in his diary that he had received "a pleasant letter from a Hindu of the Transvaal." Gandhi wrote again in April 1910, enclosing a copy of his newly published book, *Hind Swaraj*. Gandhi's third and last letter was written August 15, 1910. Though ill, Tolstoy replied on the day he received it. In his long letter he admitted that "the longer I live, and especially now, when I vividly feel the nearness of death, I want to tell others what I feel so particularly clearly and what to my mind is of great importance—namely, that which is called passive resistance, but which is in reality nothing else than the teaching of love uncorrupted by false interpretations." Gandhi received the letter several days after Tolstoy's death on November 21, 1910. For further information see Dr. Kalidas Nag, *Tolstoy and Gandhi* (Patna: Pustak Bhandar, 1950) and "Tolstoy and Gandhi" in Louis Fischer, *The Life of Mahatma Gandhi* (New York: Harper, 1950).

4. Henry Escombe, Attorney-General of Natal.

5. Gandhi's former client and owner of the S. S. *Courland*, on which he was detained.

6. In his *Autobiography*, Gandhi recalls that one song sung by Mr. Alexander at the time was "Hang old Gandhi on the sour apple tree."

7. Joseph Chamberlain.

8. Literally, the fifth caste. Since there are only four castes, the fifth caste means an outcaste or untouchable.

9. Gandhi met Albert West, a partner in a small printing firm, in a vegetarian restaurant and eventually persuaded him to take charge of the *Indian Opinion* press at Durban.

10. A printer who first proposed to Gandhi the idea of starting *Indian Opinion*.

CHAPTER 3

1. One of the leaders of the *satyagraha* movement. He was a trader, born in Mauritius (the island in the Indian Ocean between Ceylon and Madagascar), where his parents had migrated from Madras.
2. This occurred in Johannesburg.
3. Coconut-husk fiber.
4. Rev. Joseph J. Doke, a missionary and friend of Gandhi.

CHAPTER 4

1. In the Boer War Gandhi organized and led the Indian Ambulance Corps. In the Zulu "Rebellion" of 1906—a one-sided action by the government against the Zulus—Gandhi led a small Indian unit of stretcher-bearers.
2. A small stream.
3. Herman Kallenbach, an architect and close associate of Gandhi in South Africa.
4. A German professional strong man.
5. Henry S. L. Polak, an Englishman closely associated with Gandhi in South Africa.
6. An open plain.
7. Valiamma Moodaly. A memorial to her was unveiled in Johannesburg on July 15, 1914.
8. Swami Nagappan, an eighteen-year-old *satyagrahi* who contracted double pneumonia while doing road work in prison and died after his release on July 7, 1909.
9. General Louis Botha (1863–1919), a Boer leader who became Prime Minister of the Union of South Africa.
10. The Acting Viceroy of India in 1904 (April 30 to December 13) and former Governor of Madras.
11. At the time Lord Crewe was Secretary of State for the Colonies.
12. A law enacted by the Boer Republic. Its object was to prevent any non-white person from obtaining any land rights in the mining areas except in certain areas set apart for them.

CHAPTER 5

1. This is included in most editions of the pamphlet issued after 1921.
2. This is a mistaken recollection on the part of Gandhi. It must have been written in 1909.
3. Seers.
4. Moslem ascetics.
5. Doctors of indigenous medicine.
6. A custom whereby a widow, if she has no male heir, has a child by another man.

7. Using goods made in India.
8. Self-government.

CHAPTER 6

1. Later Gandhi announced that he had adopted Lakshmi as a daughter.
2. A Hindu title of respect.
3. The Indian National Congress.
4. Sir Jagadis Chandra Bose (1858–1937), an Indian scientist who showed the identity of the life mechanisms of plants and those of animals; and Janendra Nath Ray (1898–   ), well-known Indian chemist.
5. A platform or stage; usually an awning formed by grass, leaves, or cloth.
6. The story of the young boy, Prahlad, who suffered for the truth's sake, is one of the most famous in ancient Indian literature. It is well known by every Indian child, as the story of George Washington and the cherry tree is known in America.
7. Bread made without yeast, somewhat like a pancake.
8. The vow of khaddar or khadi is to spin with one's own hands and to wear nothing but homespun garments.
9. This is an honorific title.
10. Peasants.
11. Residents of the province of Bihar.
12. A kind of milk soup.
13. Split pulse—the seeds of a legume used commonly for food in India.
14. All these are names of Indian social groups.
15. A lunch carrier.
16. Clarified butter.

CHAPTER 7

1. Strike-breakers.
2. The sister of Ambalal Sarabhai, the leading millowner; she was on Gandhi's side in this dispute.
3. The practice of arbitration of labor disputes has continued in the Ahmedabad mills. In 1936, for example, the millowners asked the labor union to accept a 20 per cent cut in wages. The union refused and the dispute went to arbitration, with Gandhi representing the union on a three-man arbitration board. Gandhi suggested, in effect, a closed shop and no wage decrease, and this was accepted by the impartial chairman.
4. A form of non-violent demonstration in which work ceases, shops are closed, etc.
5. Arbitration; originally, a native court of arbitration having five members.
6. The arbitrators.
7. A Sanskrit prayer, correctly called Vishnu Sahasra Nam, which contains 1,000 names of Vishnu.
8. Orthodox.
9. Scriptures.
10. The Bhagavad Gita.

11. The God of Justice, who reputedly descended into hell and then went to heaven, but renounced it because his faithful dog was refused entrance with him. He was finally readmitted because of his compassion.

12. General R. E. H. Dyer was the military leader responsible for the Amritsar massacre. Sir Michael O'Dwyer was the British Acting Governor of the Punjab who approved Dyer's action.

13. A disciple of Ramakrishna and with him one of the leaders of the revival of Hinduism in the nineteenth century.

14. A community north of the city of Madras.

15. Freedom from the cycle of death and rebirth.

16. I.e., not as a member of one of the four castes, but as an untouchable.

17. Street-cleaning and similar work performed by untouchables.

18. Prayers recited by Brahmins thrice daily, at sunrise, noon, and sunset.

19. Non-cooperation movement.

20. Scavengers.

21. An untouchable caste of Gujarat who were originally weavers but were reduced to sweepers of streets.

22. Sacred Hindu legends.

23. Religion of caste.

24. Zoroastrian scripture.

25. Revered teacher; this title was often used for Tagore.

CHAPTER 8

1. C. Rajagopalachari, a Congress leader at whose home in Madras Gandhi was staying.

2. Mrs. Sarojini Naidu, a Congress leader. Devi is an honorific title for a woman.

3. A part of Gujarat in western India.

4. In March 1918 he had led a satyagraha campaign on behalf of peasants who had to pay taxes despite a crop failure.

5. Satyagraha Committee.

6. An Indian soldier of the Indian army (under British rule).

7. An incident in eastern Bengal when the workers in the tea gardens of Assam fled and were rounded up at Chandpur.

8. A district on the western coast of India. Here, in 1921, the Moplahs, a Moslem community, revolted against the government and this led to Hindu-Moslem riots.

9. A small community in Bihar.

10. Jawaharlal Nehru's father.

11. Lala Lajpat Rai.

12. Frederick Edwin Smith, Lord Birkenhead (1872–1930), a Tory lawyer who was, at the time, Lord High Chancellor of Britain, and later was Secretary of State for India (1924–1928).

13. Edwin S. Montagu (1879–1924), then Secretary of State for India (1917–1922), co-sponsor of the Montagu-Chelmsford reforms.

14. Indian Civil Service.

15. A South African town which was besieged by the Boers for three months in 1899–1900. Gandhi's ambulance corps assisted General Buller's operations to relieve the town.

16. In Gandhi's native Gujarat district.

17. Perhaps the outstanding Congress leader before Gandhi; he died in 1920.

18. M. R. Jayakar, a leader of the "moderates" in Indian political life.

CHAPTER 9

1. Hinduism; strictly, knowledge of God.

2. Not this.

3. Strength or ability.

4. The spinning wheel.

5. Southeast Bengal, east of Calcutta.

6. A territory under the Madras Presidency in the center of the Indian peninsula, ceded from the Hyderabad State to the British in 1903.

7. Kabir or Kabirpanthis was a weaver who lived in the fifteenth century and tried to effect a reconciliation between Hinduism and Islam.

CHAPTER 10

1. Literally, a university. This name was given to national schools created during the non-cooperation movements in the 1920s.

2. About 200 miles distant.

3. I.e., to obtain spiritual benefit from being near him.

4. A Moslem who, with Patel, had led the satyagraha campaign in Bardoli.

5. J. M. Sengupta, Mayor of Calcutta.

6. Religious sacrifice.

7. The national university founded by Gandhi at Ahmedabad in 1920.

8. A rich member of the Jain sect who was treasurer of the Gujarat Vidyapith for several years.

9. Twice president of the Indian National Congress and former Mayor of Calcutta, who went to Nazi Germany during World War II and was killed in an airplane accident on his way to Japan in 1945.

10. The seclusion of women, practiced by Moslems and some Hindus.

11. Long live the revolution!

CHAPTER 11

1. Bishop Frederick B. Fisher, author of a biography of Gandhi entitled The Strange Little Brown Man (New York, 1932).

2. Miss Madeleine Slade, a disciple of Gandhi.

3. A kind of lower garment or loincloth worn by men.

4. This presumably refers to powers reserved to the British under the proposed constitution.

5. A Moslem ruler in Delhi from 1660 to 1707.

CHAPTER 12

1. Dr. Manchershah Gilder, a Bombay physician who was Gandhi's heart specialist.
2. Rabindranath Tagore.
3. The Inspector-General of Prisons.
4. Indira Nehru, his daughter.
5. Nehru's sister.
6. The mother of Jawaharlal Nehru.
7. The wealthy textile manufacturer.
8. Perhaps Tagore's best-known work, an English translation of hymns made in 1913.

CHAPTER 13

1. A kind of legume.
2. A small community a short distance southeast of Ahmedabad.
3. A Hindu orphanage.
4. Ayurvedic medicine is a Hindu form of therapy according to the Vedas.
5. A hill station near Bombay.
6. A process of pumping air or the introduction of straw into the organ of generation of a cow so as to make it incapable of retaining even a drop of milk in the udders.
7. The district in the southwestern tip of India where untouchables had been especially badly treated.
8. Rudolf Steiner (1861–1925), a German philosopher.
9. Jenghiz Khan (1167–1227), Mongol emperor whose armies conquered from the China Sea to the banks of the Dnieper.
10. Herman Kallenbach.
11. "Gandhi also discussed the Palestine problem. 'The Jews have a good case,' he affirmed. But he hoped the Arabs too would not be wronged."
12. The American journalist and biographer of Gandhi.
13. Jayaprakash Narayan, leader of the Indian Socialist Party.
14. *Janata*, December 27, 1953, p. 3.

CHAPTER 14

1. British Prime Minister Neville Chamberlain.
2. Premier Edouard Daladier of France.
3. Dr. Eduard Benes, President of Czechoslovakia, 1935–1938 and 1940–1948.
4. "Servants of God"—the non-violent Pathan followers ("Red Shirts") of Abdul Ghaffar Khan in the Northwest Frontier Province.
5. On July 23, 1939 Gandhi had sent the following note to Hitler: "Friends have been urging me to write to you for the sake of humanity. But I have resisted their request because of the feeling that any letter from me would be an impertinence. Something tells me that I must not calculate, and that I must make my appeal for whatever it may be worth. It is quite clear

that you are today the one person in the world who can prevent a war which may reduce humanity to the savage state. Must you pay that price for an object, however worthy it may appear to you to be? Will you listen to the appeal of one who has deliberately shunned the method of war not without considerable success? Anyway I anticipate your forgiveness, if I have erred in writing to you." (*Harijan*, September 9, 1939.)

6. *What War Means: The Japanese Terror in China*, by H. J. Timperley (London: Gollancz, 1938; 288 pp.)

7. Max Müller (1823–1900), an Oxford professor who specialized in comparative Oriental philology.

CHAPTER 15

1. An island in the Indian Ocean east of Madagascar.

2. All-India Congress Committee, a large committee of the Indian National Congress which made policy; not to be confused with the smaller Working Committee.

3. A cushion, pad, or anything stuffed; used here in the sense of a sovereign's throne.

4. Leopold S. Amery (1873–1955), Secretary of State for India and Burma in 1940–1945.

5. Military atrocities, particularly on women, during the 1942 movement.

6. *The Light of Asia*, by Sir Edwin Arnold.

7. The Tata Steel Works are located at Jamshedpur.

8. The government.

9. An interview with British officials.

CHAPTER 16

1. A Christian missionary, formerly stationed in Bengal, who became a friend of both Tagore and Gandhi and died in a railroad accident in Italy in 1923 en route to India.

2. Dr. John R. Mott, the American Christian leader.

3. In the winter of 1940.

4. In the spring of 1940.

CHAPTER 17

1. Dedication or adoration.

2. The British statesman, who spent three days there in 1938. Sir Arthur Cunningham, Lord Lothian (1885–), was in 1938 resident for the British Government in Rajputana.

3. Karel Capek (1890–1938), Czechoslovak dramatist and novelist.

4. The Working Committee was the small executive committee of the Indian National Congress.

5. Shri A. W. Aryanayakam and his wife, Ashadevi, both educators.

6. A sanyasi is a religious mendicant, usually a worshipper of Siva.

7. A well-known Indian tree with bitter-tasting leaves.

8. "I submit myself to the teaching of the Hokekyo Sutra"—the so-called Lotus sutra of the Nichiren sect of Buddhism.

9. One of the translators of Gandhi's works into English.

10. A Hindu from Madras who was a religious leader.

11. A small community in the Central Provinces, southeast of Wardha and south of Nagpur.

12. An industrialist whose father was from Gandhi's birthplace and at whose beach home at Juhu, near Bombay, Gandhi occasionally stayed for convalescence.

13. Name for Krishna, derived from his pastoral avocation as a herdsman.

14. *Asthi Sinchana* is the Hindu ceremony of sprinkling the bones with water a few days after burning.

CHAPTER 18

1. An honorific title meaning Great Leader.

2. The journal of the Moslem League.

3. This letter was written in Gujarati, the native language of both Gandhi and Jinnah, and accompanied by a translation in Urdu, the Moslem version of Hindustani.

4. ". . . no constitutional plan would be workable in this country or acceptable to the Muslims unless it is designed on the following basic principle, viz., that geographically contiguous units are demarcated into regions which should be so constituted with such territorial readjustments as may be necessary that the areas in which the Muslims are numerically in a majority, as in the north-western and eastern zones of India, should be grouped to constitute 'independent States' in which the constituent units shall be autonomous and sovereign. . . ."

5. "(1) . . . The Muslim League endorses the Indian demand for independence and will co-operate with the Congress in the formation of a provisional interim Government. . . . (2) After the termination of the war, a commission shall be appointed for demarcating contiguous districts in the N.W. and E. of India, wherein the Muslim population is in absolute majority. . . . (3) a plebiscite of all the inhabitants held on the basis of adult suffrage or other practicable franchise shall ultimately decide the issue of separation from Hindustan. . . . (4) In the event of separation, mutual agreements shall be entered into for safeguarding defence and commerce and communications and for other essential purposes. . . ."

6. C. Rajagopalachari.

7. The northeastern province of India, bordering Burma.

8. Prof. J. B. Kripalani, who first aided Gandhi in Champaran in 1917.

9. Subhas Chandra Bose.

10. Rabindranath Tagore.

11. A village on the Poona-Sholapur railroad where Gandhi established a nature-cure clinic.

12. Temple.

13. The common Moslem salutation meaning, "Peace be with you."

14. Author of *Selections from Gandhi* (Ahmedabad, 1948), *Studies in Gandhism* (Calcutta, 1947), and *My Days with Gandhi* (Calcutta, 1953).

15. The wife of Kanu Gandhi, grandson of Gandhi's cousin.

16. Center of *khadi* industry.

17. Vinoba Bhave.

18. Rice.

19. A *patwari* is a village accountant responsible for keeping records.

20. Mud-built.

21. Bays.

22. Rowdies.

23. A member of the Working Committee of the Congress.

24. Annada Chaudhuri, one-time Congress minister of West Bengal.

25. Nripen Chandra Bose, a Congress worker.

26. Shaheed Surawarthy, the Moslem League Premier of Bengal just before the partition.

27. A Congress worker who lost his life in an attempt to prevent Hindu-Moslem riots at Kanpur.

28. A Bengal leader of the Hindu Mahasabha, an orthodox Hindu party.

29. A Sikh leader.

30. Suburbs of Calcutta.

31. A Hindu Mahasabha leader.

32. A Calcutta businessman.

33. One of Gandhi's physicians, a nature-cure expert, who had a clinic in Poona.

34. Chanting God's name.

CHAPTER 19

1. The head of a Moslem religious academy, the Jamia Millia Islamia, at Okla, near New Delhi. He was appointed by Gandhi chairman of the national society for basic education.

2. A constructive worker belonging to the wealthy Sarabhai family of Ahmedabad.

3. Dr. Rajendra Prasad, president of the Congress.

4. A Moslem officer of the Indian National Army.

5. An association of learned men versed in Islam.

6. A militant Hindu organization; often called R. S. S.

7. The orthodox Hindu political group which somewhat paralleled the Moslem League.

8. Prominent journalist and Congress member, who died in an airplane accident in 1951.

9. Barbarians.

10. Devils, monsters.

11. Chanting God's name.

12. A term used at the time for the President of the Indian National Congress.

13. Madan Lai, a Hindu refugee from the Punjab.

14. A Moslem temple, a mosque.

15. A plain, supposedly near Delhi, on which was staged the great conflict which forms the principal theme of the Mahabharata.

16. The wife of a grandson of Gandhi's cousin.

17. Nathuram Vinayak Godse, a 35-year-old Brahmin. He was publisher of a Hindu Mahasabha weekly in Poona.

18. Abha Gandhi.

CHAPTER 20

1. Pandit Govind Ballabh Pant (1887–   ), an active Congress leader in Uttar-Pradesh, and more recently Home Minister in the Central Government.

2. Incarnation of the Divine Spirit.

• CHRONOLOGY OF GANDHI'S LIFE

1869: Oct. 2. Born at Porbandar, Kathiawad, India, son of Karamchand (Kaba) and Putlibai Gandhi.
1876: Attended primary school in Rajkot, where his family moved.
Betrothed to Kasturbai (called Kasturba in her old age), daughter of Gokuldas Makanji, a merchant.
1881: Entered high school in Rajkot.
1883: Married to Kasturbai.
1885: Father died at age of 63.
1887: Passed matriculation examination at Ahmedabad and entered Samaldas College, Bhavnagar, Kathiawad, but found studies difficult and remained only one term.
1888: First of four sons born.
Sept. Sailed from Bombay for England to study law.

HIS TWENTIETH YEAR

1891: Summer. Returned to India after being called to bar. Began practice of law in Bombay and Rajkot.
1893: April. Sailed for South Africa to become lawyer for an Indian firm.
Found himself subjected to all kinds of color discrimination.
1894: Prepared to return to India after completing law case, but was persuaded by Indian colony to remain in South Africa and do public work and earn a living as a lawyer.
Drafted first petition sent by the Indians to a South African legislature.
May. Organized the Natal Indian Congress.
1896: Returned to India for six months to bring back his wife and two children to Natal.
Dec. Sailed for South Africa with family. Was mobbed when he disembarked at Durban for what Europeans thought he wrote about South Africa when he was in India.

HIS THIRTIETH YEAR

1899: Organized Indian Ambulance Corps for British in Boer War.
1901: Embarked with family for India, promising to return to South Africa if Indian community there needed his services again.
1901–1902: Traveled extensively in India, attended Indian National Congress meeting in Calcutta, and opened law office in Bombay.

• Reprinted with permission from Homer A. Jack, editor, *The Wit and Wisdom of Gandhi.* (Boston: Beacon Press, 1951), pp. 205-10.

1902: Returned to South Africa after urgent request from Indian community.

1903: Summer. Opened law office in Johannesburg.

1904: Established the weekly journal, *Indian Opinion.*

Organized Phoenix Farm near Durban, after reading Ruskin's *Unto This Last.*

1906: March. Organized Indian Ambulance Corps for Zulu "Rebellion." Took vow of continence for life.

Sept. First *satyagraha* campaign began with meeting in Johannesburg in protest against proposed Asiatic ordinance directed against Indian immigrants in Transvaal.

Oct. Sailed for England to present Indians' case to Colonial Secretary and started back to South Africa in December.

1907: June. Organized *satyagraha* against compulsory registration of Asians ("The Black Act").

1908: Jan. Stood trial for instigating *satyagraha* and was sentenced to two months' imprisonment in Johannesburg jail (his first imprisonment).

Jan. Was summoned to consult General Smuts at Pretoria; compromise reached; was released from jail.

Feb. Attacked and wounded by Indian extremist, Mir Alam, for reaching settlement with Smuts.

Aug. After Smuts broke agreement, second *satyagraha* campaign began with bonfire of registration certificates.

Oct. Arrested for not having certificate, and sentenced to two months' imprisonment in Volksrust jail.

1909: Feb. Sentenced to three months' imprisonment in Volksrust and Pretoria jails.

June. Sailed for England again to present Indians' case.

HIS FORTIETH YEAR

Nov. Returned to South Africa, writing *Hind Swaraj* en route.

1910: May. Established Tolstoy Farm near Johannesburg.

1913: Began penitential fast (one meal a day for more than four months) because of moral lapse of two members of Phoenix settlement.

Sept. Helped campaign against nullification of marriages not celebrated according to Christian rites, with Kasturbai and other women being sentenced for crossing the Transvaal border without permits.

Nov. Third *satyagraha* campaign begun by leading "great march" of 2,000 Indian miners from Newcastle across Transvaal border in Natal.

Nov. Arrested three times in four days (at Palmford, Standerton, and Teakworth) and sentenced at Dundee to nine months' imprisonment; tried at Volksrust in second trial and sentenced to three months' imprisonment with his European co-workers, Polak and Kallenbach. Imprisoned in Volksrust jail for a few days and then taken to Bloemfontein in Orange Free State.

Dec. Released unconditionally in expectation of a compromise settlement, C. F. Andrews and W. W. Pearson having been sent by Indians in India to negotiate.

1914: Jan. Underwent fourteen days' fast for moral lapse of members of Phoenix Farm.

Jan. Satyagraha campaign suspended, with pending agreement between Smuts, C. F. Andrews, and Gandhi, and with ultimate passage of Indian Relief Act.

July. Left South Africa forever, sailing from Capetown for London with Kasturbai and Kallenbach, arriving just at beginning of World War I.

Organized Indian Ambulance Corps in England, but was obliged to sail for India because of pleurisy.

1915: Secured removal of customs harassment of passengers at Viramgam; first incipient satyagraha campaign in India.

May. Established Satyagraha Ashram at Kochrab, near Ahmedabad, and soon admitted an untouchable family; in 1917 moved ashram to new site on Sabarmati River.

1916: Feb. Gave speech at opening of Hindu University at Benares.

1917: Helped secure removal of recruiting of South African indenture workers in India.

Led successful satyagraha campaign for rights of peasants on indigo plantations in Champaran. Defied order to leave area in April, was arrested at Motihari and tried, but case was withdrawn. Mahadev Desai joined him at Champaran.

1918: Feb. Led strike of millworkers at Ahmedabad. Millowners agreed to arbitration after his three-day fast (his first fast in India).

March. Led satyagraha campaign for peasants in Kheda.

Attended Viceroy's War Conference at Delhi and agreed that Indians should be recruited for World War I.

Began recruiting campaign, but was taken ill and came near death; agreed to drink goat's milk and learned spinning during convalescence.

1919: Spring. Rowlatt Bills (perpetuating withdrawal of civil liberties for seditious crimes) passed, and first all-India satyagraha campaign conceived.

April. Organized nation-wide hartal—suspension of activity for a day—against Rowlatt Bills.

April. Arrested at Kosi near Delhi on way to Punjab and escorted back to Bombay, but never tried.

April. Fasted at Sabarmati for three days in penitence for violence and suspended satyagraha campaign, which he called a "Himalayan miscalculation" because people were not disciplined enough.

Assumed editorship of English weekly, Young India, and Gujarati weekly, Navajivan.

HIS FIFTIETH YEAR

Oct. After five months' refusal, authorities allowed him to visit scene of April disorders in Punjab. Worked closely with Motilal Nehru. Conducted extensive inquiry into violence in many Punjab villages.

1920: April. Elected president of All-India Home Rule League.

June. Successfully urged resolution for a *satyagraha* campaign of non-cooperation at Moslem Conference at Allahabad and at Congress sessions at Calcutta (Sept.) and Nagpur (Dec.).

Aug. Second all-India *satyagraha* campaign began when he gave up Kaisar-i-Hind medal.

1921: Presided at opening of first shop selling homespun (*khadi*) in Bombay.

Aug. Presided at bonfire of foreign cloth in Bombay.

Sept. Gave up wearing shirt and cap and resolved to wear only a loincloth in devotion to homespun cotton and simplicity.

Nov. Fasted at Bombay for five days because of communal rioting following visit of Prince of Wales (later Edward VIII and Duke of Windsor).

Dec. Mass civil disobedience, with thousands in jail. Gandhi invested with "sole executive authority" on behalf of Congress.

1922: Feb. Suspended mass disobedience because of violence at Chauri Chaura and undertook five-day fast of penance at Bardoli.

March. Arrested at Sabarmati on charge of sedition in *Young India*. Pleaded guilty in famous statement at the "great trial" in Ahmedabad before Judge Broomfield. Sentenced to six years' imprisonment in Yeravda jail.

1923: Wrote *Satyagraha in South Africa* and part of his autobiography in prison.

1924: Jan. Was operated on for appendicitis and unconditionally released from prison in February.

Sept. Began 21-day "great fast" at Mohammed Ali's home near Delhi as penance for communal rioting (between Hindus and Moslems), especially at Kohat.

Dec. Presided over Congress session at Belgaum as president.

1925: Nov. Fasted at Sabarmati for seven days because of misbehavior of members of *ashram*.

Dec. Announced one-year political silence and immobility at Congress session at Cawnpore.

1927: No-tax *satyagraha* campaign launched at Bardoli, led by Sardar Patel.

1928: Dec. Moved compromise resolution at Congress session at Calcutta, calling for complete independence within one year, or else the beginning of another all-Indian *satyagraha* campaign.

1929: March. Arrested for burning foreign cloth in Calcutta and fined one rupee.

Dec. Congress session at Lahore declared complete independence and a boycott of the legislature and fixed January 26 as National Independence Day. Third all-Indian satyagraha campaign began.

1930: March 12. Set out from Sabarmati with 79 volunteers on historic salt march 200 miles to sea at Dandi.

April 6. Broke salt law by picking salt up at seashore as whole world watched.

May. Arrested by armed policemen at Karadi and imprisoned in Yeravda jail without trial.

One hundred thousand persons arrested. There was no session of Congress in December because all leaders were in jail.

1931: Jan. Released unconditionally with 30 other Congress leaders.

March. Gandhi-Irwin (Viceroy) Pact signed, which ended civil disobedience.

Aug. Sailed from Bombay accompanied by Desai, Naidu, Mira, etc., for the second Round Table Conference, arriving in London via Marseilles, where he was met by C. F. Andrews.

Autumn. Resided at Kingsley Hall in London slums, broadcast to America, visited universities, met celebrities, and attended Round Table Conference sessions.

Dec. Left England for Switzerland, where he met Romain Rolland, and Italy, where he met Mussolini.

Dec. Arrived in India. Was authorized by Congress to renew satyagraha campaign (fourth nation-wide effort).

1932: Jan. Arrested in Bombay with Sardar Patel and detained without trial at Yeravda prison.

Sept. 20. Began "perpetual fast unto death" while in prison in protest of British action giving separate electorate to untouchables.

Sept. 26. Concluded "epic fast" with historic cell scene in presence of Tagore after British accepted "Yeravda Pact."

Dec. Joined fast initiated by another prisoner, Appasaheb Patwardhan, against untouchability; but fast ended in two days.

1933: Began weekly publication of Harijan in place of Young India.

May 8. Began self-purification fast of 21 days against untouchability and was released from prison by government on first day. Fast concluded after 21 days at Poona.

July. Disbanded Sabarmati ashram, which became center for removal of untouchability.

Aug. Arrested and imprisoned at Yeravda for four days with 34 members of his ashram. When he refused to leave Yeravda village for Poona, he was sentenced to one year's imprisonment at Yeravda.

Aug. 16. Began fast against refusal of government to grant him permission to work against untouchability while in prison; on fifth day of fast he was removed to Sassoon Hospital; his health was precarious; he was unconditionally released on eighth day.

Nov. Began ten-month tour of every province in India to help end untouchability.

Nov. Kasturba arrested and imprisoned for sixth time in two years.

1934: Summer. Three separate attempts made on his life.

July. Fasted at Wardha *ashram* for seven days in penance against intolerance of opponents of the movement against untouchability.

Oct. Launched All-India Village Industries Association.

1935: Health declined; moved to Bombay to recover.

1936: Visited Segaon, a village near Wardha in the Central Provinces, and decided to settle there. (This was renamed Sevagram in 1940 and eventually became an *ashram* for his disciples.)

1937: Jan. Visited Travancore for removal of untouchability.

1938: Autumn. Tour of Northwest Frontier Province with the Khan Abdul Ghaffar Khan.

1939: March. Began fast unto death as part of *satyagraha* campaign in Rajkot; fast ended four days later when Viceroy appointed an arbitrator.

HIS SEVENTIETH YEAR

1940: Oct. Launched limited, individual civil-disobedience campaign against Britain's refusal to allow Indians to express their opinions regarding World War II—23,000 persons imprisoned within a year.

1942: *Harijan* resumed publication after being suspended for 15 months.

March. Met Sir Stafford Cripps in New Delhi but called his proposals "a post-dated check"; they were ultimately rejected by Congress.

Aug. Congress passed "Quit India" resolution—the final nation-wide *satyagraha* campaign—with Gandhi as leader.

Aug. 9. Arrested with other Congress leaders and Kasturba and imprisoned in Aga Khan Palace near Poona, with populace revolting in many parts of India. He began correspondence with Viceroy.

Aug. Mahadev Desai, Gandhi's secretary and intimate, died in Palace.

1943: Feb. 10. Began 21-day fast at Aga Khan Palace to end deadlock of negotiations between Viceroy and Indian leaders.

1944: Feb. 22. Kasturba died in detention at Aga Khan Palace at age of seventy-four.

May 6. After decline in health, was released unconditionally from detention (this was his last imprisonment; he had spent 2,338 days in jail during his lifetime).

Sept. Important talks with Jinnah of Moslem League in Bombay on Hindu-Moslem unity.

1946: March. Conferred with British Cabinet Mission in New Delhi.

Nov. Began four-month tour of 49 villages in East Bengal to quell communal rioting over Moslem representation in provisional government.

1947: March. Began tour of Bihar to lessen Hindu-Moslem tensions.

March. Began conferences in New Delhi with Viceroy (Lord Mount-batten) and Jinnah.

May. Opposed Congress decision to accept division of country into India and Pakistan.

Aug. 15. Fasted and prayed to combat riots in Calcutta as India was partitioned and granted independence.

Sept. Fasted for three days to stop communal violence in Calcutta.

Sept. Visited Delhi and environs to stop rioting and to visit camps of refugees (Hindus and Sikhs from the Punjab).

1948: Jan. 13. Fasted for five days in Delhi for communal unity.

Jan. 20. Bomb exploded in midst of his prayer meeting at Birla House, Delhi.

Jan. 30. Assassinated in 78th year at Birla House by Vinayak N. Godse.

BIBLIOGRAPHY

A selected list of the more important works by and about Gandhi.

WORKS BY GANDHI

An Appeal to Every Briton in South Africa. Durban: Natal Indian Congress, 1894.

The Indian Franchise: An Appeal. Durban: Natal Indian Congress, 1894.

The Grievances of the British Indians in South Africa: An Appeal to the Indian Public. Madras: Price Current Press; 2nd ed., 1896, 44 pp.

Hind Swaraj, or Indian Home Rule. First published in *Indian Opinion*, 1909. Rev. ed., Ahmedabad; Navajivan, 1938, 80 pp.

This pamphlet, written on a voyage from London to South Africa in 1909, consists of a dialogue between the "reader" and the "editor"—Gandhi. This brief work became the basis of Gandhi's thirty-year campaign for Indian freedom.

Speeches and Writings of Mahatma Gandhi, introduction by C. F. Andrews. Madras: Natesan, 1917; 4th rev. ed., 1934, 1072 pp.

A Guide to Health, trans. by A. Rama Iyer. Madras: Ganesan, 1920, 114 pp.

This first appeared serially in *Indian Opinion* in Gujarati. It consists of advice on food and simple treatments for disease.

Young India, 1919–1922. Madras: Ganesan, 1923, 1199 pp. 2nd ed., New York: Viking, 1923, 1471 pp. 2nd ed., New York: B. W. Huebsch, 1923, 1199 pp.

The Story of My Experiments with Truth. Ahmedabad: Navajivan, Vol. I, 1927, 602 pp.; Vol. II, 1929, 608 pp. Also under title *Gandhi's Autobiography: The Story of My Experiments with Truth.* Washington: Public Affairs Press, 1948, 640 pp.

This was begun while Gandhi was in prison and appeared serially in *Young India* beginning in December 1925. It was written in Gujarati and translated into English by Mahadev Desai.

Young India, 1924–1926. Madras: Ganesan, New York: Viking, 1927, 984 pp.

Satyagraha in South Africa, trans. by Valji G. Desai. Madras: Ganesan, 1928, 511 pp. Rev. ed., Ahmedabad: Navajivan, 1950, 351 pp. This supplements the autobiography and was also partly written in prison.

Self-Restraint versus Self-Indulgence. Ahmedabad: Navajivan, Part I, 1930, 130 pp.; Part II, 1939, 147 pp.; one-vol. ed., 1947, 232 pp.

From Yeravda Mandir, trans. by Valji G. Desai. Ahmedabad: Navajivan, 1933; 3rd ed., 1945, 68 pp. A series of weekly letters written in 1930 from prison to members of his ashram.

Songs from Prison, adapted by John Hoyland. London: Allen and Unwin; New York: Macmillan, 1934, 160 pp. Translations from the Upanishads and other Indian lyrics made in Yeravda prison in 1930.

Young India, 1927–1928. Madras: Ganesan, 1935, 1104 pp.

Cent Per Cent Swadeshi, or The Economics of Village Industries. Ahmedabad: Navajivan, 1938; 3rd ed., 1948, 132 pp.

Economics of Khadi. Ahmedabad: Navajivan, 1941, 627 pp.

Christian Missions: Their Place in India. Ahmedabad: Navajivan, 1941, 311 pp.

Constructive Programme: Its Meaning and Place. Ahmedabad: Navajivan, 1941; 2nd ed., 1948, 31 pp.

The Indian States' Problem. Ahmedabad: Navajivan, 1941, 687 pp.

Non-Violence in Peace and War. Ahmedabad: Navajivan, Vol. I, 1942, 2nd ed., 1944, 589 pp.; Vol. II, 1949, 403 pp.

Women and Social Injustice. Ahmedabad: Navajivan, 1942; 3rd ed., 1947, 216 pp.

Gandhi-Jinnah Talks, preface by C. Rajagopalachari. New Delhi: Hindustan Times, 1944, 104 pp.

Gandhiji's Correspondence with the Government, 1942–44. Ahmedabad: Navajivan; 2nd ed., 1945, 360 pp.

The Gospel of Selfless Action, or the Gita According to Gandhi, trans. by Mahadev H. Desai. Ahmedabad: Navajivan, 1946, 390 pp.

Key to Health, trans. by Sushila Nayyar. Ahmedabad: Navajivan, 1948, 83 pp.

Delhi Diary. Ahmedabad: Navajivan, 1948, 406 pp.

Prayers and speeches from September 10, 1947 to his death on January 30, 1948.

Communal Unity. Ahmedabad: Navajivan, 1949, 1006 pp.

Bapu's Letters to Mira, edited by Mira. Ahmedabad: Navajivan, 1949, 387 pp.

Also under title *Gandhi's Letters to a Disciple,* introduction by John Haynes Holmes. New York: Harper; London: Victor Gollancz, 1950, 234 pp.

Diet and Diet Reform. Ahmedabad: Navajivan, 1949, 176 pp.

To The Students. Ahmedabad: Navajivan, 1949, 324 pp.

Ramanama. Ahmedabad: Navajivan, 1949, 56 pp.

Food Shortage and Agriculture. Ahmedabad: Navajivan, 1949, 227 pp.

For Pacifists. Ahmedabad: Navajivan, 1949, 106 pp.

Hindu Dharma. Ahmedabad: Navajivan, 1950, 443 pp.

Basic Education. Ahmedabad: Navajivan, 1951, 114 pp.

Towards Non-Violent Socialism. Ahmedabad: Navajivan, 1951, 165 pp.

Satyagraha: Non-Violent Resistance. Ahmedabad: Navajivan, 1951, 406 pp.

Drink, Drugs and Gambling. Ahmedabad: Navajivan, 1952, 175 pp.

For Workers Against Untouchability. Ahmedabad: Navajivan, 1954, 34 pp.

How to Serve the Cow. Ahmedabad: Navajivan, 1954, 109 pp.

Sarvodaya. Ahmedabad: Navajivan, 1954, 200 pp.

Nature Cure. Ahmedabad: Navajivan, 1954, 68 pp.

The Removal of Untouchability. Ahmedabad: Navajivan, 1954, 304 pp.

Ashram Observances in Action, trans. by Valji G. Desai. Ahmedabad: Navajivan, 1955, 151 pp.

Gokhale: My Political Guru. Ahmedabad: Navajivan, 1955, 67 pp.

Truth is God. Ahmedabad: Navajivan, 1955, 168 pp.

WORKS ABOUT GANDHI

Ambedkar, B. R. *What Congress and Gandhi Have Done to the Untouchables.* Bombay: Thacker and Co., 1945; 2nd ed., 1946, 399 pp.

Andrews, C. F. *Mahatma Gandhi's Ideas*. London: Allen and Unwin, 1929, 382 pp.; 3rd impression, introduction by Horace Alexander, 1949, 382 pp.

————, ed. *Mahatma Gandhi: His Own Story*. London: Allen and Unwin; New York: Macmillan, 1930, 350 pp.
An abridgment of Gandhi's autobiography.

————, ed. *Mahatma Gandhi at Work: His Own Story Continued*. London: Allen and Unwin; New York: Macmillan, 1931, 407 pp.
This describes Gandhi's experiences in South Africa, and is abridged from his own writings.

Baros, Jan, ed. *Mahatma Gandhi: Pictorial History of a Great Life*. Calcutta: Gossain, 1948; 2nd ed., 1949, 206 pp.

Barr, Mary F. *Bapu: Conversations and Correspondence with Mahatma Gandhi*. Bombay: Int. Book House, 1949, 214 pp.

Birla, G. D. *In the Shadow of the Mahatma*. Bombay: Orient Longmans, 1953, 337 pp.

Bose, Nirmal K. *My Days with Gandhi*. Calcutta: Nishana, 1953, 309 pp.

————. *Studies in Gandhism*. Calcutta: India Associated Pub. Co., 1940; 2nd ed., 1947, 358 pp.

————, ed. *Selections from Gandhi*. Ahmedabad: Navajivan, 1948, 311 pp.

Bourke-White, Margaret. *Halfway to Freedom*. New York: Simon and Schuster, 1949, 245 pp.

Catlin, George. *In the Path of Mahatma Gandhi*. London: Macdonald, 1948, 332 pp.; Chicago: Regnery, 1950.

Chaturvedi, Benarsidas, and Marjorie Sykes. *Charles Freer Andrews*. London: Allen and Unwin, 1949, 334 pp.; New York: Harper, 1950.

Datta, Dhirendra Mohan. *The Philosophy of Mahatma Gandhi*. Madison: University of Wisconsin Press, 1953, 155 pp.

Desai, Mahadev H. *Gandhiji in Indian Villages*. Madras: Ganesan, 1927, 349 pp.

————. *With Gandhiji in Ceylon*. Madras: Ganesan, 1928, 159 pp.

————. *The Story of Bardoli*. Ahmedabad. Navajivan, 1929, 393 pp.

————. *The Epic of Travancore*. Ahmedabad: Navajivan, 1937, 251 pp.

Deshpande, M. S., ed. *Light of India.* Sangli: M. S. Deshpande, 1950, 293 pp.

Deshpande, P. G., ed. *Gandhiana: A Bibliography of Gandhian Literature.* Ahmedabad: Navajivan, 1948, 240 pp.

This bibliography contains 1,400 titles in English and an equal number in several Indian languages.

Dhawan, Gopi N. *The Political Philosophy of Mahatma Gandhi.* Bombay: Popular Book Depot, 1946, 354 pp.; 2nd rev. ed., 1951.

Diwakar, R. R. *Satyagraha: The Power of Truth.* Bombay: Hind Kitabs, 1946, 202 pp., Hinsdale: Regnery, 1948, 108 pp.

Doke, Joseph J. *An Indian Patriot in South Africa.* London: London Indian Chronicle, 1909, 97 pp.; Madras: Natesan, 1919, 103 pp.

Duncan, Ronald, ed. *Selected Writings of Mahatma Gandhi.* Boston: Beacon Press, 1951, 253 pp.

Eaton, Jeanette. *Gandhi: Fighter Without a Sword.* New York: Morrow, 1950, 253 pp.

A biography written especially for high-school students.

Fischer, Louis. *A Week with Gandhi.* New York: Duell, Sloan and Pearce, 1942, 122 pp.

————. *Gandhi and Stalin.* New York: Harper, 1947, 183 pp.

————. *The Life of Mahatma Gandhi.* New York: Harper, 1950, 558 pp.; London: Jonathan Cape, 1951. Abridged as *Gandhi: His Life and Message for the World.* New York: Signet Key Book, 1954, 192 pp.

The best biography of Gandhi so far published.

Gandhi, Devadas, ed. *India Unreconciled.* New Delhi: Hindustan Times, 1943, 528 pp.

A documented history of Indian political events from the crisis of August 1942 to February 1944.

————, ed. *Memories of Bapu.* New Delhi: Hindustan Times, 1948, 96 pp.

A large-sized book of photographs edited by one of Gandhi's sons.

George, S. K. *Gandhi's Challenge to Christianity.* London: Allen and Unwin, 1939, 112 pp.

Gregg, Richard B. *The Power of Non-Violence.* Philadelphia: J. B. Lippincott, 1934, 371 pp.

Holmes, John Haynes. *My Gandhi.* New York: Harper, 1953, 186 pp.

Homage. New Delhi: Ministry of Information and Broadcasting, 1948, 65 pp.

Homage to Mahatma Gandhi. New Delhi: Ministry of Information and Broadcasting, 1948, 112 pp.

Jack, Homer A., ed. *The Wit and Wisdom of Gandhi.* Boston: Beacon Press, 1951, 234 pp.

Jain, Jagdishchandra. *I Could Not Save Bapu.* Benares: Jagran S. Mandir, 1950, 242 pp.

Jones, E. Stanley. *Mahatma Gandhi: An Interpretation.* New York: Abingdon-Cokesbury, 1948, 160 pp.

Kabir, Humayun, ed. *Gandhian Outlook and Techniques.* New Delhi: Ministry of Education, 1953, 424 pp.

Kelelkar, Kaka, ed. *To a Gandhian Capitalist.* Bombay: Hind Kitabs, 1951, 204 pp.

Kripalani, J. B. *Gandhi the Statesman.* Delhi: Ranjit, 1951, 111 pp.

Mahatma Gandhi. New Delhi: Ministry of Information and Broadcasting, 1954, 303 pp.

Perhaps the most comprehensive collection of photographs of Gandhi yet published.

Manshardt, Clifford, ed. *Mahatma and the Missionary.* Chicago: Regnery, 1949, 140 pp.

Masani, Shakuntala. *Gandhi's Story.* New York: Oxford, 1950, 101 pp.

A biography for young people.

Mashruwala, K. G. *Gandhi and Marx.* Ahmedabad: Navajivan, 1951, 112 pp.

Maurer, H. *Great Soul: The Growth of Gandhi.* New York: Doubleday, 1948, 128 pp.

Morton, Eleanor. *The Women in Gandhi's Life.* New York: Dodd, Mead, 1953, 304 pp.

Muzumdar, Haridas T. *Gandhi Versus the Empire.* New York: Universal, 1932, 352 pp.

————. *Mahatma Gandhi: Peaceful Revolutionary.* New York: Scribner's, 1952, 127 pp.

Nag, Kalidas. *Tolstoy and Gandhi.* Patna: Pustak Bhandar, 1950, 136 pp.

Nayyar, see Pyarelal.

Nayyar, Sushila. *Kasturba, Wife of Gandhi.* Wallingford, Pa.: Pendle Hill, 1948, 71 pp.

Nehru, Jawaharlal. *Jawaharlal Nehru: An Autobiography.* London: John Lane, 1936, 618 pp. Also under title *Towards Freedom,* New York: John Day, 1941, 445 pp.

——. *Nehru on Gandhi.* New York: John Day, 1948, 150 pp.

Nehru, Krishna. *The Story of Gandhi.* New York: Didier, 1950, 64 pp.
A short, illustrated biography for young people.

Peare, Catherine O. *Mahatma Gandhi.* New York: Henry Holt, 1950, 229 pp.
An excellent biography for high-school students.

Polak, H. S. L., ed. *Souvenir of the Passive Resistance Movement in South Africa (1906–14).* Golden Number, Indian Opinion. Natal: Phoenix Farm, 1914, 54 pp.

——, H. N. Brailsford, and Lord Pethick-Lawrence. *Mahatma Gandhi.* London: Odhams, 1949, 320 pp.

Prabhu, R. K., ed. *Sati Kasturba.* Bombay: Hind Kitabs, 1944, 87 pp.

——. *This Was Bapu.* Ahmedabad: Navajivan, 1954, 178 pp.

Prasad, Rajendra. *Mahatma Gandhi and Bihar.* Bombay: Hind Kitabs, 1949, 132 pp.

——. *At the Feet of Mahatma Gandhi.* Bombay: Hind Kitabs, 1955, 350 pp.

Pyarelal (Nayyar). *The Epic Fast.* Ahmedabad: M. M. Bhatt, 1932, 325 pp.

——. *A Pilgrimage for Peace: Gandhi and Frontier Gandhi among N.W.F. Pathans.* Ahmedabad: Navajivan, 1950, 208 pp.

——. *Mahatma Gandhi: The Last Phase.* Ahmedabad: Navajivan, 1956, 2 vols.

Radhakrishnan, Sarvepalli, ed. *Mahatma Gandhi: Essays and Reflections on His Life and Work.* London: Allen and Unwin, 1939, 382 pp.; 2nd ed., 1949, 557 pp.
This was presented to Gandhi on his seventieth birthday in 1939 and contains contributions from well-known persons. The second edition includes memorials on his death.

Rajagopalachar[i], C., and J. C. Kumarappa, eds. *The Nation's Voice.* Ahmedabad: Navajivan, 1932; 2nd ed., 1947, 256 pp.

Contains an account of Gandhi's trip to England for the Round Table Conference in 1931.

Raman, T. A. *What Does Gandhi Want?* London: Oxford, 1943, 117 pp.

Ray, Benoy Gopal. *Gandhian Ethics.* Ahmedabad: Navajivan, 1950, 70 pp.

Reynolds, Reginald. *To Live in Mankind: A Quest for Gandhi.* London: Andre Deutsch, 1951, 215 pp.; New York: Doubleday, 1952.

Rolland, Romain. *Mahatma Gandhi.* Paris: Delamain and Boutelleau, 1924, 210 pp.

——. *Mahatma Gandhi: The Man Who Became One with the Universal Being.* New York: Century, 1924, 250 pp.

Sarma, D. S., ed. *The Gandhi Sutras.* New York: Devin-Adair, 1949, 174 pp.

Sharma, Jagdish S. *Mahatma Gandhi: A Descriptive Bibliography.* Delhi: S. Chand, 1955, 565 pp.

Sheean, Vincent. *Lead, Kindly Light.* New York: Random House, 1949, 374 pp.

Shridharani, Krishnalal J. *The Mahatma and the World.* New York: Duell, Sloan and Pearce, 1946, 247 pp.

Shukla, Chandrashankar. *Reminiscences of Gandhiji.* Bombay: Vora, 1951, 218 pp.

——, ed. *Gandhiji as We Know Him.* Bombay: Vora, 1945, 145 pp.

——, ed. *Incidents in Gandhiji's Life.* Bombay: Vora, 1949, 344 pp.

Tendulkar, Dinanath Gopal. *Mahatma: Life of Mohandas Karamchand Gandhi.* Bombay: Vithalbhai K. Jhaveri and D. G. Tendulkar, 1951–54, 8 vols.

——, et al., eds. *Gandhiji: His Life and Work.* Bombay: Karnatak, 1944, 501 pp.

Presented to Gandhi on his seventy-fifth birthday in 1944. Contains contributions from notables, a long chronology of his life, and many photographs.

Topolski. *Sketches of Gandhi.* New Delhi: Hindustan Times, 1953, 26 sketches.

Walker, Roy. *Sword of Gold: A Life of Mahatma Gandhi.* London: Indian Independence Union, 1945, 200 pp.

INDEX

Abdulla, Sheth, 28, 29, 31, 33, 36, 39-41, 48
Agriculture, 56, 133, 145-48, 221, 265, 407, 521
Ahimsa, xvii, 17, 138-39, 301, 314-15, 349, 408, 433
Ahmedabad, 125-28, 136, 154-57, 162-67, 184-86, 197-208, 237, 239, 242, 298-99, 375, 411, 429, 502, 513, 514
Alam, Mir, 72-76, 78-79, 512
Alexander, Horace, viii, xxi, 259-61
Ali, Mohammed, xxi, 189-93, 212, 276, 514
Ambedkar, B. R., 281, 290, 295-96, 521
Amritsar massacre, 182, 188
An Indian Patriot in South Africa, vii, 80-84
Anasuyabehn, 155, 157, 300, 502
Andrews, Charles F., viii, xxi, 3, 38, 101, 172-73, 178, 188, 216, 234, 259, 261-62, 266, 282, 290, 381, 388-93, 393, 397, 513, 519, 522
Anti-Semitism, 317-26
Arabs, 317-26
Arts, the, 173-75, 180-81, 286, 333, 384
Ashram, xvii, xxii, 136-44, 244, 256, 391, 404, 462; see also Kochrab, Sabarmati, Sevagram
Assam, 428
Atheism, 23
Atomic bombs, 348-49, 349-50
Attlee, Clement R., 439, 488
Azad, Maulana Abdul Kalam, 458, 461

Banker, S. G., xxi, 197-208, 292, 300
Benares University, xxi, 128-36, 295, 513
Bengal, 426-38, 438-50, 516
Besant, Anne, xxi, 22-23, 81, 128-29, 134
Bhave, Vinoba, 329-31, 434, 508
Bihar, 145-48, 149-53, 183, 438-39, 450, 502, 516
Birth control, 302-8
Black Act, 59-66, 66, 72-75, 76-79, 512
Boer War, 58, 86, 136, 202, 501, 511
Bombay, 25-27, 105, 130, 132-41, 158, 183, 188-89, 190, 199-201, 235, 242, 247, 248, 273, 281, 294, 302, 418, 420-26, 429, 454, 499, 511, 514, 515, 516
Bose, Nirmal K., 433, 522
Bose, Subhas, 241, 371, 429, 504
Bourke-White, Margaret, 480-82, 522
Broomfield, C. N., 197-208, 514
Buddha, 310, 397, 507

Calcutta, vi, 150, 193, 195, 223, 233, 234, 242, 285, 290, 294, 304, 352, 392, 427, 438-50, 451, 491, 511, 514, 517
Caste, 3, 24, 150, 168-69; see also Harijans
Celibacy, xvii, 55, 115, 140, 177, 302-308, 411, 512
Chamberlain, Joseph, 48-49
Chiang Kai-shek, 351-55
China, 326, 330, 347-48, 351-55, 358, 360, 372-74, 408

Christianity, vii, viii, 16, 22-23, 34-38,
40, 51, 54, 76, 81, 83, 85, 162, 164,
168, 178, 180, 277, 313, 314, 316,
317-19, 322, 325, 329, 386, 388-92,
415, 438, 462, 463, 466, 469, 486,
512, 520, 524
Churchill, Winston, v, viii, 255, 356,
470
Civilization, 105-10, 118, 140, 227
Color discrimination, see Gandhi, discrimination
Communal unity, vii, viii, 75, 189,
190-93, 235, 264, 271, 341-43, 417-
50, 450-64, 514, 516, 517, 521
Communism, 326-28, 328-29, 329-31;
see also Russia
Congress, Indian National, xvii, xxii-
xxiii, 130, 132, 145, 149, 178-79,
188, 190-92, 208, 224, 235, 239,
242, 254, 271-78, 281, 328, 342,
351, 357, 359-71, 404, 417-18, 426-
30, 439, 457-58, 461, 493, 511, 514,
515, 516
Cow protection, 168, 170-72, 521
Cripps, Stafford, 352-53, 356-57, 359,
404, 417, 516
Czechoslovakia, 320, 332-36, 338,
340-41

Delhi, 172-81, 202, 216, 242, 275,
282-85, 293-94, 359-71, 388, 394,
398-402, 427, 439, 450-64, 464-67,
473-75, 476, 480-82, 483-85, 513,
516, 517, 521
Desai, Mahadev, xxi, 3, 149, 172-73,
213, 234, 254, 266, 283, 292, 302,
308, 347, 352, 382, 403, 414, 513,
516, 519, 520, 522
Diet, vii, 10-13, 17, 18-19, 70, 74,
106, 140, 150, 152, 170, 297-301,
513, 521
Doke, Joseph J., vii, xxi, 73-76, 80-84,
100, 501, 523
Durban, 29, 38, 39, 42-50, 50-54, 56-
58, 85, 92, 94, 136, 389-91, 511-
12

Education, viii, 50-53, 144, 158, 406,
410
Einstein, Albert, v, 325, 488
England, vii, 18-20, 53, 97, 104, 125,
254-78, 318-21, 324, 325, 333, 337,
372, 382, 394, 511-12, 513, 515
English, the, 10-11, 19-20, 84, 99-101,
105, 107, 111, 114, 117-20, 130,
171, 195, 211, 213-15, 222-23, 231,
256, 270, 274, 277-78, 287, 312,
332, 344-47, 357, 374, 393
Escombe, Henry, 40, 42-43, 48-50

Fasts, see Gandhi, fasts
Fearlessness, 63-64, 142
Fischer, Louis, vii, 241-42, 257, 293-
96, 325, 326, 356-58, 451-57, 473-
75, 483-85, 505, 523
France, 24, 318-19, 324, 332-33, 337-
38, 397-98, 515
Friends, Society of, 34, 258, 259, 397

Germany, 202, 317-20, 322, 323-24,
333, 338, 345-46, 352, 372, 409,
470
Gandhi, Devadas (youngest son), xxi-
xxiii, 50-53, 214-15, 382, 410-14,
414-15, 476-79, 523
Gandhi, Harilal (oldest son), xxii, 25,
50-53, 411, 415
Gandhi, Karamchand (father), xxii,
4-5, 7-9, 13, 15-16, 24, 26, 499, 511
Gandhi, Karsandas (second brother),
4, 7-8, 14
Gandhi, Kasturba[i] (wife), xxii, 6-9,
11, 18, 25, 42, 50-55, 97-99, 127,
151, 208-9, 246-47, 284, 286-87,
292, 298-99, 301, 359, 408-9, 410-
16, 474, 499, 511, 512, 513, 515,
516, 525
Gandhi, Laxmidas (older brother), 4,
7, 10, 18, 24-28, 163
Gandhi, Maganlal (cousin), xxii, 58,
65, 126, 156
Gandhi, Manilal (second son), xxii,
252, 411